LEGAL PRACTICE COURSE

A Practitioner's Guide to Executorship and Administration

KU-050-593

WITHDRAWN

While every care has been taken to ensure the accuracy of this work, no responsibility for loss or damage occasioned to any person acting or refraining from action as a result of any statement in it can be accepted by the authors, editors or publishers.

Other titles in this series
A Practitioner's Guide to Advising Charities
A Practitioner's Guide to Beneficiaries' Actions
A Practitioner's Guide to Charity Fundraising
A Practitioner's Guide to Contentious Trusts and Estates
A Practitioner's Guide to the Court of Protection
A Practitioner's Guide to Drafting Trusts
A Practitioner's Guide to Inheritance Claims
A Practitioner's Guide to Legacies
A Practitioner's Guide to Money Laundering Compliance
A Practitioner's Guide to Powers and Duties of Trustees
A Practitioner's Guide to Powers of Attorney
A Practitioner's Guide to Probate
A Practitioner's Guide to Trustee Investment
A Practitioner's Guide to Trusts

A Practitioner's Guide to Executorship and Administration

John Thurston, LLB, Solicitor
Associate with Thurston & Co Solicitors

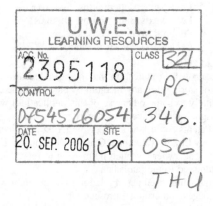

U.W.E.L.
LEARNING RESOURCES
ACC. No. 2395118
CLASS 321
LPC
346.
056
THU
CONTROL 0754526054
DATE 20. SEP. 2006
SITE LPC

LexisNexis™ UK

Members of the LexisNexis Group worldwide

United Kingdom	LexisNexis UK, a Division of Reed Elsevier (UK) Ltd, Halsbury House, 35 Chancery Lane, LONDON, WC2A 1EL, and 4 Hill Street, EDINBURGH EH2 3JZ
Argentina	LexisNexis Argentina, BUENOS AIRES
Australia	LexisNexis Butterworths, CHATSWOOD, New South Wales
Austria	LexisNexis Verlag ARD Orac GmbH & Co KG, VIENNA
Canada	LexisNexis Butterworths, MARKHAM, Ontario
Chile	LexisNexis Chile Ltda, SANTIAGO DE CHILE
Czech Republic	Nakladatelství Orac sro, PRAGUE
France	Editions du Juris-Classeur SA, PARIS
Germany	LexisNexis Deutschland GmbH, FRANKFURT and MUNSTER
Hong Kong	LexisNexis Butterworths, HONG KONG
Hungary	HVG-Orac, BUDAPEST
India	LexisNexis Butterworths, NEW DELHI
Ireland	LexisNexis, DUBLIN
Italy	Giuffrè Editore, MILAN
Malaysia	Malayan Law Journal Sdn Bhd, KUALA LUMPUR
New Zealand	LexisNexis Butterworths, WELLINGTON
Poland	Wydawnictwo Prawnicze LexisNexis, WARSAW
Singapore	LexisNexis Butterworths, SINGAPORE
South Africa	LexisNexis Butterworths, DURBAN
Switzerland	Stämpfli Verlag AG, BERNE
USA	LexisNexis, DAYTON, Ohio

© Reed Elsevier (UK) Ltd 2004

All rights reserved. No part of this publication may be reproduced in any material form (including photocopying or storing it in any medium by electronic means and whether or not transiently or incidentally to some other use of this publication) without the written permission of the copyright owner except in accordance with the provisions of the Copyright, Designs and Patents Act 1988 or under the terms of a licence issued by the Copyright Licensing Agency Ltd, 90 Tottenham Court Road, London, England W1T 4LP. Applications for the copyright owner's written permission to reproduce any part of this publication should be addressed to the publisher.

Warning: The doing of an unauthorised act in relation to a copyright work may result in both a civil claim for damages and criminal prosecution.

Crown copyright material is reproduced with the permission of the Controller of HMSO and the Queen's Printer for Scotland. Parliamentary copyright material is reproduced with the permission of the Controller of Her Majesty's Stationery Office on behalf of Parliament. Any European material in this work which has been reproduced from EUR-lex, the official European Communities legislation website, is European Communities copyright.

A CIP Catalogue record for this book is available from the British Library.

ISBN 0 7545 26054

Typeset by Kerrypress Ltd, Luton, Beds

Printed and bound in Great Britain by Antony Rowe Ltd, Chippenham, Wiltshire

Visit LexisNexis UK at www.lexisnexis.co.uk

Preface

This book is aimed at the busy professional, be they solicitor, accountant, legal executive, or will draftsman. It is intended to provide a quick and easily digestible guide to administering the estates of deceased persons.

Although some legal knowledge is assumed, it may also be of use to lay persons administering the estates of deceased relatives or friends.

Contents

Table of Cases

Table of Statutes

References in the right-hand column are to paragraph number. Paragraph references printed in **bold** type indicate where the Act is set out in part or in full.

Table of Statutory Instruments

References in the right-hand column are to paragraph number. Paragraph references printed in **bold** type indicate where the Statutory Instrument is set out in part or in full.

Chapter 1

Overview

1.1 This chapter is intended for lay persons wishing to administer an estate themselves.

The first duty of the personal representatives or relatives of a deceased person is to register the death with Registrar of Births, Deaths and Marriages. Normally this is a formality, but in certain circumstances an inquest may be held.

The next stage is to secure the assets of the deceased and to begin to collect the information required to obtain a grant of probate or letters of administration to the estate of the deceased person. If the estate is large enough, consideration will have to be given to the funding of the inheritance tax due.

It will then be necessary to draft the oath, and if required the Inland Revenue account in order to obtain the grant of probate or letters of administration.

Once the grant has been obtained, it is then necessary to pay the debts and funeral expenses of the deceased. When all the liabilities have been met, the personal representatives can then distribute the assets to those with an entitlement under the will or intestacy rules.

Accounts will have to be prepared, and approved by the executors and the residuary beneficiaries where appropriate.

Chapter 2

Immediate post-death procedure

Registering the death

2.1 Usually professionals do not become involved in registering the deaths of clients, although it can happen, for example where there are no relatives. If there are no relatives, the person arranging for the disposal of the body can register the death. This should normally be done within five days of the death in the sub-district where the death occurred. It will be necessary to supply the following information:

(a) the date and place of birth of the deceased;

(b) the full name of the deceased;

(c) the marital status of the deceased;

(d) the usual address of the deceased;

(e) the occupation of the deceased;

(f) the name and occupation of any spouse.

The Registrar will issue a certificate for burial or cremation, a certificate of notification of death for the Department of Work and Pensions, and (on payment of a fee) a copy of the entry in the Register. It is a good idea, even where a professional is involved, to obtain several copies of the death certificate, as it may be necessary to produce copies to banks or building societies where the deceased had an account, and also to any life insurance companies where the deceased was insured.

Inquests

2.2 In certain circumstances the Registrar must report a death to the coroner, for example if the deceased had not seen his doctor in the fourteen days before death, or the cause of death was unknown or uncertain. The coroner is not obliged to hold an inquest in every case, although there are some situations where an inquest must be held, for example if the death was violent or unnatural. In other cases, he has a discretion as to whether to order an inquest, but if he is satisfied that the death was due to natural causes, he can issue a certificate to the Registrar so that the death can be registered.

Disposal of the body

2.3 Anyone can express a wish as to how they would like the disposal of his or her body to take place. The wish can be expressed either orally, or in a will, or in written document not contained in the will. Whilst most personal representatives will seek to comply with the wishes of the deceased, there is no obligation on them to do so. However, it should be noted that personal representatives are under a duty to dispose of the body.

It may be that the client has expressed a wish for his body to be used for medical research, in which case the nearest medical school should be contacted on the day of death, or next day. If this is not possible, arrangements should be made for the body to be kept in refrigerated storage. Unless the relatives have expressed a wish to the contrary, the medical school will pay the cost of a simple funeral.

If the deceased has expressed a wish to donate their organs, then the nearest hospital should be notified as soon as possible after death. Where the personal representatives are not close relatives of the deceased, they should consult them to ensure that they agree to the proposed donation.

The body or ashes may be interred in a churchyard with the consent of the incumbent, or in a cemetery maintained by a local authority. Usually a fee will be charged.

Paying for the funeral

2.4 It may be that the deceased has entered into an arrangement to pay for his funeral during his lifetime. If this is not the case, then the person or persons arranging the funeral become personally liable to the undertaker for the cost of the funeral. However, reasonable funeral costs are the first charge on the estate, and many banks and building societies are prepared to release funds for this purpose before a grant has been obtained.

Occasionally, there may be dispute as to the funeral arrangements. This subject is considered in more detail in CHAPTER 11.

Preserving the assets

2.5 The executors or administrators, or the solicitors instructed by the executors or administrators should take possession of all relevant documents belonging to the deceased – share certificates, cheque books, passbooks, life insurance policies, land certificates and title deeds.

If the deceased left a house, which due to his death has become unoccupied, then the insurers should be notified. The house should also be secured, and relevant electricity, gas, water and telephone companies notified. The local authority should also be notified. If cold weather is expected, then steps should be taken to ensure that frozen pipes do not cause damage.

The personal representatives should also check the position with regard to insurance. Personal representatives now have wide powers of insurance under s 19 of the Trustee Act 1925 as amended by Trustee Act 2000. In particular, the position with regard to house insurance should be checked, as the premises may not be covered if they are unoccupied.

The will

2.6 Frequently the deceased will have told relatives about the existence of a will, and its whereabouts. If the deceased did not do so, then it will be necessary to conduct a search of his or her papers to see if there is a will, or correspondence containing any reference to a will.

Consideration should also be given to whether letters should be sent to all the solicitors' firms in areas where the deceased was living at the date of death, or has lived, enquiring if they hold a will on behalf of the deceased. Advertisements can also be inserted in the Law Society's Gazette for lost wills. Most long established firms of solicitors will hold wills executed many years ago where the testators must have died; it is possible that these testators executed later wills, but there is always a suspicion that these testators were regarded as having died intestate as the relatives were unaware of the existence of the will.

It is also possible to deposit wills at the Principal Registry. This facility is not used very much, but a search should be made for missing wills.

The beneficiaries may be keen to know the contents of the will, but personal representatives are under no duty to tell them. However, once the will has been proved, it becomes a public document and is available for inspection by all; therefore in most cases there is little point in the personal representatives refusing to disclose the contents of a will to the beneficiaries.

Solicitors as personal representatives or instructed to act by personal representatives

2.7 Rule 15 of the Solicitors Practice Rules 1990 requires solicitors to give information about costs and other matters, and to operate a complaints handling procedure in accordance with the Solicitors Costs Information and Client Care Code.

Strictly, it is the executors or administrators who are the clients of the solicitor. However, it is clearly good and desirable practice to send a client care letter to the residuary beneficiaries under the will as well.

Can a beneficiary under the will who is not an executor or administrator request the solicitor to obtain a remuneration certificate? The answer is yes, but only in limited circumstances. An entitled third party is entitled to apply for a remuneration certificate. 'An entitled third party' means a residuary beneficiary absolutely and immediately (not contingently) entitled to an inheritance, where a solicitor has charged the estate of his professional costs for acting in the administration of the estate, and either:

(a) the only personal representatives are solicitors (whether or not acting in a professional capacity); or

(b) the only personal representatives are solicitors acting jointly with partners or employees in a professional capacity.

A solicitor dealing with an estate is not obliged to provide information about the estate to a beneficiary who is not a personal representative, however, it is good practice to do so. Where the solicitor is sole executor, the solicitor should keep the beneficiaries informed about the administration of the estate.

A solicitor, who has been appointed an executor, cannot be forced to renounce the right to grant. However, the solicitor should consider whether it is in the best interests of the estate not to renounce the right to grant. The solicitor may find it embarrassing to have to deal with beneficiaries, who do not wish him to take out a grant.

(For more information please see pages 297, 449 – 450 of the Guide to the Professional Conduct of Solicitors.)

Chapter 3

Collecting the required information

3.1 In order to obtain the grant, it is necessary to collect the following various pieces of information:

— whether the deceased left a will;

— full name and address of the deceased;

— date of birth of the deceased;

— names, addresses and occupations of the executors or administrators;

— whether the deceased was survived by parents, brothers and sisters, spouse, children or grandchildren, and if so, how many;

— whether the deceased was domiciled in England and Wales;

— the National Insurance number of the deceased;

— the income tax reference of the deceased;

— the name and address of the tax district to which the deceased submitted returns;

— the assets of the deceased;

— the debts and liabilities of the deceased;

— whether there is anyone for whom the deceased should have provided but failed to do so;

— whether the deceased made *inter vivos* (lifetime) gifts in the seven years before death;

— whether the deceased was a member of a pension scheme, and whether a lump sum was payable on retirement;

— whether the deceased had taken out any life insurance policies;

— whether the deceased was in receipt of an annuity, and if so, details.

Having ascertained the assets owned by the deceased, it will then be necessary to obtain valuations of the various assets. The procedure for the valuation of assets is set out below.

Land

3.2 It is usual to obtain a valuation of any land within the estate from a qualified valuer.

Shares

3.3 It is common to obtain a valuation from brokers, who can also be requested to check the number of shares held by the deceased.

The Stock Exchange also provides a pricing service, the address is:

Historic Price Service T/4
London Stock Exchange
Old Broad Street
London EC2N 1HP
Tel no: 020 7797 1206
Fax no: 020 7797 1952
Email: historicpriceservice@londonstockexchange.com

Banks and building societies

3.4 The executors should write to all banks and building societies where it is thought the deceased held accounts requesting details of all accounts, the amount standing to the credit of the account as at the date of death, the interest due to the date of death and the interest paid or credited to the account since the deceased's last tax return.

In the case of a large estate, it may be desirable to open an executors' account.

Social security benefits/pensions

3.5 Letters should be sent to the local office of the Department of Work and Pensions and to the Recovery from Estates 'A' Wing Government Buildings, Otley Road, Lawnswood, Leeds LS16 5PU requesting details of any overpayments and/or underpayments.

Pensions

3.6 The deceased may have been a member of a pension scheme provided by his employer, or a member of a private scheme. The relevant scheme providers should be notified of the death, and asked to provide details of any overpayment or underpayment.

Life assurance policies

3.7 The insurance company should be notified of the death, and the company should be asked to provide a note of the amount due under the policy. A claim form should also be requested.

Inland Revenue

3.8 The deceased's tax office should be notified of the date of death, as there may be a refund due to the estate where the deceased was employed. However, particularly where the deceased was self-employed, additional tax may be due.

Unclaimed assets register

3.9 The deceased may have had investments or assets that are not known to the personal representatives. The unclaimed assets register will assist personal representatives to find such investments or assets. The web address is www.uar-.co.uk.

Chapter 4

Types of grant

Is a grant necessary?

4.1 Once the executors have collected the necessary information, the next stage is to apply for a grant of probate or letters of administration. The effect of a grant is to confer authority on the executors and administrators to deal with the estate of the deceased, and in the case of a grant of probate where there is a will appointing executors, it confirms that the will is valid.

However, it is sometimes possible to complete the administration of an estate without obtaining a grant. Frequently, spouses and cohabitees own the home as joint tenants, and there may also be bank and building society accounts in the joint names of both spouses or cohabitees. If everything is jointly owned, it will not be necessary to obtain a grant. The survivor will be entitled to all the jointly owned assets, and only needs to produce the death certificate to have the house or joint accounts transferred into their sole name.

If the deceased has only left a small amount of money invested in a building society account, then the building society can agree to release the money without the need for the production of a grant. This power can only be exercised where the amount in the account is less than £5,000. A similar provision applies to money invested with the National Savings Bank, Trustee Savings Bank, Savings Certificates or Premium Bonds. It may also be possible to obtain other monies without the need for the production of the grant, for example arrears of salary, or money in bank accounts.

Types of grant

4.2 There are various types of grant which can be obtained in order to administer the estate of a deceased person. They are:

(a) grant of probate;

(b) grant of letters of administration;

(c) grant of letters of administration with the will annexed;

(d) grant to the unadministered estate;

(e) grant during the minority of an executor or administrator;

(f) grants to attorneys;

(g) grants where the deceased died domiciled outside England and Wales;

(h) grant limited to certain property.

It is necessary to examine each of these grants in turn.

Grant of probate

4.3 A grant of probate will be obtained where the deceased left a will appointing executors who are able and willing to take out a grant. If there is a will, but no valid appointment of executors, for example because they have all predeceased the testator, then it is necessary to obtain a grant of letters of administration with the will annexed.

Whilst there is no limit on the number of persons who can be appointed executors, a grant will not be made out to more than four.

Strictly there are no restrictions on who can be appointed as an executor, and so a testator can appoint anyone, however undesirable they may be. However, a grant of probate will not be made to an infant; instead a grant will be made to another person, possibly the parents, for the use and benefit of the child. Such a grant will usually have a time limit, so that the infant can take a grant in his or her own right once he or she has attained the age of 18.

Grant of letters of administration

4.4 It is necessary to obtain a grant of letters of administration when the deceased did not leave a will, and died intestate.

The Non-Contentious Probate Rules (NCPR 1987) prescribe who is entitled to the grant; the order follows the order of entitlement to the estate under the intestacy rules. Rule 22(1) provides that the following are entitled:

— the surviving spouse;

— the children of the deceased or the issue of any deceased child who died before the deceased;

— the father and mother of the deceased;

— brothers and sisters of the whole blood and the issue of any deceased brother and sister of the whole blood who died before the deceased;

— brothers and sisters of the half blood and the issue of any deceased brother and sister of the half blood who died before the deceased;

— grandparents;

— uncles and aunts of the whole blood and the issue of any deceased uncle and aunt of the whole blood who died before the deceased;

— uncles and aunts of the half blood and the issue of any deceased uncle or aunt of the half blood who died before the deceased.

'Children' includes legitimate, illegitimate and adopted children.

Rule 22(2) provides that in default of any person having a beneficial interest in the estate, the Treasury Solicitor is entitled to a grant if he claims *bona vacantia* on behalf of the Crown.

Rule 22(3) provides that if all persons entitled to a grant under the foregoing provisions of the rule have been cleared off, a grant may be made to a creditor of the deceased or to any person who, notwithstanding that he has no immediate beneficial interest in the estate, may have a beneficial interest in the estate in the event of an accretion thereto.

If a person entitled to a grant dies, his or her personal representatives may be entitled to a grant. Rule 22(4) provides that subject to paragraph (5) of r 27, the personal representative of a person in any of the classes mentioned in paragraph (1) of this rule or the personal representative of a creditor of the deceased shall have the same right to a grant as the person whom he represents. However, if the spouse of the intestate has died without taking a beneficial interest in the whole estate of the deceased as ascertained at the time of the application for the grant, the other persons entitled to the grant are to be preferred to the personal representatives of the deceased spouse. Rule 27(5) provides that unless a District Judge or Registrar otherwise directs, administration is to be granted to a person of full age entitled thereto in preference to a guardian of a minor, and to a living person entitled thereto in preference to the personal representative of a deceased person.

Therefore, if the deceased died intestate leaving three children, one a minor, two adults and no spouse, a grant will be made to the two adult children rather than to the guardian of the minor child, or the personal representatives of a deceased child.

Grant of letters of administration with the will annexed

4.5 This grant can be obtained where there is a will, but there are no executors willing and able to prove the will. This might be for various reasons, for example:

- all the executors appointed in the will have predeceased the testator;
- all the executors have either predeceased the testator or are unwilling to take out a grant;
- the will did not appoint any executors (this should not be the case if the will is professionally drawn).

In this situation, r 20 of the NCPR 1987 provides the order of priority to a grant is to be determined in accordance with the following order:

(a) the executor (but subject to r 36(4)(d));

(b) any residuary legatee or devisee holding in trust for any other person;

(c) any other residuary legatee (including one for life) or where the residue is not wholly disposed of by the will, any person entitled to share in the undisposed of residue (including the Treasury Solicitor when claiming *bona vacantia* on behalf of the Crown) provided that –

  (i) unless a District Judge or Registrar otherwise directs, a residuary legatee or devisee whose legacy or devise is vested in interest shall be preferred to one entitled on the happening of a contingency, and

  (ii) where the residue is not in terms wholly disposed of, the District Judge or Registrar may, if he is satisfied that the testator has nevertheless disposed of the whole or substantially the whole of the known estate, allow a grant to be made to any legatee or devisee entitled to, or to share in the estate disposed of, without regard to the person entitled to share in any residue not disposed of by will;

(d) the personal representatives of any residuary legatee or devisee (but not one for life, or one holding in trust for any other person), or of any person entitled to share in any residue not disposed of by the will;

(e) any other legatee or devisee (including one for life or one holding in trust for any other person) or any creditor of the deceased, provided that, unless a District Judge or Registrar otherwise directs, a legatee or devisee whose legacy or devise is vested in interest shall be preferred to one entitled on the happening of a contingency;

(f) the personal representatives of any other legatee or devisee (but not one for life or one holding in trust for any other person) or any creditor of the deceased.

Rule 36 is concerned with grants to trust corporations. Rule 36(4)(a) provides that where a corporate body would, if an individual, be entitled to a grant but is not a trust corporation as defined in the rules, administration for its use and benefit, limited until further representation be granted, may be made to its nominee or to its lawfully constituted attorney. Rule 36(4)(d) provides that the provisions of paragraph (a) are not to apply where a body corporate is appointed executor jointly with an individual unless the right of the individual has been cleared off. 'Clearing off' is a process whereby the person or persons applying for a grant explain why those with a better right to a grant are not applying.

A person who is a beneficiary under a will, but is not entitled to take because he has witnessed the will, is not entitled to a grant (r 21 NCPR 1987).

Rule 20 covers three situations:

- where there is a complete disposal of the whole residuary estate;

- where there is a part disposal of the residuary estate;
- where there is no residuary gift in the will,

and there is no effective appointment of executors.

In the last situation, the person or persons entitled under the intestacy rules to the residuary estate will be entitled to the grant under this paragraph.

General points about letters of administration

4.6 Rule 27(4) of the NCPR 1987 provides that a grant of administration may be made to any person entitled thereto without notice to other persons entitled in the same degree. So if a parent dies intestate leaving five children, one child can obtain a grant of letters of administration without notice to the others. If a will appoints executors, then notice must be given to those not proving the will.

It may be that a minor and an adult are entitled to a grant. In this situation; r 27(5) provides that unless a Registrar otherwise directs, administration is to be granted to a person of full age entitled thereto in preference to a guardian of a minor.

The rules also provide that personal representatives of a deceased beneficiary are entitled to a grant just as if the beneficiary was still alive. If a living person is also entitled, then that living person must be given priority in preference to the personal representatives of a deceased person (r 27(5)). Thus if the deceased died intestate, for example, a widower leaving three children one of whom predeceased the intestate, the two surviving children have a better right to the grant than the personal representatives of the deceased child.

Rule 27(6) provides that a dispute between persons entitled to a grant in the same degree shall be brought by summons before a Registrar.

Grant to the unadministered estate

4.7 This grant is issued where part of the estate is unadministered, and the sole, or if the original grant was to more than one personal representative, the last surviving personal representative, has died. It should be noted that such a grant is not necessary where no original grant was obtained. If a sole executor has died without obtaining a grant, then a grant of letters of administration with the will annexed will be made. In this situation, the order of entitlement is governed by r 20 of the NCPR 1987. If the deceased died without leaving a will, then a simple grant of letters of administration to the next person entitled under r 22 of the NCPR will be made.

If a grant has been obtained, the order of entitlement to the grant depends on whether the deceased died leaving a will. If this was the case, it may be that the chain of executorship will apply. Section 7(1) of the Administration of Estates

Act 1925 provides that the executor of the sole or last surviving executor of a testator is the executor of that testator. However, this only applies if the executor of the original testator proves the will of that testator. In addition, it does not apply if other executors survive, and prove the will. Section 7(2) provides that so long as the chain is unbroken, the last executor in the chain is the executor of every preceding testator. Section 7(3) provides that the chain of such representation is broken by:

— an intestacy; or

— the failure of the testator to appoint an executor; or

— the failure to obtain probate of the will.

The chain of representation will not be broken by a temporary grant of administration where probate is subsequently granted.

If the chain of executorship does not apply, then the order of entitlement is governed by r 20 of the NCPR 1987 where the deceased left a will. If the deceased died intestate, the order of entitlement is governed by r 22 of the NCPR 1987.

Grant during the minority of an executor or administrator

4.8 It is to be hoped that no professionally drawn will would appoint an infant as an executor. However, it may be on intestacy that a minor is entitled to a grant. If a minor is entitled, then r 32 of the NCPR 1987 provides for the grant of letters of administration to the parents jointly or to the guardians of the infant. Such a grant will terminate when the infant attains 18. Rule 32(2) provides that a Registrar may, by order, assign any person as guardian of the minor.

Grants in case of mental incapacity

4.9 Due to the increase in longevity, there may be an increase in the number of grants under this category. An elderly couple where the husband dies intestate may leave a spouse entitled under the intestacy rules, but incapable of managing her affairs because of, for example, Alzheimer's disease. If the deceased had left a will appointing the spouse as executor, it is to be hoped that in this scenario at the very least a codicil would have been executed revoking the appointment of the spouse as executor, and appointing an adult child in his or her place, but this will not always happen.

If a person entitled to a grant is incapable of managing his affairs by reason of mental incapacity, r 35(2) of the NCPR 1987 provides that administration for his use and benefit may be granted in the following order of priority:

(a) to the person authorised by the Court of Protection to apply for a grant;

(b) where there is no person so authorised, to the lawful attorney of the incapable person acting under a registered enduring power of attorney;

(c) where there is no such attorney entitled to act, or if the attorney renounces administration for the use and benefit of the incapable person, to the person entitled to the residuary estate of the deceased.

Rule 35(1) of the NCPR 1987 provides that unless a Registrar otherwise directs, no grant shall be made in this situation unless all the persons entitled in the same degree as the incapable person have been cleared off. This would apply, for example, if the testator has appointed his wife and children as executors. If the wife is mentally incapable, then no grant will be made under r 35 until the children have been cleared off; the children might renounce their right to the grant, or possibly might have predeceased the testator. It would also apply if the deceased had died intestate leaving three children. If one is mentally incapable, then no grant will be made under r 35 if the other children wish to take out a grant.

Rule 35(3) provides that where a grant is required to be made to not less than two administrators, and there is only one person competent and willing to take a grant under the rule, administration may be granted to such person jointly with any other person nominated by him, unless a Registrar otherwise directs. Rule 35(4) provides that notwithstanding the other provisions in the rule, administration for the use and benefit of the incapable person may be granted to such two or more other persons as the Registrar may by order direct.

Rule 35(5) provides that notice of an intended application under this rule must be given to the Court of Protection.

It is also necessary to produce a medical certificate to the effect that the executor or administrator is mentally incapable. This is not required if the Court of Protection has authorised the applicant to apply for a grant, or the applicant is acting under an enduring power of attorney which has been registered (see Practice Note [1962] 2 All ER 613, Practice Direction [1969] 1 All ER 494).

Grant to an attorney

4.10 An attorney can apply for a grant for the use and benefit of the donor under r 31 of the NCPR 1987. Such a grant will be limited until further representation is granted, or in such other way as the District Judge or Registrar may direct.

If the donor is an executor, notice of the application must be given to any other executor unless the District Judge or Registrar dispenses with such notice (r 31(2)).

Rule 31(3) provides that if the donor is mentally incapable, and the attorney is acting under an enduring power of attorney, the application has to be made under r 35 (see PARA 4.9).

Grants where the deceased died domiciled outside England and Wales

4.11 Rule 30(1) of the NCPR 1987 provides that where the deceased died domiciled outside England and Wales, a District Judge or Registrar may order that a grant, limited in such way as the District Judge or Registrar may direct, should be issued to any of the following persons:

(a) to the person entrusted with the administration of the estate by the court having jurisdiction at the place where the deceased died domiciled; or

(b) where there is no person so entrusted, to the person beneficially entitled to the estate by the law of the place where the deceased died domiciled or, if there is more than one person so entitled, to such of them as the District Judge or Registrar may so direct; or

(c) if in the opinion of the District Judge or Registrar the circumstances so require, to such person as the Registrar may direct.

Rule 30(2) provides that a grant under paragraph (a) or (b) may be issued jointly with such person as the District Judge or Registrar may direct, if the grant is required to be made to not less than two administrators.

Rule 30(3) provides that without any order under r 30(1)–

(a) probate of any will which is admissible to proof may be granted:

  (i) if the will is in the English or Welsh language, to the executor named therein; or

  (ii) if the will describes the duties of a named person in terms sufficient to constitute him executor according to the tenor, to that person; and

(b) where the whole or substantially the whole of the estate in England and Wales consists of immovable property, a grant in respect of the whole estate may be made in accordance with the law which would have been applicable if the deceased had died domiciled in England and Wales.

Thus if the deceased was not domiciled in England and Wales, but leaves a will complying with the requirements of the Wills Act 1963, the will is in English or Welsh and appoints an executor, it can be proved without an order. However, affidavit evidence may be required – practitioners thinking of making use of these provisions should approach the Probate Registry they intend to use to ascertain the exact requirements.

Grants limited to certain property

4.12 Where required it is possible to obtain a grant limited to certain property, for example settled land.

It is also common for authors to appoint literary executors to deal with the copyrights of their published work, and general executors to deal with the remainder of the estate.

Very occasionally, where the deceased is in business, whether as a sole trader, in a partnership or through the medium of a limited company, separate executors may be appointed to deal with the business assets and other assets.

These types of grant are rare, and therefore are not considered in detail in this book.

Grants to assignees

4.13 Rule 24(1) of the NCPR 1987 provides that where all the persons entitled to the estate of the deceased (whether under a will or on intestacy) have assigned their whole interest in the estate to one or more persons, the assignee or assignees shall replace, in the order of priority for a grant of administration, the assignor or, if there are two or more assignors, the assignor with the highest priority. Rule 24(2) provides that where there are two or more assignees, administration may be granted with the consent of the others to any one or more (not exceeding four) of them. The original instrument of assignment must be produced, and a copy lodged in the registry (r 24(3)).

Number of executors

4.14 A testator can appoint as many executors as he or she likes, although if an excessive number were appointed, there must clearly be a doubt about the capacity of the testator! However, whilst in theory a testator can appoint as many executors as he likes, only four will be permitted to take out a grant. If more than four executors apply for a grant of probate, it will be granted to the first four to apply with power reserved to the others.

Rule 27(1) provides that where on an application for probate, power to apply for a like grant is to be reserved to such other of the executors as have not renounced probate, the oath must state that notice of the application has been given to the executor or executors to whom power is to be reserved. If power is to be reserved to the partners in a firm, notice is to be given to the partners by sending it to the firm at its principal or last known place of business (r 27(2)). Rule 27(3) provides that a District Judge or Registrar may dispense with giving notice if he is satisfied that the giving of such notice is impracticable or would result in unreasonable delay or expense.

A grant can be made to one executor, although the court has power to appoint another administrator under s 114(4) of the Supreme Court Act 1981 (SCA 1981). This should be contrasted with administrators where two have to be appointed if there is a life interest or a minority interest.

Number of administrators

4.15 Under s 114(1) of the SCA 1981 the number of administrators is limited to four. If more than four persons are entitled, the grant will be made to the first four to apply. Thus if the deceased died intestate without a spouse, but leaving six children, the first four children to apply for a grant will be the persons to whom the grant is made.

A grant can be made to a single administrator, but this cannot be done if a minority or life interest arises under the intestacy, in which event the grant must be made to at least two persons or a trust corporation.

If a minority or life interest does arise under the intestacy rules, and one of two the administrators dies, it is not necessary to appoint another administrator.

Where a deceased died intestate leaving a spouse and children, the person with the best right to the grant is the spouse. It may be that a second administrator is required because there is a life interest, or because some or all of the children are under age. If one of the children is of age, that child can be appointed an administrator without leave under r 25(1). This provides that a person entitled in priority to a grant of administration, may without leave, apply for a grant with a person entitled in a lower degree, provided there is no other person entitled in a higher degree to the person to be joined, unless every other such person has renounced.

Rule 25(2) provides that an application must be to a Registrar or District Judge in order to obtain leave to join with a person entitled in priority to a grant of administration a person having no right or no immediate right thereto. It must be supported by an affidavit by the person entitled in priority, the consent of the person who has been proposed to join as an administrator and such other evidence as the District Judge or Registrar may direct.

No leave is required if the person to be joined is a trust corporation. Leave is also not required if r 32(3) or 35(3) apply. Rule 32 applies to grants to minors, and r 32(3) provides that in this situation where there is only one person competent and willing to take a grant, such person may, unless a District Judge or Registrar otherwise directs, nominate any fit and proper person to act jointly with him in taking the grant. Rule 35 applies to grants in cases of mental incapacity, and r 35(3) provides that where a grant is required to be made to not less than two administrators, and there is only one person competent and willing to take a grant, administration may be granted to such person jointly with any other person nominated by him, unless a District Judge or Registrar otherwise directs.

Appointment of additional personal representatives

4.16 Rule 26(1) of the NCPR 1987 provides that an application under s 114(4) of the SCA 1981 to add a personal representative shall be made to a

Registrar and shall be supported by an affidavit by the applicant, the consent of the person proposed to be added as personal representative and such other evidence as the Registrar may require. Rule 26(2) provides that on any such application the Registrar may direct that a note shall be made on the original grant of the addition of a further personal representative, or he may impound or revoke the grant or make such other order as the circumstances of the case may require.

Capacity to take out the grant

4.17 A testator can appoint anyone he wishes as executor even though that person may be completely undesirable as an executor. Similarly anyone entitled to a grant of letters of administration with or without the will under the NCPR 1987 can apply even though that person may have convictions for fraud, and be unsuitable as an administrator. It should be noted that it may be that there is a duty on administrators to disclose facts about their past which may mean that they are unsuitable to be administrators (see *Shephard v Wheeler [2000] 1 WTLR 1175*).

Whilst the general rule is that anyone can be appointed as an executor or administrator, there are rules preventing some types of applicant applying, or imposing restrictions on their right to apply.

A grant will not be made to an infant. Instead, a grant will be made for the use and benefit of the minor under r 32 (see PARA 4.8 above).

A grant will not be made to a person who is incapable of managing his affairs by reason of mental disorder. Instead, a grant will be made for his use and benefit under r 35 NCPR 1987 (see PARA 4.9 above).

A grant may be made to a person resident outside the jurisdiction.

A trust corporation is also entitled to a grant. Section 128 of the SCA 1981 provides that a trust corporation means the Public Trustee or a corporation either appointed by the court in any particular case to be a trustee or authorised by rules made under s 4(3) of the Public Trustee Act 1906 to act as custodian trustee.

Renunciation

4.18 Acting as an executor and administrator can be an onerous task, and a person appointed as executor, who may have agreed to act as such, may not feel able to do so when the testator dies because of ill health.

Anyone appointed as an executor can renounce the right to take out a grant, as long as they have not intermeddled with the estate. Intermeddling means that the person has taken steps to administer the estate – it is an implied acceptance of the office of executor. A person entitled to apply for grant of letters of administration can also renounce even if that person has intermeddled with the estate as the authority of an administrator is derived from the grant.

It should be noted that acts of humanity or necessity will not constitute intermeddling. Thus arranging the funeral of the deceased, feeding the animals of the deceased, and preserving the property of the deceased will not amount to intermeddling.

Rule 37(1) provides that renunciation of probate by an executor shall not operate as renunciation of any right which he may have to a grant of administration in some other capacity unless he expressly renounces such right. A different rule applies to administrators. Rule 37(2) provides that no person who has renounced administration in one capacity may obtain a grant thereof in some other capacity.

Some testators appoint the members of firm of solicitors as executors. Rule 37(2A) of the NCPR 1987 provides that renunciation of probate or administration by members of a partnership:

- may be effected; or
- subject to paragraph (3), may be retracted by any two of them with the authority of the others and any such renunciation or retraction must recite such authority.

A renunciation of probate or administration may be retracted at any time with the leave of a District Judge or Registrar. However, if a grant has been made to some other person entitled in a lower degree, leave to retract a renunciation of probate will only be given in exceptional circumstances (r 37(3)).

Rule 37(4) provides that a direction or order giving leave under this rule may be made either by the Registrar of a district probate registry where the renunciation is filed or by a District Judge.

Grant of letters of administration to a person not entitled to it

4.19 The court has power to grant letters of administration to a person not strictly entitled to it. Rule 52 provides that an application for such a grant must be made to a District Judge or Registrar and must be supported by an affidavit setting out the grounds of the application.

Inheritance (Provision for Family and Dependants) Act 1975

4.20 Occasionally, an applicant may wish to bring proceedings against an estate where no grant has been obtained, for example if all the assets are jointly owned. In this situation, application can be made for the appointment of the Official Solicitor as administrator with his consent. However, where such a situation arises it may be possible to appoint another person to deal with the estate (see *Murphy v Holland [2003] EWCA Civ 1862*).

Chapter 5

Procedure for obtaining the grant in straightforward cases

5.1 In the great majority of cases, there is no dispute about the validity of a will, or the fact that the deceased died intestate. In these cases, obtaining a grant of probate or letters of administration is straightforward. Challenges to the validity of wills are discussed in CHAPTER 11.

Documents required to be submitted

5.2 In order to obtain a grant of probate or letters of administration, it is necessary to prepare and submit the following documents:

(a) to the Probate Registry:

- (i) oath for executors and administrators;
- (ii) any will and codicils;
- (iii) a cheque for the fees payable to the Probate Registry;
- (iv) such other affidavits as may be required;
- (v) form D18 – part of the Inland Revenue account;
- (vi) IHT 205 in the case of an excepted estate (probably as from November 2004).

(b) to the Capital Taxes Office:

- (i) Inland Revenue account – this is not required in every case;
- (ii) a cheque for any inheritance tax payable, unless the inheritance tax direct payment scheme is being used (see 5.7).

Where to apply

5.3 Application can be made to the Principal Registry, a district probate registry or a sub-registry. Registries have no territorial jurisdiction, and so an application can be made to a registry which operates in an area with which neither the deceased nor any beneficiary has any connection (r 4(1) and 5(1)

Non-Contentious Probate Rules 1987 (NCPR 1987)). The addresses and telephone numbers of all registries and sub-registries in England and Wales are set out in APPENDIX 4.

Applications by solicitors

5.4 Executors and administrators can employ a solicitor to make the application for a grant. Rule 4(2) of the NCPR 1987 provides that every solicitor through whom an application is made must give the address of his place of business in England and Wales.

Applications by lay persons

5.5 A lay person can apply for a grant without using a solicitor. Such applications are governed by r 5 of the NCPR 1987. Rule 5(2) provides that a personal applicant may not apply through an agent, whether paid or unpaid. In addition, any personal applicant must not be attended by any person acting or appearing to act as his adviser. Rule 5(3) provides that no personal application shall be proceeded with if:

(a) it becomes necessary to bring the matter before the court by action or summons, unless a District Judge or Registrar so permits …;

(b) an application has already been made by a solicitor or probate practitioner on behalf of the applicant and has not been withdrawn; or

(c) the District Judge or Registrar so directs.

Rule 5(4) provides that after a will has been deposited in a registry by a personal applicant, it may not be delivered to the applicant or to any other person unless there are special circumstances and the District Judge or Registrar so directs.

Rule 5(5) provides that a personal applicant must produce a certificate of the death of the deceased or such other evidence of the death as the District Judge or Registrar may approve.

Rule 5(6) provides that a personal applicant must supply all information necessary to enable the papers leading to the grant to be prepared by the registry.

Rule 5(7) provides that unless the District Judge or Registrar otherwise directs every oath or affidavit required on a personal application must be sworn or executed by all the deponents before an authorised officer.

Rule 5(8) provides that no legal advice must be given to a personal applicant by an officer of a registry and every such officer shall be responsible only for embodying in proper form the applicant's instructions for a grant.

Time limits

5.6 Rule 6(2) provides that except with the leave of a District Judge or Registrar, no grant of probate or of administration with the will annexed can be issued within seven days of the death of the deceased, and no grant of administration can be issued within fourteen days of the death.

There is no other time limit for applications, although penalties may be imposed if the Inland Revenue account is not submitted within twelve months.

Rule 6(1) provides that a District Judge or Registrar shall not allow any grant to be issued until all enquiries which he may see fit to make have been answered to his satisfaction.

Raising the funds to pay inheritance tax

5.7 Inheritance tax is due six months after the end of the month of death unless due to the circumstances listed below there is a right to pay by instalments. The right to pay by instalments applies to:

(a) land of any description, wherever situated;

(b) a business or an interest in a business;

(c) shares or securities in a company controlled by the deceased;

(d) unquoted shares and securities not giving control if not less than 20% of so much of the tax chargeable on the value transferred as is tax for which the person paying the tax attributable as mentioned in s 227(1) of the Inheritance Tax Act 1984 is liable (in the same capacity) consists of tax attributable to the value of the shares and securities or such other tax as may by virtue of s 227 be paid by instalments. This means that there is a right to pay by instalments if at least 20% of the tax payable on the estate of the deceased is attributable to shares not giving any control or on other assets qualifying for instalments;

(e) unquoted shares and securities in a company not controlled by the deceased if the Board are satisfied that the tax attributable to their value cannot be paid in one sum without undue hardship;

(f) unquoted shares and securities in a company not controlled by the deceased if so much of the value transferred as is attributable to the shares exceeds £20,000; and either

  (i) the nominal value of the shares is not less than 10% of the nominal value of all the shares of the company at the time of the transfer; or

  (ii) the shares are ordinary shares and their nominal value is not less than 10% of the nominal value of all ordinary shares of the company at that time;

(g) woodlands.

The most important category is the first – land of any description. The other categories apart from (g) are not so important as frequently the assets listed will qualify for 100% business property relief.

If there is a right to pay by instalments, then the tax attributable to the property must be paid by ten equal yearly instalments. The election to do so is usually made in the Inland Revenue account. If the property is sold, then the inheritance tax due in respect of that property must be paid.

Interest is due on the outstanding instalments except in the case of some property qualifying for business property relief, agricultural property relief or timber. Whether or not interest is due on the outstanding instalments, it is always due if an instalment is paid late.

If there is no right to pay by instalments, then the tax due should be paid six months after the end of the month of death. If it is not paid, interest is due. It must also be paid before the grant is obtained. Possible methods of raising the tax are:

— Building society accounts. If the deceased had any accounts with building societies, then they may be prepared to release the funds required to pay the inheritance tax.

— Banks. Approach banks with which the deceased held accounts in order to see if they are prepared to release funds. It may be that the deceased held bank accounts as a joint tenant. If this is the case, no grant is required to enable the surviving joint tenant to access the money; all that is required is the production of the death certificate. A bank loan can be obtained. Obviously the bank will charge interest and an arrangement fee.

— The Inheritance Tax Direct Payment Scheme. Most banks and building societies participate in this scheme. It is necessary to obtain a reference number by completing form D21 and sending it to the appropriate IR Capital Taxes Office, or by telephoning the Capital Taxes Office Helpline. Once the amount of inheritance tax due has been ascertained form D20 should be completed, and sent to the relevant bank or building society.

— It may be possible to obtain payment of the monies due under a life assurance policy without the need for a grant.

— It is possible to sell chattels before a grant has been obtained.

— If a receiver has been appointed by the Court of Protection to deal with the property of the deceased, the Court may be prepared to release funds in order to pay inheritance tax.

— It is possible to use moneys invested with National Savings to pay inheritance tax. A letter should be obtained from National Savings as to the appropriate value of the relevant holdings, and this should be sent to the Pre-Grant Section of the Capital Taxes Office together with the Inland Revenue account.

— It may be that the beneficiaries will have some spare cash which can be used to pay the inheritance tax. It will be cheaper to utilise this money rather than obtain a bridging loan from the bank.

If there is a possibility of a deed of variation or disclaimer, these can be entered into before the papers are submitted to the Inland Revenue. A deed of variation or disclaimer may reduce the inheritance tax payable. If the variation or disclaimer is in favour of a spouse, it may mean that no inheritance tax is payable because of spouse exemption.

Leave to swear death

5.8 Rule 53(1) of the NCPR 1987 provides that an application to swear to the death of a person in whose estate a grant is sought may be made to a District Judge or Registrar, and shall be supported by an affidavit setting out the grounds of the application and containing particulars of any policies of insurance effected on the life of the presumed deceased, together with such further evidence as the District Judge or Registrar may require.

Chapter 6

Drafting the oath, and any other affidavits required to obtain a grant

6.1 In order to obtain a grant, personal representatives must submit an executors' or administrators' oath. It may also be necessary to submit, in the form of an affidavit, evidence with regard to the following issues:

(a) if there is any doubt about compliance with the requirements of s 9 of the Wills Act 1837;

(b) if there is any doubt about the date of the will – this will be important if there is more than one will, and it is necessary to determine which is the most recent;

(c) if there are any circumstances casting doubt as to whether the testator knew and approved of the contents of the will. Normally, this is presumed, but if it appears that the testator was, for example, blind, it will probably be necessary for witnesses to swear affidavits confirming that the will was read to the testator before he signed it, and that he appeared to understand it. This may not be necessary if the attestation clause indicates that the will has been read over to the testator;

(d) if the will contains alterations – there is a presumption that they were made after the will was executed, and are invalid. However, if it can be proved that they were made before the will was executed, then they are valid;

(e) if it is apparent from the will that another document has been attached to the will – for example, if there is an indentation in the will which appears to have been made by a paperclip.

The executors' or administrators' oath

6.2 When swearing the executor's or administrator's oath it is usual to use the printed forms supplied by Law Stationers, or word processed forms. The following points are common to all forms:

— *The name of the deceased*

The true name of the deceased should be inserted.

It is not uncommon for people not to use a name, perhaps because they do not like it, and people sometimes change their surnames. If this is the case, the true name should still be inserted, unless property is vested in the name of the deceased in a name other than the true name, or the will was executed in a name other than the true name, in which event it will be necessary to include the alias in the oath. It is also necessary to specify which part of the estate was held in the other name, or give any other reason for the inclusion of the name in the grant (r 9 NCPR 1987).

— Order of names of applicants

The order should follow the order in the will.

If this is not done, the Probate Registry will treat that as an implied request to vary the order.

If the application is for a grant of letters of administration, then the order should follow the order of entitlement to the estate.

— Dates of birth and death

It is necessary to insert the dates of birth and death of the deceased. If you are taking instructions from an elderly person who appears confused, the date of birth should be checked against the birth certificate of the deceased. The date of death should be obtained from the death certificate.

— Domicile

It is important to state the correct domicile of the deceased.

Everyone has a domicile of origin, which is usually determined by the domicile of the parents. It is also possible to acquire a domicile of choice by residing in a country with the intention of living there permanently. It should be noted that residence in another country, even if it is for a long period, will not give the person concerned a domicile of choice in that country if the person does not intend to remain there permanently.

The grant will recite the domicile of the deceased; if it states that the deceased was domiciled in England and Wales, it will be recognised in Scotland and Northern Ireland.

— The will and any codicil

The oath must specify how many documents are being proved, for example a will and two codicils. The will and any codicils must be marked; this means that the applicant and the person before whom the oath is sworn must sign those documents (r 10 NCPR 1987).

Rule 10(2) provides that the Registrar may allow a facsimile copy of the will to be marked or exhibited in lieu of the original document.

— Settled land

Rule 8(3) of the NCPR 1987 requires that the oath shall state whether or not, to the best of the applicant's knowledge information and belief, there was land vested in the deceased which was settled previously to his death and not by his will and which remained settled land notwithstanding his death.

In the great majority of cases the deceased will not have been entitled to settled land, or if they were, the settlement will have terminated on the death of the life tenant. Since the Trusts of Land and Appointment of Trustees Act 1996 it has not been possible to create a strict settlement governed by the Settled Land Act 1925.

If the deceased was entitled to settled land, and if the settlement continued after death, then a grant limited to the settled land in favour of the trustees of the settlement will be required.

— Duty of personal representatives

The oath then requires that the personal representatives will administer the estate in accordance with the duties imposed by s 25 of the Administration of Estates Act 1925.

— Certificates of value

If the estate of the deceased was within certain limits, then it is not necessary to deliver an Inland Revenue account.

If the estate is an excepted estate, then the gross estate must be stated as not exceeding £240,000 for estates where the deceased died after 6 April 2003; the net value of the estate must be shown as not exceeding £ rounded up to the next whole thousand. Note that the Inland Revenue are reviewing the rules about excepted estates.

If the estate of the deceased was outside these limits, then the gross and net estate can be ascertained from the Inland Revenue account.

The fee payable to the Probate Registry depends on the value of the net estate. If it is more than £5,000, it is £50 plus £1 for every office copy required.

Grants of probate

Non proving executors

6.3 If the will appoints more than one executor, it is common for some of the executors not to take out the grant. Instead, power is reserved to them to take out the grant if they wish to do so.

If there are executors who do not want to take out the grant, r 27(1) of the NCPR 1987 provides that the oath must state that notice of the application has been given to those to whom power is to be reserved. If the partners in a firm of solicitors have been appointed executors, r 27(2) provides that notice may be given to the partners by sending it to the firm at its principal or last known place of business.

Rule 27(3) provides that a District Judge or Registrar may dispense with the giving of such notice if he is satisfied that the giving of such a notice would be impracticable or would result in unreasonable delay or expense.

Change of name of applicant

6.4 It may be that an applicant for a grant of probate has changed his or her name; for example, a woman may have changed her name on marriage. If this is the case, the oath must state that there has been a change of name, and offer an explanation. If it is marriage which has caused the name change, then the oath should state 'Wendy June Wood in the will called Wendy June Swallow having changed her name on marriage'. (See *Tolley's Administration of Estates* para C7.23).

Grants of letters of administration

6.5 The oath to lead to a grant of simple administration is very similar to that required to obtain a grant of probate. The differences are:

(a) there is no reference to any will or codicil;

(b) the oath must state in what manner all persons having a prior right to the grant have been cleared off;

(c) the oath also states in what capacity the applicants are entitled to the grant.

Rule 22 of the NCPR 1987 prescribes the order of entitlement to a grant of letters of administration. An applicant for a grant must show how anyone higher up the order has ceased to be entitled. Thus no words of clearance are necessary if the application is by the spouse of the deceased as there is no one with a better right to the grant. If it is a child who is applying then the deceased should be described as a widow or widower.

If the deceased was unmarried at the date of death, but had been divorced, then the oath must state 'that the marriage between   and   was dissolved by the final decree of the   Court in England and Wales dated the   day of   and the deceased did not thereafter remarry'. (See *Tolley's Administration of Estates* para C9.43).

If the application is made by persons other than the surviving spouse or children, the words 'or any other person entitled in priority to share in his/her estate by virtue of any enactment' must be added.

It is also necessary to state the capacity in which the applicant is claiming. It is only necessary to use the word 'lawful' if the application is by a surviving spouse, or an adopted child.

Grant of letters of administration with the will annexed

6.6 The major difference is that the oath will refer to any wills or codicils which the deceased left. In addition, the order of entitlement to the grant is determined by r 20 of the NCPR 1987. As with grants of simple administration, it is necessary to clear off anyone with a better right to the grant – to explain why they are not obtaining a grant. This might be because they were appointed executors in the will, but have renounced the right to a grant, or have predeceased.

Chapter 7

Drafting the Inland Revenue account

Introduction and overview

7.1 It is necessary to submit an account to the Inland Revenue unless the estate is excepted. An excepted estate is one where:

(a) the person died on or after 6 April 2003 domiciled in the United Kingdom. Other rules apply if the person died domiciled outside the UK (see IHT 12);

(b) the value of that person's estate is attributable wholly to property passing under his will or intestacy or under a nomination of an asset taking effect on death or under a single settlement in which he was entitled to an interest in possession in settled property or by survivorship in a beneficial joint tenancy;

(c) of that property –

   (i) not more than £100,000 represented value attributable to property which, immediately before that person's death was settled property; and

   (ii) not more than £75,000 represented value attributable to property which, immediately before that person's death, was situated outside the UK;

(d) that person died without having made any chargeable transfers during the period of seven years ending with this death other than specified transfers where the aggregate chargeable value did not exceed £100,000. 'Specified transfers' means chargeable transfers made during the period of seven years ending with that person's death where the value transferred is attributable to cash or to quoted shares or securities or an interest in or over land (and furnishings and chattels disposed of at the same time to the same donee and intended to be enjoyed with the land), save to the extent that ss 102 and 102A(2) of the Finance Act 1986 apply to the transfer, or the land or furnishings or chattels became settled property on that transfer; and

(e) the aggregate of the gross value of that person's estate and of the value transferred by any specified transfers did not exceed £240,000.

For deaths before 6 April 2003, other rules applied to determine if an estate was excepted.

It is also possible to submit a reduced account. The conditions which must be satisfied before a reduced account can be submitted are set out in IHT 19, which is reproduced in the Appendices. One situation where a reduced account can be submitted is where the deceased died domiciled in England and Wales, and all the deceased's assets pass to the surviving spouse, who is also domiciled in England and Wales.

These rules will change (probably in November 2004). The new rules will provide:

(i) No IHT 200 will be required if the gross value of the estate plus any lifetime transfers in the seven years prior to death do not exceed the NRB.

(ii) No IHT 200 will be required if the gross estate plus any lifetime transfers in the seven years prior to death do not exceed £1m and the net chargeable estate after deducting spouse or charity exemption is less than the NRB.

If the estate is an excepted estate, it will be necessary to submit an IHT 205 to the Probate Registry. This is a short four page document.

In addition, when ever an IHT 200 is delivered, a D18 must be submitted to IR Capital Taxes, even though no IHT is payable.

If it is necessary to submit an Inland Revenue account, the relevant forms can be obtained from:

IR Capital Taxes

Ferrers House

PO Box 38

Castle Meadow Road

Nottingham NG2 1BB

Tel: 0115 974 2400

Fax: 0115 974 2432

It is also possible to obtain the forms and leaflets via the internet – the address is www.inlandrevenue.gov.uk

The forms are also available on the computerised forms packages which are available commercially.

The Inland Revenue also produce some guidance notes – IHT 215 – the current edition is reproduced in APPENDIX 3.

The IHT 200 account is a summary of all the property the deceased owned in his own right, any jointly owned property, and any property in which the deceased had a life interest. The account calculates the total estate, deducts any debts due from the deceased and the funeral expenses, and then calculates the inheritance tax. This sounds very simple, but if it is done manually, it can involve considerable calculations, and carrying figures from one page to another.

There are also supplementary pages which have to be completed – D1 to D21. As the totals from these pages have to be inserted in the IHT 200, it is probably best to start by completing the supplementary pages. There is also a worksheet which has to be completed in order to calculate the inheritance tax due.

Once the forms have been completed, if no tax is payable, the forms necessary to obtain the grant and D18 must be sent to the Probate Registry. The Inland Revenue account should be sent to IR Capital Taxes at the same time.

If tax is payable, the procedure is different. The IHT 200 and the supplementary pages including D18 should be sent to IR Capital Taxes, together with the tax due.

IR Capital Taxes will complete the D18, and send it back. The D18 and the papers required to obtain the grant of probate must then be submitted to the Probate Registry.

These rules will change (probably in November 2004). The new rules will provide that is the estate is an excepted estate, it will be necessary to submit an IHT 205 to the Probate Registry. This is a short four page document.

In addition, whenever an IHT 200 is delivered, a D18 must be submitted to IR Capital Taxes, even though no IHT is payable. IR Capital Taxes will complete the D18, and return it. It must then be lodged with the Probate Registry.

Completion of the supplementary pages

7.2 The supplementary pages are:

- D1 – the will;
- D2 – domicile outside the UK;
- D3 – gifts and other transfers of value;
- D4 – joint and nominated assets;
- D5 – assets held in trust;
- D6 – pensions;
- D7 – stocks and shares;
- D8 – debts due to the estate;
- D9 – life insurance and annuities;
- D10 – household and personal goods;

— D11 – interest in another estate;

— D12 – land, buildings, and interest in land;

— D13 – agricultural relief;

— D14 – business relief, business or partnership interests;

— D15 – foreign assets;

— D16 – debts owed by the estate;

— D17 – continuation sheet;

— D18 – probate summary;

— D19 – confirmation that no inheritance tax is payable;

— D20 – application to transfer funds to pay inheritance tax;

— D21 – application for Capital Taxes reference.

It is not proposed to go through each supplementary page in detail. The requirements of IR Capital Taxes are clearly set out in IHT 215, and readers are referred to those notes, which are set out in APPENDIX 3. However, it is hoped that the following comments will assist readers.

Note: The references to numbers in brackets are references to the relevant numbered questions on the D forms.

D1 – The will

7.3 (1) It is quite common for a testator to move between making a will and death.

If no house is included as part of the estate in the IHT 200, it is necessary to explain what has happened to the proceeds, and where they appear in the IHT 200.

(2) If the will only contains a residuary gift, then tick the n/a box.

If there are specific gifts, then if they are included in the IHT 200, tick the yes box.

If the items the subject of specific gifts have been the subject of lifetime gifts, then it is necessary to give details of those lifetime gifts.

If the item has been sold, you must give details about the sale, and say where the proceeds appear in the IHT 200.

(3) If you are claiming spouse exemption, give the full name of the spouse, and the date of birth. It is also desirable to ask to see the marriage certificate to ensure that the deceased was in fact married.

If you are claiming charity exemption, and the charity is not well known, the registered number of the charity should be given.

Usually a copy of the will should be submitted with the IHT 200. However, if the gross estate is less than the NRB, and you have answered yes to questions 1 and 2, then you do not need to submit one.

If there has been a deed of variation, it should be sent with the will. More often than not a deed of variation will reduce the amount of inheritance tax payable, and if the deed of variation reduces the amount of inheritance tax payable, the inheritance tax account can be prepared on the basis that it is in force.

D2 – Domicile outside the UK

7.4 Every person has a domicile of origin, which is usually determined by the domicile of the parents. It is also possible to acquire a domicile of choice by residing in a country with the intention of permanently residing there.

There are special rules which apply for inheritance tax purposes – if the deceased has lived in the UK for 17 out of the last 20 years, he will be deemed to be domiciled in the UK. In addition, the deceased will be deemed to have been domiciled in the UK if he was domiciled in the UK at any time in the three years before death. It should be stressed that these rules only apply for the purposes of inheritance tax, and it may be that for other purposes the deceased will not be domiciled here, for example in order for an application to be made under the Inheritance (Provision for Family and Dependants) Act 1975, it must be proved that the deceased died domiciled in England and Wales. It is possible for a deceased to be domiciled here for inheritance tax purposes, but not for the purposes of an application under the 1975 Act.

Domicile is very significant – if the deceased was domiciled outside the UK, then any foreign property will not be subject to inheritance tax. If the deceased was domiciled in the UK, all the assets of the deceased, wherever situated, will be subject to inheritance tax.

If the deceased was domiciled in the UK and owned foreign assets, it is necessary to complete D15. If the deceased was domiciled elsewhere, it is only necessary to complete the D forms applying to assets in this country in addition to the D2.

D3 – Gifts and other transfers of value

7.5 IR Capital Taxes needs to know about gifts during the lifetime of the deceased as these may affect the rate of inheritance tax payable on death, and in addition if the gift is large enough, or there have been a series of gifts, then the gift or gifts may be chargeable to inheritance tax. However, if the gift is covered by an exemption, it may not need to be included.

If the personal representatives are claiming normal expenditure out of income exemption, then it need not be included if it is less than the annual exemption, and the deceased had not made any other gifts. However, if it does exceed the annual exemption, it must be included, and an additional form completed showing the income and expenditure of the deceased.

Note that the word gift has a wider meaning when used in this context than the usual accepted meaning. When it comes to lifetime transactions, inheritance tax is payable on the reduction in value of the donor's estate. It follows that transactions less than an absolute gift can give rise to a liability for inheritance tax. So if a house is sold to a child at an undervalue, that can give rise to a charge to inheritance tax as the parent's estate has been reduced in value.

(1c) One way of providing for children or grandchildren is to take out an endowment policy with a life insurance company, and make it subject to a declaration of trust in favour of children or grandchildren. The parents or grandparents continue to pay the premiums. Normally this will not have any inheritance tax consequences as the premiums will come within the annual exemption or normal expenditure out of income exemption for inheritance tax purposes.

(1d) The deceased may have been a life tenant, in which event they are deemed to own all the underlying trust assets as far as inheritance tax is concerned. If they give up any part of the life interest, they will be deemed to make a PET of whatever part of the underlying trust assets are given up. So if the life tenant surrenders 50% of the life interest, they will be deemed to make a PET of the underlying trust assets.

— *Gifts with reservation*

(2) These are ineffective as far as inheritance is concerned. The donor will still be deemed to own the assets as far as inheritance tax is concerned. So if parents give the house to children, but continue living there, it is a gift with a reservation of benefit. If the parent dies within seven years of making the gift, it should also be included in section 1. Similarly of a parent gives an antique to a child, but still uses the antique, then it must be included in his or her estate.

(3) Chargeable gifts here are lifetime transfers to discretionary trusts, and also to companies. If the deceased has during his lifetime transferred assets to the trustees of a discretionary trust, and also made other lifetime gifts within seven years of death, the amount transferred to the trustees of the discretionary trust within seven years of any other lifetime gift must be brought into account in order to determine the rate of tax. This means that in order to determine to the rate of tax on a lifetime gift, it might be necessary to go back almost 14 years.

Example:

- Z creates a discretionary trust in 1992.

- He creates another discretionary trust in 1998, or makes a PET in that year.
- He dies in 2004.

As he has died within seven years of the creation of the 1998 discretionary trust, it will be necessary to recalculate the inheritance tax payable on that discretionary trust.

If it was a PET, then it will become chargeable for the first time as the deceased has not survived for seven years after making the gift.

In order to determine the rate of tax applying to the 1998 discretionary trust on death or the PET, it will be necessary to bring into account all lifetime transfers to discretionary trusts in the seven years prior to 1998.

Accordingly, it will be necessary to bring into account the 1992 discretionary trust in order to determine the rate of tax that applies to the 1998 discretionary trust or PET.

D4 – Joint and nominated assets

7.6 There are two ways of holding property as co-owners – as joint tenants or as tenants in common. If co-owners are joint tenants, then the right of survivorship operates. This means that when one joint tenant dies, his or her interest automatically passes to the surviving joint tenant. If the co-owners are tenants in common, then if one dies his or her interest passes under his or her will, or if there is no will, under the intestacy rules to whoever is entitled to it.

All forms of property can be held as joint tenants or co-owners, so that there can be a joint tenancy or tenancy in common of land, houses, bank accounts and shareholdings.

Sometimes property is in joint names, but in fact it is all owned by one of the co-owners. This sometimes happens with bank or building society accounts which are opened in the joint names of a parent and child so as to facilitate the operation of the account because the parent is infirm. Such property should be included here.

Frequently household goods will be jointly owned. If that is the case, they should be included in the D4.

Nominated assets must also be included in the form. This is where the deceased has made use of the ability to specify who is to have the money in an account without having to comply with the requirements of the Wills Act 1837. This facility was at one time available for *inter alia* monies invested with the Post Office Savings Bank, but is now limited to sums not exceeding £5,000 invested with Industrial and Provident Societies, Friendly Societies and Trades Unions where the rules permit nomination.

Often pension schemes provide for the payment of a lump sum of up to four times the annual salary of the employee on death in service. Frequently, this lump sum is payable at the discretion of the trustees of the pension scheme as otherwise it would form part of the estate of the deceased employee for inheritance tax purposes. It is possible for the employee to request the trustees to pay the lump sum to a particular person, and whilst trustees do not have to comply with the request, frequently they will do so. These requests are sometimes incorrectly called nominations. Such lump sums should not be included here. They should be included in the D6.

D5 – Assets held in trust

7.7 The deceased may have been a life tenant under a will or settlement. If that is the case, then as far as inheritance tax is concerned, the deceased is deemed to have owned all the underlying trust assets, and they must be cumulated with the all the deceased's assets in order to determine the rate of tax.

If the deceased was within the class of beneficiaries entitled under a discretionary trust, then the members of the class are not entitled to anything as of right, and therefore it is not necessary to fill in this form.

D6 – Pensions

7.8 Pensions need to be included on this sheet if:

(a) the pension continues to be paid after death, in which event the value of the right to receive the pension must be included; note that it need not be included if the continuation is in the form of payments (usually reduced) to the surviving spouse of the deceased;

(b) if the estate of the deceased has a right to a lump sum payment on death, but not if the payment is at the discretion of the trustees of the pension scheme, although this fact should be disclosed;

(c) if the deceased had made any changes to the pension arrangements in the two years before death.

D7 – Stocks and shares

7.9 If the price of the shares is 'xd', it means that a dividend was due at the date of death, but has not been paid. The net value of the dividend must be included in this form. If the price is quoted 'cum div' it means that any future dividend is included in the price.

If the deceased died on a day when the Stock Exchange was not open, then it is permissible to take the price on the last day the Exchange was open before the date of death, or the next day the Exchange is open after the date of death.

It is common to ask brokers to value shares. Alternatively, information can be obtained from the Historic Price Service of the Stock Exchange; their address is:

4th Floor Tower
London Stock Exchange
Old Broad Street
London EC2N 1HP

Another method is to work out the value from the newspaper the day after the deceased died, or if the deceased died on a day when the Stock Exchange was closed, the price on the last day when the Exchange was open, or the price on the next day when it was open.

The value for inheritance tax purposes is either one quarter up from the lower to the higher limit of the prices quoted, or halfway between the highest and lowest bargains recorded for the day, but excluding bargains at special prices.

It is also desirable to check the deceased's actual holding in the register of each company where the deceased owned shares as one can never be certain that share certificates may have been lost or mislaid. Brokers are usually able to check the deceased's holding.

D8 – Debts due to the deceased

7.10 If there are any debts due to the deceased, they are part of the assets of the deceased as far as inheritance tax is concerned.

Parents may lend money to a child to enable that child to purchase a house. If the loan is still outstanding when the parents die, that loan is part of the surviving parent's estate as far as inheritance tax is concerned.

It will also be necessary to complete this form where the deceased was carrying on business through the medium of a limited company. Sometimes dividends are left in the company as a loan from the directors to the company. In this situation, the loan account is part of the deceased's estate as far as inheritance tax is concerned.

It will also be necessary to complete this form where the deceased has lent money to the trustees of a trust who have used it to purchase a life policy. The amount of the outstanding loan should be included here.

D9 – Life insurance and annuities

7.11 *— Life policy*

(1) The deceased may have taken out a life policy. If this has not been made the subject of a declaration of trust in favour of children or grandchildren, it will be part of the deceased's estate for inheritance tax purposes, and must be included here.

— *Joint life policy*

(2) Spouses or cohabitees may take out joint life policies which sometimes pay out on the death of the first spouse or cohabitee, and sometimes on the death of the second spouse or cohabitee.

If the policy pays out on the death of the first spouse or cohabitee, the proceeds will be part of the estate of the first spouse or cohabitee, and should have been included under question one.

If the policy pays out on the death of the second spouse or cohabitee, the value of the policy will be part of the estate of the first spouse or cohabitee to die as far as inheritance tax is concerned. The policy should also be included in D3.

If it is the spouse who is entitled to the policy, there will not be any inheritance tax implications as spouse exemption will apply provided the spouse is domiciled in the United Kingdom.

If the spouse is not domiciled in the UK, the spouse exemption is limited to £55,000 plus whatever it is left of the nil rate band.

If the deceased had paid all the premiums on a joint life policy, the deceased is in effect making a gift of half of the premiums to the other person insured, and these payments should have been recorded in D3.

(2b) Sometimes people buy policies on other people's lives. The policy will not pay out on the death of the owner, but there will be a pay out when the life assured dies.

If the deceased had bought a policy on the life of some other person, then the surrender value of that policy is part of their estate for inheritance tax purposes.

— *Pension policy*

(3) If the deceased had contributed to a personal pension policy, on retirement the deceased would have had to purchase an annuity. If the deceased was employed, and in a money purchase scheme, again on retirement the deceased would have had to purchase an annuity.

Most annuities terminate on the death of the person entitled to it. However, occasionally payments may be guaranteed for a minimum fixed period. If the deceased was entitled to an annuity with a guaranteed minimum fixed period, then if the deceased died before the expiry of that fixed minimum period, the capitalised value of the annuity will form part of the estate of the deceased for inheritance tax purposes.

If there is a surviving spouse and they are entitled to the annuity, there will be no inheritance tax consequences (this is due to the spouse exemption), provided the surviving spouse is domiciled in the United Kingdom.

— *An annuity*

(4) An annuity is a gamble. If the person entitled to it lives for 20 or 30 years after having taken out the annuity, then it may be a good buy. On the other hand, if the person entitled to it dies six months after taking out the annuity, it will be a very bad buy. On account of this, some annuities provide for the payment of a lump sum if the annuitant dies shortly after taking out the annuity. If that is the case, the lump sum will be part of the annuitant's estate for inheritance tax purposes.

Again, if the surviving spouse is entitled to the lump sum, and is domiciled in the United Kingdom, no inheritance tax will be payable on it.

However, if the lump sum is payable to a cohabitee or children, then it will be subject to inheritance tax.

— *Endowment policy*

(5) The deceased may have taken out an endowment policy, and made it subject to a declaration of trust in favour of children or grandchildren.

The initial declaration of trust would have been a PET; if it was done when the policy was first taken out, it would not usually have had any adverse inheritance tax consequences.

The parents or grandparents may have continued to pay the premiums due under the policy, and again frequently these would not have had any inheritance tax consequences as each payment would either have come within the annual exemption or the normal expenditure out of income exemption for inheritance tax purposes.

If the deceased had taken out one of these endowment policies, and put it in trust for children and grandchildren, the answer to this question is yes.

If the answer is yes, then details of the premiums paid must be included in D3.

— *Life insurance policy*

(6) This question is concerned with the situation where parents have taken out a life insurance policy, and put it in trust for children or grandchildren.

What happens if a child predeceases the parent? In such a situation, the surrender value of the policy will form part of the estate of the deceased child.

D10 – Household and personal goods

7.12 (1) and (2) – more often than not the household and personal goods will not have been sold before the personal representatives apply for the grant of probate or letters of administration.

If nothing has been sold, then it is necessary include the market value of all the household and personal goods as at the date of death. This is not the replacement cost, but what the personal representatives would receive for the assets if they were sold on the open market. For most personal representatives, this means what they would fetch if they were sold at auction.

If it is fairly standard furniture, then its value will be small. In some cases, it may even have a negative value in that it may be necessary to pay someone to take it away.

If the deceased left a motor car, then if it is necessary to include details of the make, exact model, year of registration and the registration number.

If the deceased left jewellery or antiques, then it will usually be necessary to obtain a valuation from a jeweller or specialist in antiques.

D11 – Interest in another estate

7.13 This form needs to be completed where the deceased was entitled to benefit under the will or intestacy of another person, for example a spouse who has predeceased, but has not yet received the property they are entitled to under that will or intestacy.

D12 – Land, buildings and interests in land

7.14 This form must be completed if the deceased owned any land.

It must also be completed if the deceased was entitled as a joint tenant or tenant in common to any land or house.

If the deceased was a joint owner, it would also have been necessary to complete D4.

It is essential to obtain a valuation from a qualified valuer, and a copy of that valuation should be sent to the Inland Revenue.

The valuer should value the property on the basis of the market value at the date of death.

There is a question on the second page of the form as to whether the personal representatives intend to sell the property within twelve months of death. If that is the case, in stable markets conditions, the Revenue will expect the sale price to be used as the market price as at the date of death.

If market conditions are not stable where house prices can increase dramatically between the date of death and the sale, it may not be a good idea for the sale price to be treated as the market value at the date of death. On the other hand, if this is not done, then the personal representatives will be liable for capital gains tax on the increase in value.

D11 – Agricultural relief

7.15 If the deceased was a farmer who had occupied property for agricultural purposes, and had owned it for two years, the property will qualify for agricultural property relief.

If the deceased had owned farmland which was let, it will also qualify for agriculture or property relief as long as the deceased had owned the farm land for at least seven years prior to date of death.

In summary, if the deceased had been farming the land himself then he must have owned it for two years in order to qualify for agricultural property relief. If the farmland was let, then the minimum period of ownership increases to seven years.

If the deceased was farming the land himself, and had owned it for two years, the rate of relief is 100%.

If the land was let after 31st August 1995, again it will qualify for 100% agricultural property relief, provided of course that the deceased had owned the farm land for the seven years prior to his or her death.

If the land was let before 31st August 1995, agricultural property relief will be limited to 50% of the agricultural value. However, it will be at 100% if the deceased could have obtained vacant possession within 24 months.

The questions on the D11 are designed to elicit enough information to enable the Revenue to decide if the property concerned does qualify for agricultural property relief.

(9) If you are dealing with a lifetime gift of property, and wish to claim agricultural property relief, this question must be answered.

If there has been a gift of land qualifying for agriculture or property relief, the gift will, of course, be a PET, and there is no problem if the donor survives for seven years after making the gift, because it will then be exempt from inheritance tax.

However, what is the position if the donor or dies before the seven years has expired? Is it still possible to obtain agricultural property relief? The answer to this question is yes, provided the assets are still owned by the donee at the date of death of the donor, or if they are not, that they have been replaced by other land qualifying for agricultural property relief.

D14 – business property relief

7.16 Business assets will frequently qualify for 100% business property relief. If the deceased was a sole trader then his business will qualify for 100% business property relief. If the deceased was a partner, his interest as a partner will also qualify for 100% business property relief.

In addition, any unquoted share holding, and whether or not it is a controlling shareholding, will qualify for a 100% business property relief.

However, there is one condition which must be satisfied – the deceased must have owned assets for the two years prior to the date of death.

If the deceased owned a factory or office used by a company in which the deceased had a controlling interest, that factory or office will qualify for 50% business property relief.

If the deceased had owned a factory or office, which was used by a partnership in which the deceased was a partner, again that factory or office will qualify for 50% business property relief.

Again, the deceased must have owned the factory or office for the two years prior to death.

If there has been a lifetime gift of an asset which qualifies for business property relief, as with agricultural property relief, there is no problem if the donor survives for seven years after making the gift as the gift will then be exempt. However, if the donor does not survive for seven years after making the gift, the gift will be chargeable to inheritance tax.

Business property relief will still be available if the donee still has the business property the subject of the original gift, or if it has been sold, it has been replaced with other property which qualifies for business property relief.

D15 – foreign assets

7.17 If the deceased was domiciled in England and Wales at the date death, all the assets of the deceased wherever situated will be subject to inheritance tax.

If the deceased was not domiciled in England and Wales, it is not necessary to fill in this form. Instead, all the assets of the deceased situated in England and Wales should be included in the appropriate forms.

Occasionally, a deceased who is domiciled in England and Wales may have shareholdings in foreign companies, which will have to be included in this form. More frequently, the deceased may own or have an interest in a house abroad.

If the deceased was domiciled in England and Wales and owned, or had an interest in a house abroad, then the value of that house or interest must be included in this form.

Note that the rules about paying inheritance tax by instalments apply to foreign assets as well as assets situated in England and Wales. So if the deceased owned a house in France, any inheritance tax payable on that can be paid by instalments over ten years.

The value of the asset should be shown in its foreign currency, with the English equivalent shown as well.

It may be the case that a tax similar to English inheritance tax will be payable on foreign assets in the country where they are situated. If that is the case, it may be possible to offset all or part of the foreign equivalent of inheritance tax against the English inheritance tax. This can only be done to the extent that inheritance tax is payable on the foreign asset. The foreign inheritance tax is not deducted on the D15; instead, it is deducted in the worksheet (see 7.20 below).

D16 – Debts owed by the estate

7.18 Debts owed and by the deceased are clearly deductible in calculating the amount of the estate which is subject to inheritance tax.

If the deceased owed money for the supply of electricity, gas, water etc, these are deductible in computing the amount of the deceased's estate which is subject to inheritance tax. Such debts are deducted in the IHT 200. In addition, reasonable funeral expenses and the cost of a tombstone are also deductible. Again these are deducted in the IHT 200.

However, there are some debts which may not be deductible. There are anti-avoidance provisions concerned with artificial debts. It is essential that the Revenue has these anti-avoidance provisions as otherwise it would be very easy to reduce an estate to nothing by creating artificial debts.

This form is designed to give information to the Revenue to enable them to determined if there are any artificial debts.

D20 and 21

7.19 If the deceased had an account with a bank or building society, most are prepared to release whatever is in the account in order to pay inheritance tax.

First ensure that the relevant bank or building society will operate the new procedure, then obtain a reference number from Inland Revenue Capital Taxes by telephoning the helpline, or submitting a D21. Then send the D20 to the bank or building society with the reference number.

The bank or building society then send the inheritance tax to IR Capital Taxes.

Some banks or building societies insist on using this new procedure, and will not send out cheques.

Worksheet

7.20 On the worksheet the total chargeable estate is calculated, this includes:

— All assets where tax may not be paid by instalments:

- (i) estate in the UK;
- (ii) joint property passing by survivorship;
- (iii) foreign property;
- (iv) if the deceased was a life tenant, the trust assets – optional.

— All assets where tax may be paid by instalments:

- (a) estate in the UK;
- (b) joint property passing by survivorship;
- (c) foreign property;
- (d) if the deceased was a life tenant, the trust assets – optional.

— Plus:

- gifts with reservation;
- lifetime gifts made in the seven years prior to death.

Settled assets – if the deceased was a life tenant then all the trust assets will be subject to inheritance tax. The trustees of the settlement are primarily liable for the inheritance tax due on the trust assets. It is not the deceased's personal representatives who are liable. The trustees have a choice: they can give the personal representatives of the deceased life tenant the money to pay the inheritance tax due on the settled assets, or they can elect to pay it themselves. If they elect to give the money to the personal representatives, the value of the settled property will appear on page 1. If the personal representatives elect to pay the inheritance tax themselves, it will appear on page 2.

Tax due – this includes inheritance tax at 40% in respect of lifetime gifts. The personal representatives are not initially liable for that inheritance tax; the primary liability is the donee's. So the tax attributable to the lifetime gifts must be deducted.

Double taxation relief – this applies if the deceased owned assets abroad, and was domiciled in the UK. Those foreign assets will be subject to UK inheritance tax, but it may be that the equivalent of inheritance tax has been paid on those assets in the country where they are situated. If that is the case, it is possible to offset against the UK inheritance tax the foreign equivalent payable in respect of those assets. However, the amount of deduction is limited to the amount of inheritance tax attributable to those assets.

D18 – Probate summary

7.21 Once the forms have been completed, if no tax is payable, the forms necessary to obtain the grant and D18 must be sent to the Probate Registry. The Inland Revenue account should be sent to the Capital Taxes office at the same time.

If tax is payable, the procedure is different. The IHT 200 and the supplementary pages including D18 should be sent to the IR Capital Taxes, together with the tax due, or if you are making use of the new procedure, send the D20 to the bank or building society.

The Capital Taxes Office will complete the D18, and send it back. The D18 and the papers required to obtain the grant of probate must then be submitted to the Probate Registry.

Valuation

7.22 The basic rule is that the value to be included is the market value at the date of death. If it is difficult to ascertain the value as at the date of death after making full enquiries, then an estimate can be included.

It is essential to use a professionally qualified valuer to value any house or land owned by the deceased at the date of death, and this must be an actual market valuation.

If the estate includes jewellery or antiques or other valuable chattels, then these must be valued by someone who has expertise in the relevant area. It is suggested that a good base for valuation is the price the item would have fetched if sold by auction on the date of death.

Chapter 8

Post-grant procedure

Overview

8.1 Once the grant has been obtained, then the personal representatives should register the grant with banks and building societies where the deceased held accounts, and with the registrars of any companies in which the deceased held shareholdings. If it is known that the shares may be sold, or transferred to a beneficiary in the near future, then the personal representatives may not register the grant, but instead submit it on a transfer.

It will be necessary to withdraw the monies held in any bank or building society accounts, and it may also be necessary to sell other assets in order to pay the debts of the deceased. The debts may include liability for income tax and capital gains tax.

Once the personal representatives are satisfied that all debts have been settled, they must distribute the assets to those entitled to them under the will or intestacy.

Registering the grant

8.2 The original grant or an office copy should be sent to the bank, building society, insurance company or registrar of the company together with the pass book, policy or share certificate as appropriate, with a request for the forms required to close the account or to obtain payment if appropriate and not already obtained.

If a bank has provided some form of borrowing facility to pay the inheritance tax due, then the bank should be requested to transfer the balance from any current or deposit account to pay off the loan.

Any monies not required to settle debts should be placed on deposit pending distribution to the beneficiaries.

Sale of assets

8.3 With many estates the monies withdrawn from bank and building society accounts will be enough to pay all the deceased's debts. If this is not the case, it will be necessary to sell some if not all the deceased's assets in order to pay the debts. It may also be necessary to sell assets in order to pay any legacies and to effect a distribution to the beneficiaries.

Section 39 of the Administration of Estates Act 1925 (AEA 1925) confers wide powers of sale on personal representatives for the purposes of the administration, or during a minority of any beneficiary, or the subsistence of any life interest, or until the period of distribution arrives.

The authority of personal representatives as far as personalty is concerned is joint and several, so that one can withdraw monies in a bank or building society account. However, frequently banks and building societies will insist on all the personal representatives signing all the forms required to withdraw money.

If the personal representatives have been registered as proprietors of shares, it will be necessary for all of them to sign the stock transfer form.

As far as land is concerned, all the personal representatives must sign any transfer or other document. Section 2(2) of the AEA 1925 provides that where there are two or more personal representatives, a conveyance of real estate or contract for such conveyance is not to be made without the concurrence therein of all such personal representatives without an order of the court. However, if not all the executors have proved the will, and power has been reserved to the other executors, then the proving executors can execute the conveyance or enter into a contract on their own.

Theoretically, the personal representatives can sell whichever of the deceased's assets they wish. However, they should have regard to the following factors:

(a) Any direction in the will. Usually the personal representatives are directed to pay the debts from the residuary estate.

(b) The wishes of the residuary beneficiaries. They may prefer assets to be transferred to themselves rather than sold, and the proceeds divided. This is particularly so if the Stock Market or housing prices are depressed (or rapidly increasing!).

(c) If the residuary estate is insufficient to pay off the debts, the AEA 1925 prescribes the order as to which class of gifts is to bear the debts.

(d) If there is a specific gift, the subject of the specific gift should not be sold unless it is absolutely necessary.

(e) If it is necessary to raise money urgently, for example to repay a loan from a bank, the speed of sale. Quoted shares are relatively easy to sell, but land or houses may be difficult in some market conditions.

Inheritance tax will have been paid on the market value of the deceased's assets. If land is sold within four years of the date of death, or quoted shares are sold within one year of the date of death for less than the market value as at the date of death, then that lower value can be substituted for inheritance tax purposes, and a refund of inheritance tax obtained. If more than one shareholding is sold, the prices and death values must be aggregated together to ascertain if there has been an overall loss.

Capital gains tax must also be considered. The personal representatives of the deceased will be deemed to have acquired the assets of the deceased at market value as at the date of death. If they sell the assets for more than the market value at the date of death, there is a potential liability to capital gains tax. For more details about capital gains tax on death, please see CHAPTER 14.

Payment of debts – solvent estates

Secured debts – mortgages

8.4 Frequently the deceased's assets will include a house or other residence, which may be in the sole name of the deceased, or jointly owned by spouses or cohabitees. The house may be mortgaged, and that mortgage may be linked to some form of life insurance, so that on the death of the deceased the loan is repaid.

If that is not the case, then s 35(1) of the AEA 1925 provides that where the deceased by his will disposes of an interest in property, which at the time of his death is charged with the payment of money, whether by way of legal mortgage, equitable charge or otherwise, and the deceased has not by will or other document signified a contrary intention, the interest so charged is primarily liable for the payment of the charge. Thus in the absence of any direction to the contrary, if there is a specific gift of a house subject to a mortgage, the beneficiary will take the house subject to the mortgage.

What constitutes a direction to the contrary? Section 35(2) provides that such a contrary intention shall not be deemed to be signified:

— by a general direction for the payment of debts or of all the debts of the testator out of his personal estate, or his residuary real and personal estate, or his residuary real estate; or

— by a charge of debts upon any such estate; unless such intention is further signified by words expressly or by necessary implication referring to all or some part of the charge.

Thus clear words should be used to indicate which beneficiary is to bear the burden of any charge.

Unsecured debts

8.5 Part II of the First Schedule to the AEA 1925 prescribes the order in which the assets of the deceased are to be applied in payment of the debts of the deceased where the estate of the deceased is solvent. The order is:

(a) property of the deceased undisposed of by will, but subject to the retention thereout of a fund sufficient to meet any pecuniary legacies;

(b) property of the deceased not specifically devised or bequeathed but included (either by specific or general description) in a residuary gift, subject to the retention out of such property of a fund sufficient to meet any pecuniary legacies, so far as not provided for as aforesaid;

(c) property of the deceased specifically appropriated or devised or bequeathed (either by a specific or general description) for the payment of debts – 'I give Greenacre to A and I direct that my debts shall be paid from it';

(d) property of the deceased charged with, or devised or bequeathed (either by a specific or general description) subject to a charge for the payment of debts – 'I give all the money in my account with Z Building Society to B subject to the payment of my debts therefrom';

(e) the fund, if any, retained to meet pecuniary legacies;

(f) property specifically devised or bequeathed, rateably according to value;

(g) property appointed by will under a general power, including the statutory power to dispose of entailed interests, rateably according to value.

There are some omissions from the list – property the subject of a *donatio mortis causa*, nominated property. Presumably they would come at the end of the list if it was necessary to resort to them for the payment of the debts. Such property is rarely met in practice.

The order is slightly odd in that logically property within categories (c) and (d) should come before the property within categories (a) and (b). It is clearly open to a testator to specify expressly that property within these categories should be used to pay the debts before other property. If this is not done, the courts may be prepared to find an implied intention to vary the order; this will be the case if there is a residuary gift in favour of another beneficiary.

Paragraph 8(a) provides that the order may be varied by the will of the deceased. It is very common for the order to be varied in professionally drawn wills – the usual provision is that the debts should be paid from the residuary estate.

Marshalling

8.6 The order laid down in Part II of the First Schedule to the AEA 1925 does not bind a creditor, who can enforce the debt owed to him or her against any part of the estate of the deceased. Another possibility is that the personal representatives of the deceased might resort to property higher up the order in order to satisfy the debts when there was no need to do so. For example, property the subject of a specific gift might be used to pay the debts when the residuary estate has not been exhausted. In this situation, the personal representatives must compensate the disappointed specific beneficiary out of the property which should have been used to pay the debts.

Income tax

8.7 Income tax arises in three contexts: the period up to the date of death, the administration period, and the position of the beneficiaries.

The period up to the date of death

8.8 With regard to the period up to the date of death, the Inspector of Taxes for the district in which the deceased made a tax return should be notified of the death by the personal representatives. It will probably be necessary for the personal representatives to complete a tax return or repayment claim up to the date of death. Some inspectors will accept a statement of the income up to the date of death. If all the deceased's income was taxed at source, a refund may be due, particularly if the deceased died early in the tax year having not used much of the personal allowance. On the other hand, if the deceased had untaxed income, or was a higher rate taxpayer, more may be due.

It can be difficult sometimes to establish the income of the deceased; it can be particularly difficult with regard to the state pension unless personal representatives obtain the figures quickly as the relevant government department destroys the pension records shortly after death.

It may be necessary to complete income tax returns for earlier years as well. The Inland Revenue can go back six years if the deceased has been guilty of neglect, wilful default or fraud; any such back assessment must be made within three years of the year of death.

The administration period

8.9 In almost every estate the personal representatives will receive income during the administration period, which is the period from the date of death until the residuary estate is ascertained. Frequently, this income will have been taxed at source, for example interest or dividends, and if that is the case, no more tax will be payable. If all the income accruing to the personal representatives has been taxed at source, no more tax will be due as personal representatives only pay basic rate tax. However, if the income has not been taxed at source, for example rental income from properties forming part of the assets of the deceased, then the personal representatives will have to complete a tax return, and pay the tax due.

As far as income tax is concerned, the crucial date for determining if the income should be taxed as part of the income of the deceased or as the income of the personal representatives depends on the date it is received or credited. If it is received or credited before the date of death, it is the income of the deceased. If it is received or credited after the date of death, it is the income of the personal representatives.

Note that a different rule applies for inheritance tax. All interest accrued to the date of death must be included in the IHT 200 account, and will be subject to both inheritance tax and income tax. It is possible to obtain relief against this double taxation.

Note that if the deceased was a life tenant, the income may have to be apportioned in order to ascertain which beneficiary is entitled to it. If the life tenant is entitled to it, then it will be taxed as part of the income of the life tenant. In addition, the income due before the date of death will be treated as capital for inheritance tax purposes.

The beneficiaries

8.10 Ultimately the beneficiaries will be entitled to the income.

The rules as to entitlement to income are considered in more detail later. In general the rules are:

— a beneficiary entitled to a pecuniary legacy is not usually entitled to interest from the date of death;

— if there is a specific bequest, and the assets the subject of the specific bequest produce an income, then the beneficiary is entitled to the income from the date of death. For example, if the specific bequest is of a house which is let, the beneficiary will be entitled to the rent as from the date of death;

— all other income will belong to the residuary beneficiaries.

Capital gains tax

8.11 As with income tax, it is necessary to consider capital gains tax in three contexts – the period up to the date of death, the administration period, and the position of the beneficiaries.

The period up to the date of death

8.12 It may be that the deceased has incurred a liability for capital gains tax in the tax year of death. The personal representatives must settle that liability; the deceased is entitled to the full annual exemption for capital gains tax for the year of death. There may also be a liability for capital gains tax in respect of earlier tax years.

If the deceased incurred a loss, that loss can be carried back and set off against any gains incurred in the three previous tax years. It cannot be carried forward, and set off against gains made by the personal representatives.

The administration period

8.13 The personal representatives are deemed to acquire the assets of the deceased at market value as at the date of death; this is usually the value for inheritance tax purposes. If the personal representatives sell any of the assets at more than the market value at the date of death, there is a potential liability for capital gains tax on the gain. However, they are entitled to the full annual exemption available to private individuals for the tax year of death, and for two subsequent years. If capital gains tax is payable, the rate is 40%.

If the personal representatives sell quoted shares within twelve months of death, or land within four years of death for less than the probate value, then they can elect to substitute that lower value for the probate value for inheritance tax purposes. In this situation the reduced value also becomes the value at which the personal representatives will be deemed to have acquired the land or shares for capital gains tax purposes, so that loss relief cannot be claimed. Whether the estate is small or large, the inheritance tax relief should be claimed if the personal representatives do not have any gains against which to offset the loss – its benefit will then be lost. If they do have gains against which to offset the loss, separate calculations should be made to ascertain which relief will yield the greatest benefit to the estate.

Payment of debts – insolvent estates

8.14 The number of estates which prove to be insolvent is relatively small, but as practitioners may encounter them, the relevant provisions are considered here.

What assets are available?

8.15 If a person is made bankrupt in his or her lifetime, there are various statutory provisions under which gifts made by the bankrupt prior to the bankruptcy can be set aside. Similar provisions operate if the deceased's estate proves to be insolvent. These provisions are contained in Schedule 1 to the Administration of Insolvent Estates of Deceased Persons Order 1986.

Secured creditors

8.16 Secured creditors are in a strong position if the estate is insolvent. They can rely on their security under s 285(4) of the Insolvency Act 1986, and if the security proves to be inadequate, then they can prove in the bankruptcy for the balance under r 6.109 of the Insolvency Rules 1986 (SI 1986 No 1925).

Under r 6.96–6.119 a secured creditor can value his security, and prove for the balance in the bankruptcy. If this is done, then the receiver can redeem the security at the value placed on the security by the secured creditor.

The secured creditor also has a further course of action open to him – if he voluntarily surrenders his security for the general benefit of creditors, he may prove for his whole debt, as if it were unsecured (r 6.109(2)). There must be very few situations where a secured creditor would wish to surrender their security.

Unsecured creditors

8.17 Any 'bankruptcy debt' can be proved in bankruptcy proceedings. Section 382(1) of the Insolvency Act 1986 provides that a bankruptcy debt in relation to a bankrupt means *inter alia* any debt or liability to which he is subject to at the commencement of the bankruptcy or may become subject after the commencement of the bankruptcy (including after his discharge from bankruptcy) by reason of any obligation incurred before the commencement of the bankruptcy.

There are various types of creditors – preferred, ordinary and deferred. Schedule 6 to the Insolvency Act 1986, as amended by the Enterprise Act 2002, defines preferred debts; the Crown has lost its status as a preferred creditor, but two categories which practitioners may encounter are left – contributions to occupational pension schemes and remuneration of employees.

All ordinary debts rank equally. If the assets of the deceased are insufficient to pay them in full, then they abate rateably.

Deferred debts include a loan made by the spouse of the deceased; it is immaterial that the lender was not the spouse of the deceased at the date the loan was made (s 329 of the Insolvency Act 1986).

Most debts are classed as ordinary debts now if not deferred debts.

Joint tenancies

8.18 The Enterprise Act 2002 has inserted a new section into s 421A of the Insolvency Act 1986. This applies if the deceased was a joint tenant immediately before death, and within five years of death, application is made for an insolvency administration order. The court has a wide discretion about what type of order to make, but it can order the surviving joint tenant to make good the value lost to the estate. The court is required to assume that the interests of the deceased's creditors out weigh all other considerations.

Protection of the personal representatives

8.19 Before distributing the estate to the beneficiaries, the personal representatives need to be satisfied that all the debts have been paid, and all liabilities met. In the great majority of estates, this does not cause any problem. However, in some estates, it may be difficult for the personal representatives to be certain that there are no further liabilities. In view of this, there are various statutory provisions which protect the personal representatives. These are:

(a) Personal representatives can protect themselves against claims of which they are unaware by means of advertisements under s 27 of the Trustee Act 1925 (TA 1925). Advertisements must be inserted in the *London Gazette*, and in a newspaper circulating in the district in which any land owned by the deceased is situated. The trustees must also give such other notices as would have been directed by a court of competent jurisdiction in an action for administration. The notice must require any person interested to send notice of claims to the personal representatives within the time specified in the notice, not being less than two months. The personal representatives must also make all the searches which an intending purchaser would make or be advised to make. At the expiration of the specified period, the personal representatives can distribute the estate only having regard to claims of which they had notice. Any disappointed claimant – ie, a claimant outside the time limit – may follow the property, or any property representing the same, into the hands of a beneficiary. It should be noted that s 27 only protects personal representatives and trustees from liability for claims of which they are unaware.

(b) Section 48(1) of the Administration of Justice Act 1985 provides that where:

    (i) any question of construction has arisen out of the terms of a will or a trust; and

    (ii) an opinion in writing given by a person who has a ten-year High Court qualification, within the meaning of s 71 of the Courts and Legal Services Act 1990, has been obtained on that question by the personal representatives or trustees under the will or trust, the High Court may, on the application of the personal representatives or trustees and without hearing argument, make an order authorising those persons to take such steps in reliance on the said opinion as are specified in the order;

    Subsection (2) provides that the High Court shall not make an order if it appears that a dispute exists which would make it inappropriate for the court to make the order without hearing argument.

    There is a similar provision in the Standard Provisions of the Society of Trust and Estate Practitioners; the qualification period is reduced to five years.

(c) Section 26 of the TA 1925 deals with the situation where personal representatives or trustees are liable for any rent or on any other covenant contained in a lease. If the personal representatives or trustees satisfy all liabilities under the lease or grant up to the date of the conveyance, and where necessary set apart a sufficient fund to answer any future claim that may be made in respect of any fixed and ascertained sum which the lessee agreed to lay out on the demised property, the personal representatives or trustees may then safely distribute the assets.

Section 26(1A) provides that where a personal representative or trustee has entered or may be required to enter into an authorised guarantee agreement within the Landlord and Tenant (Covenants) Act 1995 with respect to any lease comprised in the estate of a deceased testator or intestate or a trust estate –

'(a) he may distribute the residuary real and personal estate of the deceased testator or intestate, or the trust estate, to or amongst the persons entitled thereto–

(i) without appropriating any part of the estate of the deceased, or the trust estate, to meet any future liability (or, as the case may be, any liability) under any such agreement, and

(ii) notwithstanding any potential liability of his to enter into any such agreement; and

(b) notwithstanding any such distribution, he shall not be personally liable in respect of any subsequent claim (or, as the case may be, any claim) under any such agreement.'

If a personal representative or trustee has entered into such an agreement, he must have satisfied all liabilities under it which may have accrued and been claimed up to the date of distribution. The lessor has the right to follow the assets into the hands of the persons amongst whom the assets may have been distributed.

(d) Illegitimate, legitimated, and adopted children are entitled to share in a gift to children just as if they are legitimate children, subject to any contrary intention.

Section 45 of the Adoption Act 1976 provides:

(i) a trustee or personal representative is not under a duty, by virtue of the law relating to trusts or the administration of estates, to enquire, before conveying or distributing any property, whether any adoption has been effected or revoked if that fact could affect entitlement to the property;

(ii) a trustee or personal representative shall not be liable to any person by reason of a conveyance or distribution of the property made without regard to any such fact if he has not received notice of the fact before the conveyance or distribution;

(iii) this section does not prejudice the right of a person to follow the property, or any property representing it, into the hands of another person, other than a purchaser, who has received it.

There is now no protection as regards illegitimate children and so personal representatives must rely on advertisements under s 27 of the TA 1925 to protect them from claims by unknown children of the deceased.

(e) There is always a possibility that an application for financial provision will be made under the Inheritance (Provision for Family and Dependants) Act 1975. The time limit for beginning proceedings under the Act is six months from the date of the grant, but the court can grant leave to applicants to begin proceedings outside this time limit. In order to protect personal representatives, s 20(1) of the Act provides that a personal representative of a deceased person is not liable for having distributed any part of the estate of the deceased after the end of the period of six months from the date on which representation with respect to the estate of the deceased was first taken out on the ground that he ought to have taken into account the possibility that the court might permit the making of an application for an order under s 2 of the Act after the end of that period.

Under the Civil Procedure Rules a claimant has four months in which to serve any proceedings. It is possible that a claimant could begin proceedings just before the expiry of the six month period, not tell the personal representatives about the claim and then serve them just before the four month period has expired. Section 20 would not protect the personal representatives in that situation, although s 27 advertisements might.

(f) In certain circumstances, it is possible to apply for rectification of a will under s 20 of the Administration of Justice Act 1982. The time limit for such applications is six months from the date of the grant, and the court can extend that time limit if they so wish. However, as with applications out of time under the Inheritance (Provision for Family and Dependants) Act 1982 personal representatives are protected if they delay distribution until six months after the date of the grant.

The point made above about service also applies to applications for rectification.

(g) If the trustees have been unable to ascertain who is entitled, application can be made to the court for directions.

(h) If the trustees have made all reasonable enquiries, but have not been able to identify all possible beneficiaries, application can be made to the court for a 'Benjamin' order authorising the distribution of the assets in a certain manner. This procedure could be used if, for example, a possible beneficiary is almost certainly dead, for example a member of the RAF who was certified by the Air Ministry to have died in January 1943 having failed to return from a bombing raid over Germany (*Re Green's Will Trusts [1985] 3 All ER 455*).

(j) As a last resort money can be paid into court.

In the long term, the Limitation Act 1980 (LA 1980) may protect personal representatives. Section 21(1) of the LA 1980 provides that no period of limitation prescribed by the Act shall apply to an action by a beneficiary under a trust, being an action:

- in respect of any fraud or fraudulent breach of trust to which the trustee was a party or privy; or

- to recover from the trustee trust property or the proceeds of trust property in the possession of the trustee, or previously received by the trustee and converted to his use.

Section 22 provides that subject to s 21(1) and (2) of the LA 1980:

— no action in respect of any claim to the personal estate of a deceased person or to any share or interest in any such estate (whether under a will or on intestacy) shall be brought after the expiration of twelve years from the date on which the right to receive the share or interest accrued; and

— no action to recover arrears of interest in respect of any legacy, or damages in respect of such arrears, shall be brought after the expiration of six years from the date on which the interest became due.

If no period of limitation is specified in the LA 1980, then the doctrine of laches will apply. The idea behind this doctrine is that a potential claimant must not delay in bringing an action; the court will take into account various factors like hardship and the balance of justice before deciding if an action is barred by laches.

It will often be the case that the personal representatives will not be in a position to make a distribution to the beneficiaries for some time after the grant has been obtained. The personal representatives will then be able to take advantage of the protection afforded to them by s 20 of the Inheritance (Provision for Family and Dependants) Act 1975. However, some beneficiaries will not be prepared to wait six months after the date of the grant for a distribution. In what circumstances is it safe for the personal representatives to make a distribution within the six month period? It may be safe in the following circumstances:

(a) whilst personal representatives can never be completely certain that a claim under the 1975 Act will not be lodged, there are estates where the personal representatives are virtually certain that there will not be a claim;

(b) it may be clear that the claim will only affect a small part of the estate. The remainder can then be safely distributed, although it would be prudent to retain a generous amount to meet the claim;

(c) if the applicant agrees;

(d) if the beneficiary gives the personal representatives an indemnity. The difficulty with the indemnity is that unless it is secured, it may prove to be worthless;

(e) if the personal representatives and the residuary beneficiaries are the same persons;

(f) if the court agrees (it might be difficult to arrange a hearing within six months of the date of the grant).

Readers are reminded that in some circumstances personal representatives should wait until ten months have elapsed from the date of the grant before distributing the estate.

Chapter 9

Powers of the personal representatives

9.1 Certain powers are conferred on personal representatives and trustees; these powers are frequently modified in wills, and the common variations are detailed in this section.

Most of the powers apply to personal representatives and trustees; in any event personal representatives frequently become trustees – they may be expressly appointed trustees by the will, or they may become trustees because minors are entitled under the will and cannot give a valid receipt for capital money.

Advancement

9.2 Section 32 of the Trustee Act 1925 (TA 1925) empowers trustees to advance capital to a beneficiary.

When does the power of advancement arise?

9.3 Section 32(2) of the TA 1925, as amended by the Trusts of Land and Appointment of Trustees Act 1996, provides that the section does not apply to capital money arising under the Settled Land Act 1925. Thus the trustees of a strict settlement have no power to advance capital to a beneficiary under s 32.

Section 32(1) of the TA 1925 gives the trustees wide powers to apply the capital for the advancement or benefit of a beneficiary. The beneficiary may be absolutely or contingently entitled, the contingency, for example, could be attaining a specified age or some other such contingency. It is immaterial that the interest of the beneficiary is liable to be defeated by the exercise of a power of appointment or revocation, or to be diminished by the increase of the class to which he belongs.

There is a proviso to s 32(1) of the TA 1925 limiting the powers of the trustees. Only one-half of the presumptive share of a beneficiary can be advanced, and when the beneficiary becomes absolutely and indefeasibly entitled, the advancement must be brought into account. In addition, if there is a beneficiary with a prior or life interest, an advancement cannot be made without the consent of that person in writing.

What is meant by 'advancement or benefit'?

9.4 This phrase has been given a wide meaning. In *Pilkington v IRC [1964] AC 612* Lord Radcliffe at page 635 said that it meant 'any use of money which will improve the material situation of the beneficiary'. It has been held to include even the payment of a donation to a charity (*Re Clore's Settlement Trust [1966] 2 All ER 272*), and also payments to a beneficiary which will result in a saving in tax (*Re Moxon's Will Trust [1958] 1 All ER 386*).

It is also possible to exercise the power of advancement in order to resettle trust funds. Furthermore, there is no objection to the exercise of the power if other persons benefit incidentally (*Pilkington v IRC [1964] AC 612*).

It is possible that a resettlement may infringe the equitable rule that trustees must not delegate (of course statute has now conferred some powers of delegation). However, in Pilkington's case, Viscount Radcliffe said at pages 638–639:

> 'I am unconvinced by the argument that the trustees would be improperly delegating their trust by allowing the money raised to pass over to new trustees under a settlement conferring new powers on the latter. In fact I think the whole issue of delegation is here beside the mark. The law is not that trustees cannot delegate; it is that trustees cannot delegate unless they have authority to do so. If the power of advancement which they possess is so read as to allow them to raise money for the purpose of having it settled, then they do have the necessary authority to let the money pass out of the old settlement into the new trusts. No question of delegation of their powers or trusts arises. If, on the other hand, their power of advancement is read so as to exclude settled advances, *cadit quaestio*.'

The statutory power in s 32 of the TA 1925 is wide enough to permit the resettlement of trust funds, but a discretionary trust may not be permissible (see *Modern Law of Trusts*, 8th edition, by Parker and Mellows (Sweet & Maxwell) at pages 700–707).

Resettlements can fall foul of the perpetuity rules, but with settlements coming into existence after 15 July 1964 the 'wait and see' rule will apply so that the resettlement will only be invalid if it becomes clear that the perpetuity rules will be infringed. It should be noted that for perpetuity purposes the resettlement is treated as being contained in the original settlement.

Prior interests

9.5 An advancement cannot be made unless the person with a prior interest consents. Thus if there is a life tenant, no advance can be made to the remainderman unless the life tenant consents.

What is the position of discretionary beneficiaries? It is clear that they do not have any prior interest within the meaning of the section, and so their consent to an advancement is not necessary (*Re Harris' Settlement (1940) 162 LT 358*).

However, a beneficiary with a protected interest does have a prior interest, and will not forfeit it by giving consent (*Re Hastings-Bass [1975] Ch 25, Re Shaw's Settlement [1951] Ch 833*). It should be noted that the court has no power to dispense with the consent required by s 32.

In *Henley v Wardell (1988) Times, 29 January*, a power of advancement was subject to an uncontrolled discretion, but it was still necessary to obtain the consent of the life tenant before it could be exercised.

Money advanced for a particular purpose

9.6 If trustees advance money for a particular purpose, it will not be necessary for the trustees to ensure that it is applied for that particular purpose if they have grounds for thinking that this will be done. However, if money has been advanced in previous years for a particular purpose, and the trustees are aware that it was not applied for that particular purpose, the trustees must then ensure that any further advance is so applied (*Re Pauling's Settlement Trust [1964] Ch 303*).

Common alterations

9.7 It is common to include variations which:

(a) permit the personal representatives to advance the whole of the capital;

(b) dispense with the requirement that the advance should be brought into account, or give the trustees a discretion as to whether the advance should be brought into account;

(c) dispense with consents of beneficiaries with prior interests;

(d) if there is a life interest, power to advance capital to the life tenant.

Appropriation

9.8 Section 41 of the Administration of Estates Act 1925 (AEA 1925) authorises personal representatives to appropriate any part of the real or personal estate, including things in action, of the deceased in the actual state or condition or state of investment thereof at the time of appropriation in or towards satisfaction of any legacy bequeathed by the deceased. Thus if a beneficiary has a legacy of £10,000, the personal representatives can satisfy that legacy by transferring shares worth £10,000 to the beneficiary.

If the asset is worth more than the legacy, it is probable that personal representatives cannot use s 41 of the AEA 1925. Instead, they can sell the asset to the beneficiary. In addition, there is some doubt as to whether a personal representative who is also a beneficiary can make use of s 41 of the AEA 1925.

There are various limitations on the power of appropriation. An appropriation must not be made so as to affect prejudicially any specific devise or bequest (s 41(1)(i)). If the beneficiary is absolutely entitled, the appropriation can only be made with the consent of that beneficiary. If the legacy is settled, the appropriation can only be made with the consent of the trustees, or the person for the time being entitled to the income (s 41(1)(ii)).

If the person whose consent is required cannot give it because he is an infant, or incapable of managing his own affairs by reason of mental disorder within the meaning of the Mental Health Act 1983, the consent can be given by his parents or parent, testamentary or other guardian, or receiver, or, if, in the case of an infant, there is no such parent or guardian, by the court on the application of his next friend. It is not necessary to obtain consent on behalf of a person who may come into existence after the time of appropriation, or who cannot be found or ascertained at that time (s 41(1)(iii)). However, s 41(5) of the AEA 1925 provides that the personal representatives in making the appropriation shall have regard to the rights of any person who may thereafter come into existence, or who cannot be found or ascertained at the time of appropriation, and of any other person whose consent is not required by the section. Furthermore, if there is no receiver acting for a person suffering from mental disorder, and the appropriation is of an investment authorised by law or by the will, if one exists, of the deceased for the investment of money subject to the trust, no consent is required on behalf of the person suffering from mental disorder (s 41(1)(iv)). In similar circumstances, no consent is required if there is no trustee of a settled legacy, and there is no person of full age entitled to the income (s 41(1)(v)).

An appropriation made under s 41 binds all persons interested in the property whose consent is not required by the section (s 41(4)).

Assume that a beneficiary has a legacy of £20,000. The personal representatives can satisfy that legacy by transferring to the beneficiary land to the value of £20,000. If the land is worth more than the legacy, this cannot be done. Instead, the personal representatives can sell the asset to the beneficiary. If the asset is the subject of a specific devise to another beneficiary, appropriation cannot be made. If the residuary beneficiaries are entitled to the land, they are bound by any appropriation made by the personal representatives.

Valuation

9.9 Section 41(3) provides that the personal representatives may ascertain and fix the value of the respective parts of the real and personal estate and the liabilities of the deceased as they may think fit, and shall for that purpose employ a duly qualified valuer where necessary. Thus an executrix cannot value shares in an unquoted company herself, and then appropriate them in her favour at that valuation (*Re Bythway (1911) 104 LT 411*).

The date for the valuation of the assets could be very important in a volatile market. The Act does not provide any guidance, but the question was decided in the case of *Re Collins [1975] 1 WLR 309*, where it was held that the relevant date was the date of appropriation, and not the date of death. Thus if prices are rising, the beneficiary will want the appropriation to be made as soon as possible, whereas if they are dropping, the beneficiary will want the appropriation to be delayed.

Intestacy

9.10 Section 41(9) specifically provides that the section applies whether the deceased died intestate or not.

In *Kane v Radley-Kane [1999] Ch 274* James Radley-Kane died intestate in May 1994 leaving a widow, the first Defendant, and three sons. The widow was, in fact, the step-mother of the three sons.

The deceased owned 36% of the ordinary shares in a company called Shiredean Limited, which were valued for probate purposes at £50,000. The net value of the deceased's estate was £93,000. Letters of administration were granted to the widow, and she regarded herself as entitled to the whole estate under the intestacy rules.

In January 1997 the shares in Shiredean were sold for £1,131,438.

The claimant, one of the sons, issued proceedings claiming that the appropriation of the shares by the widow in her own favour was invalid.

It was held that this was the case. However, the judge stated that if the assets had been equivalent of cash, for example government stock, then the appropriation would have been valid.

Trustees and powers of appropriation

9.11 Section 41 applies only to personal representatives, and does not apply to trustees, who have the following implied powers of appropriation:

(a) If there are separate trusts of separate property, the trustees can appropriate assets to the value of the separate amounts given.

(b) If there is a trust for sale, and there is nothing in the trust instrument to indicate that an appropriation should not be made, the trustees may make an appropriation.

Normally any adult beneficiaries must agree.

For a fuller discussion see *Modern Law of Trusts*, 8th edition, by Parker and Mellows (Sweet & Maxwell) at page 709–710.

Stamp duty

9.12 Since the Stamp Duty (Exempt Instruments) Regulations 1987, stamp duty is not payable in respect of an instrument giving effect to an appropriation in or towards satisfaction of a general legacy, provided that the instrument is certified as coming within the appropriate category of the schedule to the regulations. Since 1 December 2003 stamp duty only applies to share transfers.

With regard to stamp duty land tax, it is clear that where a person takes a property under the will or intestacy of a deceased person, stamp duty land tax is not payable whether or not the property is subject to a charge. In such a case, the application for registration must be accompanied by a SDLT 60. However, if the beneficiary provides other consideration than the assumption of a charge, stamp duty land tax may be payable. For example, where a beneficiary agrees to take a house in satisfaction of a legacy, but also pays to the executors the difference between the legacy and the market value of the house, stamp duty land tax may be payable.

Businesses

Sole traders

9.13 The personal representatives can continue the business, but only for the purpose of selling it, and only for a year. The personal representatives are personally liable for debts they incur, but there is a right of indemnity from the estate. This right takes priority over the rights of the creditors if the business is being run in order to sell it. However, if the business is being run under a power in the will, the personal representatives have the right of indemnity in preference to the beneficiaries but not the creditors. Note that if the personal representatives have power to postpone the sale, they can run the business indefinitely.

The personal representatives can only use the assets employed in the business at the date of death; these could prove to be insufficient.

Common variations

9.14 It is common to include clauses which provide for the following:

(a) to run the business as long as the personal representatives like;

(b) to use other assets;

(c) to appoint a manager;

(d) indemnity.

Partnerships

9.15 The death of a partner automatically dissolves a partnership, unless the partnership agreement provides that on the death of a partner the partnership continues.

There is no need to give the personal representatives of a partner extra powers to run the business, but it should be done in the case of a small partnership as all the other partners may die or retire leaving the personal representative as a sole trader.

Companies

9.16 The testator may have shares in a company which will pass to the personal representatives. The company will continue to trade as before, and so there is no need for any extra powers, apart perhaps from empowering the personal representatives to give warranties on a sale.

Charging clauses

9.17 The traditional rule is that trustees are not entitled to profit from a trust and are entitled only to reasonable expenses. However, the Trustee Act 2000 (TA 2000) has substantially changed the law. Section 29 contains provisions entitling a trustee who is a trust corporation, or acts in a professional capacity, to remuneration. Section 29(1) provides that a trustee who–

(a) is a trust corporation, but

(b) is not a trustee of a charitable trust,

is entitled to receive reasonable remuneration out of the trust funds for any services that the trust corporation provides on behalf of the trust.

A professional trustee is similarly entitled. Section 29(2) provides that a trustee who–

(a) acts in a professional capacity, but

(b) is not a trust corporation, a trustee of a charitable trust or a sole trustee,

is entitled to receive reasonable remuneration out of the trust funds for any services that he provides on behalf of the trust.

All the other trustees must agree in writing that he may be remunerated for the services. Note that a sole trustee cannot charge.

Section 28(5) defines what is meant by acting in a professional capacity. A trustee acts in a professional capacity if he acts in the course of a profession or business which consists of or includes the provision of services in connection with–

(a) the management or administration of trusts generally or a particular kind of trust, or

(b) any particular aspect of the management or administration of trusts generally or a particular kind of trust,

and the services he provides to or on behalf of the trust fall within that description.

Section 29(3) of the TA 2000 defines reasonable remuneration. In relation to the provision of services by a trustee, it means such remuneration as is reasonable in the circumstances for the provision of those services on behalf of that trust by that trustee. If the trustee in an institution, authorised under the Banking Act 1987, and provides the services in that capacity, reasonable remuneration will be the institution's reasonable charges for the provision of such services. Section 29(4) of the TA 2000 provides that a trustee is entitled to remuneration even if the services in question are capable of being provided by a lay trustee.

A trustee who has been appointed as an agent of the trustees, or nominee or custodian under the powers conferred by Part IV of the TA 2000 or the trust instrument, is also entitled to remuneration under s 29 (s 29(6)).

Section 29(5) of the TA 2000 provides that a trustee is not entitled to remuneration under s 29 if any provision about his entitlement to remuneration has been made–

(a) by the trust instrument, or

(b) by any enactment or any provision of subordinate legislation.

It has always been the case that trustees were entitled to the reimbursement of expenses. Section 31(1) of the TA 2000 confirms this position by providing that a trustee is entitled to be reimbursed out of the trust funds or may pay out of the trust fund expenses properly incurred when acting on behalf of the trust. Section 31(2) provides that the section applies to a trustee who has been authorised under a power conferred by Part IV or the trust instrument–

(a) to exercise functions as an agent of the trustees, or

(b) to act as a nominee or custodian,

as it applies to any other trustee.

Section 28 contains provisions dealing with the situation where there is a charging clause. Section 28(1) provides that subsections (2) to (4) apply to a trustee if–

(a) there is a provision in the trust instrument entitling him to receive payment out of trust funds in respect of services provided by him on behalf of the trust, and

(b) the trustee is a trust corporation or is acting in a professional capacity.

Section 28(2) provides that the trustee is to be treated as entitled under the trust instrument to receive payment in respect of services even if they are services which are capable of being provided by a lay trustee. Section 28(6) provides that a person acts as a lay trustee if he–

(a) is not a trust corporation, and

(b) does not act in a professional capacity.

Section 15 of the Wills Act 1837 provides that a gift to an attesting witness or the spouse of an attesting witness is void. Section 28(4) provides that any payments to which the trustee is entitled in respect of services are to be treated as remuneration for services and not as a gift for the purposes of s 15 of the 1837 Act. This means that a trustee or a trustee's spouse who are not beneficiaries can safely witness the will.

Section 34(3) of the Administration of Estates Act 1925 (AEA 1925) lays down the order in which the assets are to be applied in payment of the debts of the deceased. Again, s 28(4) applies so that any payments to which the trustee is entitled in respect of services are to be treated as remuneration for services and not as a gift.

Section 33(2) of the TA 2000 provides that nothing in s 28 or s 29 is to be treated as affecting the operation of–

(a) s 15 of the Wills Act 1837, or

(b) s 34(3) of the Administration of Estates Act 1925 in relation to any death occurring before the commencement of s 28 or s 29.

Section 30 of the TA 2000 deals with the remuneration of trustees of charitable trusts. Section 30(1) provides that the Secretary of State may make regulations for the remuneration of trustees of charitable trusts who are trust corporations or act in a professional capacity. Section 30(2) provides that the power under subsection (1) includes power to make provision for the remuneration of a trustee who has been authorised under a power conferred by Part IV or the trust instrument–

(a) to exercise functions as an agent of the trustees, or

(b) to act as a nominee or custodian.

Section 30(3) of the TA 2000 provides that regulations under the section may:

(a) make different provisions for different cases;

(b) contain such supplemental, incidental, consequential and transitional conditions as the Secretary of State considers appropriate.

Section 30(4) of the TA 2000 provides that the power to make regulations under the section is exercisable by statutory instrument which will be subject to annulment in pursuance of a resolution of either House of Parliament. At the time of writing, no such regulations have been made.

If there is an express charging clause, a trustee of a charitable trust who is not a trust corporation is only entitled to receive payment for services which are capable of being provided by a lay trustee:

(a) if he is not a sole trustee, and

(b) to the extent that a majority of the other trustees have agreed that it should apply to him (s 28(3)).

Section 33(1) of the TA 2000 provides that ss 28, 29, 31 and 32 apply in relation to services provided or (as the case may be) expenses incurred on or after their coming into force on behalf of a trust whenever created.

These provisions also apply to personal representatives (s 35(1) and (2)).

Remuneration to which a personal representative would be entitled under s 28 or 29 is to be treated as an administration expense for the purposes of s 34(3) of the TA 2000. It is also to be treated as an administration expense for the purposes of any provision giving reasonable administration expenses priority over the preferential debts listed in Schedule 6 to the Insolvency Act 1986 (s 35(3)). Section 35(4) provides that nothing in subsection (3) is to be treated as affecting the operation of the provisions mentioned in paragraphs (a) and (b) of that subsection in relation to any death occurring before the commencement of s 35.

Notwithstanding the Act, an express charging clause should still be inserted in a trust instrument or will as a sole executor cannot charge. Even if there are other executors, then they might not agree that the other professional executors can charge.

Compounding liabilities

9.18 Section 15(f) of the Trustee Act 1925 empowers personal representatives or two or more trustees to, *inter alia*, 'compromise, compound, abandon, submit to arbitration, or otherwise settle any debt, account, claim, or thing whatever relating to the testator's or intestate's estate or to the trust'.

The power to delegate – collective delegation

9.19 Before 1925 there was no doubt that a trustee could delegate his powers. In *Speight v Gaunt (1883) 22 Ch D 727* Jessel MR said at pages 739–740:

> 'It seems to me that on general principles a trustee ought to conduct the business of the trust in the same manner that an ordinary prudent man of business would conduct his own, and that beyond there is no liability or obligation on the trustee … If the investment is an investment made on the Stock Exchange through a stockbroker, the ordinary course of business is

> for the investor to select a stockbroker in good credit and in a good position, having regard to the sum to be invested, and to direct him to make the investment – that is, to purchase on the Stock Exchange of a jobber or another broker the investment required.'

The Trustee Act 1925 (TA 1925) contained various provisions concerning delegation by trustees.

The Trustee Act 2000 substantially changes the law. Sections 21, 23 and 30 of the TA 1925 are repealed. Instead, Part IV of the 2000 Act contains a comprehensive code dealing with the appointment of agents, nominees and custodians.

The TA 2000 is based on the recommendations of the Law Commission. Traditionally, the law has permitted trustees to delegate administrative decisions, but not fiduciary duties. The Law Commission considered that this distinction was out of date, and that the distinction ought to be between the administrative powers and distributive powers. It is possible to delegate administrative powers; it is not possible to delegate distributive powers.

Section 11(1) of the TA 2000 provides that trustees may authorise any person to exercise any or all of their delegable functions as their agent. Section 11(2) defines the trustees' delegable functions. These are any function other than:

(a) any function relating to whether, or in what way, any assets of the trust should be distributed;

(b) power to decide whether any fees or other payment due to be made out of the trust funds should be made out of income or capital (this is a decision about the distribution of assets);

(c) any power to appoint a person to be a trustee of the trust; or

(d) any power conferred by any other enactment or the trust instrument which permits the trustees to delegate any of their functions or to appoint a person to act as nominee or custodian. (The agent cannot delegate again.)

Section 11(2) does not apply to charitable trustees. Instead, s 11(3) provides that in the case of a charitable trust, the trustees' delegable functions are:

— any function consisting of carrying out a decision that the trustees have taken;

— any function relating to the investment of assets subject to the trust (including, in the case of land acquired as an investment, managing the land and creating or disposing of an interest in the land);

— any function relating to the raising of funds for the trust otherwise than by means of profits of a trade which is an integral part of the carrying out of the trust's charitable purpose;

— any other function prescribed by an order made by the Secretary of State.

Section 11(4) of the TA 2000 provides that for the purposes of subs (3)(c) a trade is an integral part of carrying out a trust's charitable purpose if, whether carried on in the UK or elsewhere, the profits are applied solely to the purposes of the trust and either:

(a) the trade is exercised in the course of the actual carrying out of a primary purpose of the trust; or

(b) the work in connection with the trade is mainly carried out by beneficiaries of the trust.

Section 12 of the TA 2000 deals with the question of who may be appointed as an agent. The trustees can appoint one of their number, but they cannot appoint a beneficiary, even if the beneficiary is a trustee. If two or more persons are appointed as agents, they must exercise their functions jointly. A person may be appointed to act as the agent of the trustees even though he is also appointed to act as the nominee or custodian of the trustees.

Section 13 of the TA 2000 deals with linked functions. Section 13(1) provides that a person who is authorised under s 11 to exercise a function is subject to any specific duties or restrictions attached to the function. The Act then goes on to provide as an example that a person who is authorised under s 11 to exercise a general power of investment is subject to the duties under s 4 in relation to that part. This applies whatever the terms of the agency. Section 13(2) provides that a person who is authorised under s 11 to exercise a power which is subject to a requirement to obtain advice is not subject to the requirement if he is the kind of person from whom it would have been proper for the trustees, in compliance with the requirement, to obtain advice. Thus if the trustees delegate the power of investment to a person who would normally give advice about investments, that person need not himself obtain further advice. However, if that person would not normally give such advice, that person must obtain advice from someone who is qualified to advise about investments.

Section 11(1) of the Trusts of Land and Appointment of Trustees Act 1996 imposes a duty on trustees to consult beneficiaries and give effect to their wishes. Section 13(3) of the TA 2000 provides that subsection (4) and (5) apply to a trust to which s 11(1) of the 1996 Act applies. Subsection (4) provides that the trustees may not under s 11 authorise a person to exercise any of their functions on terms that prevent them from complying with s 11(1) of the 1996 Act. Subsection (5) provides that a person who is authorised under s 11 to exercise any function relating to land subject to the trust is not subject to s 11(1) of the 1996 Act. Thus trustees must still consult and give effect to the wishes of the beneficiaries even if they do delegate their powers.

Section 14(1) of the TA 2000 provides that the trustees may authorise a person to exercise functions as their agent on such terms as to remuneration and other matters as they may determine. This gives the trustees a wide discretion about the terms on which an agent is employed, but it is subject to various limitations. Section 14(2) provides that the trustees may not authorise a person to exercise functions as their agent on any of the terms mentioned in subsection (3) unless it is reasonably necessary for them to do so. The terms mentioned in subsection (3) are:

(a) a term permitting the agent to appoint a substitute;

(b) a term restricting the liability of the agent or his substitute to the trustees or any beneficiary;

(c) a term permitting the agent to act in circumstances capable of giving rise to a conflict of interest.

Asset management

9.20 Section 15 of the TA 2000 deals with asset management. Section 15(1) provides that the trustees may not authorise a person to exercise any of their asset management functions as their agent except by an agreement which is in, or is evidenced in, writing. Section 15(2) provides that the trustees may not authorise a person to exercise any of their asset management functions as their agent unless:

(a) they have prepared a statement (known as a policy statement) that gives guidance as to how a function should be exercised; and

(b) the agreement under which the agent is to act includes a term to the effect that he will secure compliance with–

  (i) the policy statement, or

  (ii) if the policy statement is revised or replaced under s 22, the revised or replacement policy statement.

Section 15(3) provides that the trustees must formulate any guidance given in the policy statement with a view to ensuring that the functions will be exercised in the best interests of the trust.

Section 15(4) provides that the policy statement must be in, or evidenced in, writing.

Section 15(5) provides that the asset management functions of trustees are their functions relating to:

(a) the investment of assets subject to the trust;

(b) the acquisition of property which is to be subject to the trust; and

(c) managing property which is subject to the trust and disposing of, or creating or disposing of an interest in, such property.

Section 16(1) provides that the trustees of a trust may:

— appoint a person to act as their nominee in relation to such of the assets of the trust as they determine; and

— take such steps as are necessary to secure that those assets are vested in a person so appointed.

An appointment under the section must be in, or evidenced in, writing, and the section does not apply to any trust having a custodian trustee or in relation to any assets vested in the official custodian for charities (s 16(2) and (3)).

Custodians

9.21 Section 17 of the TA 2000 confers on trustees the power to appoint custodians. Section 17(1) provides that the trustees of a trust may appoint a person to act as a custodian in relation to such assets of the trust as they have determined. Section 17(2) provides that a person is the custodian in relation to assets if he undertakes safe custody of the assets or of any documents or records concerning the assets. Section 17(3) provides that an appointment under the section must be in, or evidenced in, writing. Section 17(4) provides that the section does not apply to any trust having a custodian trustee or in relation to any assets vested in the official custodian for charities. Section 39(1) provides that 'custodian trustee' has the same meaning as in the Public Trustee Act 1906.

Section 18 deals with investments in bearer securities. Section 18(1) provides that if trustees retain or invest in securities payable to bearer, they must appoint a person to act as a custodian of the securities. This does not apply if the trust instrument contains a provision which permits the trustees to retain or invest in securities payable to bearer without appointing a person to act as a custodian (s 18(2)). Section 18(3) provides that an appointment under the section must be in, or evidenced in, writing. Section 18(4) provides that the section does not apply to any trust having a custodian trustee or in relation to any securities vested in the official custodian for charities. Note that s 25(2) provides that s 18 does not impose a duty on a sole trustee if that trustee is a trust corporation.

Who can be appointed?

9.22 Section 19(1) of the TA 2000 deals with the question of who may be appointed as nominees or custodians. Section 19(1) also provides that a person may not be appointed under ss 16, 17 or 18 as a nominee or custodian unless one of the relevant conditions is satisfied.

Section 19(2) provides that the relevant conditions are that:

— the person carries on business which consists of or includes acting as a nominee or custodian; or

— the person is a body corporate which is controlled by the trustees; or

— the person is a body corporate recognised under s 9 of the Administration of Justice Act 1985.

Section 19(3) provides that the question of whether a body corporate is controlled by trustees is to be determined in accordance with s 840 of the Income and Corporation Taxes Act 1988.

Section 19(4) provides that the trustees of a charitable trust which is not an exempt charity must act in accordance with any guidance given by the Charity Commission concerning the selection of a person for appointment as a nominee or custodian under ss 16, 17 or 18. This guidance has been published, and is available on the Charity Commission website.

Section 19(5) provides that subject to subsection (1) and (4), the persons whom the trustees may appoint as a nominee or custodian under ss 16, 17 or 18 include:

(a) one of their number, if that one is a trust corporation; or

(b) two (or more) of their number, if they are to act as joint nominees or joint custodians.

It will be recalled that s 16 of the TA 2000 deals with the power of trustees to appoint nominees. Section 19(6) provides that the trustees may under s 16 appoint a person to act as their nominee even though he is also:

(a) appointed to act as their custodian (under s 17 or 18 or any other power); or

(b) authorised to exercise functions as their agent under s 11 or any other power.

As already mentioned, s 17 deals with the power of trustees to appoint custodians, whilst s 18 deals with the power of trustees to retain or invest in securities payable to the bearer. Section 19(7) provides that the trustees may under those sections appoint a person to act as their custodian even though he is also:

(a) appointed to act as their nominee (under s 16 or any other power); or

(b) authorised to exercise functions as their agent (under s 11 or any other power).

Terms of appointment

9.23 Section 20 of the TA 2000 deals with the terms of appointment of nominees and custodians. Section 20(1) provides that the trustees may appoint a person to act as a nominee or custodian on such terms as to remuneration and other matters as they may determine. Section 29 contains further provisions dealing with the remuneration of a trustee who has been appointed as agent, nominee or custodian (see 9.17 above). Section 32(1) applies if a person other than a trustee has been:

(a) authorised to exercise functions as an agent of the trustees; or

(b) appointed to act as a nominee or custodian.

Section 32(2) provides that the trustees may remunerate the agent, nominee or custodian out of the trust funds for services if:

(a) he is engaged on terms entitling him to be remunerated for those services; and

(b) the amount does not exceed such remuneration as is reasonable in the circumstances for the provision of the services by him on behalf of that trust.

Section 32(3) provides that the trustees may reimburse the agent, nominee or custodian out of the trust funds for any expenses properly incurred by him in exercising functions as an agent, nominee or custodian.

Section 20(2) provides that the trustees may not appoint a person to act as a nominee or custodian on any of the terms mentioned in subsection (3), unless it is reasonably necessary for them to do so. The terms mentioned in subsection (3) are:

- a term permitting the nominee or custodian to appoint a substitute;
- a term restricting the liability of the nominee or custodian or his substitute to the trustees or to any beneficiary;
- a term permitting the nominee or custodian to act in circumstances capable of giving rise to a conflict of interest.

Section 20 is subject to ss 29–32.

Review

9.24 For the whole of the time that the agent, nominee or custodian continues to act for the trust, the trustees must keep under review the arrangements under which the agent, nominee or custodian acts, and how those arrangements are being put into effect. If circumstances make it appropriate to do so, the trustees must consider whether there is a need to exercise any power of intervention that they have, and if they consider there is a need to exercise such a power, they must do so (s 22(1) TA 2000).

Section 22(4) of the TA 2000 provides that a power of intervention includes:

(a) a power to give directions to the agent, nominee or custodian; and

(b) a power to revoke the authorisation or appointment.

If the trustees have authorised an agent to exercise asset management functions, the duty under s 22(1) includes, in particular:

(a) a duty to consider whether there is any need to revise or replace the policy statement made for the purposes of s 15;

(b) if they consider that there is a need to revise or replace a policy statement, a duty to do so; and

(c) a duty to assess whether the terms of the policy statement are being complied with.

Section 22(3) provides that s 15(3) and (4) apply to the revision or replacement of a policy statement under s 22 as they apply to the making of a policy statement under that section. Section 15(3) requires that the trustees must formulate any guidance given in the policy statement with a view to ensuring that the functions will be exercised in the best interests of the trust. Section 15(4) provides that the policy statement must be in, or evidenced in, writing.

Liability of trustees

9.25 Section 23(1) of the TA 2000 provides that a trustee is not liable for any act or default of the agent, nominee or custodian unless he has failed to comply with the duty of care applicable to him, under paragraph 3 of Schedule 1:

(a) when entering into the arrangement under which the person acts as agent, nominee or custodian; or

(b) when carrying out his duties under s 22.

The duty of care is defined in s 1. A trustee must exercise such care and skill as is reasonable in the circumstances, having regard in particular:

— to any special knowledge or experience that he has or holds himself out as having; and

— if he acts as trustee in the course of a business or profession, to any special knowledge or experience that it is reasonable to expect of a person acting in the course of that kind of business or profession.

Paragraph 3(1) of Schedule 1 provides that the duty of care applies to a trustee:

- when entering into arrangements under which a person is authorised under s 11 to exercise functions as an agent;
- when entering into arrangements under which a person is appointed under s 16 to act as a nominee;
- when entering into arrangements under which a person is appointed under s 17 or 18 to act as a custodian;
- when entering into arrangements under which, under any power conferred by the trust instrument, a person is authorised to exercise functions as an agent or is appointed to act as a nominee or custodian;
- when carrying out his duties under s 22.

Paragraph 3(2) provides that for the purposes of para 3(1), entry into arrangements under which a person is authorised to exercise functions or is appointed to act as a nominee or custodian includes, in particular:

(a) selecting a person to act;

(b) determining any terms on which he is to act; and

(c) if a person is being authorised to exercise asset management functions, the preparation of a policy statement under s 15.

Section 23(2) provides that if a trustee has agreed a term under which the agent, nominee or custodian is permitted to appoint a substitute, the trustee is not liable for any act or default of the substitute unless he has failed to comply with the duty of care applicable to him, under paragraph 3 of Schedule 1:

— when agreeing that term; or

— when carrying out his duties under s 22 in so far as they relate to the use of the substitute.

Section 24 deals with the effect of trustees exceeding their powers. If trustees exceed their powers in authorising a person to exercise a function of theirs as an agent, or in appointing a person to act as a nominee or custodian, the authorisation or appointment is still valid.

General

9.26 Section 25(1) of the TA 2000 provides that a sole trustee can exercise all the powers described above.

Section 26 provides that the powers conferred by the Act on trustees to appoint agents, nominees and custodians are in addition to powers conferred on trustees otherwise than by the Act. However, powers can be restricted or excluded by the trust instrument or by any enactment or any provision of subordinate legislation.

It is provided by s 27 that the provisions about appointing agents, nominees and custodians apply in relation to trusts whether created before or after the commencement of the Act.

Delegation by individual trustee

9.27 Section 5 of the Trustee Delegation Act 1999 has substituted a new s 25 in the Trustee Act 1925. Section 25(1) provides that notwithstanding any rule of law to the contrary, a trustee may, by power of attorney, delegate the execution or exercise of all or any of the trusts, powers and discretions vested in him as trustee either alone or jointly with another person or persons.

A delegation under s 25(1) commences with the date of execution of the power if the instrument makes no provision as to the commencement of the delegation, and lasts for twelve months or any shorter period specified by the instrument creating the power (s 25(2)).

Section 25(3) provides that the persons who may be donees of a power of attorney under the section include a trust corporation.

Section 25(6) sets out a form which can be used. If a donor uses this form, or a form to the like effect but expressed to be made under s 25(5), it operates to delegate to the person identified in the form as the donee of the power the execution and exercise of all the trusts, powers and discretions vested in the donor as trustee (either alone or jointly with any other person or persons) under the trust so identified.

The donor must give written notice of the giving of the power to–

(a) each person (other than himself), if any, who under any instrument creating the trust has power (whether alone or jointly) to appoint a new trustee; and

(b) each of the other trustees, if any.

The written notice must specify:

— the date on which the power comes into operation;

— its duration;

— the donee of the power;

— the reason why the power is given;

— where some only are delegated, the trusts, powers and discretions delegated.

The notice must be given within seven days of the giving of the power (s 25(4)).

Failure to comply with subsection (4) does not invalidate any act done or instrument executed by the donee in favour of a person dealing with the donee of the power.

What happens if the donee of the power commits a breach of trust? Section 25(7) provides that the donor of the power is liable for the acts or defaults of the donee in the same manner as if they were the acts or defaults of the donor.

Section 25(8) provides that for the purpose of executing or exercising the trusts or powers delegated to him, the donee may exercise any of the powers conferred on the donor as trustee by statute or by the instrument creating the trust. This includes the power, for the purpose of the transfer of any inscribed stock, himself to delegate to an attorney power to transfer, but not including the power of delegation conferred by this section.

Section 25(9) provides that the fact that it appears from any power of attorney given under s 25, or from any evidence required for the purposes of any such power of attorney or otherwise, that in dealing with any stock the donee of the power is acting in the execution of a trust shall not be deemed for any purpose to affect any person in whose books the stock is inscribed or registered with any notice of the trust.

Section 25(10) provides that s 25 applies to a personal representative, tenant for life and statutory owner as it applies to a trustee. However, the written notice as required by s 25(4) must be given–

- in the case of a personal representative, to each of the other personal representatives, if any, except any executor who has renounced probate;
- in the case of a tenant for life, to the trustees of the settlement and to each person, if any, who together with the person giving the notice constitutes the tenant for life; and
- in the case of a statutory owner, to each of the persons, if any, who together with the person giving the notice constitute the statutory owner and, in the case of a statutory owner by virtue of s 23(1)(a) of the Settled Land Act 1925, to the trustees of the settlement.

Readers are reminded that s 7 of the Trustee Delegation Act 1999 preserves the two trustees rule so that if land is to be sold, delegation to a sole co-trustee does not mean that the sole co-trustee can give a valid receipt for capital money. Thus if spouses are holding the legal estate on trust for themselves, and one grants a power of attorney under s 25 to the other, the donee of the power cannot give a valid receipt for capital money.

Delegation to beneficiary with an interest in possession

9.28 Section 9 of the Trusts of Land and Appointment of Trustees Act 1996 has extended the powers of trustees to delegate, although it is a limited power.

Section 9(1) provides that trustees of land can delegate any of their functions by power of attorney. The attorney must be a beneficiary of full age, and must also be entitled to an interest in possession in land subject to the trust. The power must be given by all the trustees jointly, and may be revoked by one or more of them, unless expressed to be irrevocable and to be given by way of security. If another person is appointed trustee, the power is revoked, although the death of any of the original appointors will not cause a revocation. Similarly, if an appointor ceases to be a trustee for any reason, the power will not be revoked (s 9(3)).

The delegation can be for any period or can be indefinite (s 9(5)), but an enduring power cannot be used (s 9(6)) for the purposes of delegation of their functions under s 9(1).

Section 9(4) provides that if the beneficiary ceases to be a person beneficially entitled to an interest in possession in land, and is the sole attorney, the power is revoked. If there is more than one attorney, the power is still exercisable by the other beneficiaries, provided that the functions delegated to them are specified to be exercised by them jointly and not separately, and they continue to be beneficially entitled to an interest in possession in the land in question.

Section 9(7) provides that the beneficiaries to whom functions have been delegated under s 9(1) are in the same position as trustees with the same duties and liabilities. However, they are not regarded as trustees for any other purpose, including in particular any enactment permitting the delegation of functions by trustees or imposing requirements relating to the payment of capital money.

The TA 2000 has inserted s 9A into the Trusts of Land and Appointment of Trustees Act 1996. This provides that the duty of care under s 1 of the TA 2000 applies to trustees of land in deciding whether to delegate any of their functions under s 9. If the trustees of land delegate any of their functions under s 9, and the delegation is not irrevocable, while the delegation continues, the trustees–

— must keep the delegation under review;

— if circumstances make it appropriate to do so, must consider whether there is a need to exercise any power of intervention that they have; and

— if they consider that there is a need to exercise such a power, must do so (s 9A(3)).

Section 9A(5) provides that the duty of care under s 1 of the TA 2000 applies to the carrying out of any of these duties by trustees. 'Power of intervention' includes–

(a) a power to give directions to the beneficiary; and

(b) a power to revoke the delegation.

Section 9A(6) provides that a trustee of land is not liable for any act or default of the beneficiary, or beneficiaries, unless the trustee fails to comply with the duty of care in deciding to delegate any of the trustees' functions under s 9 or in carrying out any duty under subsection (3).

Section 9(2) provides protection for persons dealing with the attorney. It provides that if a person deals with the attorney in good faith, the attorney shall be presumed to have been a person to whom the function could be delegated unless that other person has knowledge at the time of the transaction that he was not such a person.

Subsequent purchasers of land are also protected if the person dealing with the attorney makes a statutory declaration before or within three months after completion of the purchase that they dealt in good faith and did not know that the attorney was a person to whom the functions could not be delegated.

The section applies to trusts where a beneficiary has a life interest, and also to co-ownership, but there is little point in using it where the trustees and beneficiaries are the same. In the great majority of co-ownership situations the beneficiaries and trustees will be the same person.

Delegation by trustee who is also beneficially interested

9.29 Section 1(1) of the Trustee Delegation Act 1999 provides that the donee of an ordinary or an enduring power of attorney can exercise the trustee functions of the donor in relation to:

- land;
- capital proceeds of a conveyance of land; or
- income from land.

It is immaterial whether the donor is a sole trustee or a joint trustee (s 1(2)(b)). However, the donor must have a beneficial interest in the land, proceeds or income when the act is done.

Thus if spouses hold land on trust for themselves as joint tenants, and one executes a power of attorney in favour of a child, that child will be able to exercise the trustee functions of the parent, and will be able to give a valid receipt for capital money if the land is sold. Note that s 7 preserves the two trustee rule so that if one spouse grants a power of attorney to the other and becomes mentally incapable, that spouse cannot give a valid receipt for capital money by himself or herself.

Section 1(1) can be excluded by the instrument which created the power of attorney, and has effect subject to the terms of that instrument (s 1(3)).

What is the position if the donee of the power does an act which would be a breach of trust if committed by the donor? Section 1(4) provides that the donor will be liable in this situation. However, the donor is not liable by reason only that the function is exercised by the donee. Section 1(4) is subject to any contrary intention expressed in the trust instrument, and has effect subject to the terms of such an instrument (s 1(5)).

Section 1(6) provides that the fact that it appears that, in dealing with any shares or stock, the donee of a power of attorney is exercising a function by virtue of s 1(1) does not affect with any notice of any trust a person in whose books the shares are, or stock is, registered or inscribed.

If the donee of a power of attorney is acting under (a) a statutory provision or (b) a provision in the instrument (if any) creating a trust, under which the donor of the power is expressly authorised to delegate the exercise of all or any of his trustee functions by power of attorney, he is acting under a trustee delegation power, and is not to be regarded as exercising a trustee function by virtue of s 1(1). Thus the attorney cannot usually delegate again.

Section 1 applies only if the donor of the power has a beneficial interest in the land. How can a purchaser from the attorney be certain that this is the case? Section 2 provides that an appropriate statement is, in favour of a purchaser, conclusive evidence that the donor of the power had a beneficial interest in the property at the time of doing the act. An 'appropriate statement' means a signed statement made by the donee–

(a) when doing the act in question; or

(b) at any other time within the period of three months beginning with the day on which the act is done.

that the donor has a beneficial interest in the property at the time of the donee doing the act (s 2(3)). If the appropriate statement is false, the donee is liable in the same way as he would be if the statement were contained in a statutory declaration.

Section 10(2) of the Powers of Attorney Act 1971 provides that a general power of attorney in the form set out in Schedule 1 to that Act, or a similar form, does not confer on the donee of the power any authority to exercise functions of the donor as trustee. Section 3 of the Trustee Delegation Act 1999 provides that s 10 of the 1971 Act is now subject to s 1 of the 1999 Act.

Insurance

9.30 Section 19 of the TA 1925 conferred on trustees a power to insure the trust property. The TA 2000 has replaced the original s 19 with a new section. The substituted s 19 provides that a trustee may insure any property which is subject to the trust against risk of loss or damage due to any event. The premiums may be paid out of the trust funds (s 19(1)). Section 19(5) provides that 'trust funds' means any income or capital funds of the trust.

Special rules apply to property held on a bare trust. Section 19(3) provides that property is held on a bare trust if it is held on trusts for–

(a) a beneficiary who is of full age and capacity and absolutely entitled to the property which is subject to the trust; or

(b) beneficiaries each of whom is of full age and capacity and who (taken together) are absolutely entitled to the property subject to the trust.

If property is held on a bare trust, the beneficiary or each of the beneficiaries may direct that any property specified in the direction is not to be insured, or that it is only to be insured on such conditions as may be specified (s 19(2)). If such a direction is given, the power to insure ceases to be a delegable function for the purposes of s 11 of the TA 2000 (power to employ agents).

Section 34(3) provides that the amendments made by the section apply in relation to trusts whether created before or after the commencement of the Act.

Section 20 deals with the application of any trust money. It is to be regarded as capital money, and under s 20(4) it may be applied by the trustees in rebuilding, reinstating, replacing or repairing the property lost or damaged, but any such application by the trustees shall be subject to the consent of any person whose consent is required – by the instrument, if any, creating the trust – to the investment of money subject to the trust. If it is a settlement within the Settled Land Act, any such application of the money is subject to the provisions of that Act.

Section 20(5) preserves the rights of third parties to require the insurance money to be applied in rebuilding, reinstating, replacing or repairing the property lost or damaged. Mortgagees, lessors and lessees may have the right to insist on rebuilding or reinstatement.

Possible amendments

9.31 It is common to make the following variations to the power:

(a) section 19 does not impose any duty on the trustees to insure; such a duty could be imposed. However, this could cause difficulties if, for example, they hold property in an area prone to flooding and cannot obtain insurance. Trustees who fail to insure when they could do so are probably guilty of a breach of the duty of care;

(b) the trustees may be given an express discretion as to whether insurance money should be used to reinstate the settled property.

Investment

9.32 The TA 2000 has substantially amended the law with regard to investment.

Section 3(1) provides that subject to the provisions of Part II of the Act, a trustee may make any kind of investment that he could make if he were absolutely entitled to the assets of the trust. Subsection (2) provides that the power under subsection (1) is called 'the general power of investment'. Section 3(3) provides that the general power of investment does not permit a trustee to make investments in land other than in loans secured on land. However, s 8 does contain a power to invest in land. Section 8 is discussed below.

There are provisions concerned with the powers of trustees to make loans secured on land. Section 3(4) provides that a person invests in a loan secured on land if he has rights under any contract under which –

(a) one person provides another with credits; and

(b) the obligation of the borrower to repay is secured on land.

'Credit' is given a wide meaning in s 3(5), where it is defined as including any cash loan or other financial accommodation. Section 3(6) provides that cash includes money in any form.

The general power of investment is subject to various restrictions. Section 4 lays down the standard investment criteria. Section 4(1) provides that in exercising any power of investment, a trustee must have regard to the standard investment criteria. This duty applies whether or not the powers under the Act are being exercised, and so it applies to trustees who invest under an express investment clause in a will or settlement. Section 4(2) provides that a trustee must from time to time review the investments of the trust and consider whether, having regard to the standard investment criteria, they should be varied. Section 4(3) provides that the standard investment criteria, in relation to a trust, are –

(a) the suitability to the trust of investments of the same kind as any particular investment proposed to be made or retained and of that particular investment as an investment of that kind; and

(b) the need for diversification of investments of the trust in so far as is appropriate to the circumstances of the trust.

A trustee is also under a duty to obtain advice, whether investing under the Act, or an express power of investment. Section 5(1) provides that before exercising any power of investment, a trustee must obtain and consider proper advice about the way in which, having regard to the standard investment criteria, the power should be exercised. The duty to obtain and consider advice also applies when trustees are reviewing the investments of the trust. Section 5(2) provides that a trustee must obtain and consider proper advice about whether, having regard to the standard investment criteria, the investments should be varied. Section 5(3) provides that a trustee need not obtain such advice if he reasonably concludes that in all the circumstances it is unnecessary or inappropriate do so. If the trust fund is large, trustees cannot reasonably claim it is inappropriate. On the other hand, if the trust fund is under £100 it would be reasonable for a trustee to conclude that it was unnecessary and inappropriate. 'Proper advice' is defined in s 5(4) as the advice of a person who is reasonably believed by the trustee to be qualified to give it due to his ability and practical experience of financial and other matters relating to the proposed investment.

The general power of investment is in addition to powers conferred on trustees otherwise than by the Act, but it is subject to any restriction or exclusion imposed by the trust instrument or by any enactment or any provision of subordinate legislation (s 6(1)). Section 6(2) provides that for the purposes of the Act, an enactment or a provision of subordinate legislation is not to be regarded as being, or as being part of, a trust instrument.

What effect do ss 3, 4, 5 and 6 have on existing trusts? Section 7(1) provides that they apply to trusts whether created before or after the commencement of the Act. However, there are various exceptions to this provision.

Section 7(2) provides that no provision relating to the powers of a trustee contained in a trust instrument made before 3 August 1961 is to be treated (for the purposes of s 6(1)(b)) as restricting or excluding the general power of investment. This means that trustees of a trust made before 3 August 1961 have the general power of investment.

Section 7(3) provides that a provision contained in a trust instrument made before the commencement of Part II which–

(a) has effect under s 3(2) of the Trustee Investments Act 1961 as a power to invest under that Act; or

(b) confers power to invest under that Act;

is to be treated as conferring the general power of investment on a trustee.

This means that if trustees are authorised to invest under the Trustee Investments Act 1961, they now have the general powers of investment as a trustee.

It should be noted that Part II of Schedule 2 to the Act contains provisions dealing with the investment of the proceeds of sale of settled land.

Acquisition of land

9.33 Part III of the Act contains default powers for trustees to acquire freehold and leasehold land.

Section 8(1) provides that a trustee may acquire freehold or leasehold land in the UK–

- as an investment;
- for occupation by a beneficiary; or
- or any other reason.

Section 8(2) provides that 'freehold or leasehold land' means–

(a) in relation to England and Wales, a legal estate in land;

(b) in relation to Scotland;

 (i) the estate or interest of the proprietor of the *dominium utile* or, in the case of land not held on feudal tenure, the estate or interest of the owner; or

 (ii) a tenancy; and

(c) in relation to Northern Ireland, a legal estate in land, including land held under a fee farm grant.

Generally, the Act applies to personal representatives administering an estate according to the law as it applies to a trustee carrying out a trust for beneficiaries (s 35(1)). However, the definition of a beneficiary under s 8(1)(b) is to be read as a reference to the person who under the will of the deceased or under the law relating to intestacy is beneficially interested in the estate. This provision is necessary as otherwise a creditor might come within the definition of a beneficiary.

Section 9(a) provides that the powers conferred by Part III are in addition to powers conferred on trustees otherwise than by that part. This means that if the trustees already have power to invest in land under the will or settlement, they do not need to make use of the powers contained in the Act. However, if the will or settlement specifically prohibits the trustees from investing in land, then they cannot do so.

Section 9(b) provides that the powers conferred by the Act are subject to any restriction or exclusion imposed by the trust instrument or by any enactment or any provision of subordinate legislation.

Section 10 contains provisions dealing with existing trusts. Section 10(1) provides that Part III of the Act does not apply in relation to a trust of property which consists of or includes land which is settled land (despite s 2 of the Trusts of Land and Appointment of Trustees Act 1996). Nor does it apply to a trust to which the Universities and Colleges Estates Act 1925 applies.

Subject to this, Part III applies to trusts whether created before or after its commencement (s 10(2)).

Section 8(3) provides that for the purpose of exercising his functions as a trustee, a trustee who acquires land under this section has all the powers of an absolute owner in relation to the land.

Section 6(3) of the Trusts of Land and Appointment of Trustees Act 1996 provides that trustees of land have the power to acquire land under the power conferred by s 8 of the Trustee Act 2000.

Section 6(5) provides that in exercising the powers conferred by the section, the trustees must have regard to the rights of the beneficiaries. Section 6(6) provides that the powers conferred by the section shall not be exercised in contravention of, or of any order made in pursuance of, any other enactment or any rule of law or equity.

Section 6(7) states that the reference to an order in subsection (6) includes an order of any court or of the Charity commissioners. Section 6(8) provides that where any enactment other than s 6 confers on trustees authority to act subject to any restriction, limitation or condition, trustees of land may not exercise the powers conferred by s 6 to do any act which they are prevented from doing under the other enactment by reason of the restriction, limitation or condition. Section 6(9) (inserted by the Trustee Act 2000) provides that the duty of care under s 1 of the Trustee Act 2000 applies to trustees of land when exercising the powers conferred by this section.

General duties with regard to investment

9.34 The duty of care applies to a trustee–

(a) when exercising the general power of investment conferred on him by the trust instrument;

(b) when carrying out a duty to which he is subject under ss 4 or 5 (duties relating to the exercise of a power of investment or to the review of investments) (Sch 1 para 1).

Section 1 defines the duty of care. A trustee must exercise such care and skill as is reasonable in the circumstances, having regard in particular–

(a) to any special knowledge or experience that he has or holds himself out as having; and

(b) if he acts as trustee in the course of a business or profession, to any special knowledge or experience that it is reasonable to expect of a person acting in the course of that kind of business or occupation.

Express powers of investment

9.35 Most, if not all, professionally drawn wills and settlements contain an express investment clause; frequently these will authorise the trustees to invest the trust funds as if they were the absolute owners. It has now been established that this means what it says – trustees can invest in appropriate investments (*Re Harari's Settlement Trusts [1949] 1 All ER 430*).

There is also some doubt about the meaning of the word 'invest'. Is it confined to assets which yield income, or does it include assets which are purchased in the hope that they will show large capital gains? There are some old cases where it has been held that assets purchased in the hope that they will increase in value are not 'investments'. However, in *Marson v Morton [1986] 1 WLR 1343*, a tax case, at page 1350 Sir Nicolas Browne-Wilkinson said 'But in my judgement in 1986 it is not any longer self-evident that unless land is producing income it cannot be an investment'.

Even though trustees may have wide powers of investment, it should be remembered that trustees are still subject to s 4 of the TA 2000, and the general duties imposed on trustees with regard to investment.

Express power to lend money on mortgage

9.36 Express investment powers frequently include a power to lend money to a beneficiary. The trustees may also be empowered not to charge any interest, and to make the loan without any security. Even though the express power may be very wide, the trustees must still have regard to the duties imposed by s 4 of the TA 2000. Thus it would normally be wrong for trustees to lend all the trust money on mortgage, although there may be exceptional circumstances where this is justified. Furthermore, trustees are under a duty to hold the balance fairly between the life tenant and the remainderman, and whilst a mortgage may satisfy the needs of a life tenant for income, there will be little capital appreciation to satisfy the needs of the remainderman. A mortgage where the amount of capital to be repaid and the rate of interest are both linked to other currencies as in *Multiservice Bookbinding Ltd v Marden [1979] Ch 84* may satisfy both the remainderman and the life tenant, but equally could disappoint depending on currency movements – unless carefully drafted, such a mortgage may not be permitted.

An unsecured loan to a beneficiary may be unfair to the remainderman as it may never be repaid. On the other hand, an interest free loan to the remainderman, or a loan at a low rate of interest to a beneficiary, may be unfair to the life tenant.

The power of maintenance

9.37 Section 31 of the TA 1925 contains a power of maintenance. This authorises the trustees to apply the whole of the income of a trust fund for the maintenance, education or benefit of a beneficiary.

When does s 31 apply?

9.38 Section 31 clearly applies to vested gifts, where the beneficiary will be entitled to the income, but in the case of a contingent interest s 31(3) states that it applies to a contingent interest only if the limitation or trust carries the intermediate income of the property.

Which contingent gifts carry the intermediate income? The law in this area is quite complicated, but the following gifts will carry the intermediate income:

(a) a contingent or future specific devise or bequest of real or personal property – 'I give Blackacre to A if he becomes a doctor', or 'I give Blackacre to A after B has qualified as a doctor';

(b) a contingent residuary devise of freehold land;

(c) a specific or residuary devise of freehold land to trustees upon trust for persons whose interests are contingent or executory (s 175 of the Law of Property Act 1925);

(d) contingent bequest of residuary personalty (*Re Adams [1893] 1 Ch 329*).

A contingent pecuniary legacy – 'I give £10,000 to A if he qualifies as a doctor' – does not normally carry interest until the time when it is payable. However, in the following situations, the gift will carry the intermediate income:

(i) If the donor has shown an intention that the income should be applied for the maintenance of the beneficiary;

(ii) If the testator is the parent of the beneficiary, or stands in loco parentis to the beneficiary, the testator has not made any other provision for the beneficiary, the gift is directly to the beneficiary, and the condition to be satisfied is attaining an age no greater than 18;

(iii) If the testator has directed that the legacy should be set aside for the benefit of a beneficiary.

Section 31(3) provides that the section also applies to a future or contingent legacy by the parent of, or by a person standing *in loco parentis* to, the legatee, if and for such period as, under the general law, the legacy carries interest for the maintenance of the legatee. This is very similar to (ii) above.

How is the power exercisable?

9.39 Section 31(1) TA 1925 provides that the trustees may, at their sole discretion, pay to the beneficiary's parent or guardian, if any, or otherwise apply for his benefit or towards his maintenance, education or benefit, the whole or such part, if any, of the income of that property as may, in all the circumstances, be reasonable, whether or not there is:

(a) any other fund applicable for the same purpose; or

(b) any person bound by law to provide for his maintenance or education.

What factors should the trustees take into account in deciding whether or not to exercise their discretion?

9.40 There is a proviso to s 31 of the TA 1925 which requires trustees to have regard to the following matters in deciding whether or not to apply the income for the maintenance, education or benefit of a beneficiary. These are as follows:

— the age of the infant;
— the requirements of the infant;
— the circumstances of the case;
— other income applicable for the same purpose;
— if the income of more than one fund is applicable for the maintenance, education or benefit of the infant, a proportionate part only of the income of each fund shall be so paid or applied.

The effect of that proviso is to impose an objective test on the trustees, and to remove some of their discretion.

Entitlement at 18

9.41 A beneficiary who does not attain a vested interest at 18 is entitled to the income until he either attains a vested interest or dies, or until the failure of his interest (s 31(1)(ii) TA 1925).

Thus if there is a gift to a beneficiary contingent on the beneficiary attaining 30, and s 31 applies, the beneficiary will be entitled to the income at the age of 18, although he will not be entitled to the capital until the age of 30.

What happens to any income which is not applied for the benefit of the beneficiaries?

9.42 If any of the income is not applied for the maintenance, education or benefit of the beneficiary, it must be accumulated and invested. It must then be paid to a beneficiary who:

(a) attains the age of 18 years, or marries under that age, if his interest in such income during his infancy or until his marriage is a vested interest; or

(b) on attaining the age of 18 years or on marriage under that age becomes entitled to the property from which such income arose in fee simple, absolute or determinable, or absolutely, or for an entailed interest (s 31(2)).

Note that under (b) a beneficiary must become absolutely entitled to personalty, or have an entailed interest; a beneficiary with a conditional or determinable interest in personalty will not be entitled to the accumulated income on attaining 18 or marriage. The position is different if the subject matter of the gift is land. 'Absolute' means complete beneficial ownership and dominion over property. It does not include an interest which can be destroyed at any time by the exercise of a power or the fulfilment of a condition with the consequence that the property must be retained by the trustees until the power or condition is spent (*Re Sharp's Settlement Trust [1972] 3 WLR 765* at page 769).

Section 31(2)(ii) provides that in any other case the trustees shall, notwithstanding that such person had a vested interest in such income, hold the accumulations as an accretion to the capital of the property from which such accumulations arose, and as one fund with such capital for all purposes. If such property is settled land, such accumulations are to be held upon the same trusts as if the same were capital money arising from the settled land.

The receipt of a married infant is a good discharge.

Class gifts

9.43 If there is a contingent class gift, the trustees are entitled to treat the share of each potential beneficiary separately, and to apply the income of each potential beneficiary's share for the maintenance of that beneficiary even if one or more beneficiary has satisfied the contingency (*Re Holford [1894] 3 Ch 30*). So if there is a contingent gift to three children, and the eldest satisfies the contingency, he is not entitled to the whole income. If a beneficiary dies without satisfying the contingency, any accumulated income accrues to the other beneficiaries as capital.

Express power of maintenance and prohibition on benefiting settlor

9.44 In *Fuller v Evans [2000] 1 All ER 636* the settlor created an accumulation and maintenance settlement for the benefit of his children. The trustees had power to provide for the maintenance and education of the children. Clause 12 of the settlement prohibited the trustees from exercising their power in such manner that the settlor would or might become entitled either directly or indirectly to any benefit in any manner or in any circumstances whatsoever. There was a divorce, and the settlor agreed to pay for the children's maintenance and school fees. The trustees were concerned that if they exercised their power of maintenance, they would indirectly benefit the settlor, and would infringe clause 12 of the settlement. It was held that if the trustees did exercise their power of maintenance, they would not infringe clause 12.

Common variations

9.45 It is common to make the following variations to the statutory power of maintenance:

(a) the trustees are given a complete discretion as to whether the income should be applied for the maintenance, education or benefit of a beneficiary;

(b) the entitlement to income may be postponed to an age greater than 18.

Powers with regard to minors

9.46 Personal representatives and trustees cannot pay the income or hand the capital to a minor, but there are various exceptions to this rule. They are:

— under s 21 of the Law of Property Act 1925 a married infant has power to give a valid receipt for all income but not capital. As an infant has to be 16 years of age to marry, this is a very limited exception as it can only apply for two years;

— section 31 of the Trustee Act 1925 authorises trustees to apply income for the maintenance of an infant beneficiary. Such payments are to be made to the parent or guardian of the child. Section 32 authorises the advancement of a maximum of one-half of the capital;

— payment into court. Section 63(1) of the Trustee Act 1925 provides that trustees, or the majority of trustees, having in their hands or under their control money or securities belonging to a trust, may pay the same into court. Section 63(2) provides that the receipt of the proper officer shall be a sufficient discharge to trustees for the money or securities so paid into court;

— the will or trust instrument may authorise payment to the infant or to the guardian or parent of the child;

— section 42 of the Administration of Estates Act 1925 applies where the will does not appoint trustees, and the infant is absolutely entitled. The personal representatives can then appoint a trust corporation or two or more individuals not exceeding four (whether or not including the personal representatives) to be trustees.

  Note that s 42 only applies if the will does not appoint trustees, and the infant must be absolutely entitled;

— section 41 of the Administration of Estates Act 1925 enables personal representatives to appropriate any asset in satisfaction of any legacy if the beneficiaries agree. In the case of an infant beneficiary, the consent can be given by the parent or guardian of the infant.

Power of trustees to give receipts

9.47 Section 14(1) of the TA 1925 provides that the receipt in writing of a trustee for any money, securities, investments or other personal property or effects payable, transferable, or deliverable to him under any trust or power shall be a sufficient discharge to the person paying, transferring, or delivering the same and shall effectually exonerate him.

Section 14(2) provides that the section does not, except where the trustee is a trust corporation, enable a sole trustee to give a valid receipt for:

(a) the proceeds of sale or other capital money arising under a trust of land;

(b) capital money arising under the Settled Land Act 1925.

It is not possible to displace this section by a provision in the trust deed.

Thus a sole trustee of personalty can give a valid receipt.

Note that a sole personal representative can give a valid receipt for capital; see paragraph 8.3.

Sale

The powers

9.48 Trustees have extensive powers to sell trust property. If the trust property consists of land, it will be a Settled Land Act settlement, or a trust for sale, or a trust of land. As a result of the Trusts of Land and Appointment of Trustees Act 1996 (TLATA 1996), it has not been possible since 1 January 1997 to create Settled Land Act settlements, although those created before that date remain in existence. If it is a Settled Land Act settlement, the tenant for life can sell the property (s 38(1) of the Settled Land Act 1925 (SLA 1925)), although the purchase price will have to be paid to at least two trustees or a trust corporation (s 94(1) SLA 1925). If it is a trust of land or trust for sale, the trustees have the power to sell the trust property (s 6(1) TLATA 1996), although again the purchaser must pay the purchase price to at least two trustees or a trust corporation (s 27(2) of the Law of Property Act 1925).

Section 8(1) of the TLATA 1996 provides that s 6 of the 1996 Act can be modified, and s 8(2) provides that if any consent is required for the exercise of the power, the power may not be exercised without that consent. Section 10(1) of the TLATA 1996 provides that if the consent of more than two persons is required for the exercise by the trustees of any function relating to land, a purchaser need only satisfy himself that the consent of any two has been obtained. However, purchasers dealing with trustees of land held on charitable, ecclesiastical or public trusts must ensure that all appropriate consents have been obtained (s 10(2) TLATA 1996)).

It should be noted that the provisions of the 1996 Act apply to all trusts whenever created, apart from land which is settled land or land to which the Universities and Colleges Estates Act 1925 applies (s 1 TLATA 1996).

The 1996 Act provides that trustees are also under a duty to consult the beneficiaries of full age and beneficially entitled to an interest in possession in the land so far as practicable (s 11(1)). They must give effect to the wishes of those beneficiaries so far as consistent with the general interest of the trust; if there is a dispute, the views of the majority by value prevail (s 11(1)). The duty to consult can be excluded, and will not normally apply to a trust created before the TLATA 1996 came into force (1 January 1997), or to a trust created or arising under a will made before 1 January 1997 (s 11(2)), or in the case of a transfer to all the beneficiaries if they are of full age and capacity and absolutely entitled.

Suppose that T1 and T2 are the trustees of a settlement under which A is the life tenant. T1 and T2 are under a duty to consult A about the operation of the trust. If A wants any land in the trust to be sold, T1 and T2 must give effect to those wishes unless advised by a valuer that it would be best not to sell the land until the next year.

Section 18(1) of the TLATA 1996 provides that ss 10 and 11 of the Act do not apply to personal representatives. A sole personal representative can sell and give a valid receipt for capital.

Chattels may also be subject to an express trust with a power of sale, or it may be implied – for example, under s 33 of the Administration of Estates Act 1925 when a person dies intestate. In the case of other property, for example stocks and shares, it is probable that there is an implied power of sale.

Section 16 of the TA 1925 provides that where trustees are authorised by the trust instrument or by law to pay capital money subject to the trust, they can raise such money by the sale or mortgage of all or any part of the trust property for the time being in possession.

Section 212 of the Inheritance Tax Act 1984 provides that a person liable for inheritance tax other than the transferor or the transferor's spouse has power to sell the property for the purpose of paying the inheritance tax.

Method of sale

9.49 Section 12 of the Trustee Act 1925 confers a wide discretion on the trustees as to the mode of sale. It provides that where a trustee has a duty or power to sell property, he may sell or concur with any other person in selling all or any part of the property, either subject to prior charges or not, and either together or in lots, by public auction or by private contract, subject to any such conditions respecting title or evidence of title or other matter as the trustee thinks fit, with power to vary any contract for sale, and to buy in at any auction, or to rescind any contract for resale and to resell, without being answerable for any loss.

Section 12(2) provides that a trust or power to sell or dispose of land includes a trust or power to sell or dispose of part thereof, whether the division is horizontal, vertical, or made in any other way.

Duty of trustees

9.50 It is the duty of trustees to obtain the best possible price for trust property (*Buttle v Saunders [1950] 2 All ER 193*). Thus although trustees have a wide discretion as to the mode of sale, they should choose the method which is likely to yield the best price.

Protection of purchasers of land

9.51 Section 16 of the TLATA 1996 contains provisions for the protection of purchasers. It does not apply if the title is registered.

Section 16(1) provides that a purchaser of land which is or has been subject to a trust need not be concerned to see that any requirement imposed on the trustees by ss 6(5), 7(3) or 11(1) has been complied with. Section 6(5) provides that, in exercising the powers conferred by the section, the trustees must have regard to the rights of the beneficiaries. Section 7 is concerned with the partition of the land subject to a trust, and provides that before exercising their powers, the trustees must obtain the consent of the beneficiaries. Section 11(1) imposes a duty on trustees to consult the beneficiaries.

Section 16(2) provides that if trustees convey land and contravene s 6(6) or (8), but the purchaser from the trustees has no actual notice of contravention, the contravention does not invalidate the conveyance. Section 6(6) provides that the powers conferred by s 6 must not be exercised in contravention of, or of any order made in pursuance of, any enactment or any rule of law or equity. Section 6(8) provides that where any enactment other than s 6 confers on the trustees authority to act subject to any restriction, limitation or condition, trustees of land may not exercise the powers conferred by s 6 to do any act which they are prevented from doing under the other enactment by reason of the restriction, limitation or condition.

Section 16(3) provides that where the powers of the trustees of land are limited:

(a) the trustees must take all reasonable steps to bring the limitation to the notice of any purchaser of the land from them; but

(b) the limitation does not invalidate any conveyance by the trustees to a purchaser who has no actual notice of the limitation.

Section 16(2) and 16(3) do not apply to land held on charitable, ecclesiastical or public trusts.

Section 16(4) provides that where land which is subject to the trust is conveyed by the trustees to persons believed by them to be beneficiaries absolutely entitled to the land and of full age and capacity, the trustees must execute a deed declaring that they are discharged from the trust in relation to the land. If they fail to do so, the court may make an order requiring them to do so. Section 16(5) provides that a purchaser of land to which a deed under subsection (4) relates is entitled to assume that, as from the date of the deed, the land is not subject to the trust unless he has actual notice that the trustees were mistaken in their belief that the land was conveyed to beneficiaries absolutely entitled to the land under the trust and of full age and capacity.

Power to convey the land to beneficiaries

9.52 Section 6(2) of the TLATA 1996 permits the trustees to convey the land to the beneficiaries if they are all of full age and capacity, even if the beneficiaries have not required the trustees to do so. The beneficiaries must do whatever is necessary to ensure that the land vests in them – for example, they must get themselves registered as proprietors of the land. If the beneficiaries fail to do so, the court may make an order requiring them to do so.

Power to partition land

9.53 The trustees have power to partition the land under s 7 of the TLATA 1996 where the beneficiaries (i) are of full age and absolutely entitled in undivided shares to land subject to the trust, and (ii) agree to the partition. The trustees may provide for the payment of any equality money by way of mortgage or otherwise.

Where a share in the land is affected by an incumbrance, the trustees may either give effect to it, or provide for its discharge from the property allotted to that share as they think fit (s 7(4)).

If a share in land is absolutely vested in a minor, the provisions of s 7 apply as if he were of full age, except that the trustees may act on his behalf and retain land or other property representing his share in trust for him (s 7(5)).

Are trustees under a duty to exercise powers of appointment?

9.54 There may be an express power in a will or settlement authorising a person to appoint the property amongst the members of a class of beneficiaries.

If there is a discretionary trust, the trustees have a discretion as to which member of the class of beneficiaries they benefit, and in what proportions.

The cases distinguish between trust or fiduciary powers and bare or ordinary powers as the duties owed by the person holding the power depend on whether it is a trusts power or bare or ordinary power. It can be very difficult to decide if a power is a trust power or an ordinary power. The distinction between trustee powers and bare powers is to a large extent irrelevant if the power is held by a trustee as the trustee will owe duties to the beneficiaries because they are trustees.

Duties of donees with a trust power of appointment

9.55 If it is a trust power, or the power is held by trustees, then the trustees owe duties to the beneficiaries.

However, this does not mean that the trustee must exercise the power, although they cannot refuse to exercise it. The trustees must consider whether to exercise the power, and should they decide not to, there is little the beneficiaries can do. The trustees could also decide to benefit one member of the class of beneficiaries excluding all the others. A beneficiary excluded in such a way, and wishing to challenge such a decision would find it very difficult to do so, as the trustees have not refused to exercise the power.

A court would find it difficult to make an order stating that the trustees must exercise the power. Therefore, where a person with a trustee power refuses to exercise it, it is unusual for a court to order them to do otherwise. However, the court may remove the trustees, and appoint new ones, or it may exercise the power of appointment itself. The court may also invite the beneficiaries if of full age and capacity to agree on a scheme of distribution.

Trustees of discretionary trusts

9.56 Trustees of a discretionary trust have a discretion as to which member or members of the class they benefit. Trustees are under certain duties with regard to this discretion.

Trustees cannot ignore the discretion, they must consider whether or not to exercise the power. If, after taking all relevant factors into consideration, they decide not to exercise the discretion, the courts will not intervene. However, if the trustees do nothing, then the courts will intervene.

Chapter 10

Completion of the administration

10.1 Once the personal representatives have settled all the liabilities including the liability for income tax, capital gains tax or inheritance tax, then they can distribute the assets to the beneficiaries. Often this is the easy stage in administering an estate, but there can be problems.

Time limit for completing the administration of the estate

10.2 Section 44 of the Administration of Estates Act 1925 (AEA 1925) provides that a personal representative is not bound to distribute the estate of the deceased before the expiration of one year from the date of death.

If there are few assets in the estate, it should be possible to distribute them within the year. However, in more complicated estates, the personal representatives may struggle to complete the administration within a year; it may take several years.

Who is entitled?

10.3 Personal representatives are under a duty to distribute the assets of the deceased to the correct persons, and if they do not do so, they may be personally liable to the disappointed beneficiaries.

In the great majority of cases, there is no problem with regard to this. However, even in apparently straightforward cases, caution may be desirable.

Gifts to children

10.4 Where a gift is made in a will to children or grandchildren, it will include legitimate, legitimated, illegitimate, adopted children, and in the case of a man, children conceived before death but not born until after death. It will not usually include stepchildren.

The same rule applies if the deceased died intestate, although it is clear that stepchildren cannot take on the intestacy of a stepparent.

It may be difficult for personal representatives to ascertain the exact number of children and grandchildren. Some protection is afforded to personal representatives as regards adopted and legitimated children – see paragraph 8.19. However, this protection does not extend to illegitimate children, and so personal representatives must rely upon advertisements under s 27 of the Trustee Act 1925 (TA 1925) (see paragraph 8.19) for protection against claims by unknown children of the deceased.

If there is any doubt about paternity, then it may be that DNA analysis will have to be used to determine fatherhood.

It may be desirable to check birth certificates, particularly with adopted children.

Frequently gifts in wills to grandchildren, or the children of a named person, will specify that it is only the children or grandchildren living at the date of death of the testator who are to take. If that is not the case, personal representatives must have regard to the class closing rules. These close the class, and are necessary because otherwise it might be impossible to complete the administration of the estate. A gift to all my grandchildren would be very hard to operate if there were no class closing rules – the gift would have to remain open until the personal representatives were certain that there would be no more grandchildren. However, even with class closing rules, the gift may have to remain open for years. If there is a gift to all my grandchildren, and there are grandchildren living at the date of death, then those living at that date or *en ventre sa mère* take. If there are no such grandchildren, then the class remains open indefinitely.

Portions

10.5 There is a rule against double portions. A portion is a gift made by a father or person in loco parentis to a child, which is made for the purpose of establishing the child in life, or of making a permanent provision for him. If the will of the father or person in loco parentis to the child contains a legacy or gift of residue to that child, there is a presumption that the legacy or gift of the residue is satisfied by the portion either wholly or in part. This is all subject to contrary intention.

In *Casimir v Alexander [2001] WTLR 939* in September 1985 L provided the finance to enable his daughter S to purchase a house as a residence for L, S and her children. He made a will in June 1985 appointing S as his executor. The will contained a specific bequest to of all his furniture, and the residuary estate was given in different proportions to S, her two brothers, G and S, and any grandchildren living at the date of L's death.

L died in 1990. G commenced proceedings alleging that S had exerted undue influence in order to persuade L to purchase the house in her name. He also alleged that if the purchase had been a gift, it should be brought into account on the distribution of the residuary estate.

Both these allegations were dismissed.

The evidence showed that L had intended to make a gift, and also that this gift should not be brought into account on the distribution of the residuary estate.

In *Race v Race [2002] WTLR 1193* MR and JR were brother and sister. Their father executed a will providing that JR could live in a public house for the rest of her life, and that the proceeds should then be treated as part of the residue, which was to be divided equally between MR and JR.

Subsequently father gave the public house to JR.

It was held that both gifts were portions, and that the one adeemed the other. A portion was defined as gift intended to establish a child in life, or make some provision for him. It was distinguished from a gift, or present.

Deceased beneficiaries

10.6 Normally, if a beneficiary predeceases a testator, the gift to that beneficiary lapses. However, there are the following exceptions to this rule:

(a) wills frequently contain an express substitution clause;

(b) section 33 of the Wills Act 1837 (WA 1837) provides that if a child or remoter issue of the testator predeceases leaving issue the issue will take the share their parent would have taken had he or she survived. Section 33(1) provides that where:

— a will contains a devise or bequest to a child or remoter descendant of the testator; and

— the intended beneficiary dies before the testator, leaving issue; and

— issue of the intended beneficiary are living at the testator's death;

then, unless a contrary intention appears by the will, the devise or bequest shall take effect as a devise or bequest to the issue living at the testator's death.

Section 33(2) provides that where:

- a will contains a devise or bequest to a class of persons consisting of children or remoter descendants of the testator; and
- a member of the class dies before the testator leaving issue; and
- issue of that member are living at the testator's death;

then, unless a contrary intention appears by the will, the devise or bequest shall take effect as if the class included the issue of its deceased member living at the testator's death.

Section 33(3) provides that issue shall take under this section through all degrees, according to their stock, in equal shares if more than one, any gift or share which their parent would have taken and so that no issue shall take whose parent is living at the testator's death and so capable of taking.

Section 33(4) provides that for the purposes of the section:

(a) the illegitimacy of any person is to be disregarded; and

(b) a person conceived before the testator's death and born living thereafter is to be taken to have been living at the testator's death.

Note that there is no contingent entitlement under the section. If it applies, the issue of a deceased beneficiary are entitled even though they may be very small children.

If the deceased died intestate, the children of the deceased are entitled on the statutory trusts. Section 47(1)(i) of the AEA 1925 defines these as in trust, in equal shares if more than one, for all or any children or child of the intestate, living at the death of the intestate, who attain the age of 18 years or marry under that age. If any child of the intestate predeceases the intestate leaving issue living at the death of the intestate, the issue are entitled provided they attain the age of 18 years or marry under that age. The issue take through all degrees, according to their stocks, in equal shares if more than one, the share their parent would have taken if living at the death of the intestate. In addition, no issue can take whose parent was living at the death of the intestate and so capable of taking.

Thus if a child of the intestate has predeceased the intestate leaving three children, those children will take the share their parent would have taken had he or she survived. Each grandchild must attain 18 or marry under that age in order to take; if one does not, then his or her share will accrue to his or her brothers and sisters.

Construction of wills

10.7 It is to be hoped that if the will has been professionally drafted there will not be any problems with regard to interpretation. However, if there are problems, the following approaches can be adopted:

(a) if all the affected beneficiaries are of full age and capacity, they could be asked to agree to one particular interpretation. If they are not of full age and capacity because they are minors, and the amount of money or property involved is small, then the parents may be asked to agree to a compromise on their behalf with suitable indemnities to the personal representatives;

(b) make use of s 48 of the Administration of Justice Act 1985 (AJA 1985).

Section 48(1) of the AJA 1985 provides that where:

(i) any question of construction has arisen out of the terms of a will or a trust; and

(ii) an opinion in writing given by a person who has a ten-year High Court qualification, within the meaning of s 71 of the Courts and Legal Services Act 1990, has been obtained on that question by the personal representatives or trustees under the will or trust, the High Court may, on the application of the personal representatives or trustees and without hearing argument, make an order authorising those persons to take such steps in reliance on the said opinion as are specified in the order.

Subsection (2) of the AJA 1985 provides that the High Court shall not make an order if it appears that a dispute exists which would make it inappropriate for the court to make the order without hearing argument.

(c) In certain circumstances it is possible to apply for rectification of a will. Section 20(1) of the AJA 1982 provides that if a court is satisfied that a will is so expressed that it fails to carry out the testator's intentions, in consequence of:

(a) a clerical error; or

(b) a failure to understand his instructions;

it may order the will to be rectified so as to carry out his intentions.

Section 20(2) provides that an application for an order under the section shall not, except with the leave of the court, be made after the end of the period of six months from the date on which representation with respect to the estate of the deceased is first taken out. In deciding if leave should be granted, the courts apply the same principles as they would in deciding whether to grant leave for an application out of time under the Inheritance (Provision for Family and Dependants) Act 1975.

Rule 55(1) of the NCPR 1987 provides that an application for an order that a will be rectified by virtue of s 20(1) of the AJA 1982 may be made to a District Judge or Registrar, unless a probate action has been commenced. Rule 55(2) provides that the application must be supported by an affidavit, setting out the grounds of the application, together with such evidence as to the testator's intentions and as to whichever of the following matters as are in issue:

(a) in what respects the testator's intentions were not understood; or

(b) the nature of an alleged clerical error.

Rule 55(3) provides that unless otherwise directed, notice of the application must be given to every person having an interest under the will whose interests might be prejudiced, or such other person who might be prejudiced, by the rectification applied for and any comments in writing by any such person must be exhibited to the affidavit in support of the application.

Rule 55(4) provides that if the District Judge or Registrar is satisfied that, subject to any direction to the contrary, notice has been given to every person mentioned in paragraph (3) above, and that application is unopposed, he may order that the will be rectified accordingly.

Missing beneficiaries

10.8 It is sometimes difficult to trace missing beneficiaries. This is particularly true of the person who has died intestate in their eighties without a spouse or children, but with many brothers and sisters. In such a situation it may be wise to take out a missing beneficiary indemnity policy. In all cases where this is a possibility, ask the insurance company what enquiries they require to be made before they will issue the policy. Subject to this:

(a) make enquiries of the living relatives;

(b) make use of the various search facilities available through the internet;

(c) advertise in appropriate newspapers and other publications;

(d) employ enquiry agents, or tracing agencies;

(e) distribute the estate to those entitled as if the missing beneficiary had died without issue having first obtained an indemnity from the persons to whom the estate is distributed. Ideally, the indemnity should be secured by a charge over property. The disadvantage of this is that it might be difficult to enforce the indemnity, particularly if it is not supported by a charge, but this may be the easiest and cheapest solution if the value of the assets involved is small;

(f) apply to the court for an order to distribute the estate on the basis that a beneficiary is dead. These orders are known as Benjamin orders.

Divorce

10.9 The divorce of the testator does not automatically revoke a will. Instead, any gift to the former spouse lapses, and any appointment of the former spouse as executor or trustee also lapses. Section 18A of the Wills Act 1837 (WA 1837) provides:

> '(1) Where, after a testator has made a will, an order or decree of a court of civil jurisdiction in England and Wales dissolves or annuls his marriage or his marriage is dissolved or annulled and the divorce or annulment is entitled to recognition in England and Wales by virtue of Part II of the Family Law Act 1986, –
>
> (a) provisions of the will appointing executors or trustees or conferring a power of appointment, if they appoint or confer the power on the former spouse, shall take effect as if the former spouse had died on the date on which the marriage is dissolved or annulled, and
>
> (b) any property which, or an interest in which, is devised or bequeathed to the former spouse shall pass as if the former spouse had died on that date'.

Section 18A(2) of the WA 1837 provides that subsection (1)(b) is without prejudice to any right of the former spouse under the Inheritance (Provision for Family and Dependants) Act 1975.

If the testator has given the spouse a life interest with remainder to the children, then if the testator and his spouse are divorced, the effect is to accelerate the interest in remainder, so that the children will be absolutely entitled even though the former spouse is still alive at the date of death of the testator.

Marriage

10.10 Marriage revokes any existing wills of the testator and the testatrix. However, s 18(3) of the WA 1837 provides that where it appears from a will that at the time it was made the testator was expecting to be married to a particular person and that he intended that the will should not be revoked by the marriage, the will is not revoked by marriage to that person. Thus if the testator marries someone else, then the will will be revoked by the marriage not contemplated by the will.

Section 18(4) deals with a will where one provision but not the whole will is expressed to in expectation of marriage to a particular person, and that the testator intends that provision should not be revoked by the marriage. It provides that where it appears from a will that at the time it was made the testator was expecting to be married to a particular person and that he intended that a disposition in the will should not be revoked by his marriage to that person:

(a) that disposition shall take effect notwithstanding the marriage; and

(b) any other disposition in the will shall take effect also, unless it appears from the will that the testator intended the disposition to be revoked by the marriage.

Thus where only one provision in a will is expressed to be made in expectation of marriage to a particular person, and it is clear that the testator intended that provision should not be revoked by the marriage, then normally the whole will will not be revoked by the marriage.

Intestacy

Total intestacy

Overview

10.11 This is dealt with in s 33 of the Administration of Estates Act 1925. This section imposes a trust, and gives the personal representatives power to sell all the assets. The personal representatives must then pay the funeral, testamentary and administration expenses and the debts of the deceased.

If a minority or life interest arises under the intestacy, the personal representatives can invest the assets in accordance with the Trustee Act 2000.

Section 33(1) of the Administration of Estates Act 1925 (AEA 1925) imposes a trust in the case of a person who dies intestate. It provides that on the death of a person intestate as to any real or personal estate, such estate shall be held in trust by his personal representatives with the power to sell it – with power to postpone such sale and conversion for such period as the personal representatives, without being liable to account, may think proper.

Section 33(2) provides that out of the ready money of the deceased (so far as not disposed of by his will, if any) and any net money arising from disposing of any other part of his estate (after payment of costs), the personal representatives must pay all such funeral, testamentary and administration expenses, debts and other liabilities as are properly payable thereout, having regard to the rules of administration contained in that Part of the AEA 1925. Having done that, the personal representatives are then required to set aside a fund sufficient to provide for any pecuniary legacies bequeathed by the will, if any.

Section 33(3) directs that during the minority of any beneficiary, or the subsistence of any life interest, the money, or so much thereof as may not have been distributed, may be invested under the Trustee Act 2000.

Section 33(5) of the AEA 1925 provides that the income of so much of the real and personal estate of the deceased as may not be disposed of by his will, if any, or may not be required for administration purposes, may as from the death of the deceased be treated and applied as income. If necessary, the income must be apportioned between the life tenant and the remainderman. This applies however the estate is invested.

Partial intestacy

10.12 Section 33 of the AEA 1925 clearly contemplates that the section will apply to a partial intestacy, as subsection (2) refers to setting aside a fund for any pecuniary legacies bequeathed by the will. However, s 49(1) of the AEA 1925 provides that 'where any person dies leaving a will effectively disposing of part of his property, this Part of this Act shall have effect as respects the part of his property not so disposed of …'. The Part referred to is Part IV, whereas s 33 is in Part III. Notwithstanding the apparent conflict between the two sections, it is considered that a court would impose a trust under s 33(1) in a partial intestacy.

What is the position if the will imposes an express trust? It may be that the terms of the trust imposed by the will are identical to the statutory implied trust, in which event there is no problem. However, the terms may differ, in which event it is probable that the terms of the express trust will prevail.

Order of entitlement

10.13 The AEA 1925 as amended prescribes the order of entitlement. The order is as follows:

(a) If the intestate left a spouse who survived the intestate by 28 days, and issue, then the surviving spouse is entitled to the personal chattels (see below for a definition of 'personal chattels'), a statutory legacy of £125,000 free of death duties and costs, but with interest thereon at the rate of 6% and a life interest in one half of the residue.

The remainder of the estate (one half of the residuary estate and the interest in reversion after the death of the surviving spouse) is held on the statutory trusts for the issue. The statutory trusts are discussed below.

(b) If the deceased left a spouse and no issue, but did leave a parent or brother and sister of the whole blood, or issue of a brother or sister of the whole blood, if the spouse survives for 28 days after the death of the intestate, the surviving spouse is entitled to the personal chattels, a statutory legacy of £200,000 free of death duties and costs, but with interest thereon at the rate of 6%, and one half of the residue.

Note that if the deceased and his or her spouse were involved in divorce proceedings, they are still married until the decree absolute is granted.

Section 55(1)(x) of the AEA 1925 defines personal chattels as 'carriages, horses, stable furniture and effects (not used for business purposes), motor cars and accessories (not used for business purposes), garden effects, domestic animals, plate, plated articles, linen, china, glass, books, pictures, prints, furniture, jewellery, articles of household or personal use or ornament, musical and scientific instruments and apparatus, wines, liquors, and consumable stores', but do not include any chattels used at the death of the intestate for business purposes, or money or security for money.

It should be noted that assets used for business purposes, money and security for money are not included. The other half of the residue is held on trust –

(i) where the intestate leaves one parent or both parents (whether or not brothers or sisters of the intestate or their issue also survive) in trust for the parent absolutely or, as the case may be, for the two parents in equal shares absolutely;

(ii) where the intestate leaves no parent, on the statutory trusts for the brothers and sisters of the whole blood of the intestate.

(c) If the intestate leaves no issue and no parent or brother and sister of the whole blood or issue of a brother and sister of the whole blood, the surviving spouse is entitled to the whole estate provided he or she survives the testator by 28.

(d) If the deceased did not leave a spouse, then the order of entitlement is:

(i) the issue on the statutory trusts;

(ii) the parents in equal shares if more than one;

(iii) brothers and sisters of the whole blood on the statutory trusts;

(iv) brothers and sisters of the half blood on the statutory trusts;

(v) the grandparents, and if more than one in equal shares;

(vi) the uncles and aunts of the whole blood;

(vii) the uncles and aunts of the half blood;

(viii) the Crown or the Duchy of Lancaster or the Duke of Cornwall as *bona vacantia*.

If both spouses are killed at the same time, and the order of death is uncertain, then if the intestate is the older spouse, for intestacy purposes, the younger spouse is deemed not to have survived the older spouse.

Where there is a possibility that the beneficiaries might be under age, then the residuary estate is directed to be held on the statutory trusts. Section 47(1) of the AEA 1925 defines these trusts as –

> '(i) in trust, in equal shares if more than one, for all or any children or child of the intestate, living at the death of the intestate, who attain the age of eighteen years or marry under that age, and for all or any of the issue living at the death of the intestate who attain the age of eighteen years or marry under that age of any child of the intestate who predeceases the intestate, such issue to take through all degrees, according to their stocks, in equal shares if more than one, the share which their parent would have taken if living at the death of the intestate, and so that no issue shall take whose parent is living at the death of the intestate and so capable of taking'.

Thus if an intestate died without a spouse, leaving two children and three grandchildren – the children of a child who predeceased him – the residuary estate will be divided into three parts. Each of his two children will be entitled to a part, provided he or she has attained the age of 18, or married under that age; if not it will be held in trust until the contingency is satisfied. The grandchildren will be entitled to the third share their parent would have taken, subject to them attaining the age of 18 or marrying under that age.

If one of the children, or grandchildren, fails to satisfy the contingency, then his or her share goes to swell the share of the others.

The surviving spouse has the right to redeem the life interest. Section 47A(1) of the AEA 1925 provides where a surviving husband or wife is entitled to a life interest in part of the residuary estate, and so elects, the personal representative shall purchase or redeem the life interest by paying the capital value thereof to the tenant for life, or the persons deriving title under the tenant for life, and the costs of the transaction. Thereupon the residuary estate of the intestate may be dealt with and distributed free from the life interest. Regulations have been made as to the calculation of the capital value (Intestate Succession (Interest and Capitalisation) Order 1977 (SI 1977 No 1491).

The election must be made within twelve months of the date of the grant, although the court has power to extend that time limit in certain circumstances (s 47(3)). The tenant for life must give notice to the personal representatives other than himself or herself, or if he or she is the sole personal representative, the Senior Registrar of the Family Division of the High Court. Rule 56(1) provides that where a surviving spouse who is the sole or sole surviving personal representative of the deceased is entitled to a life interest in part of the residuary estate and elects under s 47A of the AEA 1925 to have the life interest redeemed, he may give written notice of the election to the Senior District Judge in pursuance of subsection (7) of that section by filing a notice in Form 6 in the Principal Registry or in the district probate registry from which the grant issued. Rule 56(2) provides that where the grant issued from a district probate registry, the notice shall be filed in duplicate. Rule 56(3) provides that a notice filed under this rule shall be noted on the grant and the record and shall be open to inspection.

Under the Intestates' Estates Act 1952 (IEA 1952) a surviving spouse has the right to acquire the matrimonial home. Paragraph 1 of the Second Schedule provides that where the residuary estate of the intestate comprises an interest in a dwelling-house in which the surviving spouse was resident at the time of the intestate's death, the surviving spouse may require the personal representative, in exercise of the power conferred by s 41 of the AEA 1925 (and with due regard to the requirements of that section as to valuation) to appropriate the said interest in the dwelling-house in or towards satisfaction of any absolute interest of the surviving spouse in the real and personal estate of the intestate. Under paragraph 1(2) the right is not exercisable where the interest is:

— a tenancy which at the date of the death of the intestate was a tenancy which would determine within the period of two years from that date; or

— a tenancy which the landlord by notice given after that date could determine within the remainder of that period.

'Absolute interest' in the real and personal estate includes a reference to the capital value of a life interest which the surviving spouse has elected to have redeemed (para 1(4) IEA 1952).

Paragraph 1(5) provides that where part of a building was, at the date of the death of the intestate, occupied as a separate dwelling, that dwelling shall be treated as a dwelling-house for the purposes of the schedule.

Paragraph 2 provides that where:

(a) the dwelling-house forms part of a building and an interest in the whole of the building is comprised in the residuary estate; or

(b) the dwelling-house is held with agricultural land and an interest in the agricultural land is comprised in the residuary estate; or

(c) the whole or part of the dwelling was at the time of the intestate's death used as a hotel or lodging house; or

(d) a part of the dwelling-house was at the time of the intestate's death used for purposes other than domestic purposes,

the right conferred by paragraph 1 of the Schedule is not exercisable unless the court, on being satisfied that the exercise of that right is not likely to diminish the value of assets in the residuary estate (other than the interest in the dwelling-house) or make them more difficult to dispose of, so orders.

The right must be exercised within twelve months of the date of the grant by the surviving spouse giving notice to the other personal representatives. The court can extend the period of twelve months. If the spouse is the sole personal representative, then a spouse wishing to exercise the right should obtain the consent of the other beneficiaries if of full age and capacity, or arrange for the appointment of another administrator, or apply to the court.

Once given the notice is irrevocable except with the consent of the personal representatives. If the spouse is uncertain whether to give the notice, he or she can require the personal representatives to obtain a valuation of the house. The date for valuing the house is the date of appropriation (*Re Collins [1975] 1 WLR 309*).

The dwelling house must not be sold during the period of twelve months after that date of the grant except with the consent of the surviving spouse unless it is necessary to do so in the course of administration owing to want of other assets.

Paragraph 5(1) provides that where the surviving spouse is one of two or more personal representatives, the rule that a trustee may not be a purchaser of trust property shall not prevent the surviving spouse from purchasing out of the estate of the intestate an interest in a dwelling-house in which the surviving spouse was resident at the time of the intestate's death.

Paragraph 5(2) provides that the power of appropriation under s 41 of the AEA 1925 includes a power to appropriate an interest in a dwelling-house in which the surviving spouse was resident at the time of the intestate's death partly in satisfaction of an interest of the surviving spouse in the real and personal estate of the intestate and partly in return for a payment of money by the surviving spouse to the personal representative. So if the house is worth more than the surviving spouse's entitlement, the surviving spouse can pay the difference between the market value and the surviving spouse's entitlement.

Entitlement to income or interest

10.14 It is highly unlikely that the personal representatives will be able to distribute the assets within a day or so of death, and so the law prescribes rules as to entitlement to income or interest. The entitlement varies according to the type of gift.

Specific gifts

10.15 If there is a specific gift in a will, then the beneficiary is entitled to all the income accruing since the date of death. Thus if there is a specific gift of a house which is let, the beneficiary is entitled to the rental income accruing since the date of death.

Note that it may be necessary to apportion the income if a payment relates to the period before and after death, and is made after death as the residuary beneficiaries are entitled to the income due up to the date of death. An example may be of help:

- specific gift of shares in Z plc to A;
- the company pays a dividend every six months on in respect of the period up to 1 September and the period up to 1 March;
- the testator dies on 1 August.

The dividend payment due on 1 September will have to be apportioned as one month relates to the period after death, and five months to the period before death.

Note that if the testator had died on 2 September no apportionment of the 1 September dividend would have been required as the dividend related to the period before death even though it may not have been paid until after death.

Other legacies and bequests

10.16 Other legacies do not carry interest until the time when they are due. As from that date, they bear interest at the rate payable on funds lodged in court. When is a legacy due? The normal rule is that a legacy is due for payment one year after the date of death, but there are the following exceptions to this rule:

(a) there may be a specific direction in the will as to the payment of interest or income;

(b) the terms of the gift may indicate that interest is not to be paid until a later date. If there is a pecuniary legacy to a child contingent on attaining 25, interest will not be payable until the child has attained 25;

(c) the following gifts will carry interest as from the date of the testator's death:

(i) where the legacy is to the testator's infant child or child to whom he stands *in loco parentis*. It is immaterial that the legacy is absolute, contingent or deferred, although if the legacy is contingent, then the contingency must be on attaining the age of 18. In addition, the will must make no other provision for the maintenance of the child. (*Re Pollock [1943] Ch 338*);

(ii) where the legacy is to an infant, and the testator has shown an intention to provide for the maintenance of the child. There must not be any other provision for the maintenance of the child, and it is immaterial that the child is not the testator's or one to whom the testator stood *in loco parentis*, or that the gift is contingent (*Re Churchill [1909] 2 Ch 431*);

(iii) where the will contains an immediate legacy payable to a creditor of the testator in satisfaction of a debt (*Re Rattenberry [1906] 1 Ch 667*);

(iv) where the legacy is immediate and charged on realty (*Turner v Buck (1874) LR 18 Eq 301*), but not if the realty is given on trust for sale.

Interest should be paid gross to a beneficiary. Tax should be deducted from other income.

The residue

10.17 The residuary beneficiaries are entitled to all the interest and income accruing to the personal representatives, whether or not there interests are immediate, contingent or deferred. There is one exception – a deferred gift of residuary personalty.

Burden of pecuniary legacies

10.18 Out of which property should the pecuniary legacies be paid?

It is to be hoped that a professionally drawn will will include a direction as to which assets are to bear the pecuniary legacies. The normal direction is that they should be paid out of the residuary estate.

If there is no such direction, then it is possible that the pre-1925 rules still apply. These state that the pecuniary legacies must be paid out of residuary personalty. Residuary realty did not have to bear the burden. The reason for this rule was historical: originally the realty did not vest in the personal representatives, and therefore was not available to satisfy the pecuniary legacies. However, the rule was easily displaced as if there was a mixed residuary gift of personalty and realty, then the rule did not apply, although the residuary personalty had to be used first.

If there was a partial intestacy, then s 33(2) of the AEA 1925 provides that after payment of costs funeral testamentary and administration expenses and other liabilities, the personal representatives must set aside a fund sufficient to provide for any pecuniary legacies bequeathed by the will of the deceased.

Adempion of specific gifts

10.19 Section 24 of the Wills Act 1837 provides that every will shall be construed, with reference to the real and personal estate comprised in it, to speak and take effect as if it had been executed immediately before the death of the testator, unless a contrary intention appears.

Thus as far as the property the subject matter of the gift is concerned, s 24 provides that the will speaks from the death of the testator. However, it is very easy to displace the section. A gift of 'my piano' will be construed as meaning the piano owned by the testator at the date of the will rather than one owned at the date of death. This means that if the testator sells the piano and buys another after having made the will, the gift will fail, and the beneficiary will receive nothing.

However, if the gift had been generic, then s 24 will apply, and the gift will include the property owned at the date of death and not the date of the will. Thus a gift of all my golfing equipment will include the golfing equipment owned by the testator at the date of death.

Specific gifts of shares in companies, be they small or large, can cause difficulties if the company is taken over, and the shareholders receive shares or shares and cash. Are the beneficiaries entitled to these shares? The answer is no, unless the change is nominal, and the shareholding is in substance intact.

A draftsman drafting a will including a gift of shares in a company may wish to include a provision dealing with what happens if the company is taken over or amalgamates with another.

Inheritance tax corrective account

10.20 It may be necessary to file a corrective account, for example if assets or liabilities unknown to the personal representatives come to light.

Inheritance tax clearance

10.21 If the personal representatives consider that no tax is payable, they should complete form D19, and submit it to the Capital Taxes Office.

If inheritance tax is payable, once the personal representatives are certain that all inheritance tax due has been paid, they can apply to the Capital Taxes Office for a clearance certificate.

Costs

10.22 Rule 15 of the Solicitors Practice Rules 1990, the written professional standards and the cost information code mean that solicitors must give adequate costs information to the personal representatives. It is also desirable that this information is given to the residuary beneficiaries if they are not the personal representatives.

There is no uniform method of charging for administering an estate. Some firms charge solely according to the hours spent on the administration, whereas others also include a mark up or a percentage value element.

In *Jemma Trust Company Ltd v Liptrott and others [2002] WTLR 235* the question to be decided was whether solicitors are entitled to include an additional element calculated according to the value of the estate. At first instance, it was held that it was wrong to include an additional element calculated by reference to the value of the estate. This has been reserved on appeal.

It was suggested that the appropriate percentages would be:

£1 million	1½%
£4 million	½%
£8 million	⅙%
£12 million	1/12%

It was also made clear that it would not be right to include an additional charge according to the value of the estate for every estate.

If the major asset in the estate is the matrimonial home worth £750,000, and the surviving spouse is entitled to it, it would be wrong to charge an hourly rate and then add 1.5% of the value of the house.

It was also made clear that the correct procedure was for the solicitors to agree the costs or basis for charging at the outset.

Most wills direct that the costs of administering the estate should be paid from the residuary estate. In the great majority of estates, all the costs incurred will be chargeable against the residuary estate, but problems can arise. Two situations where this may happen are:

(a) where there is a gift to a beneficiary who cannot be found;

(b) where there is a dispute about ownership of a chattel the subject matter of a specific gift.

One method of dealing with a missing beneficiary is to take out a missing beneficiary indemnity policy, and this will usually be a proper administration expense. However, if there is a small legacy to a missing beneficiary, it would clearly be unreasonable for the personal representatives to spend a large amount of the residuary estate in a fruitless search for the missing beneficiary. It may be that the most appropriate way of dealing with that problem is to transfer the residuary estate to the residuary beneficiaries with suitable indemnities for the personal representatives.

With regard to (b) above, in the matter of the estate of the late *Cara Prunella Cough-Taylor [2003] WTLR 15*, D left a chattel to A. B removed the chattel after D's death claiming that D had given the chattel to him during her life. It was held that the executors were not obliged to begin proceedings to recover the chattel unless it was at the expense of A. However, they could assign the cause of action to A.

Distribution

10.23 Once the personal representatives are satisfied that they have taken account of all debts and liabilities of the deceased, and taken advantage of any protection available to then (see PARA 8.19) they can begin to distribute the assets. It should be possible to pay the pecuniary legacies and transfer assets the subject of a specific gift at an early stage in the administration. It should also be possible to make an interim distribution to the residuary beneficiaries.

Estate accounts

10.24 There is no set form for the accounts, but the aim should be to make them easily understandable by lay personal representatives and residuary beneficiaries, and to this end should be as simple as possible. The following guidelines may help:

(a) If the estate comprises only a few assets, and the residuary beneficiaries are absolutely entitled, then simple accounts showing receipts and payments will suffice. However, it should clearly distinguish between income and capital, and the tax year to which income relates as the beneficiaries will have to include any income to which they are entitled in their income tax return for the relevant year.

Note that the crucial date for determining liability for income tax is the date when it is received or credited (see PARAS 8.7– 8.10). However, all interest due up to the date of death must be included in the inheritance tax account, even though it may not be paid until after death.

(b) In larger estates, the following accounts may have to be prepared:

- a statement setting out the name of the deceased, the date of the will, if any, the date of the grant and summarising the main provisions of the will;
- capital account – showing the value of the assets at the date of death, and the sale price if the assets have been sold;

- liabilities and expenses – showing the debts incurred by the deceased, the funeral, administration and testamentary expenses;
- income account – showing the income received since the date of death, the tax year, and the beneficiary entitled to it;
- distribution account – showing the entitlement of the various beneficiaries.

Receipt and discharge

10.25 Normally a specific monetary legatee will be asked to sign a receipt for the legacy. If there is a specific bequest of a chattel or land, then the beneficiary should be asked to sign an acknowledgment.

It is common to request the personal representatives and residuary beneficiaries to sign the accounts.

Power of appropriation

10.26 There is a statutory power of appropriation under s 41 of the AEA 1925. This authorises personal representatives to appropriate any part of the real or personal estate, including things in action, of the deceased in the actual state or condition or state of investment thereof at the time of appropriation in or towards satisfaction of any legacy bequeathed by the deceased. Thus if a beneficiary has a legacy of £10,000, the personal representatives can satisfy that legacy by transferring shares worth £10,000 to the beneficiary.

If the asset is worth more than the legacy, it is probable that personal representatives cannot use s 41. Instead, they can sell the asset to the beneficiary. In addition, there is some doubt as to whether a personal representative who is also a beneficiary can make use of s 41.

There are various limitations on the power of appropriation. An appropriation must not be made so as to affect prejudicially any specific devise or bequest (s 41(1)(i)). If the beneficiary is absolutely entitled, the appropriation can only be made with the consent of that beneficiary. If the legacy is settled, the appropriation can only be made with the consent of the trustees, or the person for the time being entitled to the income (s 41(1)(ii)).

If the person whose consent is required cannot give it because he is an infant, or incapable of managing his own affairs by reason of mental disorder within the meaning of the Mental Health Act 1983, the consent can be given by his parents or parent, testamentary or other guardian, or receiver, or, if, in the case of an infant, there is no such parent or guardian, by the court on the application of his next friend. It is not necessary to obtain consent on behalf of a person who may come into existence after the time of appropriation, or who cannot be found or ascertained at that time (s 41(1)(iii)). However, s 41(5) provides that the personal representatives in making the appropriation shall have regard to the rights of any person who may thereafter come into existence, or who cannot be found or ascertained at the time of appropriation, and of any other person whose consent is not required by the section. Furthermore, if there is no receiver acting for a person suffering from mental disorder, and the appropriation is of an investment authorised by law or by the will, if any, of the deceased for the investment of money subject to the trust, no consent is required on behalf of the person suffering from mental disorder (s 41(1)(iv)). In similar circumstances, no consent is required if there is no trustee of a settled legacy, and there is no person of full age entitled to the income (s 41(1)(v)).

An appropriation made under s 41 of the AEA 1925 binds all persons interested in the property whose consent is not required by the section (s 41(4)).

Assume that a beneficiary has a legacy of £20,000. The personal representatives can satisfy that legacy by transferring to the beneficiary land to the value of £20,000. If the land is worth more than the legacy, this cannot be done. Instead, the personal representatives can sell the asset to the beneficiary. If the asset is the subject of a specific devise, appropriation cannot be made. If the residuary beneficiaries are entitled to the land, they are bound by any appropriation made by the personal representatives.

Valuation

10.27 Section 41(3) of the AEA 1925 provides that the personal representatives may ascertain and fix the value of the respective parts of the real and personal estate and the liabilities of the deceased as they may think fit, and shall for that purpose employ a duly qualified valuer where necessary. Thus an executrix cannot value shares in an unquoted company herself, and then appropriate them in her favour at that valuation (*Re Bythway (1911) 104 LT 411*).

The date for the valuation of the assets could be very important in a volatile market. The Act does not provide any guidance, but the question was decided in the case of *Re Collins [1975] 1 WLR 309*, where it was held that the relevant date was the date of appropriation, and not the date of death. Thus if prices are rising, the beneficiary will want the appropriation to be made as soon as possible, whereas if they are dropping, the beneficiary will want the appropriation to be delayed.

Intestacy

10.28 Section 41(9) of the AEA 1925 specifically provides that the section applies whether the deceased died intestate or not.

In Kane v Radley-Kane [1999] Ch 274 James Radley-Kane died intestate in May 1994 leaving a widow, the first defendant, and three sons. The widow was, in fact, the step-mother of the three sons.

The deceased owned 36% of the ordinary shares in a company called Shiredean Limited, which were valued for probate purposes at £50,000. The net value of the deceased's estate was £93,000. Letters of Administration were granted to the widow, and she regarded herself as entitled to the whole estate under the intestacy rules.

In January 1997 the shares in Shiredean were sold for £1,131,438.

The claimant, one of the sons, issued proceedings claiming that the appropriation of the shares by the widow in her own favour was invalid.

It was held that this was the case. However, the judge stated that if the assets had been equivalent of cash, for example government stock, then the appropriation would have been valid.

What would have been the position if the widow had obtained another valuation of the shares on the day of appropriation, or shortly before, and the value had been £50,000? It is possible that the appropriation might have been valid.

The widow could also have asked the sons to agree to the appropriation; presumably they would have refused if they had any idea about the likely sale price of the shares.

Another possibility, albeit expensive, would have been to apply to the court for permission for the widow to appropriate in her favour.

A surviving spouse can also elect to take the matrimonial home in satisfaction of their statutory legacy or a capitalised life interest or both. The date for valuing the house is the date of appropriation, and the right must be exercised within twelve months of the date of issue of the grant of administration.

Transferring the assets

10.29 The personal representatives may have to sell all the assets of the deceased, but this is unusual, and it is more common for the personal representatives to transfer the assets of the deceased to the beneficiaries entitled to them. The formalities required for this are:

(a) *Chattels* – frequently no formalities will be required. Ownership can be simply transferred by delivery. However, in the case of some chattels, there may be further requirements. If a car is transferred, for example, it will be necessary to notify DVLC about the change of registered keeper.

(b) *Bank and building society accounts* – if these were in joint names, all that is necessary is to produce the death certificate.

If the account was not in joint names, then it is difficult to transfer the account. Unless use is made of the Administration of Estates (Small Payments) Act 1965, it will be necessary to produce the grant, and complete the forms required by the bank or building society in order to close the account. It will also be necessary to submit the passbook.

(c) *Shares* – the personal representatives may have submitted the grant to the Registrar. If not, it will have to be submitted together with the appropriate transfer form. If the appropriate certificate on the back of the form is completed, no stamp duty should be payable.

(d) *Land – title already registered* – If the deceased was solely entitled, the personal representatives can be registered as proprietors of the land, but usually they will not apply for registration as either the land will be sold, or will be vested in a beneficiary.

If the land is sold, the purchaser will have to produce at least a certified copy of the grant.

If the personal representatives assent to the property vesting in a beneficiary, the following documents will have to be lodged with the Land Registry:

— Form AS1 or TR1, or if the transfer only relates to part of the land on the title, AS3 or TP1;

— the grant or an official copy or a certified copy;

— Form AP1;

— SDLT 60;

— the fee.

If the deceased was a joint tenant, the following must be submitted to the Land Registry:

- the original death certificate or written confirmation by a conveyancer of the fact of the death which should include the full name of the deceased, the date and place of death and either the date of birth or the age at death of the deceased; or
- the original grant of representation; or
- a certificate given by the conveyancer that he holds the original or an official copy of such grant of representation; and
- Form AP1;
- SDLT 60 (see below);

There is no fee payable.

It is clear that no stamp duty land tax is payable if a surviving joint tenant is absolutely entitled to a property not subject to any charge. However, the position if the property is subject to a charge is not clear as this is not covered by section 285 of the Finance Act 2004, which provides:

> '(1) In Schedule 3 the Finance Act 2003 (stamp duty land tax: transactions exempt from charge), after paragraph 3 insert–

3A(1) The acquisition of property by a person in or towards satisfaction of his entitlement under or in relation to the will of the deceased person, or on the intestacy of a deceased person, is exempt from charge.

(2) Subparagraph (1) does not apply if the person acquiring the property gives any consideration for it, other than the assumption of secured debt.

(3) In this paragraph–

"debt" means an obligation, whether certain or contingent, to pay a sum of money either immediately at a future date, and

"secured debt" means debt that, immediately after the death of the deceased person is secured on the property.

(2) In Schedule 4 to that Act (Stamp Duty Land Tax: chargeable consideration), in paragraph 8 (debt as consideration), after sub-paragraph (2) insert–

"(2A) Where a land transaction would be exempt from charge under paragraph 3 A of Schedule (assents and appropriations by personal representatives) but for sub-paragraph (2) of that paragraph (cases where a person acquiring property gives consideration for it), the chargeable consideration for the transaction does not include the amount of any secured debt assumed.

"Secured debt" has same meaning as in that paragraph.'

Schedule 4 of the Finance Act 2003 paragraph 8 provides that the assumption of existing debt by a purchaser is chargeable consideration, and it could be argued that a surviving joint tenant is a purchaser assuming an existing debt, and that therefore stamp duty land tax is payable. However, it is the author's opinion that, stamp duty land tax is not payable as the vesting occurs by operation of law, and as far as joint tenants who are absolutely entitled are concerned, the survivor is already liable on the charge, and is not assuming any further debt.

If the deceased was a tenant in common, a restriction would have been entered on the register. This will be removed if the Registrar is satisfied that the other person or persons in whom the legal estate is vested is solely entitled to the property.

(e) *Land – If the title is unregistered* – If the personal representatives intend to sell the land, then they need do nothing, although the purchaser will have to register the title.

If they assent to the land vesting in a beneficiary, then it will have to be registered. The appropriate assent should be used, and this should be submitted to the Land Registry with From FR1, the usual pre-registration documents and the grant or an official copy or a certified copy.

If the deceased was a joint tenant in equity, then the personal representatives need take no further action as the right of survivorship operates.

If the deceased was a trustee holding on trust for himself as a tenant in common, the legal estate would have been vested in the deceased as a joint tenant, and therefore the right of survivorship operates as far as the legal estate is concerned. If a new trustee is appointed, s 40 of the Trustee Act 1925 normally operates to vest any land in the new trustees. This is not an occasion of compulsory registration.

Nil rate band discretionary trust, coupled with power to accept an IOU, residue to spouse

10.30 This type of will is very common as it enables the nil rate band of both spouses to be utilised.

If the trustees are going to accept an IOU from the surviving spouse, then all the assets of the deceased spouse can be vested in the surviving spouse, who should give the personal representatives a written IOU; preferably a charge in favour of the trustees if the nil rate band discretionary trust should be created.

It is probably best if there are some other assets in the trust apart from the IOU.

The trustees should also take advice from someone authorised to advise about investments, and have regular meetings of the trustees as required by the Trustee Act 2000.

While it is believed that IR Capital Taxes is prepared to accept such schemes, there are uncertainties associated with it.

Chapter 11

Problems with wills and other disputes

11.1 The validity of a will may be challenged because the deceased did not have capacity to make it, or on the ground of non-compliance with the formal requirements, or on the ground that the testator did not know and approve of the contents of the will. Each possible ground of challenge will be considered in turn.

Capacity

11.2 A testator must normally be over 18 to make a valid will, although there are exceptions for soldiers, sailors and airmen.

The testator must also have the requisite mental capacity. This means that the testator must be able to understand three issues:

(a) that he is making a will, which will only come into effect on death;

(b) he has some idea of the persons he should be benefiting in his will;

(c) he has some idea of the extent of his property. It is not necessary to know down to the last penny.

Normally testators must possess this capacity at the date of execution of the will, but under the rule in *Parker v Felgate* a will can be valid if the testator had capacity at the time he gave instructions for a will, even if he did not have capacity at the time he came to execute the will, provided that the will is in accordance with the instructions given by the testator.

There are two rebuttable presumptions that assist those wishing to prove wills – if the will is rational, there is a presumption that the testator had capacity. In addition, if the testator had capacity, there is a presumption that that capacity continued.

If the capacity of the testator to make the will is challenged, then it may be necessary to obtain medical reports as to the capacity of the testator to execute a will.

Formalities

11.3 Section 9 of the Wills Act 1837 (WA 1837) as amended provides:

'No will shall be valid unless –

(a) it is in writing, and signed by the testator, or by some other person in his presence and by his direction; and

(b) it appears that the testator intended by his signature to give effect to the will; and

(c) the signature is made or acknowledged by the testator in the presence of two or more witnesses present at the same time; and

(d) each witness either –

(i) attests and signs the will; or

(ii) acknowledges his signature,

in the presence of the testator (but not necessarily in the presence of any other witness),

but no form of attestation shall be necessary.'

At its simplest all that is required is that the testator should execute the will in the presence of two witnesses, who should then sign the will in the presence of the testator.

If the will was professionally drawn, then the person responsible for drawing up the will should have ensured compliance with the formalities, and if they have not done so, there is the possibility that they may be liable for negligence.

Note the following points:

— *Writing*

Whilst a will is normally written, typed or printed on paper, the only requirement under the WA 1837 is that it should be in writing, so it could be written on other media.

— *Signature*

The WA 1837 does not define what is meant by a signature. Anything the testator intends to be his signature will suffice, for example a thumbprint.

— *Signatures by persons other than the testator*

There is no requirement that the testator should sign the will. Another person can do it on his behalf as long as that person signs in the presence of, and at the request of the testator. This means that a blind person, or a person who cannot sign his or her name, can make a will.

— Position of signature

Normal practice is for the testator to sign the will at the end. However, a signature in another place will be effective as long as the testator intended it to give effect to the will.

— Witnesses

The testator must sign the will in the presence of two witnesses, who must then sign the will in the presence of the testator.

Anyone who can comprehend the procedure can witness a will, and so a child of mature years can act as a witness. A blind person cannot witness a will.

— Acknowledgement of signatures

It is also possible for the testator and the witnesses to acknowledge a signature made in private. Clearly an express acknowledgement will be effective, but it has also been held that protests by a witness that the will was invalid amount to an acknowledgement of that witness's signature.

— Attestation clause

It is not essential for the validity of a will that it should contain an attestation clause. However, it is desirable that a will should contain one, as on the death of the testator there is a rebuttable presumption that there had been compliance with the formal requirements of the WA 1837 if there is one.

If there is no attestation clause, then it may be necessary to lodge affidavit evidence from the witnesses or other persons present at the date of execution as to compliance with the formalities of the WA 1837.

Rule 12(1) of the Non-Contentious Probate Rules 1987 (NCPR 1987) provides that where a will contains no attestation clause, or the attestation clause is insufficient, or where it appears to the District Judge or Registrar that there is doubt about the due execution of the will, he must before admitting it to proof require an affidavit as to due execution from one or more of the attesting witnesses. If no attesting witness is conveniently available, an affidavit from any other person who was present when the will was executed should be lodged. Having considered the evidence, if the District Judge or Registrar is satisfied that the will was not duly executed, he must refuse probate and mark the will accordingly.

Rule 12(2) provides that if no affidavit can be obtained in accordance with paragraph (1), the District Judge or Registrar may accept evidence on affidavit from any person he may think fit to show that the signature on the will is in the handwriting of the deceased, or of any other matter which may raise a presumption in favour of due execution of the will. If he thinks fit he may require that notice of the application be given to any person who may be prejudiced by the will.

Rule 12(3) provides that a District Judge or Registrar may accept a will for proof without evidence if he is satisfied that the distribution of the estate is not thereby affected.

Knowledge and approval

11.4 A testator must know and approve of the contents of a will. Normally, there is a presumption that this is the case, but the presumption does not apply in the following circumstances:

(a) where the testator is blind or illiterate or the will was signed by another person on behalf of the testator. In these cases, the will should be read to the testator before he executes it, and the attestation clause altered to indicate that this has been done. If this is not done, affidavit evidence will be required;

(b) where there are suspicious circumstances – for example, it would be seen as suspicious where the draftsman was a major or sole beneficiary under a will. It does not mean that the beneficiary cannot take under the will, but it will be necessary for the beneficiary to dispel the doubt. The beneficiary must prove that the testator knew and approved of the contents of the will.

Rule 13 of the NCPR 1987 provides that before admitting to proof a will which appears to have been signed by a blind or illiterate testator, or which for any other reason raises doubts as to the testator having had knowledge of the contents of the will at the time of its execution, the District Judge or Registrar must satisfy himself that the testator had such knowledge.

Alterations and obliterations to the will

11.5 The words in a will may have been altered or obliterated by the testator.

If it is an alteration, the rules are:

- if it can be proved that the alteration was made before the will was executed, the alteration will be valid. It will be necessary to produce evidence from the attesting witnesses or other persons present when the will was executed. If a codicil to the will has been executed confirming the original will, then the alteration will be valid;

- if the alteration has been signed or initialled by the testator and two witnesses, then it will be upheld. The witnesses need not be the same persons as originally witnessed the will;

- if neither of the above apply, then the alteration will be invalid, and the original wording will be admitted to probate.

If it is an obliteration, then the rules are:

(i) if it can be proved that the obliteration was made before the will was executed, it will be valid. If a codicil to the will has been executed confirming the original will, then again the obliteration will be valid;

(ii) if the obliteration has been initialled by the testator and the witnesses, then it will be upheld. The witnesses need not be the same persons as originally witnessed the will;

(iii) if (i) and (ii) do not apply, then if the original wording is apparent, that wording will be admitted to probate. 'Apparent' means that the original wording can be read by natural means without the use of artificial aids;

(iv) If (i), (ii) and (iii) do not apply, probate will be granted with a blank if the testator intended to revoke the wording;

(v) If (i), (ii), (iii) and (iv) do not apply, extrinsic evidence will be admissible to prove the original contents. This evidence may be a copy of the original will, or the testator's instructions to the draftsman.

In unusual circumstances, the doctrine of conditional revocation may apply. If the testator obliterates the amount of a legacy in a will, and substitutes another figure, that substitution may be invalid. If it is, extrinsic evidence will be admissible to as to the original amount as the testator's revocation was conditional on the validity of the substitution.

Rule 14(1) of the NCPR 1987 provides that where there appears in a will any obliteration, interlineations or other alteration which is not authenticated in the manner prescribed by s 21 of the WA 1837, or by the re-execution of the will or by the execution of a codicil, the District Judge or Registrar shall require evidence to show whether the alteration was present at the time the will was executed and shall give directions as to the form in which the will is to be proved. These provisions do not apply to any alteration which appears to the District Judge or Registrar to be of no practical importance.

Rule 11(1) provides that where the District Judge or Registrar considers that in any particular case a facsimile copy of the original will would not be satisfactory for purposes of record, he may require an engrossment suitable for facsimile reproduction to be lodged.

Rule 11(2) provides that where a will:

(a) contains alterations which are not to be admitted to proof; or

(b) has been ordered to be rectified by virtue of s 20(1) of the Administration of Justice Act 1982;

there shall be lodged an engrossment of the will in the form in which it is to be proved. Such engrossment must reproduce the punctuation, spacing, and division into paragraphs of the will and must follow continuously from page to page on both sides of the paper.

Incorporation of documents in a will

11.6 It is possible for a document to be incorporated in a will if the document is in existence at the date of the will, is referred to in the will as an existing document and can be easily identified.

Rule 14(3) of the NCPR 1987 provides that if a will contains any reference to another document in such terms as to suggest that it ought to be incorporated in the will, the District Judge or Registrar must require the document to be produced and may call for such evidence in regard to the incorporation of the document as he may think fit.

Doubt as to date of will

11.7 Rule 14(4) of the NCPR 1987 provides that where there is doubt as to the date on which a will was executed, the District Judge or Registrar may require such evidence as he thinks necessary to establish the date.

Lost or damaged wills

11.8 Sometimes a will cannot be found after death. In this situation, a copy may be admitted to probate.

There is a presumption that a will last known to have been in the possession of the testator has been revoked if it cannot be found after death. It is necessary to rebut this presumption.

Rule 54(1) of the NCPR 1987 provides that subject to paragraph (2) below, an application for an order admitting to proof a nuncupative will, or a will contained in a copy or reconstruction thereof where the original is not available, shall be made to a District Judge or Registrar.

Rule 54(2) provides that in any case where a will is not available owing to its being retained in the custody of a foreign court or official, a duly authenticated copy of the will may be admitted to proof without the order referred to in paragraph (1) above.

Rule 54(3) provides that an application under paragraph (1) above shall be supported by an affidavit setting out the grounds of the application, and by such evidence on affidavit as the applicant can adduce as to:

(a) the will's existence after the death of the testator or, where there is no such evidence, the facts on which the applicant relies to rebut the presumption that the will has been revoked by destruction;

(b) in respect of a nuncupative will, the contents of that will; and

(c) in respect of a reconstruction of a will, the accuracy of that reconstruction.

The District Judge or Registrar may require additional evidence in the circumstances of a particular case as to due execution of the will or as to the accuracy of the copy will, and may direct that notice be given to persons who would be prejudiced by the application (r 54(4)).

Other matters affecting the validity of a will

11.9 There are other factors which may affect the validity of a will, but are rarely encountered in practice. A will will be invalid if the testator was induced by fraud or undue influence to execute a will. It will also be invalid if the testator was forced to execute it against his will.

Disputes about funeral arrangements

11.10 Occasionally, there are disputes about the funeral arrangements for the deceased. These disputes sometimes reach the courts.

In Buchanan v Milton [1999] 2 FLR 844 the deceased was born in Australia of Aboriginal parents. He was adopted very shortly after his birth, and brought up in England. He did return to Australia for a month, when he was 23, but he did not enjoy the experience and returned to England. He died intestate leaving a child, H.

The deceased's adoptive mother wanted him to be cremated, but his natural mother wanted him to be returned to Australia for burial there. His natural mother applied to be appointed as Administrator in place of H's mother and the deceased's adoptive mother. The application was made under s 116 of the Supreme Court Act 1981 on the basis that there were special circumstances justifying the displacement of an Administrator. If the natural mother was appointed the Administrator, she could decide on the funeral arrangements.

It was held that the special circumstances in s 116 could include all relevant circumstances. However, the application was refused.

In Fessi v Whitmore [1999] 1 FLR 767 the parents of a child lived in Nuneaton. They separated, and the father went to live in Wales with the child. The child was killed very shortly after the move. The child had been very close to his paternal grandfather. The father wanted the ashes scattered in Wales; the mother wanted them scattered near those of the paternal grandfather at Nuneaton.

It was held that the ashes should be scattered at Nuneaton.

In *Re Blagdon Cemetery [2002] 4 All ER 482* the son of the petitioners had been killed in an industrial accident, and buried where they lived. They moved to another part of the country, and wanted their son's body to be exhumed and reburied where they now lived. Their petition was granted.

In *Re Christ Church Harwood LSG 16 May 2002* page 32 the daughter of the petitioners had died young. They wanted to incorporate an engraved photographic image of the deceased in the memorial. The petition was granted.

In the matter of *Crawley Green Road Cemetery, Luton [2001] Fam 308* S's ashes were interred in consecrated ground in Luton. S's wife moved to London, and wanted the ashes to be interred in a cemetery where she now lived.

It was stated that there was a presumption against exhumation, but it could be ordered if there were medical grounds justifying exhumation; no medical grounds existed in this case.

However, the family were humanists, and there had been a humanist funeral service. As such they were unhappy that the ashes were interred in consecrated ground, something they had not appreciated earlier. It would be contrary to the European Convention on Human Rights to refuse exhumation.

The disinherited stepchildren

11.11 A frequent legal problem faced by practitioners is that of disinherited children. This situation usually arises when parties who have been married before, and have children from a previous relationship, marry each other or cohabit. The couple may make wills giving everything to each other, with a gift in default to their respective children. However, after one individual dies the survivor then changes his or her will excluding the children of the first spouse to die, and giving all his other assets to his or her own children. What can the excluded step children do in this situation?

The following courses of action are open to the disappointed stepchildren:

(a) check to ensure that the testator had capacity to make a will;

(b) check to ensure that the testator knew and approved of the contents of the will;

(c) check to see if there was any agreement to enter into mutual wills;

(d) check for any possibility of a claim under the Inheritance (Provision for Family and Dependants) Act 1975;

(e) check to see if there is any room for the application of the equitable doctrine of promissory estoppel;

(f) check to ensure compliance with s 9 of the Wills Act 1837.

Capacity

11.12 If a medical report was obtained at the time the testator executed the will confirming that the testator had capacity, there is very little which can be done to challenge the will under this head.

If that is not the case, further enquiries should be made as to whether the deceased was mentally capable at the time the deceased made the will.

For further discussion of this aspect, please see 11.2.

Knowledge and approval

11.13 Normally knowledge and approval are presumed if the testator had capacity to make the will, however, there are some situations where there is no such presumption. For example, where the draftsman of the will is a major beneficiary. In this case, it will be necessary for the beneficiary to prove that the deceased knew and approved of the contents of the will.

For further discussion, please see 11.4.

Mutual wills

11.14 It may be that the parties have agreed to make mutual wills, if such an agreement exists the surviving party will be bound by the agreement. However, the mere fact that the parties have made mirror image wills giving each other absolute interests with the residue split equally between their respective children does not mean that mutual wills have been created.

If there is an agreement to create mutual wills, the effect is that the survivor is entitled to a life interest in the property of the first one to die. The survivor may also be limited to a life interest in their own property.

In *Re Goodchild (deceased) Goodchild and another v Goodchild [1997] 3 All ER 63* Dennis and Joan Goodchild had a successful business. Their only child, Gary, the first Plaintiff in these proceedings, worked in the business. They made mirror image wills giving their estate to each other, but if they did not survive each other by 28 days, Gary was entitled. Joan died first, and Dennis inherited all her property under her will. Dennis then married Enid, and then died less than two months later. It was argued that Dennis and Joan had executed mutual wills. Gary also claimed to be entitled to claim under the Inheritance (Provision for Family and Dependants) Act 1975.

It was held that in order for the doctrine of mutual wills to apply, there had to be a contract at law between the two testators that both wills would be irrevocable and remain unaltered. The judge at first instance had held that there was no evidence of any such agreement, and his decision was upheld on appeal.

However, it was held that Gary was entitled to succeed under the 1975 Act as Gary was barely able to meet his financial requirements from his existing income. It was held that there was a moral obligation on Dennis to leave Gary the property he had received from Joan, and he was awarded £185,000.

In *Birch v Curtis [2002] 2 FLR 847* H and W had both been married before, they made wills together in 1986. W died first, and H remarried. He subsequently made further wills. On his death, W's children alleged that where H and W had agreed to make wills in a certain format, the doctrine of mutual wills applied. It was held that this was not the case.

Inheritance (Provision for Family and Dependants) Act 1975

11.15 It is possible that the disinherited stepchildren might have a claim under the Inheritance (Provision for Family and Dependants) Act 1975.

However, there are two major hurdles which must be overcome. The first is that the stepchildren will have to prove that they come within the category of persons entitled to claim – usually the appropriate category will be children of the family. The second hurdle is that it will be necessary for the children to prove that reasonable financial provision has not been made for their maintenance.

With regard to the first issue, s 1(1) of the 1975 Act prescribes the persons entitled to claim. They include:

> 'any person (not being a child of the deceased) who, in the case of any marriage to which the deceased was at any time a party, was treated as a child of the family in relation to that marriage;'

This applies where the deceased had married someone with children from a previous relationship, and treated those children as his or her own. Note that it does not matter that the marriage ended either by divorce or the death of the other party sometime earlier. If there was a child of the other party to the marriage, and the deceased treated the child as a child of the family, the child will still be able to claim, even though the marriage ended in divorce, or the death of the parent of the child.

What test is applied to decide if the applicant is a child of the family? In *Re Leach (deceased) [1985] 2 All ER 754* at page 762 Slade LJ said:

> 'I can see no reason why even an adult applicant who has at all material times been an adult person may not be capable of qualifying under that subsection, provided that the deceased has, as wife or husband (or widow or widower) under the relevant marriage, expressly or impliedly, assumed the position of parent towards the applicant, with the attendant responsibilities and privileges of that relationship'.

Maintenance does not necessarily mean subsistence level. Regard must be had to the standard of living enjoyed by the applicant prior to the death, and it can include the provision of luxuries (*Re Borthwick (deceased) [1949] 1 All ER 472*).

In *Re Christie (deceased) [1979] 1 All ER 546* it was defined as:

> '… reasonable financial provision for the applicant in the sense that of such financial provision as it would be reasonable in all the circumstances of the case for the applicant to receive for the maintenance of his way of life and well-being, his health and financial security and well-being, the health and financial security of his immediate family for which he is responsible.' [page 550].

Even if the stepchildren can prove that they come within the category of those entitled to claim, if they are otherwise adequately provided for, stepchildren stand little chance in succeeding in a claim under the 1975 Act.

There are also guidelines which the court must consider in deciding whether or not reasonable financial provision has been made for an applicant, and if reasonable financial provision has not been made for an applicant, what order should be made. If the applicant is a child of the family of the deceased, the court must have regard to:

(a) to whether the deceased had assumed any responsibility for the applicant's maintenance and, if so, the extent to which and the basis upon which the deceased had assumed responsibility and to the length of time for which the deceased discharged that responsibility;

(b) to whether in assuming and discharging that responsibility the deceased did so knowing that the applicant was not his own child;

(c) to the liability of any other person to maintain the applicant.

Equity

11.16 What happens if the parties agree to make mutual wills, and the survivor does something which prevents the implementation of the mutual wills? In this scenario the court may impose a constructive trust.

In *Healey v Brown [2002] WTLR 849* H and W owned the matrimonial home as beneficial joint tenants. H had a son by a previous marriage, PB, and W had a niece, JH. They executed mutual wills under which their interest in the house went to JH, and the residue to PB. W died first, and H transferred the property into the joint names of himself and PB. On his death, JH claimed that she was entitled to the property absolutely.

It was held that any contract between H and W was unenforceable because of non compliance with s 2 of the Law of Property (Miscellaneous Provisions) Act 1989. However, equity would impose a constructive trust so that JH was entitled to one half of the property.

The doctrine of proprietary estoppel may also be relevant. If promises have been made to a stepchild, and a stepchild has acted to his or her detriment relying on the promise, the estate of the person making the promise may not be allowed to refuse to implement the promise. In *Campbell v Griffin [2001] WTLR 981* C, who had spent part of his childhood in a children's home, became Mr and Mrs A's lodger. Initially, this had been a commercial arrangement, but gradually Mr and Mrs A became to regard C as their son. He helped with domestic chores, and towards the end of Mr and Mrs A's life became a carer. Both Mr and Mrs A made promises to him that he would have a home for life.

It was held that the doctrine of proprietary estoppel applied, and C was awarded £35,000 from the sale proceeds of the house (about £160,000).

The court held that once it had been proved that promises had been made, and that there had been conduct by the applicant of such nature that inducement may be inferred, then there is a presumption of reliance.

In *Jiggins v Brisley [2003] WTLR 1141* H and W were tenants of a council flat. They decided to purchase it with the benefit of the statutory discount, and one of their sons, B and his wife P, provided the purchase price and the costs. It was the understanding of the parties that H and W would live in the house for the rest of their joint lives, and that it would then pass to B and P.

In 1992 or 1993, H and W were asked to transfer the flat into the name of P, but they refused, although assurances were given to B and P that the flat would be left to them on the death of the survivor. As a result of these assurances B and P spent money on repairs to the flat.

B died in 2000, and H died shortly thereafter. W then changed her will so that P received a legacy of £20,000 with the residue going to her grandchildren.

It was held the doctrine of proprietary estoppel was applied, and the personal representatives of W held the flat on trust for P.

Compliance with Wills Act 1837

11.17 It is probably worth checking with witnesses to ensure that the will was validly executed. This, of course, will not apply if it is clear that the will has been executed in the presence of a solicitor.

Chapter 12

Standing searches, caveats, citations and applications for an order to attend for examination or for a subpoena to bring in a will

12.1 In the great majority of probates there is no dispute about the validity of the will, or the construction of the will. If there are any, they are frequently resolved without reference to the court.

There are various precautionary steps which are commonly taken in the initial stages of any probate dispute. They are:

(a) *standing searches* – this procedure is used if a relative or any other person wishes to be notified of the issue of a grant;

(b) *caveats* – these are lodged if someone wishes to challenge the issue of a grant;

(c) *citations* – this is where someone is cited to take out a grant.

Rule 43(1) of the NCPR 1987 provides that any person who wishes to be notified of the issue of a grant may enter a standing search for the grant by lodging at, or sending by post to, any registry or sub-registry a notice in Form 2.

Rule 43(2) provides that a person who has entered a standing search will be sent an office copy of any grant which corresponds with the particulars given on the completed Form 2 and which was:

— issued not more than twelve months before the entry of the standing search; or

— issued within a period of six months after the entry of the standing search.

It is possible to renew the standing search by written application made within the last month of the original period.

Caveats

12.2 Rule 44 of the NCPR 1987 enables anyone to enter a caveat. Rule 44(1) provides that any person who wishes to show cause against the sealing of a grant may enter a caveat in any registry or sub-registry, and the District Judge or Registrar must not allow any grant to be sealed if he has knowledge of an effective caveat. However, a grant can still be issued on the day on which the caveat is entered.

Rule 44(2) provides that any person wishing to enter a caveat (the caveator) or a solicitor or probate practitioner on his behalf, may effect entry of a caveat –

- by completing Form 3 in the appropriate book at any registry or sub-registry; or
- by sending by post at his own risk a notice in Form 3 to any registry or sub-registry. The proper officer must provide an acknowledgement of the entry of the caveat.

The caveat is effective for a period of six months, and can be renewed by lodging a written application within the last month of the period of six months. Subsequent renewals are also permissible.

An index of caveats is maintained. Whenever anyone applies for a grant, the registry or sub-registry at which the application is made must cause a search of the index to be made. The appropriate District Judge or Registrar must be notified of the entry of a caveat against the sealing of the grant for which application has been made (r 44(4)).

Rule 44(5) provides that where a person other than the caveator claims to have an interest in the estate a warning in Form 4 may be issued against the caveat. The person warning must state his interest in the estate of the deceased, and the caveator must be required to give particulars of any contrary interest in the estate. The warning or a copy must be served on the caveator forthwith.

Rule 44(6) provides that a caveator who has no interest contrary to that of the person warning, but who wishes to show the cause against the sealing of a grant to that person, may within eight days of service of the warning upon him (inclusive of the day of service), or at any time thereafter if no affidavit has been filed under paragraph 12, issue and serve a summons for directions.

Rule 44(7) provides that on the hearing of any summons for directions the District Judge or Registrar may give a direction for the caveat to cease to have any effect. Rule 44(8) provides that any caveat in force when a summons for directions is issued shall remain in force unless a direction has been given under paragraph (7) or until it is withdrawn under paragraph (11).

Rule 44(10) provides that a caveator having an interest contrary to that of the person warning may within eight days of the service of a warning upon him (inclusive of the day of service) or at any time thereafter if no affidavit has been filed under paragraph (12) enter an appearance in the nominated registry by filing Form 5. The caveator must serve on the person warning a copy of Form 5 sealed with the seal of the court.

Rule 44(11) provides that a caveator who has not entered an appearance to a warning may at any time withdraw his caveat by giving notice at the registry or sub-registry at which it was entered, and the caveat thereupon ceases to have effect. Where the caveat has been so withdrawn, the caveator must forthwith give notice of withdrawal to the person warning.

Rule 44(12) provides that if no appearance has been entered by the caveator, or no summons has been issued by him under paragraph (6), the person warning may at any time after eight days of service of the warning upon the caveator (inclusive of the day of service) file an affidavit in the nominated registry as to such service. The caveat then ceases to have effect provided that there is no pending summons under paragraph (6).

Rule 44(13) provides that unless a District Judge or, where application to discontinue a caveat is made by consent, a Registrar, by order made on summons otherwise directs, any caveat in respect of which an appearance to a warning has been entered is to remain in force until the commencement of a probate action.

If a probate action is commenced, the senior District Judge must give notice of the action to every caveator other than the plaintiff in the action in respect of each caveat that is in force upon being advised by the court concerned of the commencement of a probate action (r 45(1)). If a caveat is entered subsequent to the commencement of a probate action, the senior District Judge must give notice to that caveator of the existence of the action (r 45(2)). Unless a District Judge by order made on summons otherwise directs, the commencement of a probate action operates to prevent the sealing of a grant until application for a grant is made by the person shown to be entitled to it by the decision of the court in such action (r 45(4)). This does not prevent the issue of a grant of administration pending suit under s 117 of the Supreme Court Act 1981.

Citations

12.3 Rule 46(1) of the NCPR 1987 provides that any citation may issue from the Principal Registry or a district probate registry. It must be settled by a District Judge or Registrar before being issued.

Rule 44(2) provides that every averment in a citation, and such other information as the Registrar may require, shall be verified by an affidavit sworn by the person issuing the citation ('the citor'). In special circumstances the District Judge or the Registrar may accept an affidavit sworn by the citor's solicitor or probate practitioner.

Rule 46(3) provides that the citor must enter a caveat before entering a citation. Unless a District Judge by order made on summons otherwise directs, any caveat in force at the beginning of the citation proceedings, unless withdrawn pursuant to paragraph (11) of r 44, remains in force until application for a grant is made by the person shown to be entitled thereto by the decision of the court in such proceedings. Upon such application any caveat entered by a party who had notice of the proceedings ceases to have effect.

Rule 46(4) requires every citation to be served personally on the person cited unless the District Judge or Registrar, on cause shown by affidavit, directs some other mode of service, which may include notice by advertisement.

Rule 46(5) provides that every will referred to in a citation must be lodged in a registry before the citation is issued, except where the will is not in the citor's possession and the District Judge or Registrar is satisfied that it is impracticable to require it to be lodged.

Rule 46(6) provides that a person who has been cited to appear may, within eight days of service of the citation upon him (inclusive of the day of such service), or at any time thereafter if no application has been made by the citor under paragraph (5) of r 47 or paragraph (2) of r 48, enter an appearance in the registry from which the citation issued by filing Form 5. A copy of Form 5 sealed with a seal of the registry must be served on the citor.

Rule 47 deals with citations to accept or refuse or to take a grant. Rule 47(1) provides that a citation to accept or refuse a grant may be issued at the instance of any person who would himself be entitled to a grant in the event of the person cited renouncing his right thereto.

Rule 47(2) provides that where power to make a grant to an executor has been reserved, a citation calling on him to accept or refuse a grant may be issued at the instance of the executors who have proved the will or the survivor of them or of the executors of the last survivor of deceased executors who have proved.

Rule 47(3) provides that a citation calling on an executor who has intermeddled in the estate of the deceased to show cause why he should not be ordered to take a grant may be issued at the instance of any person interested in the estate at any time after the expiration of six months from the death of the deceased. However, no citation to take a grant can be issued whilst proceedings as to the validity of the will are pending.

Rule 47(4) provides that a person cited who is willing to accept or take a grant may, after entering an appearance, apply *ex parte* by affidavit to a District Judge or Registrar for an order for a grant to himself.

Rule 47(5) sets out what happens if the time limited for appearance has expired, and the person cited has not entered an appearance. If the citation has been issued at the instance of any person who would himself be entitled to a grant in the event of the person cited renouncing his right to the grant, the citor may apply for an order for a grant to himself.

If the citation has been to an executor to whom power has been reserved, the citor may apply to a District Judge or Registrar for an order that a note be made on the grant that the executor in respect of whom power was reserved has been duly cited and has not appeared and that all his rights in respect of the executorship have wholly ceased.

If the citation is to someone who has intermeddled in the estate, the citor may apply to a District Judge or Registrar by summons (which must be served on the person cited) for an order requiring such person to take a grant within a specified time or for a grant to himself or to some other person specified in the summons. Intermeddling is taking active steps in the administration of the estate, but it does not include acts of humanity like feeding the animals belonging to the deceased.

Rule 47(6) provides that an application under r 47(5) must be supported by an affidavit showing that the citation was duly served.

Rule 47(7) sets out what happens if the person cited has entered an appearance but has not applied for a grant under paragraph (4), or has failed to prosecute his application with reasonable diligence. If the citation has been issued at the instance of any person who would himself be entitled to a grant in the event of the person cited renouncing his right to the grant, the citor may apply by summons to a District Judge or Registrar for an order for a grant to himself.

If the citation has been to an executor to whom power has been reserved, the citor may apply to a District Judge or Registrar for an order striking out the appearance and for the endorsement on the grant of a note that the executor in respect of whom power was reserved has been duly cited and that all his rights in respect of the executorship have wholly ceased.

If the citation is to someone who has intermeddled in the estate, the citor may apply to a District Judge or Registrar for an order requiring the person cited to take a grant within a specified time or for a grant to himself or to some other person specified in the summons.

The summons must be served on the person cited.

Rule 48 deals with citations to propound a will. Rule 48(1) provides that a citation to propound a will shall be directed to the executors named in the will and to all persons interested thereunder, and may be issued at the instance of any citor having an interest contrary to that of the executors or such other persons.

Rule 48(2) provides that if the time limited for appearance has expired, the citor may –

(a) in the case where no person has entered an appearance, apply to a District Judge or Registrar for an order for a grant as if the will were invalid and such application shall be supported by an affidavit showing that the citation was duly served; or

(b) in the case where no person who has entered an appearance proceeds with reasonable diligence to propound the will, apply to a District Judge or Registrar by summons, which shall be served on every person cited who has entered an appearance, for such an order as is mentioned in paragraph (a).

Application for an order to attend for examination or for subpoena to bring in a will

12.4 Section 122(1) of the Supreme Court Act 1981 (SCA 1981) provides that where there are reasonable grounds for believing that any person has knowledge of any document which is or purports to be a testamentary document, the High Court may, whether or not any legal proceedings are pending, order him to attend for the purpose of being examined in open court. Section 122(2) provides that the court may –

(a) require any person who is before it, in compliance with an order under subsection, (1) to answer any question relating to the document concerned; and

(b) if appropriate, order him to bring in the document in such manner as the court may direct.

Section 122(3) provides that any person, who having been required by the court to do so under this section, fails to attend for examination, answer any question or bring in any document is guilty of contempt of court.

Section 123 provides that where it appears that any person has in his possession, custody or power any document which is or purports to be a testamentary document, the High Court may, whether or not any legal proceedings are pending, issue a subpoena requiring him to bring in the document in such manner as the court may in the subpoena direct.

Rule 50(1) of the NCPR 1987 provides that an application under s 122 of the SCA 1981 for an order requiring a person to attend for examination may, unless a probate action has been commenced, be made to a District Judge or Registrar by summons which shall be served on every such person.

Rule 50(2) provides that an application under s 123 of the SCA 1981 for the issue by a District Judge or Registrar of a subpoena to bring in a will must be supported by an affidavit setting out the grounds of the application, and if any person served with the subpoena denies that the will is in his possession or control he may file an affidavit to that effect in the registry from which the subpoena issued.

Chapter 13

Inheritance tax

Death estate

13.1 Section 4(1) of the Inheritance Tax Act 1984 (ITA 1984) provides that on the death of any person tax shall be charged as if, immediately before his death, he had made a transfer of value and the value transferred by it had been equal to the value of his estate immediately before his death. Thus inheritance tax is payable on the value of all the property comprised in the estate of a deceased person.

The rate of tax is determined by cumulating all the PETS and *inter vivos* or lifetime chargeable transfers (in general terms transfers to trustees of a discretionary trust) in the seven years preceding the date of death. If they amount to more than the nil rate band, the whole of the estate is taxable at 40%; if less, the unused part of the nil rate band can be offset against the death estate, and only the balance will be taxable at 40%.

Assume that T dies leaving an estate of £613,000. Assuming that there have been no *inter vivos* gifts, inheritance tax will be payable on £613,000 – the 2004–2005 nil rate band of £263,000 = £350,000 at 40% = £140,000.

If the deceased had made *inter vivos* or lifetime gifts in the seven years before death amounting to £400,000, the nil rate band would have been absorbed by these gifts, and so the whole death estate would have been taxable at 40%.

Potentially exempt transfers

13.2 A potentially exempt transfer is a transfer of value:

(a) which is made by an individual on or after 18 March 1986; and

(b) which, apart from this section, would be a chargeable transfer (or to the extent to which, apart from this section, it would be such a transfer); and

(c) to the extent that it constitutes either a gift to another individual or a gift into an accumulation and maintenance trust or a disabled trust (s 3A ITA 1984).

Gifts to individuals, to trusts with an interest in possession and to accumulation and maintenance trusts are thus all PETS. If the donor survives for seven years, no inheritance tax is payable. If the donor dies within the seven years, inheritance tax is payable. However, tapering relief may operate to reduce the amount of inheritance tax payable (s 7(4) ITA 1984). The amount of relief is:

PET within 0 – 3 years of death	*100% of inheritance tax payable – no reduction*
3 – 4	80%
4 – 5	60%
5 – 6	40%
6 – 7	20%

Note that tapering relief only reduces the amount of inheritance tax payable; it does not reduce the value for inheritance tax purposes, nor does it affect the value for cumulation purposes.

Rate of tax

13.3 There are two rates of tax applicable to the death estate at the moment – nil or 40%. The nil rate band limit for 2004–2005 is £263,000.

In order to determine the rate of tax on death, the PET must be cumulated with:

(a) all *inter vivos* or lifetime chargeable transfers made in the seven years preceding the PET; and

(b) previous PETs provided they are within seven years of death.

If a PET was made more than seven years before death, the PET is ignored for all inheritance tax purposes.

Examples:

a e = annual exemption

(i)	1995	*inter vivos* or lifetime chargeable transfer
	1996	PET
	2001	PET
	2004	Death

It will be necessary to calculate the inheritance tax payable on the 2001 PET.

It will have to be cumulated with the 1995 *inter vivos* or lifetime chargeable transfer, but not the 1996 PET as this was more than seven years before death.

(ii)	2001	*inter vivos* chargeable transfer £119,000
	2003	PET £196,000

2004 Death

No inheritance tax will be payable on the *inter vivos* chargeable transfer as it is within nil rate band.

How much of nil rate band is left to offset against 2003 PET?

Nil rate band (2004/05)		£263,000
Deduct 2001 *inter vivos* chargeable transfer	£119,000	
Less a e × 2 (if not used in one year, annual exemption or balance of annual exemption can be carried forward to next year)	£6,000	£113,000
		£150,000
2003 PET		£196,000
Less a e × 2		£6,000
		£190,000
Less balance of nil rate band		£150,000
		£40,000
Inheritance tax at 40% =		£16,000

(iii)	1999 PET	£319,000
	2004 Death	
	PET	£319,000
	Less a e × 2	£6,000
		£313,000
	Less nil rate band	£263,000
		£50,000
	Inheritance tax at 40% =	£20,000
	4–5 years: 60% of tax payable £20,000 × $\frac{60}{100}$	£12,000

Note that the rates of inheritance tax payable are the rates in force at the date of death, unless they have increased. The value on which inheritance tax is payable in the case of a PET is the value at the date of the gift; thus the value is frozen. Relief is available if the asset has gone down in value since the date of the gift. Even if the donor is not likely to survive for seven years, it is thus still a good idea to give away assets which may increase in value.

It may be possible to insure against the donor dying within seven years of the PET.

Gifts with reservation of benefit

13.4 Be careful not to infringe the rules relating to gifts with reservation of benefit – otherwise the PET will be ineffective as far as saving inheritance tax is concerned.

Section 102 of the Finance Act 1986 applies where an individual disposes of any property by way of gift and either:

(a) possession and enjoyment of the property are not *bona fide* assumed by the donee at or before the beginning of the relevant period; or

(b) at any time in the relevant period the property is not enjoyed to the entire exclusion, or virtually to the entire exclusion, of the donor and of any benefit to him by contract or otherwise.

The effect of these provisions is that such a gift is ineffective as far as inheritance tax is concerned; at the date of death the donor will still be deemed to own the property. Furthermore, the original gift is still a PET. However, the donee still owns the property for other purposes, and so there will be no free uplift to market value for capital gains tax purposes.

If the donor releases the reserved benefit, it will be deemed to be a PET as from the date when the reservation was released.

The Finance Act 1999 inserted special provisions dealing with land. Section 102 A applies where an individual disposes of an interest in land by way of a gift on or after the 9 March 1999. Section 102 A (2) provides that at any time in the relevant period when a donor or spouse enjoys a significant right or interest, or is party to a significant arrangement, in relation to the land:

(a) the interest disposed of is referred to (in relation to the gift and the donor) as property subject to a reservation; and

(b) section 102 (3) and (4) above shall apply.

Section 102 A (3) provides that subject to subsections (4) and (5), a right, interest or arrangement in relation to land is significant for the purposes of subsection (2) if (and only if) it entitles or enables the donor to occupy all or part of the land, or to enjoy some right in relation to all or part of the land, otherwise than for full consideration in money, or money's worth.

Subsection (4) provides that a right, interest or arrangement is not significant for the purposes of subsection (2) if:

(a) it does not and cannot prevent the enjoyment of the land to the entire exclusion, or virtually to the entire exclusion of the donor; or

(b) it does not entitle or enable the donor to occupy all or part of the land immediately after the disposal, but would do so were it not for the interest disposed of.

Subsection (5) provides that a right or interest is not significant for the purposes of subsection (2) if it was granted or acquired before the period of seven years ending with the date of the gift.

Thus if a parent grants a lease of his house to himself, and then gives the freehold to a child, the donor will be deemed to have reserved a benefit, and the house will form part of the donor's estate on death. However, if the lease is granted on the same terms as a lease between strangers, no benefit will have been reserved in the gift of the freehold.

What is the position if the parents execute a declaration of trust declaring that they hold the property on trust for themselves and their children? The declaration of trust will be a PET, but the reservation of benefit provisions will not apply if:

(a) the parents and the children occupy the land; and

(b) the parents do not receive any benefit, other than a negligible one, which is provided by or at the expense of the children for some reason connected with the gift.

Thus both the parents and the children must occupy the house. If the children do not do so, the parents will be deemed to have reserved a benefit. The parents must not receive any collateral benefit. Thus if the child has a 50% interest in the property, this child must not bear more than 50% of the running expenses of the home. If they do bear more than 50%, the reservation of benefit provisions will apply.

If a child moves out, the parents will have to provide full consideration to prevent the application of the reservation of benefit rules.

Exemptions and reliefs applying on death

13.5 It may be possible to claim the following exemptions and reliefs:

(a) *The spouse exemption.* If the spouse of the deceased succeeds to the property, the spouse exemption will apply. Section 18(1) of the ITA 1984 provides that a transfer of value is an exempt transfer to the extent that the value transferred is attributable to property which becomes comprised in the estate of the transferor's spouse, or, so far as the value transferred is not so attributable, to the extent that the estate is increased.

Note that spouse exemption only applies if the donee spouse is domiciled in the United Kingdom. If the donee spouse is not domiciled in the United Kingdom, spouse exemption is limited to £55,000. This means that an amount equal to the nil rate band plus £55,000 can be given to a spouse not domiciled here without incurring any liability for inheritance tax.

(b) *Reverter to settlor*. The charge under s 52 of the ITA 1984 will not apply if the interest comes to an end during the settlor's life and on the same occasion the property in which the interest subsisted reverts to the settlor (s 53(3)). Section 52 deals with the effect of a termination of an interest in possession during the life of the person entitled to the interest in possession.

What happens if the settlor assigns his interest to his spouse, or dies before the other interest has terminated? Section 53(4) of the ITA provides that inheritance tax is not payable if on the occasion when the interest comes to an end the settlor's spouse or, where the settlor has died less than two years earlier, the settlor's widow or widower becomes beneficially entitled to the settled property and is domiciled in the UK.

This exemption will not apply if the settlor or his spouse had acquired the reversionary interest for a consideration in money or money's worth (s 53(5)(a)).

Section 54 has a similar provision dealing with the situation where a person is entitled to an interest in possession in settled property which on his death, but during the settlor's life, reverts to the settlor.

(c) *Gifts of excluded property*. No inheritance tax is payable in respect of gifts of excluded property. Excluded property comprises the following:

(i) property situated outside the UK if the person beneficially entitled to it is an individual domiciled outside the UK (s 6(1)).

Note that both conditions must be satisfied for property to be treated as excluded as property – the property must be situated outside the UK, and the person beneficially entitled to it must be domiciled outside the UK. If a person is domiciled in the UK, all the assets of that person wherever situated will be subject to inheritance tax. If a person is not domiciled in the UK, it is only the assets in this country which will be subject to inheritance tax;

(ii) a reversionary interest unless:

— it has at any time been acquired (whether by the person entitled to it or by a person previously entitled to it) for a consideration in money or money's worth; or

— it is one to which the settlor or his spouse is or has been beneficially entitled (s 48(1)).

(iii) section 48(3) of the ITA 1984 provides that where property comprised in a settlement is situated outside the UK:

- the property (but not a reversionary interest in the property) is excluded property unless the settlor was domiciled in the UK at the time when the settlement was made; and
- s 6(1) applies to a reversionary interest in the property, but does not otherwise apply in relation to that property.

Thus normally there is no charge to inheritance tax on any transfers of reversionary interests. The life tenant is deemed to own the underlying assets for inheritance tax purposes, and therefore it would be wrong to charge dealings with reversionary interests.

(d) *Charities and political parties*. Gifts to charities and political parties are exempt.

(e) *Business property relief and agricultural property relief*. Business property relief operates to reduce the value of the property by 100% in the following cases:

(i) property consisting of a business or an interest in a business;

(ii) shares in or securities of a company which are unquoted and which (either by themselves or together with other such shares or securities owned by the transferor) gave the transferor control of the company immediately before the transfer;

(iii) any unquoted shares in a company.

Relief of 50% is available on the following:

— shares in or securities of a company which are quoted and which (either by themselves or together with other such shares or securities owned by the transferor) gave the transferor control of the company immediately before the transfer;

— any land, or building, machinery or plant which, immediately before the transfer, was used wholly or mainly for the purposes of a business carried on by a company of which the transferor then had control or by a partnership of which he was then a partner;

— any land or building, machinery or plant which, immediately before the transfer, was used wholly or mainly for the purposes of a business carried on by the transferor and was settled property in which he was then beneficially entitled to an interest in possession (s 105(1) ITA 1984).

Shares are quoted if they are quoted on a recognised stock exchange (s 105(1ZA) ITA 1984).

Section 106 provides that property is not relevant business property in relation to a transfer of value unless it has been owned by the transferor for the two years immediately preceding the transfer.

Section 116 of the ITA 1984 permits the value of agricultural property to be reduced by 100% if:

- the interest of the transferor in the property immediately before the transfer carries the right to vacant possession or the right to obtain it within the next twenty-four months; or
- it is notwithstanding the terms of the tenancy valued at an amount broadly equivalent to vacant possession value; or

- the interest of the transferor in the property immediately before the transfer does not carry the right to vacant possession within twenty-four months because the property is let on a tenancy beginning on or after 1 September 1995 (see ESC F17).

In other cases the relief is 50%.

Section 117 provides that relief is not available unless:

— it was occupied by the transferor for the purposes of agriculture throughout the period of two years ending with the date of transfer; or

— it was owned by him throughout the period of seven years ending with that date and was throughout that period occupied (by him or another) for the purposes of agriculture.

A farmer who is an owner-occupier will qualify for 100% relief if he has owned the land for two years.

If the land is let, it will still qualify for 100% relief if the owner has owned it for seven years and can recover possession within 24 months, or the tenancy was granted after 1 September 1995.

(f) *Loss on sale relief.* This applies if quoted shares or land are sold for less than the market value at the date of death. It is considered more fully at PARA 14.1.

Liability for inheritance tax

13.6 This section deals with who is liable to pay any inheritance tax due to the Inland Revenue.

Lifetime chargeable transfers

13.7 These are usually lifetime transfers to the trustees of a discretionary trust. Inheritance tax may have been paid when the transfer was first made, and if the settlor dies within seven years of the transfer, then the inheritance tax has to be recalculated using the death rate. If this calculation results in more tax being payable, the primary liability falls on the transferee trustees, but if they do not satisfy the liability within twelve months of death, then the personal representatives of the deceased become liable for the tax. Although it is uncertain, it would seem only right that the personal representatives should be able to recover the tax from the transferee trustees if they should be bearing the burden.

Potentially exempt transfers

13.8 If the donor dies within seven years of making a gift, the primary liability for any inheritance tax due falls on the donee. However, as with lifetime transfers, if the donee does not pay within twelve months of the tax becoming due, then it becomes the liability of the personal representatives. Again, although it is not absolutely certain, it seems that the personal representatives should be able to recover the tax from the donee if they should be bearing the burden.

The death estate

13.9 Section 200(1) of the ITA 1984 provides that the persons liable for tax on the value transferred by a chargeable transfer made on the death of any person are:

(a) so far as the tax is attributable to the value of property which either –

   (i) was not immediately before the death comprised in a settlement; or

   (ii) was so comprised and consists of land in the UK which devolves upon or vests in the deceased's personal representatives, the deceased's personal representatives;

(b) so far as the tax is attributable to the value of property which, immediately before the death, was comprised in a settlement, the trustees of the settlement;

(c) so far as the tax is attributable to the value of any property, any person in whom the property is vested (whether beneficially or otherwise) at any time after the death, or who at any such time is beneficially entitled to an interest in possession in the property;

(d) so far as the tax is attributable to the value of any property which, immediately before the death, was comprised in a settlement, any person for whose benefit any of the property or income from it is applied after death.

Burden of inheritance tax

13.10 Which beneficiary has to bear the burden of inheritance tax? Normally the inheritance tax payable on the free estate of the deceased is a testamentary expense, and is payable out of the residuary estate.

Inheritance tax due in respect of property situated abroad is usually borne by the foreign property.

If property passes by survivorship, any inheritance tax due is normally borne by the survivor or survivors.

It is of course open to testators to direct that the burden of inheritance tax should fall on particular beneficiaries to the exclusion of others. The personal representatives must give effect to this direction, but it does not affect the Inland Revenue, who can take proceedings against whoever is liable for the tax.

Time for payment

13.11 Inheritance tax is due in respect of the death estate six months after the end of the month of death. If it is not paid then, interest is due.

It is possible to elect to pay the inheritance tax due in respect of certain property by instalments over ten years; for a fuller description of the property to which the instalment option applies, see PARA 5.7.

Inland Revenue charge

13.12 Section 237(1) of the ITA 1984 provides that a charge in respect of unpaid inheritance tax is imposed on –

(a) any property to the value of which the value transferred is wholly or partly attributable; and

(b) where the chargeable transfer is made by the making of a settlement or is made under Part III of the Act, any property comprised in the settlement.

Section 237(2) provides that where the chargeable transfer is made on death, personal or moveable property situated in the UK which was beneficially owned by the deceased immediately before his death and which vests in his personal representatives is not subject to the charge. 'Personal property' includes leaseholds.

The charge does not bind the purchasers of land in England and Wales unless it was registered as a land charge or, in the case of registered land, protected by notice on the register.

Position where there are gifts in a will to exempt beneficiaries and non-exempt beneficiaries

13.13 Section 41 of the ITA 1984 provides that notwithstanding the terms of any disposition:

(a) none of the tax on the value transferred shall fall on any specific gift if or to the extent that the transfer is exempt with respect to the gift; and

(b) none of the tax attributable to the value of the property comprised in the residue shall fall on any gift of a share of residue if or to the extent that the transfer is exempt with respect to the gift.

Whilst the theory behind this section is correct – a gift which would otherwise be exempt should not bear its own tax – it has caused difficulties in its application to mixed gifts of residue to exempt beneficiaries and non-exempt beneficiaries.

— Part residue going to exempt beneficiaries, part to non-exempt

For example, suppose a will contains the following residuary gift:

> 'I give half of my residuary estate to my son and half to the RSPCA.'

There are two ways of dealing with this gift:

(a) the son's share could be grossed up so that the son receives the same amount as the charity;

(b) all the inheritance tax is paid form the son's share so that the son receives less than the charity.

According to *Re Ratcliffe* it is a question of the construction of the will as to which method should be adopted, and in that particular case it was held that method (b) was the correct way of dealing with it.

— Specific gift to exempt beneficiary, residue to non-exempt beneficiary

Section 42(1) of the ITA 1984 defines a specific gift as any gift other than a gift of residue or of a share of residue.

If there is a specific gift in a will to an exempt beneficiary, like the spouse or a charity, then the value of the specific gift does not bear any inheritance tax, but the residue bears tax at whatever rate is appropriate.

If a will contains a specific legacy of £400,000 to the spouse, that will be exempt because of spouse exemption. If the residue of £500,000 goes to the children, then the balance of that after deducting the nil rate band will be chargeable to inheritance at 40%.

— Specific gift to non-exempt beneficiary bearing its own tax, residue to exempt beneficiary

No inheritance tax will be payable on the residue, and the value of the non-exempt gift will be subject to inheritance. Thus if the specific gift is worth £663,000, inheritance tax at 40% will be payable on £400,000 – the amount of the specific gift less the nil rate band for 2004/2005 – £160,000.

— Specific gift to non-exempt beneficiary free of tax, residue to exempt beneficiary

It may be that the specific gift is expressed to be free of tax, or if nothing is said, then it will be treated as being free of tax. In this situation, the specific gift must be grossed up to find the amount which after deducting the tax will leave the amount of the gift.

Thus if a will contains a legacy of £300,000 to a child, and that gift is expressed to be free of tax, or nothing is said, and the residue is given to an exempt beneficiary, assuming that the nil rate band has been absorbed by lifetime gifts, the legacy will have to be grossed up.

$$£300{,}000 \times \frac{100}{100-40} = £500{,}000$$

The beneficiary will receive the £300, 000 legacy in full, but the residuary beneficiary will have to bear the burden of the inheritance tax.

— Specific gift to exempt beneficiary, part of residue to exempt beneficiary

If there is a specific gift to an exempt beneficiary, the spouse, and a gift of part of the residue to a charity, the share of the residue passing to the non-exempt beneficiary is taxed on the actual amount.

— Specific gift to non-exempt beneficiary subject to tax, part of residue to exempt beneficiary

In order to calculate the inheritance tax, the specific gift should be deducted from the residue, and the part of the residue going to the non-exempt beneficiary calculated. The specific gift should then be added to the non-exempt residue, and the inheritance tax calculated.

— Specific gifts to non-exempt beneficiaries, some subject to tax, some not, residue to exempt beneficiary

— Specific gifts to non-exempt beneficiaries, some subject to tax, some not, residue to exempt and non-exempt beneficiaries

— Specific gift to non-exempt beneficiaries free of tax, residue to exempt and non-exempt beneficiaries

These will all involve complicated calculations in order to determine the rate of inheritance tax. As they are met infrequently in practice, they are not considered in this book.

Chapter 14

Capital gains tax

14.1 After death, the personal representatives will need to settle any liability for capital gains tax incurred by the deceased when he was alive. The personal representatives will of course be able to offset the deceased's annual exemption against the liability, and it may be that other exemptions and reliefs will be available.

Any losses incurred by the deceased can be offset against any gains made by the deceased in the tax year of death, but they cannot be carried forward and set off against any losses incurred by the personal representatives. However, s 62(2) of the Taxation of Chargeable Gains Act 1992 permits allowable losses sustained by an individual in the year of assessment in which he dies to be deducted from chargeable gains accruing to the deceased in the three years of assessment preceding the year of assessment in which the death occurs, taking chargeable gains accruing in a later year before those accruing in an earlier year.

The personal representatives are deemed to acquire the assets at market value at the date of death (s 62(1)). Normally the value for inheritance tax purposes will be accepted as being the market value for both inheritance tax and capital gains tax. Frequently the personal representatives will vest the property in the legatees, in which event s 62(4) provides that no chargeable gain shall accrue to the personal representatives, but instead the legatees are treated as acquiring the asset at the market value at the date of death. 'Legatee' is widely defined in s 64(2) as including any person taking under a testamentary disposition or on an intestacy or partial intestacy, whether he takes beneficially or as trustee, and a person taking under a *donatio mortis causa* shall be treated (except for the purposes of s 62) as a legatee and his acquisition as made at the time of the donor's death.

Section 64(1) permits the legatee to deduct:

(a) any expenditure within s 38(2) incurred by him in relation to the transfer of the asset to him by the personal representatives or trustees; and

(b) any such expenditure incurred in relation to the transfer of the asset by the personal representatives or trustees.

Sections 71(1), 72(1) and 73(1) provide that on the death of the life tenant there is a deemed disposal by the trustees, but no chargeable gain accrues. However, s 74(2) provides that if hold-over relief has been claimed, these provisions do not apply, but any chargeable gain accruing to the trustees is restricted to the amount of the held-over gain. Thus if a settlement was created *inter vivos*, and any gain made by the settlor was held over, the held-over gain becomes chargeable on the death of the life tenant, but not the gain accruing from the date of transfer to the date of death.

It may be necessary for the personal representatives to sell assets in order to complete the administration of the estate. Any gain will be computed in accordance with normal principles, and the personal representatives are entitled to the annual exemption for the year of death, and the two subsequent tax years; the remaining gain will be subject to tax at 40%. Note that s 64(1) does not apply in this situation, but the Revenue has issued Statements of Practice, SP 7/81 and SP 8/94, which contain a scale of permitted deductions. In addition, in *IRC v Richards Executors [1971] 1 WLR 571* executors paid fees to solicitors for investigations, valuations, the obtaining of a confirmation in Scotland and the resealing of the confirmation in England. It was held that the proportion of fees applicable to some stocks and shares was deductible in calculating the capital gains of the executors.

Personal representatives are not allowed to claim the private residence exemption, but by Statutory Concession D5 they can still claim it if the house is occupied by the beneficiary entitled to the house under the will or intestacy, as his only or main residence, and was so occupied before the death of the deceased. This concession has now been incorporated into the Taxation of Chargeable Gains Act 1992 by the Finance Act 2004. The 2004 Act has inserted a new section after s 225 of the Taxation of Chargeable Gains Act 1992, which provides that personal representatives can claim private residence exemption if the following conditions are satisfied:

(a) Immediately before and immediately after the death of the deceased person the dwelling house or part of the dwelling house was the only or main residence of one or more individuals.

(b) That one of those individuals has a relevant entitlement, two or more of those individuals have relevant entitlements, and the relevant entitlement, or relevant entitlements together, accounts/account for 75% of the proceeds of disposal.

    'Relevant entitlement' means an entitlement as legatee of the deceased person to, or to an interest in possession in, the whole or any part of the net proceeds of disposal.

    'Net proceeds of sale' is defined as:

    (i) the proceeds of the disposal of the asset realised by the personal representatives; less

    (ii) any incidental costs allowable as a deduction in accordance with s 38 (1)(c) in computing in the gain accruing to the personal representatives on that disposal.

It is to be assumed that none of the proceeds are required to meet liabilities of the deceased (including any liability for inheritance tax).

Sections 178 and 179 of the Inheritance Tax Act 1984 provide that if shares quoted on the Stock Exchange or the Unlisted Securities Market are sold at a loss within twelve months of death, the lower value can be substituted for inheritance tax purposes. Where this is done, the lower value also becomes the acquisition value of the personal representatives for capital gains tax purposes, so that they cannot claim loss relief as well. If several shareholdings are sold, the gains and losses must be aggregated. There is a similar provision with regard to the sale of land within four years of death, but it is unclear whether the sale price also becomes the acquisition value for capital gains tax purposes as well. Section 187 of the ITA 1984 provides that the market value for the purposes of capital gains tax of shares for which the relief is claimed shall be their sale value; there is no similar provision with regard to land, and so it could be argued that the lower value did not have to be substituted for capital gains tax purposes. However, s 274 of the Taxation of Chargeable Gains Act 1992 provides that where on the death of any person inheritance tax is chargeable on the value of his estate immediately before his death and the value of an asset has been ascertained (whether in any proceedings or otherwise) for the purposes of that tax, the value so ascertained shall be taken for the purposes of this Act to be the market value of that asset at the date of death. Thus it is probable that personal representatives cannot claim a loss for both capital gains tax and inheritance tax as far as land is concerned. (See Barlow, King & King *Wills Administration and Taxation*, 7th edition, Sweet & Maxwell page 229.)

It should be noted that losses incurred by personal representatives cannot be transferred to beneficiaries.

Chapter 15

Income tax

Income arising before death

15.1 It is the duty of personal representatives to ensure that any income tax due to the date of death is paid or, if a repayment is due, that it is claimed (s 74(1) Taxes Management Act 1970). Payment or repayment may affect the amount of inheritance tax due on death.

The personal representatives should report the death to the Inspector of Taxes, and submit a return for the period from 6 April to the date of death. The Revenue can assess personal representatives within three tax years from the end of the tax year in which death occurred; assessments can go back six years from date of assessment.

Personal allowances

15.2 The deceased is entitled to full personal allowances for the year of death.

How do you distinguish between income of the deceased and income of the estate?

15.3 The crucial date is the date when it is received or credited. For succession purposes it may have to be apportioned, but for income tax purposes the crucial date is the date when the payment should be received or credited.

Dividends or interest paid after death in respect of periods before or after death will have to be apportioned, and the part apportioned to the period before death will be subject to inheritance tax. When the dividend or interest is paid, it will be subject to income tax. This can result in an element of double taxation. Section 699 of the Income and Corporation Taxes Act 1988 (ICTA 1988) affords some relief, but only to a residuary beneficiary who is absolutely entitled.

The administration period

15.4 This runs from the date of death to the date when the administration of the estate is complete, or in other words, when the residue is ascertained (s 695(1) ICTA 1988). The personal representatives are liable only for basic rate tax, but they cannot claim any personal allowances. However, they may be able to offset interest on money borrowed to pay inheritance tax.

The personal representatives are responsible for completing any income tax return. If basic rate tax has been deducted at source, it need not be included in any tax return by the personal representatives. However, if the personal representatives are in receipt of untaxed income, for example rents, they must notify the appropriate tax district, and complete a return.

Note that the rule in *Re Earl of Chesterfield's Trusts* does not affect liability for income tax.

If the personal representatives have had to borrow money in order to pay the inheritance tax due on personalty, the interest is deductible in computing the income tax liability of the personal representatives. Note that it is only the interest paid in respect of a period ending within one year of the making of the loan (s 364(1) ICTA 1988).

If inheritance tax is payable on realty, use should be made of the right to pay by instalments so that there is no need to borrow.

Taxation of beneficiaries

General legacies

15.5 General legacies usually do not carry interest or income. However, if interest is payable, it is assessable under Schedule D Case III of the ICTA 1988. Normally the interest should be paid gross.

Specific legatees

15.6 Specific legatees are entitled to the income from the date of death, but they are not liable for income tax until the asset is vested in them. The income will then be taxed as part of the specific legatee's income in the year in which it arises.

Annuities

15.7 Annuities are chargeable under Schedule D Case III. The personal representatives should deduct tax at basic rates when paying.

Annuities may be expressed in different ways. For example:

(a) the annuitant is to have such sum as after deduction of basic rate income tax will leave £750;

(b) the annuitant is to have £750 free of income tax.

Residuary beneficiaries with a limited interest

15.8 The personal representatives must deduct income tax at basic rate before paying any income to a beneficiary, and the beneficiary includes the grossed up amount in his return. All the income paid to a beneficiary in a year of assessment is taxed in that year. Personal representatives should therefore be wary of saving up income, and paying it all in one tax year. It could mean that the beneficiary will have to pay higher rate tax, which he would not have had to pay if the income had been paid regularly.

Residuary beneficiaries with an absolute interest

15.9 Income tax is payable only on the income, not on distributions of capital. Under s 696 and s 697 of the ICTA 1988 personal representatives must calculate the residuary income each year. Residuary income is all income less any annual interest, annuity, or other annual payment for that year which is a charge on residue, and management expenses properly chargeable to income. 'Properly chargeable' means properly chargeable under the general law.

The residuary beneficiary is taxed on the income paid to him in the relevant year of assessment regardless of when it was received by the personal representatives. In order to determine if a distribution is of income or capital, it is necessary to calculate the aggregate residuary income since the commencement of the administration. If the payments or transfers to the beneficiary exceed that total, then the excess is capital. If it does not, then it is income. This means that the transfer of a chattel such as an antique could be classed as an income distribution. The value of the antique will have to be grossed up at the appropriate rate. The income bearing the highest rate of tax is deemed to have been paid to the beneficiary first.

Tax deduction certificates

15.10 Personal representatives can be required to supply beneficiaries with Form R185 showing the amount of income paid and the tax deducted.

Chapter 16

Tax consequences of different gifts. Variations and disclaimers

Spouse – absolute or life interest?

Inheritance tax

16.1 It makes no difference initially, as far as inheritance tax is concerned, whether the spouse has an absolute interest or a life interest under the will of a deceased spouse. No inheritance tax will be payable because of the spouse exemption. However, if the spouse has an absolute interest, the spouse can make use of the *inter vivos* exemptions from inheritance tax and, in addition, can make PETs. A spouse with a life interest, as opposed to an absolute, will not be able to do so out of the capital – the subject of the life interest – unless the trustees have the power to advance capital to the life tenant and do so.

Note that the spouse exemption is limited to £55,000 if the spouse is not domiciled in the United Kingdom.

Capital gains tax

16.2 Where a spouse has an absolute interest, any gain belongs to the spouse.

Where a spouse has a life interest, any gain belongs to the trustees. The trustees will be entitled to half the annual exemption available to private individuals, but the rate of tax on the gains will be 40%.

The spouse will also be entitled to the annual exemption in his or her own right.

Income tax

16.3 It makes no difference, as far as income tax is concerned, whether the spouse has an absolute interest or only a life interest. The spouse will be liable to income tax on all income received.

Nil rate band gift

16.4 A very effective method of saving inheritance tax is for the will to contain a legacy up to the nil rate band to the children, with the residue to the spouse.

Note the following points:

(a) PETs and *inter vivos* chargeable transfers made in the seven years before death will reduce the nil rate band;

(b) be careful not to exceed the nil rate band – grossing up may apply if there is a gift free of tax to children or grandchildren with the residue going to the spouse;

(c) consider imposing a limit on the legacy in case the nil rate band is substantially increased;

(d) be careful also to ensure that a nil rate band legacy does not include agricultural property and business property qualifying for 100% relief as it is a waste of the relief.

Nil rate band discretionary trust

16.5 This is where an amount not exceeding the nil rate band is settled on a discretionary trust for the benefit of the spouse and children. Usually the trustees are given power to accept an IOU from the surviving spouse or a charge on the matrimonial home for the amount of the nil rate band legacy. On the death of the surviving spouse, the amount due under the IOU or charge is deductible from the estate of the surviving spouse.

Inheritance tax

16.6 No inheritance tax falls due on creation, but there is a possibility of a charge on distributions and on each tenth anniversary. However, the amount of inheritance tax payable should be small.

When a member of the class of beneficiaries dies, the trust property will not form part of the beneficiary's estate for inheritance tax purposes.

Capital gains tax

16.7 The trustees will be entitled to half of the annual exemption available to an individual.

If the trustees dispose of any assets, and become liable to capital gains tax, the rate of tax is 40%.

Death normally wipes out any capital gain, so that a beneficiary acquires the assets at market value as at the date of death. This will not happen with discretionary trusts.

Income tax

16.8 The trustees will pay income tax at 40% (dividends 32.5%), but if the income is paid to a beneficiary who is not a basic rate taxpayer, the beneficiary will be able to recover the tax paid, although the 10% paid on dividends is not recoverable.

Two-year discretionary trust

Inheritance tax

16.9 Section 144 of the ITA 1984 provides that any termination of a discretionary trust within two years of death is not a transfer of value for inheritance tax purposes. Any termination is read back into the will.

Inheritance tax may have to be paid on the death of the testator. If there is an appointment in favour of the spouse, the spouse exemption will apply.

Appointments should not be made within three months of death. The reason for this is that s 65(4) provides that there is no charge when property leaves the settlement if the event in question occurs within a quarter beginning with the day on which the settlement commenced. Section 144(2) provides that the section does not apply in that situation.

Capital gains tax

16.10 There is no special treatment for capital gains tax purposes. If the administration of the estate has been completed, the trustees will be deemed to acquire the assets at market value as at the date of death. If there is an appointment, the trustees will be deemed to dispose of the assets at market value on the date of the appointment.

If the administration of the estate has not been completed, the position is unclear. It is arguable that the trustees are disposing of a chose in action, which has a nil base cost for capital gains tax purposes as it is a new type of property coming into existence on death, but the market value of which is near the value of the assets the trustees will ultimately receive if the estate is solvent. If this argument is correct, and it is the author's opinion that the Inland Revenue will argue this, it means that the trustees could incur a large liability for capital gains tax.

Absolute gifts to children and grandchildren

16.11 As the children or grandchildren will not be able to give a valid receipt for capital until they are 18, the personal representatives will usually become trustees of the gift.

Inheritance tax

16.12 If the beneficiary dies under the age of 18, the property will still form part of the beneficiary's estate for inheritance tax purposes. However, there will be no charge when the beneficiary attains 18, or if the trustees exercise their power of advancement.

Capital gains tax

16.13 Any gain made by the trustees will belong to the beneficiary. There will not be a deemed disposal when the beneficiary attains 18.

Income tax

16.14 Trustees pay income tax at basic rate; depending on his or her income, the beneficiary will be able to recover the tax paid, or may be liable to higher rate tax.

Contingent gifts to children and grandchildren

Inheritance tax

16.15 Frequently this type of gift will be an accumulation and maintenance settlement, and will receive special treatment as far as inheritance tax is concerned. Where gifts are contingent they are usually set out as follows 'to my grandson A if he attains 21'. If the beneficiary dies under the age of 18, the gift will not form part of the beneficiary's estate. Where s 31 of the Trustee Act (TA 1925) 1925 applies, the beneficiary will be entitled to the income on attaining 18. In this situation, if the contingent beneficiary dies between the ages of 18 and the specified age, the trust property will form part of the beneficiary's estate. However, when the beneficiary attains the specified age, no inheritance tax will be payable.

Capital gains tax

16.16 The trustees are entitled to a maximum of half the annual exemption available to an individual; the rate of tax is 40%.

When a beneficiary satisfies the contingency and becomes absolutely entitled, there is a deemed disposal by the trustees at market value. Hold-over relief will be available if the trust assets are business assets; it will apply to all assets if the settlement is an accumulation and maintenance settlement up to the time when the contingency is satisfied. If a beneficiary obtains an interest in possession at say 18 under an accumulation and maintenance settlement, but does not become entitled to the capital until say 25, hold-over relief will be limited to business assets.

Income tax

16.17 Trustees will pay income tax at 40%. The beneficiary may be able to recover this tax; alternatively, the beneficiary may be liable for more if his income is large enough.

Free of tax legacies

16.18 The basic rule is that any gift in a will of property in the UK is free of inheritance tax. However, if a legacy is tax free, and the residue goes to an exempt beneficiary, the legacy will have to be grossed up – see paragraph 13.13.

Variations and disclaimers

Inheritance tax

16.19 Section 142(1) of the ITA 1984 provides that:

'Where within the period of two years after a person's death –

(a) any of the dispositions (whether effected by will, under the law relating to intestacy or otherwise) of the property comprised in his estate immediately before his death are varied, or

(b) the benefit conferred by any of those dispositions is disclaimed,

by an instrument in writing made by the persons or any of the persons who benefit or would benefit under the dispositions, the Act shall apply as if the variation had been effected by the deceased or, as the case may be, the disclaimed benefit had never been conferred.'

Variations

16.20 The following points should be noted with regard to variations:

— section 142(1) of the ITA 1984 applies to both intestacies and wills;

— a surviving joint tenant can use s 142(1);

— the variation must be made within two years of the date of death;

— there must be an instrument in writing;

— the section does not apply to a settlement where the deceased was the life tenant;

— the section does not permit the variation of a gift where the deceased reserved a benefit;

— the section does not apply if consideration was given for the variation. An indemnity as regards inheritance tax or income tax might infringe this provision.

— the parties to a variation must be of full age and capacity. If not, the court may be prepared to sanction a variation under the Variation of Trusts Act 1958. To be effective, any order must be made within two years of death;

— if extra inheritance tax is payable, the personal representatives must join in the election;

— the election must be in the deed of variation. Since the 1 August 2002 there is no need for notice to be given to the Revenue unless the variation means that more inheritance tax is payable;

— once property has been varied, it cannot be varied again; however, there can be several variations as long as the property is different.

Disclaimers

16.21 Any beneficiary can refuse to accept a gift, unless he has expressly or impliedly accepted the gift, or fails to disclaim within a reasonable time. As long as gifts are unconnected, a beneficiary can accept one gift and refuse another. If a non-residuary gift is disclaimed, the gift becomes part of the residue; if a residuary gift is disclaimed, the property passes to those persons entitled under the intestacy rules.

Section 142 of the ITA 1984 applies to disclaimers as well as variations.

Capital gains tax

16.22 Section 62(6) of the Taxation of Chargeable Gains Act 1992 provides that:

> 'Where within the period of two years after a person's death any of the dispositions (whether effected by will, under the law relating to intestacy or otherwise) of the property of which he was competent to dispose are varied, or the benefit conferred by any of those dispositions is disclaimed, by an instrument in writing made by the persons or any of the persons who benefit under the dispositions:

(a) the variation or disclaimer shall not constitute a disposal for the purposes of this Act; and

(b) this section shall apply as if the variation had been effected by the deceased or, as the case may be, the disclaimed benefit had never been conferred.'

Note that the section applies to property held by the deceased as a joint tenant.

Income tax

Variations

16.23 Income arising between the date of death and the variation belongs to the original beneficiary.

A variation may be deemed to be a settlement, and the anti-avoidance provisions in the ICTA 1988 may apply.

Disclaimers

16.24 The income belongs to the beneficiary who takes as a result of the disclaimer.

Chapter 17

Taxation of settlements

Interest in possession trusts

Inheritance tax

Inheritance tax on the creation of interest in possession trusts

17.1 If the settlement is created on death, the usual charging rules apply, so that if the spouse is the life tenant no inheritance tax will be payable because of the spouse exemption, provided the spouse is domiciled in the United Kingdom.

Position of the life tenant

17.2 For inheritance tax purposes the life tenant is deemed to own the trust assets (s 49(1) Inheritance Tax Act 1984 (ITA 1984)). As a consequence, the remainderman owns nothing – a reversionary interest is normally excluded property for inheritance tax purposes (s 48 ITA 1984). If a person is entitled to the income for a period less than life, he will still be deemed to own the trust assets. If there is more than one life tenant, they will be deemed to own the appropriate share of the trust fund (ss 50(1) and (2) ITA 1984).

Death of the life tenant

17.3 On the death of the life tenant, for inheritance tax purposes, he is treated as being the owner of all the underlying trust assets (ss 5 and 49 ITA 1984). The trustees are liable for the proportion of inheritance tax due in respect of the trust property, if any.

Exemptions and reliefs

17.4 It may be possible to claim the following exemptions and reliefs:

(a) Section 52(1) of the ITA 1984 provides that where at any time during the lifetime of a person beneficially entitled to an interest in possession his interest comes to an end, inheritance tax is payable as if at that time he had made a transfer of value. Section 53(2) provides that tax shall not be chargeable under s 52 if the person whose interest in the property comes to an end becomes on the same occasion beneficially entitled to the property or to another interest in possession in the property. So if the life tenant becomes absolutely entitled to the trust assets, there will be no charge to inheritance tax.

(b) Reverter to settlor – the charge under s 52 will not apply if the interest comes to an end otherwise than on of the death of the life tenant during the settlor's life and on the same occasion the property in which the interest subsisted reverts to the settlor (s 53(3)).

Section 53(4) provides that inheritance tax is not payable if on the occasion when the interest comes to an end the settlor's spouse or, where the settlor has died less than two years earlier, the settlor's widow or widower becomes beneficially entitled to the settled property and is domiciled in the UK. This exemption will not apply if the settlor or his spouse had acquired the reversionary interest for a consideration in money or money's worth (s 53(5)(a) ITA 1984).

Section 54 has a similar provision which deals with the situation where a person is entitled to an interest in possession in settled property which on his death, but during the settlor's life, reverts to the settlor.

(c) The spouse exemption – if the spouse of the life tenant succeeds to the property, the spouse exemption will apply. Section 18(1) of the ITA 1984 provides that a transfer of value is an exempt transfer to the extent that the value transferred is attributable to property which becomes comprised in the estate of the transferor's spouse, or, so far as the value transferred is not so attributable, to the extent that the estate is increased. Note that the spouse must be domiciled in the UK.

(d) Gifts of excluded property. No inheritance tax is payable in respect of gifts of excluded property. Excluded property comprises the following:

(i) property situated outside the UK if the person beneficially entitled to it is an individual domiciled outside the UK (s 6(1));

(ii) a reversionary interest unless:

— it has at any time been acquired (whether by the person entitled to it or by a person previously entitled to it) for a consideration in money or money's worth; or

— it is one to which the settlor or his spouse is or has been beneficially entitled (s 48(1));

(iii) section 48(3) of the ITA 1984 provides that where property comprised in a settlement is situated outside the UK:

- the property (but not a reversionary interest in the property) is excluded property unless the settlor was domiciled in the UK at the time when the settlement was made; and
- s 6(1) applies to a reversionary interest in the property, but does not otherwise apply in relation to that property.

Thus normally there is no charge to inheritance tax on any transfers of reversionary interests. The life tenant is deemed to own the underlying assets for inheritance tax purposes, and therefore it would be wrong to charge dealings with reversionary interests.

(e) Charities. Gifts to charities are exempt.

(f) Variations and disclaimers. It is only settlements created on death which can be varied. Settlements in which the deceased had been a beneficiary cannot be varied. Disclaimers apply to both.

(g) Business property relief and agricultural property relief.

Property qualifying for 100% relief can be transferred to a settlement without incurring any charge to inheritance tax. However, in order to claim the relief on death within seven years of a lifetime transfer, the trustees must still own the property or replacement property, and the trustees will have to satisfy the qualifying conditions themselves before they can claim the reliefs.

What happens if the taxpayer is the life tenant under a settlement and uses the settled property in his business? For inheritance tax purposes, a life tenant is deemed to be beneficially entitled to the property in which the life interest subsists. In *Fetherstonaugh v IRC [1984] STC 261, CA* a life tenant used 1,845 acres of settled property for his farming business. It was held that the settled property was 'property consisting of a business or an interest in a business'.

Section 105(1)(e) provides that any land or building, machinery or plant, which, immediately before the transfer, was used wholly or mainly for the purposes of a business carried on by the transferor and was settled property in which he was then beneficially entitled to an interest in possession qualifies for business property relief at 50%.

What is the relationship between the Fetherstonaugh decision and s 105(1)(e)? It seems that where the settled property and the rest of the life tenant's business are transferred together at the same time, 100% business property relief is available. Thus if the life tenant of a settlement comprising a factory carries on business there as a sole trader, 100% relief will be available if the business and factory are transferred together. However, if the factory is transferred separately, only 50% relief will be available. On the other hand, if the life tenant dies owning the business, 100% relief will apply to both the factory and the business.

The Revenue take the view that the person with the interest in possession is the owner of the property for the purposes of claiming agricultural property relief. Thus if the life tenant farms the settled property for at least two years before death, 100% agricultural property relief will be available on his death. 100% relief is still available if the property is tenanted, and the tenancy was granted after 1 September 1995. On the other hand, if the tenancy was granted before 1 September 1995, only 50% agricultural property relief will be available if there is no right to obtain vacant possession within twenty-four months. In addition, the life tenant must have been entitled to the property for seven years.

For more information, readers are referred to Butterworth's *Inheritance Tax*, para E2.71 *et seq*.

(h) Section 90 of the ITA 1984 provides that where under the terms of a settlement a person is entitled by way of remuneration for his services as trustee to an interest in possession in property comprised in the settlement, then except to the extent that the interest in possession represents more than a reasonable amount of remuneration;

   (i) the interest shall be left out of account in determining for the purpose of the ITA 1984 the value of his estate immediately before his death; and

   (ii) tax shall not be charged under s 52 when the interest comes to an end.

(j) Section 146(6) of the ITA 1984 provides that anything which is done in compliance with an order under the Inheritance (Provision for Family and Dependants) Act 1975 or occurs on the coming into force of such an order, and which would (apart from this subsection) constitute an occasion on which tax is chargeable under any provision, other than s 79, shall not constitute such an occasion; and where an order under the 1975 Act provides for property to be settled or for the variation of a settlement, and (apart from this subsection) tax would be charged under s 52(1) on the coming into force of the order, s 52(1) shall not apply.

Capital gains tax

The creation of the settlement

17.5 If a settlement is created by will or arises on an intestacy, then the normal rule applies – no capital gains tax is payable on death. The personal representatives will be deemed to acquire the assets at market value as at the date of death, and when they become trustees, they will be deemed to acquire the trust assets at market value as at the date of death.

Death of the life tenant

17.6 There is a deemed disposal and reacquisition by the trustees on the death of a life tenant, but no chargeable gain or allowable loss accrues (s 72(1) TCGA 1992). If more than one beneficiary is entitled to the settled property, there will be a deemed disposal and reacquisition of the appropriate part of the fund.

Section 73(1)(b) of the TCGA 1992 provides that if on the death of the life tenant, the property reverts to the settlor, the deemed disposal and reacquisition are to be for such consideration as to secure that neither gain nor loss accrues to the trustees. The settlor thus takes over the acquisition costs and subsequent expenditure of the trustees.

If hold-over relief has been claimed in respect of settled property, any held over gain becomes chargeable on the death of the life tenant, but not any gain accruing since the date of the settlement (s 74 Taxation of Chargeable Gains Act 1992).

Section 38(4) provides that any provision introducing the assumption that assets are sold and immediately reacquired shall not imply that any expenditure is incurred as incidental to the sale or reacquisition.

Termination of a life interest on death when the settlement continues

17.7 Where a life interest terminates on death and settlement continues there is a deemed disposal and reacquisition by the trustees, but no chargeable gain accrues. Section 72(3) and (4) of the TCGA 1992 defines what is meant by a life interest; it can include property out of which the trustees are paying an annuity. Any held-over gain will be chargeable.

Taxation of settlements without an interest in possession

Inheritance tax

Inheritance tax on the creation of the trust

17.8 If the settlement is created by will, the settled assets will be part of the testator's estate, and will be subject to inheritance tax in accordance with the normal principles; these are discussed in CHAPTER 13.

The ten-yearly charge

17.9 Section 64 of the ITA 1984 imposes a charge on relevant property, which is defined by s 58(1) as settled property in which no qualifying interest in possession subsists. The value charged is the value of the relevant property comprised in the settlement, less agricultural property relief and business property relief.

The settlement has its own cumulative total, which is defined in s 66(5) as the aggregate of:

(a) the values transferred by any chargeable transfers made by the settlor in the period of seven years ending with the day on which the settlement commenced; and

(b) the amounts on which any charges to tax were imposed under s 65 in respect of the settlement in the ten years before the anniversary concerned.

Section 65 imposes a charge to inheritance tax *inter alia* when property leaves a settlement. This is examined in more detail in the next section.

The rate of tax is 30% of the rate which would be charged on a lifetime chargeable transfer (6%).

Exit charges

17.10 These arise in two situations:

(a) where property comprised in a settlement ceases to be relevant property; and

(b) if (a) does not apply, where the trustees of the settlement make a disposition as a result of which the value of relevant property comprised in the settlement is less than it would be but for the disposition (s 65(1) ITA 1984).

A termination of the settlement, or the distribution of some of the property to the beneficiaries, both fall within (a).

When (a) does not apply, (b) will catch any disposition by the trustees of the settlement which reduces the value of the relevant property comprised in the settlement.

Section 65(4) of the ITA 1984 provides that there is no charge if the event in question occurs within a quarter, beginning with the day on which the settlement commenced or with a ten-year anniversary. Thus there will be no charge if the event giving rise to the charge occurs within three months of the establishment of the settlement, or an anniversary charge.

Section 65(5) provides that tax will not be charged in respect of a payment of costs and expenses so far as fairly attributable to relevant property. Neither is tax payable if the payment is income of any person for the purposes of income tax.

The amount chargeable is the amount by which the value of the relevant property in the settlement is less immediately after the event in question than it would be but for the event (s 65(2)(a)).

The rate of tax is a proportion of the rate charged on the last ten-year anniversary. The proportion is so many fortieths as there are complete successive quarters in the period beginning with the most recent anniversary and ending with the day before the occasion of the charge (s 69(4)). Thus, if four years have elapsed since the last ten-yearly charge, the rate of tax will be 16/40 of the rate charged on the last ten-year anniversary, sixteen quarters having elapsed since the last ten-yearly charge.

Special rules apply to the calculation of the exit charge before the tenth anniversary.

Capital gains tax

17.11 The rules applicable to trusts with an interest in possession apply to trusts without an interest in possession. However, hold-over relief may apply to all assets. It is not limited to business assets.

Appendices

Contents

Appendix 1

Non-Contentious Probate Rules 1987

Arrangement of sections

30. Grants where deceased died domiciled outside England and Wales

31. Grants to attorneys

32. Grants on behalf of minors

33. Grants where a minor is co-executor

34. Renunciation of the right of a minor to a grant

35. Grants in case of mental capacity

36. Grants to trust corporations and other corporate bodies

37. Renunciation of probate and administration

38. Notice to Crown of intended application for grant

39. Resealing under Colonial Probates Acts 1892 and 1927

40. Application for leave to sue on guarantee

41. Amendment and revocation of grant

42. Certificate of delivery of Inland Revenue affidavit

43. Standing searches

44. Caveats

45. Probate actions

46. Citations

47. Citation to accept or refuse to take a grant

48. Citation to propound a will

49. Address for service

50. Application for order to attend for examination or for a subpoena to bring in a will

51. Grants to part of an estate under s 113 of the Act

52. Grants of administration under discretionary powers of court, and grants ad collingenda bona

53. Applications for leave to swear death

54. Grants in respect of nuncupative wills and copies of wills

55. Application for rectification of a will

56. Notice of election by surviving spouse to redeem life interest

57. Index of grant applications

58. Inspection of copies of original wills and other documents

59. Issue of copies of original wills

60. Taxation of costs

61. Power to require applications to be made by summons

62. Transfer of applications

62A. Exercise of a Registrar's jurisdiction by another Registrar

63. Power to make orders for costs

64. Exercise of powers of judge during Long Vacation

65. Appeals from District Judges or Registrars

66. Service of summons

67. Notices, etc

Schedules

1987 No 2024

Non-Contentious Probate Rules 1987

1 Citation and commencement

These Rules may be cited as the Non-Contentious Probate Rules 1987 and shall come into force on 1st January 1988.

2 Interpretation

(1) In these Rules, unless the context otherwise requires—

"the Act" means the Supreme Court Act 1981;

"authorised officer" means any officer of a registry who is for the time being authorised by the President to administer any oath or to take any affidavit required for any purpose connected with his duties;

"the Crown" includes the Crown in right of the Duchy of Lancaster and the Duke of Cornwall for the time being;

["district judge" means a district judge of the Principal Registry;]

"grant" means a grant of probate or administration and includes, where the context so admits, the resealing of such a grant under the Colonial Probates Acts 1892 and 1927;

"gross value" in relation to any estate means the value of the estate without deduction for debts, incumbrances, funeral expenses or inheritance tax (or other capital tax payable out of the estate);

["judge" means a judge of the High Court;]

"oath" means the oath required by rule 8 to be sworn by every applicant for a grant;

"personal applicant" means a person other than a trust corporation who seeks to obtain a grant without employing a solicitor [or probate practitioner], and "personal application" has a corresponding meaning;

["probate practitioner" means a person to whom section 23(1) of the Solicitors Act 1974 does not apply by virtue of section 23(2) of that Act] ["registrar" means the district probate registrar of the district probate registry—

(i) to which an application for a grant is made or is proposed to be made,

(ii) in rules 26,40,41 and 61(2), from which the grant issued, and

(iii) in rules 46,47 and 48, from which the citation has issued or is proposed to be issued;]

"registry" means the Principal Registry or a district probate registry;

["the senior district judge" means the Senior District Judge of the Family Division or, in his absence, the senior of the district judges in attendance at the Principal Registry;]

< ... >

< ... >

"the Treasury Solicitor" means the solicitor for the affairs of Her Majesty's Treasury and includes the solicitor for the affairs of the Duchy of Lancaster and the solicitor of the Duchy of Cornwall;

"trust corporation" means a corporation within the meaning of section 128 of the Act as extended by section 3 of the Law of Property (Amendment) Act 1926.

(2) A form referred to by number means the form so numbered in the First Schedule; and such forms shall be used wherever applicable, with such variation as a [district judge or] registrar may in any particular case direct or approve.

NOTES

Amendment

Para (1): definition "district judge" inserted by SI 1991/1876, r 6(a).

Para (1): definition "judge" inserted by SI 1991/1876, r 6(b).

Para (1): in definition "personal applicant" words "or probate practitioner" in square brackets inserted by SI 1998/1903, r 3(a).

Date in force: 14 September 1998: see SI 1998/1903, r 1(1).

Para (1): definition "probate practitioner" inserted by SI 1998/1903, r 3(b).

Date in force: 14 September 1998: see SI 1998/1903, r 1(1).

Para (1): definition "registrar" substituted by SI 1991/1876, r 6(c).

Para (1): definition "the senior district judge" substituted, for definition "the Senior Registrar" as originally enacted, by SI 1991/1876, r 6(d).

Para (1): definition "statutory guardian" omitted revoked by SI 1991/1876, r 2.

Para (1): definition "testamentary guardian" omitted revoked by SI 1991/1876, r 2.

Para (2): words in square brackets substituted by SI 1991/1876, r 7(1).

Modification

References to solicitors etc modified to include references to bodies recognised under the Administration of Justice Act 1985, s 9, by the Solicitors' Incorporated Practices Order 1991, SI 1991/2684, arts 4, 5, Sch 1.

[3 Application of other rules]

[(1) Subject to the provisions of these rules and to any enactment, the Rules of the Supreme Court 1965 as they were in force immediately before 26th April 1999 shall apply, with any necessary modifications to non-contentious probate matters, and any reference in these rules to those rules shall be construed accordingly.

(2) Nothing in Order 3 of the Rules of the Supreme Court shall prevent time from running in the Long Vacation.]

NOTES

Amendment

Substituted by SI 1999/1015, r 2.

Date in force: 26 April 1999: see SI 1999/1015, r 1.

4 Applications for grants through solicitors [or probate practitioners]

(1) A person applying for a grant through a solicitor [or probate practitioner] may apply at any registry or sub-registry.

(2) Every solicitor [or probate practitioner] through whom an application for a grant is made shall give the address of his place of business within England and Wales.

NOTES

Amendment

Provision heading: words "or probate practitioners" in square brackets inserted by SI 1998/1903, r 4(a).

Date in force: 14 September 1998: see SI 1998/1903, r 1(1).

Para (1): words "or probate practitioner" in square brackets inserted by SI 1998/1903, r 4(b).

Date in force: 14 September 1998: see SI 1998/1903, r 1(1).

Para (2): words "or probate practitioner" in square brackets inserted by SI 1998/1903, r 4(b).

Date in force: 14 September 1998: see SI 1998/1903, r 1(1).

Modification

References to solicitors etc modified to include references to bodies recognised under the Administration of Justice Act 1985, s 9, by the Solicitors' Incorporated Practices Order 1991, SI 1991/2684, arts 4, 5, Sch 1.

5 Personal applications

(1) A personal applicant may apply for a grant at any registry or sub-registry.

(2) Save as provided for by rule 39 a personal applicant may not apply through an agent, whether paid or unpaid, and may not be attended by any person acting or appearing to act as his adviser.

(3) No personal application shall be proceeded with if—

- (a) it becomes necessary to bring the matter before the court by action or summons[, unless a judge, district judge or registrar so permits];
- (b) an application has already been made by a solicitor [or probate practitioner] on behalf of the applicant and has not been withdrawn; or
- (c) the [district judge or] registrar so directs.

(4) After a will has been deposited in a registry by a personal applicant, it may not be delivered to the applicant or to any other person unless in special circumstances the [district judge or] registrar so directs.

(5) A personal applicant shall produce a certificate of the death of the deceased or such other evidence of the death as the [district judge or] registrar may approve.

(6) A personal applicant shall supply all information necessary to enable the papers leading to the grant to be prepared in the registry.

(7) Unless the [district judge or] registrar otherwise directs, every oath or affidavit required on a personal application shall be sworn or executed by all the deponents before an authorised officer.

(8) No legal advice shall be given to a personal applicant by an officer of a registry and every such officer shall be responsible only for embodying in proper form the applicant's instructions for the grant.

NOTES

Amendment

Para (3): in sub-para (a) words ", unless a judge, district judge or registrar so permits" in square brackets inserted by SI 1998/1903, r 5.

Date in force: 14 September 1998: see SI 1998/1903, r 1(1).

Para (3): in sub-para (b) words "or probate practitioner" in square brackets inserted by SI 1998/1903, r 6.

Date in force: 14 September 1998: see SI 1998/1903, r 1(1).

Para (3): in sub-para (c) words "district judge or" in square brackets inserted by SI 1991/1876, r 7(1).

Para (4): words "district judge or" in square brackets inserted by SI 1991/1876, r 7(1).

Para (5): words "district judge or" in square brackets inserted by SI 1991/1876, r 7(1).

Para (7): words "district judge or" in square brackets inserted by SI 1991/1876, r 7(1).

Modification

References to solicitors etc modified to include references to bodies recognised under the Administration of Justice Act 1985, s 9, by the Solicitors' Incorporated Practices Order 1991, SI 1991/2684, arts 4, 5, Sch 1.

6 Duty of [district judge or] registrar on receiving application for grant

(1) A [district judge or] registrar shall not allow any grant to issue until all inquiries which he may see fit to make have been answered to his satisfaction.

(2) Except with the leave of a [district judge or] registrar, no grant of probate or of administration with the will annexed shall issue within seven days of the death of the deceased and no grant of administration shall issue within fourteen days thereof.

NOTES

Amendment

Provision heading: words in square brackets inserted by SI 1991/1876, r 7(1).

Paras (1), (2): words in square brackets inserted by SI 1991/1876, r 7(1).

7 Grants by district probate registrars

(1) No grant shall be made by a … registrar—

(a) in any case in which there is contention, until the contention is disposed of; or

(b) in any case in which it appears to him that a grant ought not to be made without the directions of a judge or a [district judge].

(2) In any case in which paragraph (1)(b) applies, the … registrar shall send a statement of the matter in question to the Principal Registry for directions.

(3) A [district judge] may either confirm that the matter be referred to a judge and give directions accordingly or may direct the … registrar to proceed with

the matter in accordance with such instructions as are deemed necessary, which may include a direction to take no further action in relation to the matter.

NOTES

Amendment

Paras (1), (3): words omitted revoked, and words in square brackets substituted, by SI 1991/1876, r 7(2), (3).

Para (2): words omitted revoked by SI 1991/1876, r 7(2).

8 Oath in support of grant

(1) Every application for a grant other than one to which rule 39 applies shall be supported by an oath by the applicant in the form applicable to the circumstances of the case, and by such other papers as the [district judge or] registrar may require.

(2) Unless otherwise directed by a [district judge or] registrar, the oath shall state where the deceased died domiciled.

(3) Where the deceased died on or after 1st January 1926, the oath shall state whether or not, to the best of the applicant's knowledge, information and belief, there was land vested in the deceased which was settled previously to his death and not by his will and which remained settled land notwithstanding his death.

(4) On an application for a grant of administration the oath shall state in what manner all persons having a prior right to a grant have been cleared off and whether any minority or life interest arises under the will or intestacy.

NOTES

Amendment

Paras (1), (2): words in square brackets inserted by SI 1991/1876, r 7(1).

9 Grant in additional name

Where it is sought to describe the deceased in a grant by some name in addition to his true name, the applicant shall depose to the true name of the deceased and shall specify some part of the estate which was held in the other name, or give any other reason for the inclusion of the other name in the grant.

10 Marking of wills

(1) Subject to paragraph (2) below, every will in respect of which an application for a grant is made—

(a) shall be marked by the signatures of the applicant and the person before whom the oath is sworn; and

(b) shall be exhibited to any affidavit which may be required under these Rules as to the validity, terms, condition or date of execution of the will.

(2) The [district judge or] registrar may allow a facsimile copy of a will to be marked or exhibited in lieu of the original document.

NOTES

Amendment

Para (2): words in square brackets inserted by SI 1991/1876, r 7(1).

11 Engrossments for purposes of record

(1) Where the [district judge or] registrar considers that in any particular case a facsimile copy of the original will would not be satisfactory for purposes of record, he may require an engrossment suitable for facsimile reproduction to be lodged.

(2) Where a will—

(a) contains alterations which are not to be admitted to proof; or

(b) has been ordered to be rectified by virtue of section 20(1) of the Administration of Justice Act 1982,

there shall be lodged an engrossment of the will in the form in which it is to be proved.

(3) Any engrossment lodged under this rule shall reproduce the punctuation, spacing and division into paragraphs of the will and shall follow continuously from page to page on both sides of the paper.

NOTES

Amendment

Para (1): words in square brackets inserted by SI 1991/1876, r 7(1).

12 Evidence as to due execution of will

(1) Subject to paragraphs (2) and (3) below, where a will contains no attestation clause or the attestation clause is insufficient, or where it appears to the [district judge or] registrar that there is doubt about the due execution of the will, he shall before admitting it to proof require an affidavit as to due execution from one or more of the attesting witnesses or, if no attesting witness is conveniently available, from any other person who was present when the will was executed; and if the [district judge or] registrar, after

considering the evidence, is satisfied the will was not duly executed, he shall refuse probate and mark the will accordingly.

(2) If no affidavit can be obtained in accordance with paragraph (1) above, the [district judge or] registrar may accept evidence on affidavit from any person he may think fit to show that the signature on the will is in the handwriting of the deceased, or of any other matter which may raise a presumption in favour of due execution of the will, and may if he thinks fit require that notice of the application be given to any person who may be prejudiced by the will.

(3) A [district judge or] registrar may accept a will for proof without evidence as aforesaid if he is satisfied that the distribution of the estate is not thereby affected.

NOTES

Amendment

Para (3): words in square brackets inserted by SI 1991/1876, r 7(1).

13 Execution of will of blind or illiterate testator

Before admitting to proof a will which appears to have been signed by a blind or illiterate testator or by another person by direction of the testator, or which for any other reason raises doubt as to the testator having had knowledge of the contents of the will at the time of its execution, the [district judge or] registrar shall satisfy himself that the testator had such knowledge.

NOTES

Amendment

Words in square brackets inserted by SI 1991/1876, r 7(1).

14 Evidence as to terms, condition and date of execution of will

(1) Subject to paragraph (2) below, where there appears in a will any obliteration, interlineation, or other alteration which is not authenticated in the manner prescribed by section 21 of the Wills Act 1837, or by the re-execution of the will or by the execution of a codicil, the [district judge or] registrar shall require evidence to show whether the alteration was present at the time the will was executed and shall give directions as to the form in which the will is to be proved.

(2) The provisions of paragraph (1) above shall not apply to any alteration which appears to the [district judge or] registrar to be of no practical importance.

(3) If a will contains any reference to another document in such terms as to suggest that it ought to be incorporated in the will, the [district judge or] registrar shall require the document to be produced and may call for such evidence in regard to the incorporation of the document as he may think fit.

(4) Where there is a doubt as to the date on which a will was executed, the [district judge or] registrar may require such evidence as he thinks necessary to establish the date.

NOTES

Amendment

Paras (1), (4): words in square brackets inserted by SI 1991/1876, r 7(1).

15 Attempted revocation of will

Any appearance of attempted revocation of a will by burning, tearing, or otherwise destroying and every other circumstance leading to a presumption of revocation by the testator, shall be accounted for to the [district judge's or] registrar's satisfaction.

NOTES

Amendment

Words in square brackets inserted by SI 1991/1876, r 7(5).

16 Affidavit as to due execution, terms etc, of will

A [district judge or] registrar may require an affidavit from any person he may think fit for the purpose of satisfying himself as to any of the matters referred to in rules 13, 14 and 15, and in any such affidavit sworn by an attesting witness or other person present at the time of the execution of a will the deponent shall depose to the manner in which the will was executed.

NOTES

Amendment

Words in square brackets inserted by SI 1991/1876, r 7(1).

17 Wills proved otherwise than under section 9 of the Wills Act 1837

(1) Rules 12 to 15 shall apply only to a will that is to be established by reference to section 9 of the Wills Act 1837 (signing and attestation of wills).

(2) A will that is to be established otherwise than as described in paragraph (1) of this rule may be so established upon the [district judge or]

registrar being satisfied as to its terms and validity, and includes (without prejudice to the generality of the foregoing)—

(a) any will to which rule 18 applies; and

(b) any will which, by virtue of the Wills Act 1963, is to be treated as properly executed if executed according to the internal law of the territory or state referred to in section 1 of that Act.

NOTES

Amendment

Para (2): words in square brackets inserted by SI 1991/1876, r 7(1).

18 Wills of persons on military service and seamen

Where the deceased died domiciled in England and Wales and it appears to the [district judge or] registrar that there is prima facie evidence that a will is one to which section 11 of the Wills Act 1837 applies, the will may be admitted to proof if the registrar is satisfied that it was signed by the testator or, if unsigned, that it is in the testator's handwriting.

NOTES

Amendment

Words in square brackets inserted by SI 1991/1876, r 7(1).

19 Evidence of foreign law

Where evidence as to the law of any country or territory outside England and Wales is required on any application for a grant, the [district judge or] registrar may accept—

(a) an affidavit from any person whom, having regard to the particulars of his knowledge or experience given in the affidavit, he regards as suitably qualified to give expert evidence of the law in question; or

(b) a certificate by, or an act before, a notary practising in the country or territory concerned.

NOTES

Amendment

Words in square brackets inserted by SI 1991/1876, r 7(1).

20 Order of priority for grant where deceased left a will

Where the deceased died on or after 1 January 1926 the person or persons entitled to a grant in respect of a will shall be determined in accordance with the following order of priority, namely—

(a) the executor (but subject to rule 36(4)(d) below);

(b) any residuary legatee or devisee holding in trust for any other person;

(c) any other residuary legatee or devisee (including one for life) or where the residue is not wholly disposed of by the will, any person entitled to share in the undisposed of residue (including the Treasury Solicitor when claiming bona vacantia on behalf of the Crown), provided that—

(i) unless a [district judge or] registrar otherwise directs, a residuary legatee or devisee whose legacy or devise is vested in interest shall be preferred to one entitled on the happening of a contingency, and

(ii) where the residue is not in terms wholly disposed of, the [district judge or] registrar may, if he is satisfied that the testator has nevertheless disposed of the whole or substantially the whole of the known estate, allow a grant to be made to any legatee or devisee entitled to, or to share in, the estate so disposed of, without regard to the persons entitled to share in any residue not disposed of by the will;

(d) the personal representative of any residuary legatee or devisee (but not one for life, or one holding in trust for any other person), or of any person entitled to share in any residue not disposed of by the will;

(e) any other legatee or devisee (including one for life or one holding in trust for any other person) or any creditor of the deceased, provided that, unless a [district judge or] registrar otherwise directs, a legatee or devisee whose legacy or devise is vested in interest shall be preferred to one entitled on the happening of a contingency;

(f) the personal representative of any other legatee or devisee (but not one for life or one holding in trust for any other person) or of any creditor of the deceased.

NOTES

Amendment

Paras (c), (e): words in square brackets inserted by SI 1991/1876, r 7(1).

21 Grants to attesting witnesses, etc

Where a gift to any person fails by reason of section 15 of the Wills Act 1837, such person shall not have any right to a grant as a beneficiary named in the will, without prejudice to his right to a grant in any other capacity.

22 Order of priority for grant in case of intestacy

(1) Where the deceased died on or after 1 January 1926, wholly intestate, the person or persons having a beneficial interest in the estate shall be entitled to a grant of administration in the following classes in order of priority, namely—

(a) the surviving husband or wife;

(b) the children of the deceased and the issue of any deceased child who died before the deceased;

(c) the father and mother of the deceased;

(d) brothers and sisters of the whole blood and the issue of any deceased brother or sister of the whole blood who died before the deceased;

(e) brothers and sisters of the half blood and the issue of any deceased brother or sister of the half blood who died before the deceased;

(f) grandparents;

(g) uncles and aunts of the whole blood and the issue of any deceased uncle or aunt of the whole blood who died before the deceased;

(h) uncles and aunts of the half blood and the issue of any deceased uncle or aunt of the half blood who died before the deceased.

(2) In default of any person having a beneficial interest in the estate, the Treasury Solicitor shall be entitled to a grant if he claims bona vacantia on behalf of the Crown.

(3) If all persons entitled to a grant under the foregoing provisions of this rule have been cleared off, a grant may be made to a creditor of the deceased or to any person who, notwithstanding that he has no immediate beneficial interest in the estate, may have a beneficial interest in the event of an accretion thereto.

(4) Subject to paragraph (5) of rule 27, the personal representative of a person in any of the classes mentioned in paragraph (1) of this rule or the personal representative of a creditor of the deceased shall have the same right to a grant as the person whom he represents provided that the persons mentioned in sub-paragraphs (b) to (h) of paragraph (1) above shall be preferred to the personal representative of a spouse who has died without

taking a beneficial interest in the whole estate of the deceased as ascertained at the time of the application for the grant.

23 Order of priority for grant in pre-1926 cases

Where the deceased died before 1st January 1926, the person or persons entitled to a grant shall, subject to the provisions of any enactment, be determined in accordance with the principles and rules under which the court would have acted at the date of death.

24 Right of assignee to a grant

(1) Where all the persons entitled to the estate of the deceased (whether under a will or on intestacy) have assigned their whole interest in the estate to one or more persons, the assignee or assignees shall replace, in the order of priority for a grant of administration, the assignor or, if there are two or more assignors, the assignor with the highest priority.

(2) Where there are two or more assignees, administration may be granted with the consent of the others to any one or more (not exceeding four) of them.

(3) In any case where administration is applied for by an assignee the original instrument of assignment shall be produced and a copy of the same lodged in the registry.

25 Joinder of administrator

(1) A person entitled in priority to a grant of administration may, without leave, apply for a grant with a person entitled in a lower degree, provided that there is no other person entitled in a higher degree to the person to be joined, unless every other such person has renounced.

(2) Subject to paragraph (3) below, an application for leave to join with a person entitled in priority to a grant of administration a person having no right or no immediate right thereto shall be made to a [district judge or] registrar, and shall be supported by an affidavit by the person entitled in priority, the consent of the person proposed to be joined as administrator and such other evidence as the [district judge or] registrar may direct.

(3) Unless a [district judge or] registrar otherwise directs, there may without any such application be joined with a person entitled in priority to administration—

- (a) any person who is nominated under paragraph (3) of rule 32 or paragraph (3) of rule 35;
- (b) a trust corporation.

NOTES

Amendment

Paras (2), (3): words in square brackets inserted by SI 1991/1876, r 7(1).

26 Additional personal representatives

(1) An application under section 114(4) of the Act to add a personal representative shall be made to a [district judge or] registrar and shall be supported by an affidavit by the applicant, the consent of the person proposed to be added as personal representative and such other evidence as the [district judge or] registrar may require.

(2) On any such application the [district judge or] registrar may direct that a note shall be made on the original grant of the addition of a further personal representative, or he may impound or revoke the grant or make such other order as the circumstances of the case may require.

NOTES

Amendment

Words in square brackets inserted by SI 1991/1876, r 7(1).

27 Grants where two or more persons entitled in same degree

[(1) Subject to paragraphs (1A), (2) and (3) below, where, on an application for probate, power to apply for a like grant is to be reserved to such other of the executors as have not renounced probate, notice of the application shall be given to the executor or executors to whom power is to be reserved; and, unless the district judge or registrar otherwise directs, the oath shall state that such notice has been given.

(1A) Where power is to be reserved to executors who are … partners in a firm, … notice need not be given to them under paragraph (1) above if probate is applied for by another partner in that firm.]

(2) Where power is to be reserved to partners of a firm, notice for the purposes of paragraph (1) above may be given to the partners by sending it to the firm at its principal or last known place of business.

(3) A [district judge or] registrar may dispense with the giving of notice under paragraph (1) above if he is satisfied that the giving of such a notice is impracticable or would result in unreasonable delay or expense.

(4) A grant of administration may be made to any person entitled thereto without notice to other persons entitled in the same degree.

(5) Unless a [district judge or] registrar otherwise directs, administration shall be granted to a person of full age entitled thereto in preference to a

guardian of a minor, and to a living person entitled thereto in preference to the personal representative of a deceased person.

(6) A dispute between persons entitled to a grant in the same degree shall be brought by summons before a [district judge or] registrar.

[(7) The issue of a summons under this rule in a registry shall be noted forthwith in the index of pending grant applications.]

(8) If the issue of a summons under this rule is known to the [district judge or] registrar, he shall not allow any grant to be sealed until such summons is finally disposed of.

NOTES

Amendment

Paras (1), (1A): substituted for original para (1) by SI 1991/1876, r 8(1).

Para (1A): words omitted revoked by SI 1998/1903, r 7(1).

Date in force: 14 September 1998: see SI 1998/1903, r 1(1).

Paras (3), (5), (6), (8): words in square brackets inserted by SI 1991/1876, r 7(1).

Para (7): substituted by SI 1998/1903, r 7(2).

Date in force: 14 September 1998: see SI 1998/1903, r 1(1).

28 Exceptions to rules as to priority

(1) Any person to whom a grant may or is required to be made under any enactment shall not be prevented from obtaining such a grant notwithstanding the operation of rules 20, 22, 25 or 27.

(2) Where the deceased died domiciled outside England and Wales rules 20, 22, 25 or 27 shall not apply except in a case to which paragraph (3) of rule 30 applies.

[29 Grants in respect of settled land]

[(1) In this rule "settled land" means land vested in the deceased which was settled prior to his death and not by his will, and which remained settled land notwithstanding his death.

(2) The person or persons entitled to a grant of administration limited to settled land shall be determined in accordance with the following order of priority:

(i) the special executors in regard to settled land constituted by section 22 of the Administration of Estates Act 1925;

(ii) the trustees of the settlement at the time of the application for the grant; and

(iii) the personal representatives of the deceased.

(3) Where there is settled land and a grant is made in respect of the free estate only, the grant shall expressly exclude the settled land.]

NOTES

Amendment

Substituted by SI 1991/1876, r 9.

30 Grants where deceased died domiciled outside England and Wales

(1) Subject to paragraph (3) below, where the deceased died domiciled outside England and Wales, [a district judge or registrar may order that a grant, limited in such way as the district judge or registrar may direct,] do issue to any of the following persons—

(a) to the person entrusted with the administration of the estate by the court having jurisdiction at the place where the deceased died domiciled; or

(b) where there is no person so entrusted, to the person beneficially entitled to the estate by the law of the place where the deceased died domiciled or, if there is more than one person so entitled, to such of them as the [district judge or] registrar may direct; or

(c) if in the opinion of the [district judge or] registrar the circumstances so require, to such person as the [district judge or] registrar may direct.

(2) A grant made under paragraph (1)(a) or (b) above may be issued jointly with such person as the [district judge or] registrar may direct if the grant is required to be made to not less than two administrators.

(3) Without any order made under paragraph (1) above—

(a) probate of any will which is admissible to proof may be granted—

(i) if the will is in the English or Welsh language, to the executor named therein; or

(ii) if the will describes the duties of a named person in terms sufficient to constitute him executor according to the tenor of the will, to that person; or

(b) where the whole or substantially the whole of the estate in England and Wales consists of immovable property, a grant in respect of the whole estate may be made in accordance with the law which would have been applicable if the deceased had died domiciled in England and Wales.

NOTES

Amendment

Para (*1*)*: first words in square brackets substituted and other words in square brackets inserted by SI 1991/1876, rr 7*(*1*)*, 10.*

Para (2)*: words in square brackets inserted by SI 1991/1876, r 7*(*1*)*.*

31 Grants to attorneys

(1) Subject to paragraphs (2) and (3) below, the lawfully constituted attorney of a person entitled to a grant may apply for administration for the use and benefit of the donor, and such grant shall be limited until further representation be granted, or in such other way as the [district judge or] registrar may direct.

(2) Where the donor referred to in paragraph (1) above is an executor, notice of the application shall be given to any other executor unless such notice is dispensed with by the [district judge or] registrar.

(3) Where the donor referred to in paragraph (1) above is mentally incapable and the attorney is acting under an enduring power of attorney, the application shall be made in accordance with rule 35.

NOTES

Amendment

Paras (*1*), (*2*)*: words in square brackets inserted by SI 1991/1876, r 7*(*1*)*.*

32 Grants on behalf of minors

(1) Where a person to whom a grant would otherwise be made is a minor, administration for his use and benefit, limited until he attains the age of eighteen years, shall, unless otherwise directed, and subject to paragraph (2) of this rule, be granted to

[(a) a parent of the minor who has, or is deemed to have, parental responsibility for him in accordance with—

(i) section 2(1), 2(2) or 4 of the Children Act 1989,

(ii) paragraph 4 or 6 of Schedule 14 to that Act, or

(iii) an adoption order within the meaning of section 12(1) of the Adoption Act 1976, or

[(aa) a person who has, or is deemed to have, parental responsibility for the minor by virtue of section 12(2) of the Children Act 1989(a) where the court has made a residence order under section 8 of that Act in respect of the minor in favour of that person; or]

(b) a guardian of the minor who is appointed, or deemed to have been appointed, in accordance with section 5 of the Children Act 1989 or in accordance with paragraph 12, 13 or 14 of Schedule 14 to that Act]; [or]

[(c) a local authority which has, or is deemed to have, parental responsibility for the minor by virtue of section 33(3) of the Children Act 1989 where the court has made a care order under section 31(1)(a) of that Act in respect of the minor and that local authority is designated in that order;]

provided that where the minor is sole executor and has no interest in the residuary estate of the deceased, administration for the use and benefit of the minor limited as aforesaid, shall, unless a [district judge or] registrar otherwise directs, be granted to the person entitled to the residuary estate.

[(2) A district judge or registrar may by order appoint a person to obtain administration for the use and benefit of the minor, limited as aforesaid, in default of, or jointly with, or to the exclusion of, any person mentioned in paragraph (1) of this rule; and the person intended shall file an affidavit in support of his application to be appointed.]

(3) Where there is only one person competent and willing to take a grant under the foregoing provisions of this rule, such person may, unless a [district judge or] registrar otherwise directs, nominate any fit and proper person to act jointly with him in taking the grant.

NOTES

Amendment

Para (1): sub-paras (a), (b) substituted by SI 1991/1876, r 3.

Para (1): sub-para (aa) inserted by SI 1998/1903, r 8(1).

Date in force: 14 September 1998: see SI 1998/1903, r 1(1).

Para (1): in sub-para (b) word "or" in square brackets inserted by SI 1998/1903, r 8(2).

Date in force: 14 September 1998: see SI 1998/1903, r 1(1).

Para (1): sub-para (c) inserted by SI 1998/1903, r 8(3).

Date in force: 14 September 1998: see SI 1998/1903, r 1(1).

Para (1): words "district judge or" in square brackets inserted by SI 1991/1876, r 7(1).

Para (2): substituted by SI 1991/1876, r 4.

Para (3): words in square brackets inserted by SI 1991/1876, r 7(1).

33 Grants where a minor is a co-executor

(1) Where a minor is appointed executor jointly with one or more other executors, probate may be granted to the executor or executors not under

disability with power reserved to the minor executor, and the minor executor shall be entitled to apply for probate on attaining the age of eighteen years.

(2) Administration for the use and benefit of a minor executor until he attains the age of eighteen years may be granted under rule 32 if, and only if, the executors who are not under disability renounce or, on being cited to accept or refuse a grant, fail to make an effective application therefor.

34 Renunciation of the right of a minor to a grant

(1) The right of a minor executor to probate on attaining the age of eighteen years may not be renounced by any person on his behalf.

(2) The right of a minor to administration may be renounced only by a person [appointed] under paragraph (2) of rule 32, and authorised by the [district judge or] registrar to renounce on behalf of the minor.

NOTES

Amendment

Para (2): first word in square brackets substituted and second words in square brackets inserted by SI 1991/1876, rr 5, 7(1).

35 Grants in case of mental incapacity

(1) Unless a [district judge or] registrar otherwise directs, no grant shall be made under this rule unless all persons entitled in the same degree as the incapable person referred to in paragraph (2) below have been cleared off.

(2) Where a [district judge or] registrar is satisfied that a person entitled to a grant is by reason of mental incapacity incapable of managing his affairs, administration for his use and benefit, limited until further representation be granted or in such other way as the [district judge or] registrar may direct, may be granted in the following order of priority—

(a) to the person authorised by the Court of Protection to apply for a grant;

(b) where there is no person so authorised, to the lawful attorney of the incapable person acting under a registered enduring power of attorney;

(c) where there is no such attorney entitled to act, or if the attorney shall renounce administration for the use and benefit of the incapable person, to the person entitled to the residuary estate of the deceased.

(3) Where a grant is required to be made to not less than two administrators, and there is only one person competent and willing to take a grant under the

foregoing provisions of this rule, administration may, unless a [district judge or] registrar otherwise directs, be granted to such person jointly with any other person nominated by him.

(4) Notwithstanding the foregoing provisions of this rule, administration for the use and benefit of the incapable person may be granted to such [other person] as the [district judge or] registrar may by order direct.

(5) [Unless the applicant is the person authorised in paragraph (2)(a) above,] Notice of an intended application under this rule shall be given to the Court of Protection.

NOTES

Amendment

Para (1): words "district judge or" in square brackets inserted by SI 1991/1876, r 7(1).

Para (2): words "district judge or" in square brackets in both places they occur inserted by SI 1991/1876, r 7(1).

Para (3): words "district judge or" in square brackets inserted by SI 1991/1876, r 7(1).

Para (4): words "other person" in square brackets substituted by SI 1998/1903, r 9(1).

Date in force: 14 September 1998: see SI 1998/1903, r 1(1).

Para (4): words "district judge or" in square brackets inserted by SI 1991/1876, r 7(1).

Para (5): words from "Unless" to "paragraph (2)(a) above," in square brackets inserted by SI 1998/1903, r 9(2).

Date in force: 14 September 1998: see SI 1998/1903, r 1(1).

36 Grants to trust corporations and other corporate bodies

(1) An application for a grant to a trust corporation shall be made through one of its officers, and such officer shall depose in the oath that the corporation is a trust corporation as defined by these Rules and that it has power to accept a grant.

(2)

(a) Where the trust corporation is the holder of an official position, any officer whose name is included on a list filed with the [senior district judge] of persons authorised to make affidavits and sign documents on behalf of the office holder may act as the officer through whom the holder of that official position applies for the grant.

(b) In all other cases a certified copy of the resolution of the trust corporation authorising the officer to make the application shall be lodged, or it shall be deposed in the oath that such certified copy has been filed with the [senior district judge], that the officer is therein identified by the position he holds, and that such resolution is still in force.

(3) A trust corporation may apply for administration otherwise than as a beneficiary or the attorney of some person, and on any such application there shall be lodged the consents of all persons entitled to a grant and of all persons interested in the residuary estate of the deceased save that the [district judge or] registrar may dispense with any such consents as aforesaid on such terms, if any, as he may think fit.

(4)

(a) Subject to sub-paragraph (d) below, where a corporate body would, if an individual, be entitled to a grant but is not a trust corporation as defined by these Rules, administration for its use and benefit, limited until further representation be granted, may be made to its nominee or to its lawfully constituted attorney.

(b) A copy of the resolution appointing the nominee or the power of attorney (whichever is appropriate) shall be lodged, and such resolution or power of attorney shall be sealed by the corporate body, or be otherwise authenticated to the [district judge's or] registrar's satisfaction.

(c) The nominee or attorney shall depose in the oath that the corporate body is not a trust corporation as defined by these Rules.

(d) The provisions of paragraph (4)(a) above shall not apply where a corporate body is appointed executor jointly with an individual unless the right of the individual has been cleared off.

NOTES

Amendment

Para (2): words in square brackets substituted by SI 1991/1876, r 7(4).

Paras (3), (4): words in square brackets inserted by SI 1991/1876, r 7(1), (5).

37 Renunciation of probate and administration

(1) Renunciation of probate by an executor shall not operate as renunciation of any right which he may have to a grant of administration in some other capacity unless he expressly renounces such right.

(2) Unless a [district judge or] registrar otherwise directs, no person who has renounced administration in one capacity may obtain a grant thereof in some other capacity.

[(2A) Renunciation of probate or administration by members of a partnership—

(a) may be effected, or

(b) subject to paragraph (3) below, may be retracted by any two of them with the authority of the others and any such renunciation or retraction shall recite such authority.]

(3) A renunciation of probate or administration may be retracted at any time with the leave of a [district judge or] registrar; provided that only in exceptional circumstances may leave be given to an executor to retract a renunciation of probate after a grant has been made to some other person entitled in a lower degree.

(4) A direction or order giving leave under this rule may be made either by the registrar of a district probate registry where the renunciation is filed or by a [district judge].

NOTES

Amendment

Paras (2), (3): words in square brackets inserted by SI 1991/1876, r 7(1).

Para (2A): inserted by SI 1998/1903, r 10.

Date in force: 14 September 1998: see SI 1998/1903, r 1(1).

Para (4): words in square brackets substituted by SI 1991/1876, r 7(3).

38 Notice to Crown of intended application for grant

In any case in which it appears that the Crown is or may be beneficially interested in the estate of a deceased person, notice of intended application for a grant shall be given by the applicant to the Treasury Solicitor, and the [district judge or] registrar may direct that no grant shall issue within 28 days after the notice has been given.

NOTES

Amendment

Words in square brackets inserted by SI 1991/1876, r 7(1).

39 Resealing under Colonial Probates Acts 1892 and 1927

(1) An application under the Colonial Probates Acts 1892 and 1927 for the resealing of probate or administration granted by the court of a country to which those Acts apply may be made by the person to whom the grant was made or by any person authorised in writing to apply on his behalf.

(2) On any such application an Inland Revenue affidavit or account shall be lodged.

(3) Except by leave of a [district judge or] registrar, no grant shall be resealed unless it was made to such a person as is mentioned in sub-paragraph (a) or (b) of paragraph (1) of rule 30 or to a person to whom a grant could be made under sub-paragraph (a) of paragraph (3) of that rule.

(4) No limited or temporary grant shall be resealed except by leave of a [district judge or] registrar.

(5) Every grant lodged for resealing shall include a copy of any will to which the grant relates or shall be accompanied by a copy thereof certified as correct by or under the authority of the court by which the grant was made, and where the copy of the grant required to be deposited under subsection (1) of section 2 of the Colonial Probates Act 1892 does not include a copy of the will, a copy thereof shall be deposited in the registry before the grant is resealed.

(6) The [district judge or] registrar shall send notice of the resealing to the court which made the grant.

(7) Where notice is received in the Principal Registry of the resealing of a grant issued in England and Wales, notice of any amendment or revocation of the grant shall be sent to the court by which it was resealed.

NOTES

Amendment

Paras (3), (4), (6): words in square brackets inserted by SI 1991/1876, r 7(1).

40 Application for leave to sue on guarantee

An application for leave under section 120(3) of the Act or under section 11(5) of the Administration of Estates Act 1971 to sue a surety on a guarantee given for the purposes of either of those sections shall, unless the [district judge or] registrar otherwise directs under rule 61, be made by summons to a [district judge or] registrar and notice of the application shall be served on the administrator, the surety and any co-surety.

NOTES

Amendment

Words in square brackets inserted by SI 1991/1876, r 7(1).

41 Amendment and revocation of grant

(1) Subject to paragraph (2) below, if a [district judge or] registrar is satisfied that a grant should be amended or revoked he may make an order accordingly.

(2) Except on the application or with the consent of the person to whom the grant was made, the power conferred in paragraph (1) above shall be exercised only in exceptional circumstances.

NOTES

Amendment

Para (1): words in square brackets inserted by SI 1991/1876, r 7(1).

42 Certificate of delivery of Inland Revenue affidavit

Where the deceased died before 13th March 1975 the certificate of delivery of an Inland Revenue affidavit required by section 30 of the Customs and Inland Revenue Act 1881 to be borne by every grant shall be in Form 1.

43 Standing searches

[(1) Any person who wishes to be notified of the issue of a grant may enter a standing search for the grant by lodging at, or sending by post to any registry or sub-registry, a notice in Form 2.]

(2) A person who has entered a standing search will be sent an office copy of any grant which corresponds with the particulars given on the completed Form 2 and which—

(a) issued not more than twelve months before the entry of the standing search; or

(b) issues within a period of six months after the entry of the standing search.

(3)

(a) Where an applicant wishes to extend the said period of six months, he or his solicitor [or probate practitioner] may lodge at, or send by post to, [the registry or sub-registry at which the standing search was entered] written application for extension.

(b) An application for extension as aforesaid must be lodged, or received by post, within the last month of the said period of six months, and the standing search shall thereupon be effective for an additional period of six months from the date on which it was due to expire.

(c) A standing search which has been extended as above may be further extended by the filing of a further application for extension subject to the same conditions as set out in sub-paragraph (b) above.

NOTES

Amendment

Para (1): substituted by SI 1991/1876, r 11(1).

Para (3): in sub-para (a) words "or probate practitioner" in square brackets inserted by SI 1998/1903, r 6.

Date in force: 14 September 1998: see SI 1998/1903, r 1(1).

Para (3): in sub-para (a) words from "the registry" to "search was entered" in square brackets substituted by SI 1991/1876, r 11(2).

Modification

References to solicitors etc modified to include references to bodies recognised under the Administration of Justice Act 1985, s 9, by the Solicitors' Incorporated Practices Order 1991, SI 1991/2684, arts 4, 5, Sch 1.

44 Caveats

(1) Any person who wishes to show cause against the sealing of a grant may enter a caveat in any registry or sub-registry, and the [district judge or] registrar shall not allow any grant to be sealed (other than a grant ad colligenda bona or a grant under section 117 of the Act) if he has knowledge of an effective caveat; provided that no caveat shall prevent the sealing of a grant on the day on which the caveat is entered.

(2) Any person wishing to enter a caveat (in these Rules called "the caveator"), or a solicitor [or probate practitioner] on his behalf, may effect entry of a caveat—

(a) by completing Form 3 in the appropriate book at any registry or sub-registry; or

(b) by sending by post at his own risk a notice in Form 3 to any registry or sub-registry and the proper officer shall provide an acknowledgement of the entry of the caveat.

(3)

(a) Except as otherwise provided by this rule or by rules 45 or 46, a caveat shall be effective for a period of six months from the date of entry thereof, and where a caveator wishes to extend the said period of six months, he or his solicitor [or probate practitioner] may lodge at, or send by post to, the registry or sub-registry at which the caveat was entered a written application for extension.

(b) An application for extension as aforesaid must be lodged, or received by post, within the last month of the said period of six months, and the caveat shall thereupon (save as otherwise provided by this rule) be effective for an additional period of six months from the date on which it was due to expire.

(c) A caveat which has been extended as above may be further extended by the filing of a further application for extension subject to the same conditions as set out in sub-paragraph (b) above.

[(4) An index of caveats entered in any registry or sub-registry shall be maintained and upon receipt of an application for a grant, the registry or sub-registry at which the application is made shall cause a search of the index to be made and the appropriate district judge or registrar shall be notified of the entry of a caveat against the sealing of a grant for which the application has been made.]

(5) Any person claiming to have an interest in the estate may cause to be issued from the [nominated registry] a warning in Form 4 against the caveat, and the person warning shall state his interest in the estate of the deceased and shall require the caveator to give particulars of any contrary interest in the estate; and the warning or a copy thereof shall be served on the caveator forthwith.

(6) A caveator who has no interest contrary to that of the person warning, but who wishes to show cause against the sealing of a grant to that person, may within eight days of service of the warning upon him (inclusive of the day of such service), or at any time thereafter if no affidavit has been filed under paragraph (12) below, issue and serve a summons for directions.

(7) On the hearing of any summons for directions under paragraph (6) above the [district judge or] registrar may give a direction for the caveat to cease to have effect.

(8) Any caveat in force when a summons for directions is issued shall remain in force until the summons has been disposed of unless a direction has been given under paragraph (7) above [or until it is withdrawn under paragraph (11) below].

(9) The issue of a summons under this rule shall be notified forthwith to the [nominated registry].

(10) A caveator having an interest contrary to that of the person warning may within eight days of service of the warning upon him (inclusive of the day of such service) or at any time thereafter if no affidavit has been filed under paragraph (12) below, enter an appearance in the [nominated registry] by filing Form 5 < … > ; and he shall serve forthwith on the person warning a copy of Form 5 sealed with the seal of the court.

(11) A caveator who has not entered an appearance to a warning may at any time withdraw his caveat by giving notice at the registry or sub-registry at which it was entered, and the caveat shall thereupon cease to have effect; and, where the caveat has been so withdrawn, the caveator shall forthwith give notice of withdrawal to the person warning.

(12) If no appearance has been entered by the caveator or no summons has been issued by him under paragraph (6) of this rule, the person warning may at any time after eight days of service of the warning upon the caveator

(inclusive of the day of such service) file an affidavit in the [nominated registry] as to such service and the caveat shall thereupon cease to have effect provided that there is no pending summons under paragraph (6) of this rule.

(13) Unless a [district judge or, where application to discontinue a caveat is made by consent, a registrar] by order made on summons otherwise directs, any caveat in respect of which an appearance to a warning has been entered shall remain in force until the commencement of a probate action.

(14) Except with the leave of a [district judge], no further caveat may be entered by or on behalf of any caveator whose caveat is either in force or has ceased to have effect under paragraphs (7) or (12) of this rule or under rule 45(4) or rule 46(3).

[(15) In this rule, "nominated registry" means the registry nominated for the purpose of this rule by the senior district judge or in the absence of any such nomination the Leeds District Probate Registry.]

NOTES

Amendment

Para (1): words "district judge or" in square brackets inserted by SI 1991/1876, r 7(1).

Para (2): words "or probate practitioner" in square brackets inserted by SI 1998/1903, r 6.

Date in force: 14 September 1998: see SI 1998/1903, r 1(1).

Para (3): in sub-para (a) words "or probate practitioner" in square brackets inserted by SI 1998/1903, r 6.

Date in force: 14 September 1998: see SI 1998/1903, r 1(1).

Para (4): substituted by SI 1998/1903, r 11(1).

Date in force: 14 September 1998: see SI 1998/1903, r 1(1).

Para (5): words "nominated registry" in square brackets substituted by SI 1998/1903, r 11(2).

Date in force: 14 September 1998: see SI 1998/1903, r 1(1).

Para (7): words "district judge or" in square brackets inserted by SI 1991/1876, r 7(1).

Para (8): words in square brackets inserted by SI 1991/1876, r 12(1).

Para (9): words "nominated registry" in square brackets substituted by SI 1998/1903, r 11(2).

Date in force: 14 September 1998: see SI 1998/1903, r 1(1).

Para (10): words "nominated registry" in square brackets substituted by SI 1998/1903, r 11(2).

Date in force: 14 September 1998: see SI 1998/1903, r 1(1).

Para (10): words omitted revoked by SI 1991/1876, r 12(2).

Para (12): words "nominated registry" in square brackets substituted by SI 1998/1903, r 11(2).

Date in force: 14 September 1998: see SI 1998/1903, r 1(1).

Para (13): words in square brackets substituted by SI 1991/1876, rr 7(3), 12(3).

Para (14): words in square brackets substituted by SI 1991/1876, r 7(3).

Para (15): inserted by SI 1998/1903, r 11(3).

Date in force: 14 September 1998: see SI 1998/1903, r 1(1).

Modification

References to solicitors etc modified to include references to bodies recognised under the Administration of Justice Act 1985, s 9, by the Solicitors' Incorporated Practices Order 1991, SI 1991/2684, arts 4, 5, Sch 1.

45 Probate actions

(1) Upon being advised by the court concerned of the commencement of a probate action the [senior district judge] shall give notice of the action to every caveator other than the plaintiff in the action in respect of each caveat that is in force.

(2) In respect of any caveat entered subsequent to the commencement of a probate action the [senior district judge] shall give notice to that caveator of the existence of the action.

(3) Unless a [district judge] by order made on summons otherwise directs, the commencement of a probate action shall operate to prevent the sealing of a grant (other than a grant under section 117 of the Act) until application for a grant is made by the person shown to be entitled thereto by the decision of the court in such action.

(4) Upon such application for a grant, any caveat entered by the plaintiff in the action, and any caveat in respect of which notice of the action has been given, shall cease to have effect.

NOTES

Amendment

Paras (1), (2): words in square brackets substituted by SI 1991/1876, r 7(4).

Para (3): words in square brackets substituted by SI 1991/1876, r 7(3).

46 Citations

(1) Any citation may issue from the Principal Registry or a district probate registry and shall be settled by a [district judge or] registrar before being issued.

(2) Every averment in a citation, and such other information as the registrar may require, shall be verified by an affidavit sworn by the person issuing the

citation (in these Rules called the "citor"), provided that the [district judge or] registrar may in special circumstances accept an affidavit sworn by the citor's solicitor [or probate practitioner].

(3) The citor shall enter a caveat before issuing a citation and, unless a [district judge] by order made on summons otherwise directs, any caveat in force at the commencement of the citation proceedings shall, unless withdrawn pursuant to paragraph (11) of rule 44, remain in force until application for a grant is made by the person shown to be entitled thereto by the decision of the court in such proceedings, and upon such application any caveat entered by a party who had notice of the proceedings shall cease to have effect.

(4) Every citation shall be served personally on the person cited unless the [district judge or] registrar, on cause shown by affidavit, directs some other mode of service, which may include notice by advertisement.

(5) Every will referred to in a citation shall be lodged in a registry before the citation is issued, except where the will is not in the citor's possession and the [district judge or] registrar is satisfied that it is impracticable to require it to be lodged.

(6) A person who has been cited to appear may, within eight days of service of the citation upon him (inclusive of the day of such service), or at any time thereafter if no application has been made by the citor under paragraph (5) of rule 47 or paragraph (2) of rule 48, enter an appearance in the registry from which the citation issued by filing Form 5 and shall forthwith thereafter serve on the citor a copy of Form 5 sealed with the seal of the registry.

NOTES

Amendment

Para (1): words "district judge or" in square brackets inserted by SI 1991/1876, r 7(1).

Para (2): words "district judge or" in square brackets inserted by SI 1991/1876, r 7(1).

Para (2): words "or probate practitioner" in square brackets inserted by SI 1998/1903, r 6.

Date in force: 14 September 1998: see SI 1998/1903, r 1(1).

Para (3): words in square brackets substituted by SI 1991/1876, r 7(3).

Para (4): words "district judge or" in square brackets inserted by SI 1991/1876, r 7(1).

Para (5): words "district judge or" in square brackets inserted by SI 1991/1876, r 7(1).

47 Citation to accept or refuse or to take a grant

(1) A citation to accept or refuse a grant may be issued at the instance of any person who would himself be entitled to a grant in the event of the person cited renouncing his right thereto.

(2) Where power to make a grant to an executor has been reserved, a citation calling on him to accept or refuse a grant may be issued at the instance of the executors who have proved the will or the survivor of them or of the executors of the last survivor of deceased executors who have proved.

(3) A citation calling on an executor who has intermeddled in the estate of the deceased to show cause why he should not be ordered to take a grant may be issued at the instance of any person interested in the estate at any time after the expiration of six months from the death of the deceased, provided that no citation to take a grant shall issue while proceedings as to the validity of the will are pending.

(4) A person cited who is willing to accept or take a grant may, after entering an appearance, apply ex parte by affidavit to a [district judge or] registrar for an order for a grant to himself.

(5) If the time limited for appearance has expired and the person cited has not entered an appearance, the citor may—

(a) in the case of a citation under paragraph (1) of this rule, apply to a [district judge or] registrar for an order for a grant to himself;

(b) in the case of a citation under paragraph (2) of this rule, apply to a [district judge or] registrar for an order that a note be made on the grant that the executor in respect of whom power was reserved has been duly cited and has not appeared and that all his rights in respect of the executorship have wholly ceased; or

(c) in the case of a citation under paragraph (3) of this rule, apply to a [district judge or] registrar by summons (which shall be served on the person cited) for an order requiring such person to take a grant within a specified time or for a grant to himself or to some other person specified in the summons.

(6) An application under the last foregoing paragraph shall be supported by an affidavit showing that the citation was duly served.

(7) If the person cited has entered an appearance but has not applied for a grant under paragraph (4) of this rule, or has failed to prosecute his application with reasonable diligence, the citor may—

(a) in the case of a citation under paragraph (1) of this rule, apply by summons to a [district judge or] registrar for an order for a grant to himself;

(b) in the case of a citation under paragraph (2) of this rule, apply by summons to a [district judge or] registrar for an order striking out the appearance and for the endorsement on the grant of such a note as is mentioned in sub-paragraph (b) of paragraph (5) of this rule; or

(c) in the case of a citation under paragraph (3) of this rule, apply by summons to a [district judge or] registrar for an order requiring the person cited to take a grant within a specified time or for a grant to himself or to some other person specified in the summons;

and the summons shall be served on the person cited.

NOTES

Amendment

Paras (4), (5), (7): words in square brackets inserted by SI 1991/1876, r 7(1).

48 Citation to propound a will

(1) A citation to propound a will shall be directed to the executors named in the will and to all persons interested thereunder, and may be issued at the instance of any citor having an interest contrary to that of the executors or such other persons.

(2) If the time limited for appearance has expired, the citor may—

(a) in the case where no person has entered an appearance, apply to a [district judge or] registrar for an order for a grant as if the will were invalid and such application shall be supported by an affidavit showing that the citation was duly served; or

(b) in the case where no person who has entered an appearance proceeds with reasonable diligence to propound the will, apply to a [district judge or] registrar by summons, which shall be served on every person cited who has entered an appearance, for such an order as is mentioned in paragraph (a) above.

NOTES

Amendment

Para (2): words in square brackets inserted by SI 1991/1876, r 7(1).

49 Address for service

All caveats, citations, warnings and appearances shall contain an address for service in England and Wales.

50 Application for order to attend for examination or for subpoena to bring in a will

(1) An application under section 122 of the Act for an order requiring a person to attend for examination may, unless a probate action has been

commenced, be made to a [district judge or] registrar by summons which shall be served on every such person as aforesaid.

(2) An application under section 123 of the Act for the issue by a [district judge or] registrar of a subpoena to bring in a will shall be supported by an affidavit setting out the grounds of the application, and if any person served with the subpoena denies that the will is in his possession or control he may file an affidavit to that effect in the registry from which the subpoena issued.

NOTES

Amendment

Words in square brackets inserted by SI 1991/1876, r 7(1).

51 Grants to part of an estate under section 113 of the Act

An application for an order for a grant under section 113 of the Act to part of an estate may be made to a [district judge or] registrar, and shall be supported by an affidavit setting out the grounds of the application, and

(a) stating whether the estate of the deceased is known to be insolvent; and

(b) showing how any person entitled to a grant in respect of the whole estate in priority to the applicant has been cleared off.

NOTES

Amendment

Words in square brackets inserted by SI 1991/1876, r 7(1).

52 Grants of administration under discretionary powers of court, and grants ad colligenda bona

An application for an order for—

(a) a grant of administration under section 116 of the Act; or

(b) a grant of administration ad colligenda bona,

may be made to a [district judge or] registrar and shall be supported by an affidavit setting out the grounds of the application.

NOTES

Amendment

Words in square brackets inserted by SI 1991/1876, r 7(1).

53 Applications for leave to swear to death

An application for leave to swear to the death of a person in whose estate a grant is sought may be made to a [district judge or] registrar, and shall be supported by an affidavit setting out the grounds of the application and containing particulars of any policies of insurance effected on the life of the presumed deceased together with such further evidence as the [district judge or] registrar may require.

NOTES

Amendment

Words in square brackets inserted by SI 1991/1876, r 7(1).

54 Grants in respect of nuncupative wills and copies of wills

(1) Subject to paragraph (2) below, an application for an order admitting to proof a nuncupative will, or a will contained in a copy or reconstruction thereof where the original is not available, shall be made to a [district judge or] registrar.

(2) In any case where a will is not available owing to its being retained in the custody of a foreign court or official, a duly authenticated copy of the will may be admitted to proof without the order referred to in paragraph (1) above.

(3) An application under paragraph (1) above shall be supported by an affidavit setting out the grounds of the application, and by such evidence on affidavit as the applicant can adduce as to—

- (a) the will's existence after the death of the testator or, where there is no such evidence, the facts on which the applicant relies to rebut the presumption that the will has been revoked by destruction;
- (b) in respect of a nuncupative will, the contents of that will; and
- (c) in respect of a reconstruction of a will, the accuracy of that reconstruction.

(4) The [district judge or] registrar may require additional evidence in the circumstances of a particular case as to due execution of the will or as to the accuracy of the copy will, and may direct that notice be given to persons who would be prejudiced by the application.

NOTES

Amendment

Paras (1), (4): words in square brackets inserted by SI 1991/1876, r 7(1).

55 Application for rectification of a will

(1) An application for an order that a will be rectified by virtue of section 20(1) of the Administration of Justice Act 1982 may be made to a [district judge or] registrar, unless a probate action has been commenced.

(2) The application shall be supported by an affidavit, setting out the grounds of the application, together with such evidence as can be adduced as to the testator's intentions and as to whichever of the following matters as are in issue:—

(a) in what respects the testator's intentions were not understood; or

(b) the nature of any alleged clerical error.

(3) Unless otherwise directed, notice of the application shall be given to every person having an interest under the will whose interest might be prejudiced[, or such other person who might be prejudiced,] by the rectification applied for and any comments in writing by any such person shall be exhibited to the affidavit in support of the application.

(4) If the [district judge or] registrar is satisfied that, subject to any direction to the contrary, notice has been given to every person mentioned in paragraph (3) above, and that the application is unopposed, he may order that the will be rectified accordingly.

NOTES

Amendment

Paras (1), (4): words in square brackets inserted by SI 1991/1876, r 7(1).

Para (3): words ", or such other person who might be prejudiced," in square brackets inserted by SI 1998/1903, r 12.

Date in force: 14 September 1998: see SI 1998/1903, r 1(1).

56 Notice of election by surviving spouse to redeem life interest

(1) Where a surviving spouse who is the sole or sole surviving personal representative of the deceased is entitled to a life interest in part of the residuary estate and elects under section 47A of the Administration of Estates Act 1925 to have the life interest redeemed, he may give written notice of the election to the [senior district judge] in pursuance of subsection (7) of that section by filing a notice in Form 6 in the Principal Registry or in the district probate registry from which the grant issued.

(2) Where the grant issued from a district probate registry, the notice shall be filed in duplicate.

(3) A notice filed under this rule shall be noted on the grant and the record and shall be open to inspection.

NOTES

Amendment

Para (1): words in square brackets substituted by SI 1991/1876, r 7(4).

[57 Index of grant applications]

[(1) The senior district judge shall maintain an index of every pending application for a grant made in any registry or sub-registry.

(2) Every registry or sub-registry in which an application is made shall cause the index to be searched and shall record the result of the search.]

NOTES

Amendment

Substituted by SI 1998/1903, r 13.

Date in force: 14 September 1998: see SI 1998/1903, r 1(1).

58 Inspection of copies of original wills and other documents

An original will or other document referred to in section 124 of the Act shall not be open to inspection if, in the opinion of a [district judge or] registrar, such inspection would be undesirable or otherwise inappropriate.

NOTES

Amendment

Words in square brackets inserted by SI 1991/1876, r 7(1).

59 Issue of copies of original wills and other documents

Where copies are required of original wills or other documents deposited under section 124 of the Act, such copies may be facsimile copies sealed with the seal of the court and issued either as office copies or certified under the hand of a [district judge or] registrar to be true copies.

NOTES

Amendment

Words in square brackets inserted by SI 1991/1876, r 7(1).

60 Costs

(1) Order 62 of the Rules of the Supreme Court 1965 shall not apply to costs in non-contentious probate matters, and Parts 43, 44 (except rules 44.9 to 44.12), 47 and 48 of the Civil Procedure Rules 1998 ("the 1998 Rules") shall apply to costs in those matters, with the modifications contained in paragraphs (3) to (7) of this rule.

(2) Where detailed assessment of a bill of costs is ordered, it shall be referred—

(a) where the order was made by a district judge, to a district judge, a costs judge or an authorised court officer within rule 43.2(1)(d)(iii) or (iv) of the 1998 Rules;

(b) where the order was made by a registrar, to that registrar or, where this is not possible, in accordance with sub-paragraph (a) above.

(3) Every reference in Parts 43, 44, 47 and 48 of the 1998 Rules to a district judge shall be construed as referring only to a district judge of the Principal Registry.

(4) The definition of "costs officer" in rule 43.2(1)(c) of the 1998 Rules shall have effect as if it included a paragraph reading—

"(iv) a district probate registrar."

(5) The definition of "authorised court officer" in rule 43.2(1)(d) of the 1998 Rules shall have effect as if paragraphs (i) and (ii) were omitted.

(6) Rule 44.3(2) of the 1998 Rules (costs follow the event) shall not apply.

(7) Rule 47.4(2) of the 1998 Rules shall apply as if after the words "Supreme Court Costs Office" there were inserted ", the Principal Registry of the Family Division or such district probate registry as the court may specify".

(8) Except in the case of an appeal against a decision of an authorised court officer (to which rules 47.20 to 47.23 of the 1998 Rules apply), an appeal against a decision in assessment proceedings relating to costs in non-contentious probate matters shall be dealt with in accordance with the following paragraphs of this rule.

(9) An appeal within paragraph (8) above against a decision made by a district judge, a costs judge (as defined by rule 43.2(1)(b) of the 1998 Rules) or a registrar, shall lie to a judge of the High Court.

(10) Part 52 of the 1998 Rules applies to every appeal within paragraph (8) above, and any reference in Part 52 to a judge or a district judge shall be taken to include a district judge of the Principal Registry of the Family Division.

(11) The 1998 Rules shall apply to an appeal to which Part 52 or rules 47.20 to 47.23 of those Rules apply in accordance with paragraph (8) above in the same way as they apply to any other appeal within Part 52 or rules 47.20 to

47.23 of those Rules as the case may be; accordingly the Rules of the Supreme Court 1965 and the County Court Rules 1981 shall not apply to any such appeal.

NOTES

Amendment

Substituted by SI 2003/185, rr 4, 5.

Date in force: 24 February 2003: see SI 2003/185, r 1.

61 Power to require applications to be made by summons

(1) [Subject to rule 7(2),] a [district judge or] registrar may require any application to be made by summons to a [district judge or] registrar in chambers or a judge in chambers or open court.

(2) An application for an inventory and account shall be made by summons to a [district judge or] registrar.

(3) A summons for hearing by a [district judge or] registrar shall be issued out of the registry in which it is to be heard.

(4) A summons to be heard by a judge shall be issued out of the Principal Registry.

NOTES

Amendment

Paras (1)–(3): words in square brackets inserted by SI 1991/1876, rr 7(1), 14.

62 Transfer of applications

A registrar to whom any application is made under these Rules may order the transfer of the application to another [district judge or] registrar having jurisdiction.

NOTES

Amendment

Words in square brackets inserted by SI 1991/1876, r 7(1).

[62A Exercise of a registrar's jurisdiction by another registrar]

[A registrar may hear and dispose of an application under these Rules on behalf of any other registrar by whom the application would otherwise have been heard, if that other registrar so requests or an application in that behalf is made by a party making an application under these Rules; and where the circumstances require it, the registrar shall, without the need for any such request or application, hear and dispose of the application.]

NOTES

Amendment

Inserted by SI 1998/1903, r 14.

Date in force: 14 September 1998: see SI 1998/1903, r 1(1).

63 Power to make orders for costs

On any application dealt with by him on summons, the … registrar shall have full power to determine by whom and to what extent the costs are to be paid.

NOTES

Amendment

Words omitted revoked by SI 1991/1876, r 7(2).

64 Exercise of powers of judge during Long Vacation

All powers exercisable under these Rules by a judge in chambers may be exercised during the Long Vacation by a [district judge].

NOTES

Amendment

Words in square brackets substituted by SI 1991/1876, r 7(3).

65 Appeals from [district judges or] registrars

(1) An appeal against a decision or requirement of a [district judge or] registrar shall be made by summons to a judge.

(2) If, in the case of an appeal under the last foregoing paragraph, any person besides the appellant appeared or was represented before the [district judge or] registrar from whose decision or requirement the appeal is brought, the summons shall be issued within seven days thereof for hearing on the first available day and shall be served on every such person as aforesaid.

NOTES

Amendment

Words in square brackets inserted by SI 1991/1876, r 7(1), (6).

66 Service of summons

(1) A judge or [district judge] or, where the application is to be made to a district probate registrar, that registrar, may direct that a summons for the service of which no other provision is made by these Rules shall be served on such person or persons as the [judge, district judge or registrar] [may direct].

(2) Where by these Rules or by any direction given under the last foregoing paragraph a summons is required to be served on any person, it shall be served not less than two clear days before the day appointed for the hearing, unless a judge or [district judge or] registrar at or before the hearing dispenses with service on such terms, if any, as he may think fit.

NOTES

Amendment

Para (1): words "district judge" in square brackets substituted by SI 1991/1876, r 7(3).

Para (1): words "judge, district judge or registrar" in square brackets substituted by SI 1998/1903, r 15.

Date in force: 14 September 1998: see SI 1998/1903, r 1(1).

Para (1): words "may direct" in square brackets substituted by SI 1991/1876, r 7(7).

Para (2): words "district judge or" in square brackets inserted by SI 1991/1876, r 7(1).

67 Notices, etc

Unless a [district judge or] registrar otherwise directs or these Rules otherwise provide, any notice or other document required to be given to or served on any person may be given or served in the manner prescribed by Order 65 Rule 5 of the Rules of the Supreme Court 1965.

NOTES

Amendment

Words in square brackets inserted by SI 1991/1876, r 7(1).

68 Application to pending proceedings

Subject in any particular case to any direction given by a judge or [district judge or] registrar, these Rules shall apply to any proceedings which are pending on the date on which they come into force as well as to any proceedings commenced on or after that date.

NOTES

Amendment

Words in square brackets inserted by SI 1991/1876, r 7(1).

69 Revocation of previous rules

(1) Subject to paragraph (2) below, the rules set out in the Second Schedule are hereby revoked.

(2) The rules set out in the Second Schedule shall continue to apply to such extent as may be necessary for giving effect to a direction under rule 68.

SCHEDULE 1
FORMS

Rule 2(2)

Form 1 Certificate of Delivery of Inland Revenue Affidavit

Rule 42

And it is hereby certified that an Inland Revenue affidavit has been delivered wherein it is shown that the gross value of the said estate in the United Kingdom (exclusive of what the said deceased may have been possessed of or entitled to as a trustee and not beneficially) amounts to £ … … and that the net value of the estate amounts to £ … ..

And it is further certified that it appears by a receipt signed by an Inland Revenue officer on the said affidavit that £ … … on account of estate duty and interest on such day has been paid.

Form 2 Standing Search

Rule 43(1)

In the High Court of Justice Family Division

[The Principal (or … … … … … … … … District Probate) Registry]

I/We apply for the entry of a standing search so that there shall be sent to me/us an office copy of every grant of representation in England and Wales in the estate of—

Full name of deceased: … … … … … … … … …

Full address: … … … … … … … … …

Alternative or alias names: … … … … … … … … …

Exact date of death: … … … … … … … … …

which either has issued not more than 12 months before the entry of this application or issues within 6 months thereafter.

Signed … … … … … … … … …

Name in block letters … … … … … … … … …

Full address … … … … … … … … …

Reference No. (if any) … … … … … … … … …

NOTES

Amendment

Words in square brackets substituted by SI 1991/1876, r 11(3).

Form 3 Caveat

Rule 44(2)

In the High Court of Justice Family Division

The Principal (*or* … … … … … … … … … District Probate) Registry.

Let not grant be sealed in the estate of (*full name and address*) deceased, who died on the … … … … … … … … … day of 19 … … without notice to (*name of party by whom or on whose behalf the caveat is entered*).

Dated this … … … … … … … … … day of … … … … … … … … … 19 … …

(*Signed*) … … … … … … … … … (*to be signed by the caveator's solicitor* [*or probate practitioner*] *or by the caveator if acting in person*)

whose address for service is: … … … … … … … … …

Solicitor[/probate practitioner] for the said … … … … … … … … … (*If the caveator is acting in person, substitute "In person"*.)

NOTES

Amendment

Words "or probate practitioner" in square brackets inserted by SI 1998/1903, r 16(a).
Date in force: 14 September 1998: see SI 1998/1903, r 1(1).
Words "/probate practitioner" in square brackets inserted by SI 1998/1903, r 16(b).
Date in force: 14 September 1998: see SI 1998/1903, r 1(1).

Form 4 Warning to Caveator

Rule 44(5)

In the High Court of Justice Family Division

[(The nominated registry as defined by rule 44(15))]

To … … … … … … … … … of … … … … … … … … … a party who has entered a caveat in the estate of … … … … … … … … … deceased.

You have eight days (starting with the day on which this warning was served on you):

(i) to enter an appearance either in person or by your solicitor [or probate practitioner], at the [(name and address of the nominated registry)] setting out what interest you have in the estate of the above-named … … … … … … … … … of … … … … … … … … … deceased contrary to that of the party at whose instance this warning is issued; or

(ii) if you have no contrary interest but wish to show cause against the sealing of a grant to such party, to issue and serve a summons for [directions by a district judge of the Principal Registry or a registrar of] a district probate registry.

If you fail to do either of these, the court may proceed to issue a grant of probate or administration in the said estate notwithstanding your caveat.

Dated the … … … … … … … … … day of … … … … … … … … … 19 … … .

Issued at the instance of … … … … … … … … …

(*Here set out the name and interest* (*including the date of the will, if any, under which the interest arises*) *of the party warning, the name of his solicitor* [*or probate practitioner*] *and the address for service. If the party warning is acting in person, this must be stated.*) … … … … … … … … Registrar

NOTES

Amendment

Words "(The nominated registry as defined by rule 44(15))" in square brackets substituted by SI 1998/1903, r 17(b).

Date in force: 14 September 1998: see SI 1998/1903, r 1(1).

Words "or probate practitioner" in square brackets in both places they occur inserted by SI 1998/1903, r 17(a).

Date in force: 14 September 1998: see SI 1998/1903, r 1(1).

Words "(name and address of the nominated registry)" in square brackets substituted by SI 1998/1903, r 17(c).

Date in force: 14 September 1998: see SI 1998/1903, r 1(1).

Words from "directions by" to "a registrar of" in square brackets substituted by SI 1991/1876, r 7(8).

Form 5 Appearance to Warning or Citation

Rules 44(10), 46(6)

In the High Court of Justice Family Division

The Principal (*or* … … … … … … … … … District Probate) Registry
Caveat No … … … … … … … … … dated the … … … … … … … … …
day of … … … … … … … … … 19 … … (Citation dated the … … … …
… … … … … day of … … … … … … … … … 19 … …)

Full name and address of deceased: … … … … … … … …

Full name and address of person warning (*or* citor): … … … … … … … …

(*Here set out the interest of the person warning, or citor, as shown in warning or citation.*)

Full name and address of caveator (or person cited).

(*Here set out the interest of the caveator or person cited, stating the date of the will* (*if any*) *under which such interest arises.*)

Enter an appearance for the above-named caveator (*or* person cited) in this matter.

Dated the … … … … … … … … … day of … … … … … … … … 19 … … .

(*Signed*) … … … … … … … … …

whose address for service is: … … … … … … … … …

… … … … … … … … … Solicitor[/probate practitioner] (*or* In person).

NOTES

Amendment

Words "/probate practitioner" in square brackets inserted by SI 1998/1903, r 18.
Date in force: 14 September 1998: see SI 1998/1903, r 1(1).

Form 6 Notice of Election to Redeem Life Interest

Rule 56

In the High Court of Justice Family Division

The Principal (*or* … … … … … … … … … District Probate) Registry

In the estate of … … … … … … … … … deceased.

Whereas … … … … … … … … … … of … … … … … … … … … died on the … … … … … … … … … … day of … … … … … … … … … 19 … … wholly/partially intestate leaving his/her/lawful wife/husband and … … … … … … … … … lawful issue of the said deceased;

And whereas Probate/Letters of Administration of the estate of the said … … … … … … … … … … were granted to me, the said … … … … … … … … … … (and to … … … … … … … … … … of … … … … … … … … … …) at the Probate Registry on the … … … … … … … … … … day of … … … … … … … … … 19 … … ;

And whereas (the said … … … … … … … … … … has ceased to be a personal representative because … … … … … … … … … …) and I am (now) the sole personal representative;

Now I, the said … … … … … … … … … … hereby given notice in accordance with section 47A of the Administration of Estates Act 1925 that I elect to redeem the life interest to which I am entitled in the estate of the late … … … … … … … … … by retaining £ … … its capital value, and £ … … the costs of the transaction.

Dated the … … … … … … … … … … day of … … … … … … … … … 19 … … … .

(Signed) … … … … … … … … … …

To the [senior district judge] of the Family Division.

NOTES

Amendment

Words in square brackets substituted by SI 1991/1876, r 7(4).

SCHEDULE 2
REVOCATIONS

Rule 69

Rules revoked	*References*
The Non-Contentious Probate Rules 1954	*SI 1954/796*
The Non-Contentious Probate (Amendment) Rules 1961	*SI 1961/72*
The Non-Contentious Probate (Amendment) Rules 1962	*SI 1962/2653*
The Non-Contentious Probate (Amendment) Rules 1967	*SI 1967/748*
The Non-Contentious Probate (Amendment) Rules 1968	*SI 1968/1675*
The Non-Contentious Probate (Amendment) Rules 1969	*SI 1969/1689*
The Non-Contentious Probate (Amendment) Rules 1971	*SI 1971/1977*
The Non-Contentious Probate (Amendment) Rules 1974	*SI 1974/597*
The Non-Contentious Probate (Amendment) Rules 1976	*SI 1976/1362*
The Non-Contentious Probate (Amendment) Rules 1982	*SI 1982/446*
The Non-Contentious Probate (Amendment) Rules 1983	*SI 1983/623*
The Non-Contentious Probate (Amendment) Rules 1985	*SI 1985/1232*

Appendix 2.1

Wills Act 1837

Arrangement of sections

[9 Signing and attestation of wills]

[No will shall be valid unless—

(*a*) *it is in writing, and signed by the testator, or by some other person in his presence and by his direction; and*

(*b*) *it appears that the testator intended by his signature to give effect to the will; and*

(*c*) *the signature is made or acknowledged by the testator in the presence of two or more witnesses present at the same time; and*

(*d*) *each witness either—*

(*i*) *attests and signs the will; or*

(*ii*) *acknowledges his signature,*

in the presence of the testator (*but not necessarily in the presence of any other witness*),

but no form of attestation shall be necessary.]

NOTES

Amendment

Substituted, in relation to England and Wales, by the Administration of Justice Act 1982, s 17.

Repealed, in relation to Northern Ireland, by the Wills and Administration Proceedings (NI) Order 1994, SI 1994/1899, art 38, Sch 3.
Extent
This Act does not extend to Scotland: see s 35.

[18 Will to be revoked by marriage]

[(1) Subject to subsections (2) to (4) below, a will shall be revoked by the testator's marriage.

(2) A disposition in a will in exercise of a power of appointment shall take effect notwithstanding the testator's subsequent marriage unless the property so appointed would in default of appointment pass to his personal representatives.

(3) Where it appears from a will that at the time it was made the testator was expecting to be married to a particular person and that he intended that the will should not be revoked by the marriage, the will shall not be revoked by his marriage to that person.

(4) Where it appears from a will that at the time it was made the testator was expecting to be married to a particular person and that he intended that a disposition in the will should not be revoked by his marriage to that person,—

- *(a) that disposition shall take effect notwithstanding the marriage; and*
- *(b) any other disposition in the will shall take effect also, unless it appears from the will that the testator intended the disposition to be revoked by the marriage.]*

NOTES
Amendment
Substituted, in relation to England and Wales, by the Administration of Justice Act 1982, s 18(1).
Repealed, in relation to Northern Ireland, by the Wills and Administration Proceedings (NI) Order 1994, SI 1994/1899, art 38, Sch 3.
Extent
This Act does not extend to Scotland: see s 35.

[18A Effect of dissolution or annulment of marriage on wills]

[(1) Where, after a testator has made a will, *a decree* [an order or decree] of a court [of civil jurisdiction in England and Wales] dissolves or annuls his marriages [or his marriage is dissolved or annulled and the divorce or annulment is entitled to recognition in England and Wales by virtue of Part II of the Family Law Act 1986],—

- [(a) provisions of the will appointing executors or trustees or conferring a power of appointment, if they appoint or confer the power on the former spouse, shall take effect as if the former spouse had died on the date on which the marriage is dissolved or annulled, and

(b) any property which, or an interest in which, is devised or bequeathed to the former spouse shall pass as if the former spouse had died on that date,]

except in so far as a contrary intention appears by the will.

(2) Subsection (1)(b) above is without prejudice to any right of the former spouse to apply for financial provision under the Inheritance (Provision for Family and Dependants) Act 1975.

(3) …]

NOTES

Amendment

Inserted, in relation to England and Wales, by the Administration of Justice Act 1982, s 18(2).

Sub-s (1): first words in italics prospectively repealed with savings and subsequent words in square brackets prospectively substituted with savings by the Family Law Act 1996, s 66(1), Sch 8, para 1, as from a day to be appointed, for savings see s 66(2), Sch 9, para 5 thereof; second words in square brackets inserted, and third words in square brackets substituted, by the Family Law Act 1986, s 53; paras (a), (b) substituted by the Law Reform (Succession) Act 1995, s 3.

Sub-s (3): repealed by the Law Reform (Succession) Act 1995, s 5, Schedule.

Extent

This Act does not extend to Scotland: see s 35.

24 Wills shall be construed, as to the estate comprised, to speak from the death of the testator

< … > every will shall be construed, with reference to the real estate and personal estate comprised in it, to speak and take effect as if it had been executed immediately before the death of the testator, unless a contrary intention shall appear by the will.

NOTES

Initial Commencement

Specified date

Specified date: 1 January 1838 (with effect in relation to wills made after that date): see s 34.

Amendment

Repealed, in relation to Northern Ireland, by the Wills and Administration Proceedings (NI) Order 1994, 1994/1899, art 38, Sch 3.

Words omitted repealed by the Statute Law Revision (No 2) Act 1888.

Extent

This Act does not extend to Scotland: see s 35.

[33 Gifts to children or other issue who leave issue living at the testator's death shall not lapse]

[(1) Where—

(a) a will contains a devise or bequest to a child or remoter descendant of the testator; and

(b) the intended beneficiary dies before the testator, leaving issue; and

(c) issue of the intended beneficiary are living at the testator's death,

then, unless a contrary intention appears by the will, the devise or bequest shall take effect as a devise or bequest to the issue living at the testator's death.

(2) Where—

(a) a will contains a devise or bequest to a class of person consisting of children or remoter descendants of the testator; and

(b) a member of the class dies before the testator, leaving issue, and

(c) issue of that member are living at the testator's death,

then, unless a contrary intention appears by the will, the devise or bequest shall take effect as if the class included the issue of its deceased member living at the testator's death.

(3) Issue shall take under this section through all degrees, according to their stock, in equal shares if more than one, any gift or share which their parent would have taken and so that no issue shall take whose parent is living at the testator's death and that no issue shall take whose parent is living at the testator's death and so capable of taking.

(4) For the purposes of this section—

(a) the illegitimacy of any person is to be disregarded; and

(b) a person conceived before the testator's death and born living thereafter is to be taken to have been living at the testator's death.]

NOTES

Amendment

Substituted, in relation to England and Wales, by the Administration of Justice Act 1982, s 19.

Repealed, in relation to Northern Ireland, by the Wills and Administration Proceedings (NI) Order 1994, SI 1994/1899, art 38, Sch 3.

Extent

This Act does not extend to Scotland: see s 35.

Appendix 2.2

Administration of Estates Act 1925

Arrangement of sections

Administration of Assets

35 Charges on property of deceased to be paid primarily out of the property charged

(1) Where a person dies possessed of, or entitled to, or, under a general power of appointment (including the statutory power to dispose of entailed interests) by his will disposes of, an interest in property, which at the time of his death is charged with the payment of money, whether by way of legal mortgage, equitable charge or otherwise (including a lien for unpaid purchase money), and the deceased has not by will deed or other document signified a contrary or other intention, the interest so charged, shall as between the different persons claiming through the deceased, be primarily liable for the payment of the charge; and every part of the said interest, according to its value, shall bear a proportionate part of the charge on the whole thereof.

(2) Such contrary or other intention shall not be deemed to be signified—

(a) by a general direction for the payment of debts or of all the debts of the testator out of his personal estate, or his residuary real and personal estate, or his residuary real estate; or

(b) by a charge of debts upon any such estate;

unless such intention is further signified by words expressly or by necessary implication referring to all or some part of the charge.

(3) Nothing in this section affects the right of a person entitled to the charge to obtain payment or satisfaction thereof either out of the other assets of the deceased or otherwise.

NOTES

Initial Commencement

Specified date

Specified date: 1 January 1926.

Extent

This Act does not extend to Scotland: see s 58(3).

36 Effect of assent or conveyance by personal representative

(1) A personal representative may assent to the vesting, in any person who (whether by devise, bequest, devolution, appropriation or otherwise) may be entitled thereto, either beneficially or as a trustee or personal representative, of any estate or interest in real estate to which the testator or intestate was entitled or over which he exercised a general power of appointment by his will, including the statutory power to dispose of entailed interests, and which devolved upon the personal representative.

(2) The assent shall operate to vest in that person the estate or interest to which the assent relates, and, unless a contrary intention appears, the assent shall relate back to the death of the deceased.

(3) …

(4) An assent to the vesting of a legal estate shall be in writing, signed by the personal representative, and shall name the person in whose favour it is given and shall operate to vest in that person the legal estate to which it relates; and an assent not in writing or not in favour of a named person shall not be effectual to pass a legal estate.

(5) Any person in whose favour an assent or conveyance of a legal estate is made by a personal representative may require that notice of the assent or conveyance be written or endorsed on or permanently annexed to the probate or letters of administration, at the cost of the estate of the deceased, and that the probate or letters of administration be produced, at the like cost, to prove that the notice has been placed thereon or annexed thereto.

(6) A statement in writing by a personal representative that he has not given or made an assent or conveyance in respect of a legal estate, shall, in favour of a purchaser, but without prejudice to any previous disposition made in favour of another purchaser deriving title mediately or immediately under the personal representative, be sufficient evidence that an assent or conveyance has not been given or made in respect of the legal estate to which the statement relates, unless notice of a previous assent or conveyance affecting that estate has been placed on or annexed to the probate or administration.

A conveyance by a personal representative of a legal estate to a purchaser accepted on the faith of such a statement shall (without prejudice as aforesaid and unless notice of a previous assent or conveyance affecting that estate has been placed on or annexed to the probate or administration) operate to transfer or create the legal estate expressed to be conveyed in like manner as if no previous assent or conveyance had been made by the personal representative.

A personal representative making a false statement, in regard to any such matter, shall be liable in like manner as if the statement had been contained in a statutory declaration.

(7) An assent or conveyance by a personal representative in respect of a legal estate shall, in favour of a purchaser, unless notice of a previous assent or conveyance affecting that legal estate has been placed on or annexed to the probate or administration, be taken as sufficient evidence that the person in whose favour the assent or conveyance is given or made is the person entitled to have the legal estate conveyed to him, and upon the proper trusts, if any, but shall not otherwise prejudicially affect the claim of any person rightfully entitled to the estate vested or conveyed or any charge thereon.

(8) A conveyance of a legal estate by a personal representative to a purchaser shall not be invalidated by reason only that the purchaser may have notice that all the debts, liabilities, funeral, and testamentary or administration expenses, duties, and legacies of the deceased have been discharged or provided for.

(9) An assent or conveyance given or made by a personal representative shall not, except in favour of a purchaser of a legal estate, prejudice the right of the personal representative or any other person to recover the estate or interest to which the assent or conveyance relates, or to be indemnified out of such estate or interest against any duties, debts, or liability to which such estate or interest would have been subject if there had not been any assent or conveyance.

(10) A personal representative may, as a condition of giving an assent or making a conveyance, require security for the discharge of any such duties, debt, or liability, but shall not be entitled to postpone the giving of an assent merely by reason of the subsistence of any such duties, debt or liability if reasonable arrangements have been made for discharging the same; and an assent may be given subject to any legal estate or charge by way of legal mortgage.

(11) This section shall not operate to impose any stamp duty in respect of an assent, and in this section "purchaser" means a purchaser for money or money's worth.

(12) This section applies to assents and conveyances made after the commencement of this Act, whether the testator or intestate died before of after such commencement.

NOTES

Initial Commencement

Specified date

Specified date: 1 January 1926.

Amendment

Sub-s (3): repealed by the Law of Property (Miscellaneous Provisions) Act 1994, s 21(2), Sch 2.

Extent

This Act does not extend to Scotland: see s 58(3).

41 Powers of personal representative as to appropriation

(1) The personal representative may appropriate any part of the real or personal estate, including things in action, of the deceased in the actual

condition or state of investment thereof at the time of appropriation in or towards satisfaction of any legacy bequeathed by the deceased, or of any other interest or share in his property, whether settled or not, as to the personal representative may seem just and reasonable, according to the respective rights of the persons interested in the property of the deceased:

Provided that—

(i) an appropriation shall not be made under this section so as to affect prejudicially any specific devise or bequest;

(ii) an appropriation of property, whether or not being an investment authorised by law or by the will, if any, of the deceased for the investment of money subject to the trust, shall not (save as hereinafter mentioned) be made under this section except with the following consents:—

(a) when made for the benefit of a person absolutely and beneficially entitled in possession, the consent of that person;

(b) when made in respect of any settled legacy share or interest, the consent of either the trustee thereof, if any (not being also the personal representative), or the person who may for the time being be entitled to the income:

If the person whose consent is so required as aforesaid is an infant or [is incapable by reason of mental disorder within the meaning of [the Mental Health Act 1983], of managing and administering his property and affairs] the consent shall be given on his behalf by his parents or parent, testamentary or other guardian… or receiver, or if, in the case of an infant, there is no such parent or guardian, by the court on the application of his next friend;

(iii) no consent (save of such trustee as aforesaid) shall be required on behalf of a person who may come into existence after the time of appropriation, or who cannot be found or ascertained at that time;

(iv) if no [receiver is acting for a person suffering from mental disorder] then, if the appropriation is of an investment authorised by law or by the will, if any, of the deceased for the investment of money subject to the trust, no consent shall be required on behalf of the [said person];

(v) if, independently of the personal representative, there is no trustee of a settled legacy share or interest, and no person of full age and capacity entitled to the income thereof, no consent shall be required to an appropriation in respect of such legacy share or interest, provided that the appropriation is of an investment authorised as aforesaid.

[(1A) The county court has jurisdiction under proviso (ii) to subsection (1) of this section where the estate in respect of which the application is made does not exceed in amount or value the county court limit.]

(2) Any property duly appropriated under the powers conferred by this section shall thereafter be treated as an authorised investment, and may be retained or dealt with accordingly.

(3) For the purposes of such appropriation, the personal representative may ascertain and fix the value of the respective parts of the real and personal estate and the liabilities of the deceased as he may think fit, and shall for that purpose employ a duly qualified valuer in any case where such employment may be necessary; and may make any conveyance (including an assent) which may be requisite for giving effect to the appropriation.

(4) An appropriation made pursuant to this section shall bind all persons interested in the property of the deceased whose consent is not hereby made requisite.

(5) The personal representative shall, in making the appropriation, have regard to the rights of any person who may thereafter come into existence, or who cannot be found or ascertained at the time of appropriation, and of any other person whose consent is not required by this section.

(6) This section does not prejudice any other power of appropriation conferred by law or by the will (if any) of the deceased, and takes effect with any extended powers conferred by the will (if any) of the deceased, and where an appropriation is made under this section, in respect of a settled legacy, share or interest, the property appropriated shall remain subject to all [trusts] and powers of leasing, disposition, and management or varying investments which would have been applicable thereto or to the legacy, share or interest in respect of which the appropriation is made, if no such appropriation had been made.

(7) If after any real estate has been appropriated in purported exercise of the powers conferred by this section, the person to whom it was conveyed disposes of it or any interest therein, then, in favour of a purchaser, the appropriation shall be deemed to have been made in accordance with the requirements of this section and after all requisite consents, if any, had been given.

(8) In this section, a settled legacy, share or interest includes any legacy, share or interest to which a person is not absolutely entitled in possession at the date of the appropriation, also an annuity, and "purchaser" means a purchaser for money or money's worth.

(9) This section applies whether the deceased died intestate or not, and whether before or after the commencement of this Act, and extends to property over which a testator exercises a general power of appointment, including the statutory power to dispose of entailed interests, and authorises the setting apart of a fund to answer an annuity by means of the income of that fund or otherwise.

NOTES

Initial Commencement

Specified date

Specified date: 1 January 1926.

Amendment

Sub-s (1): in para (ii) words omitted repealed, and first words in square brackets substituted, by the Mental Health Act 1959, s 149(1), Sch 7, Part I, words in square brackets therein substituted by the Mental Health Act 1983, s 148, Sch 4, para 7; in para (iv) words in square brackets substituted by the Mental Health Act 1959, s 149(1), Sch 7, Part I.

Sub-s (1A): inserted by the County Courts Act 1984, s 148(1), Sch 2, Part III, para 13.

Sub-s (6): word "trusts" in square brackets substituted by the Trusts of Land and Appointment of Trustees Act 1996, s 25(1), Sch 3, para 6(1), (3); for savings in relation to entailed interests created before the commencement of that Act, and savings consequential upon the abolition of the doctrine of conversion, see s 25(4), (5) thereof.

Date in force: 1 January 1997: see SI 1996/2974, art 2.

Extent

This Act does not extend to Scotland: see s 58(3).

Appendix 2.3

Trustee Act 1925

Arrangement of sections

[19 Power to insure]

[(1) A trustee may—

(a) insure any property which is subject to the trust against risks of loss or damage due to any event, and

(b) pay the premiums out of the trust funds.

(2) In the case of property held on a bare trust, the power to insure is subject to any direction given by the beneficiary or each of the beneficiaries—

(a) that any property specified in the direction is not to be insured;

(b) that any property specified in the direction is not to be insured except on such conditions as may be so specified.

(3) Property is held on a bare trust if it is held on trust for—

(a) a beneficiary who is of full age and capacity and absolutely entitled to the property subject to the trust, or

(b) beneficiaries each of whom is of full age and capacity and who (taken together) are absolutely entitled to the property subject to the trust.

(4) If a direction under subsection (2) of this section is given, the power to insure, so far as it is subject to the direction, ceases to be a delegable function for the purposes of section 11 of the Trustee Act 2000 (power to employ agents).

(5) In this section "trust funds" means any income or capital funds of the trust.]

NOTES

Amendment

Substituted by the Trustee Act 2000, s 34(1).

Date in force: 1 February 2001 (in relation to trusts created before or after that date): see the Trustee Act 2000, s 34(3) and SI 2001/49, art 2.

31 Power to apply income for maintenance and to accumulate surplus income during a minority

(1) Where any property is held by trustees in trust for any person for any interest whatsoever, whether vested or contingent, then, subject to any prior interests or charges affecting that property—

(i) during the infancy of any such person, if his interest so long continues, the trustees may, at their sole discretion, pay to his parent or guardian, if any, or otherwise apply for or towards his maintenance, education, or benefit, the whole or such part, if any, of the income of that property as may, in all the circumstances, be reasonable, whether or not there is—

(a) any other fund applicable to the same purpose; or

(b) any person bound by law to provide for his maintenance or education; and

(ii) if such person on attaining the age of [eighteen years] has not a vested interest in such income, the trustees shall thenceforth pay the income of that property and of any accretion thereto under subsection (2) of this section to him, until he either attains a vested interest therein or dies, or until failure of his interest:

Provided that, in deciding whether the whole or any part of the income of the property is during a minority to be paid or applied for the purposes aforesaid, the trustees shall have regard to the age of the infant and his requirements and generally to the circumstances of the case, and in particular to what other income, if any, is applicable for the same purposes; and where trustees have notice that the income of more than one fund is applicable for those purposes, then, so far as practicable, unless the entire income of the funds is paid or applied as aforesaid or the court otherwise directs, a proportionate part only of the income of each fund shall be so paid or applied.

(2) During the infancy of any such person, if his interest so long continues, the trustees shall accumulate all the residue of that income [by investing it, and any profits from so investing it] from time to time in authorised investments, and shall hold those accumulations as follows:—

(i) If any such person—

(a) attains the age of [eighteen years], or marries under that age, and his interest in such income during his infancy or until his marriage is a vested interest; or

(b) on attaining the age of [eighteen years] or on marriage under that age becomes entitled to the property from which such income arose in fee simple, absolute or determinable, or absolutely, or for an entailed interest;

the trustees shall hold the accumulations in trust for such person absolutely, but without prejudice to any provision with respect thereto contained in any settlement by him made under any statutory powers during his infancy, and so that the receipt of such person after marriage, and though still an infant, shall be a good discharge; and

(ii) In any other case the trustees shall, notwithstanding that such person had a vested interest in such income, hold the accumulations as an accretion to the capital of the property from which such accumulations arose, and as one fund with such capital for all purposes, and so that, if such property is settled land, such accumulations shall be held upon the same trusts as if the same were capital money arising therefrom;

but the trustees may, at any time during the infancy of such person if his interest so long continues, apply those accumulations, or any part thereof, as if they were income arising in the then current year.

(3) This section applies in the case of a contingent interest only if the limitation or trust carries the intermediate income of the property, but it applies to a future or contingent legacy by the parent of, or a person standing in loco parentis to, the legatee, if and for such period as, under the general law, the legacy carries interest for the maintenance of the legatee, and in any such case as last aforesaid the rate of interest shall (if the income available is sufficient, and subject to any rules of court to the contrary) be five pounds per centum per annum.

(4) This section applies to a vested annuity in like manner as if the annuity were the income of property held by trustees in trust to pay the income thereof to the annuitant for the same period for which the annuity is payable, save that in any case accumulations made during the infancy of the annuitant shall be held in trust for the annuitant or his personal representatives absolutely.

(5) This section does not apply where the instrument, if any, under which the interest arises came into operation before the commencement of this Act.

NOTES

Initial Commencement

Specified date

Specified date: 1 January 1926.

Amendment

Sub-s (1): words in square brackets substituted by the Family Law Reform Act 1969, s 1(3), Sch 1, Part I.

Sub-s (2): words "by investing it, and any profits from so investing it" in square brackets substituted by the Trustee Act 2000, s 40(1), Sch 2, Pt II, para 25.

Date in force: 1 February 2001: see SI 2001/49, art 2.

Sub-s (2): in para (i)(a) words "eighteen years" in square brackets substituted by the Family Law Reform Act 1969, s 1(3), Sch 1, Part I.

Sub-s (2): in para (i)(b) words "eighteen years" in square brackets substituted by the Family Law Reform Act 1969, s 1(3), Sch 1, Part I.

Extent

This section does not extend to Scotland: see s 71(3).

32 Power of advancement

(1) Trustees may at any time or times pay or apply any capital money subject to a trust, for the advancement or benefit, in such manner as they may, in their absolute discretion, think fit, of any person entitled to the capital of the trust property or of any share thereof, whether absolutely or contingently on his attaining any specified age or on the occurrence of any other event, or subject to a gift over on his death under any specified age or on the occurrence of any other event, and whether in possession or in remainder or reversion, and such payment or application may be made notwithstanding that the interest of such person is liable to be defeated by the exercise of a power of appointment or revocation, or to be diminished by the increase of the class to which he belongs:

Provided that—

(a) the money so paid or applied for the advancement or benefit of any person shall not exceed altogether in amount one-half of the presumptive or vested share or interest of that person in the trust property; and

(b) if that person is or becomes absolutely and indefeasibly entitled to a share in the trust property the money so paid or applied shall be brought into account as part of such share; and

(c) no such payment or application shall be made so as to prejudice any person entitled to any prior life or other interest, whether vested or contingent, in the money paid or applied unless such person is in existence and of full age and consents in writing to such payment or application.

[(2) This section does not apply to capital money arising under the Settled Land Act 1925.]

(3) This section does not apply to trusts constituted or created before the commencement of this Act.

NOTES

Initial Commencement

Specified date

Specified date: 1 January 1926.

Amendment

Sub-s (2): substituted by the Trusts of Land and Appointment of Trustees Act 1996, s 25(1), Sch 3, para 3(8); for savings in relation to entailed interests created before the commencement of that Act, and savings consequential upon the abolition of the doctrine of conversion, see s 25(4), (5) thereof.

Extent

This section does not extend to Scotland: see s 71(3).

Appendix 2.4

Trustee Act 2000

Arrangement of sections

3 General power of investment

(1) Subject to the provisions of this Part, a trustee may make any kind of investment that he could make if he were absolutely entitled to the assets of the trust.

(2) In this Act the power under subsection (1) is called "the general power of investment".

(3) The general power of investment does not permit a trustee to make investments in land other than in loans secured on land (but see also section 8).

(4) A person invests in a loan secured on land if he has rights under any contract under which—

(a) one person provides another with credit, and

(b) the obligation of the borrower to repay is secured on land.

(5) "Credit" includes any cash loan or other financial accommodation.

(6) "Cash" includes money in any form.

NOTES

Initial Commencement

To be appointed

To be appointed: see s 42(2).

Appointment

Appointment: 1 February 2001: see SI 2001/49, art 2.

Extent

This section does not extend to Scotland: see s 42(4).

4 Standard investment criteria

(1) In exercising any power of investment, whether arising under this Part or otherwise, a trustee must have regard to the standard investment criteria.

(2) A trustee must from time to time review the investments of the trust and consider whether, having regard to the standard investment criteria, they should be varied.

(3) The standard investment criteria, in relation to a trust, are—

- (a) the suitability to the trust of investments of the same kind as any particular investment proposed to be made or retained and of that particular investment as an investment of that kind, and
- (b) the need for diversification of investments of the trust, in so far as is appropriate to the circumstances of the trust.

NOTES

Initial Commencement

To be appointed

To be appointed: see s 42(2).

Appointment

Appointment: 1 February 2001: see SI 2001/49, art 2.

Extent

This section does not extend to Scotland: see s 42(4).

5 Advice

(1) Before exercising any power of investment, whether arising under this Part or otherwise, a trustee must (unless the exception applies) obtain and consider proper advice about the way in which, having regard to the standard investment criteria, the power should be exercised.

(2) When reviewing the investments of the trust, a trustee must (unless the exception applies) obtain and consider proper advice about whether, having regard to the standard investment criteria, the investments should be varied.

(3) The exception is that a trustee need not obtain such advice if he reasonably concludes that in all the circumstances it is unnecessary or inappropriate to do so.

(4) Proper advice is the advice of a person who is reasonably believed by the trustee to be qualified to give it by his ability in and practical experience of financial and other matters relating to the proposed investment.

NOTES

Initial Commencement

To be appointed

To be appointed: see s 42(2).

Appointment

Appointment: 1 February 2001: see SI 2001/49, art 2.

Extent

This section does not extend to Scotland: see s 42(4).

6 Restriction or exclusion of this Part etc

(1) The general power of investment is—

(a) in addition to powers conferred on trustees otherwise than by this Act, but

(b) subject to any restriction or exclusion imposed by the trust instrument or by any enactment or any provision of subordinate legislation.

(2) For the purposes of this Act, an enactment or a provision of subordinate legislation is not to be regarded as being, or as being part of, a trust instrument.

(3) In this Act "subordinate legislation" has the same meaning as in the Interpretation Act 1978.

NOTES

Initial Commencement

To be appointed

To be appointed: see s 42(2).

Appointment

Appointment: 1 February 2001: see SI 2001/49, art 2.

Extent

This section does not extend to Scotland: see s 42(4).

7 Existing trusts

(1) This Part applies in relation to trusts whether created before or after its commencement.

(2) No provision relating to the powers of a trustee contained in a trust instrument made before 3rd August 1961 is to be treated (for the purposes of section 6(1)(b)) as restricting or excluding the general power of investment.

(3) A provision contained in a trust instrument made before the commencement of this Part which—

(a) has effect under section 3(2) of the Trustee Investments Act 1961 as a power to invest under that Act, or

(b) confers power to invest under that Act,

is to be treated as conferring the general power of investment on a trustee.

NOTES

Initial Commencement

To be appointed

To be appointed: see s 42(2).

Appointment

Appointment: 1 February 2001: see SI 2001/49, art 2.

Extent

This section does not extend to Scotland: see s 42(4).

Part III Acquisition of Land

8 Power to acquire freehold and leasehold land

(1) A trustee may acquire freehold or leasehold land in the United Kingdom—

(a) as an investment,

(b) for occupation by a beneficiary, or

(c) for any other reason.

(2) "Freehold or leasehold land" means—

(a) in relation to England and Wales, a legal estate in land,

(b) in relation to Scotland—

(i) the estate or interest of the proprietor of the dominium utile or, in the case of land not held on feudal tenure, the estate or interest of the owner, or

(ii) a tenancy, and

(c) in relation to Northern Ireland, a legal estate in land, including land held under a fee farm grant.

(3) For the purpose of exercising his functions as a trustee, a trustee who acquires land under this section has all the powers of an absolute owner in relation to the land.

NOTES

Initial Commencement

To be appointed

To be appointed: see s 42(2).

Appointment

Appointment: 1 February 2001: see SI 2001/49, art 2.

Extent

This section does not extend to Scotland: see s 42(4).

9 Restriction or exclusion of this Part etc

The powers conferred by this Part are—

(a) in addition to powers conferred on trustees otherwise than by this Part, but

(b) subject to any restriction or exclusion imposed by the trust instrument or by any enactment or any provision of subordinate legislation.

NOTES

Initial Commencement

To be appointed

To be appointed: see s 42(2).

Appointment

Appointment: 1 February 2001: see SI 2001/49, art 2.

Extent

This section does not extend to Scotland: see s 42(4).

Appendix 3

Inland Revenue form IHT215 – Practitioner's Guide

Inland
Revenue
Capital Taxes

Practitioner's Guide

The Guide contains the following notes
to help you fill in form IHT 2000,
the supplementary pages and form IHT (WS).

IHT 210
D1(Notes)
D2(Notes)
D3(Notes)
D4(Notes)
D5(Notes)
D6(Notes)
D7(Notes)
D8(Notes)
D9(Notes)
D10(Notes)
D11(Notes)
D12(Notes)
D13(Notes)
D14(Notes)
D15(Notes)
D16(Notes)
D17(Notes)
D18(Notes)
IHT213
IHT214

IHT215 **(Substitute)(LexisNexis UK)**

Index of supplementary pages

How to fill in form IHT200

This Guide will help you to fill in form **IHT200**. It will help you to follow the correct procedure to apply for a grant of probate and to pay the right amount of inheritance tax if there is any to pay. You may also need to fill in some of the supplementary pages that go with form **IHT200**.

The notes in this Guide are numbered and match the boxes in the form **IHT200**. There are separate notes for each of the supplementary pages.

We refer to the person who has died in both this Guide and form **IHT200** as "the deceased".

We hope this Guide will answer most of your questions. If you need more help, please telephone our Helpline (see page 2).

If you need any more of the supplementary pages or leaflets, please telephone our Orderline (see page 2).

These notes apply only where a person died on or after 18 March 1986. If a person died before this date, telephone our Helpline (see page 2) who can tell you which forms you will need.

IHT210

This Guide is for general information only. It cannot explain everything about inheritance tax. We publish a number of leaflets that give more detailed information about particular topics. There is a list on page 46 of this Guide.

If you would like a copy of one or more of the leaflets, or need a copy of any of our forms, please telephone or fax our Orderline

0845 234 1000
0845 234 1010 (fax)

Our forms and leaflets are also available on the Internet at www.inlandrevenue.gov.uk

If you want to know more about any particular aspect of inheritance tax, please telephone our Helpline, or write to one of the addresses below

Our Helpline numbers

Nottingham	0115 974 2400 0115 974 2432 (fax)
Edinburgh	0131 777 4050/4060
Belfast	028 9050 5353

Our addresses (including DX addresses for solicitors and banks etc)

Nottingham	IR Capital Taxes Ferrers House PO Box 38 Castle Meadow Road Nottingham NG2 1BB DX 701201 NOTTINGHAM 4
Edinburgh	IR Capital Taxes Meldrum House 15 Drumsheugh Gardens Edinburgh EH3 7UG DX ED 542001 EDINGUBRH 14
Belfast	IR Capital Taxes Level 3 Dorchester House 52-58 Great Victoria Street Belfast BT2 7QL DX 2001 NR BELFAST 2

2

Contents

3

The grant of representation

- You need a grant of representation to get access to most assets in the deceased's estate. There are a number of different types of grant. In England, Wales and Northern Ireland, the two most common types are

  - a grant of probate, where the deceased has left a Will and
  - a grant of letters of administration, where the deceased has not left a Will.

  In Scotland, the grant is a grant of Confirmation. Throughout this Guide, we refer to all types of grant of representation as the "grant".

Inheritance tax and the grant

- You must pay any inheritance tax and interest that is due before you can get a grant. Tax on certain assets may be paid by instalments. We tell you more about this on page 13 of the guide *"How to fill in form IHT(WS)"*. The law says that we must charge interest from six months after the end of the month in which the person died. For example, if a person dies on the 7 January, we charge interest from 1 August. It does not matter why you have not paid the tax by then: interest will still be due.

What you have received

- If you are applying for a grant without the help of a solicitor or other agent, you have received form **IHT200**, this Guide, a separate guide called *"How to fill in form IHT(WS)"*, an inheritance tax worksheet form **IHT(WS)** and some of the supplementary pages that we find apply to most estates. It is your responsibility to make sure you fill in the right supplementary pages. You do not need to fill in any that do not apply, even if we have included them with this pack.

  If you need any of the other supplementary pages you should telephone our Orderline (see page 2 of this Guide).

How to fill in the forms

- **You must answer all the questions on the form. You must fill in all the boxes on the form and on any supplementary pages that apply.** We need your answers so that we can work out the value of the estate. Please write the figure "0" or put a dash in the box if the deceased did not own any of the assets described. You should make full enquiries so you can show that the figures you give and the statements you make are right.

  If you do not answer all the questions and fill in all the boxes, we may not be able to process the form.

When you may not need to fill in form IHT200

- You do not need to fill in form **IHT200** if the estate is an excepted estate. In some estates you may only need to fill in part of form **IHT200**. You will need to fill in a different form of account for some special types of grant. We tell you more about all this starting on page 42 of this Guide.

4

Step by step guide to filling in the forms

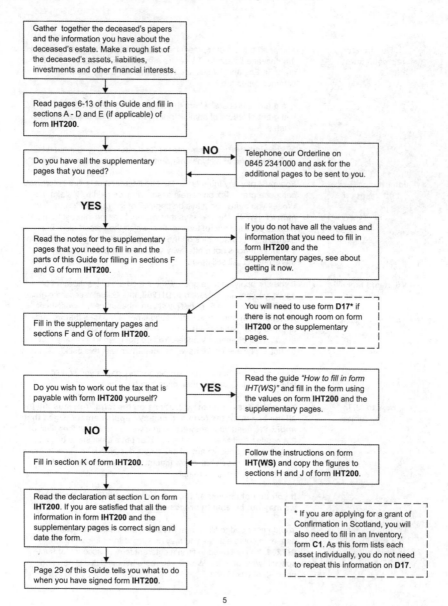

Gather together the deceased's papers and the information you have about the deceased's estate. Make a rough list of the deceased's assets, liabilities, investments and other financial interests.

Read pages 6-13 of this Guide and fill in sections A - D and E (if applicable) of form **IHT200**.

Do you have all the supplementary pages that you need?

NO — Telephone our Orderline on 0845 2341000 and ask for the additional pages to be sent to you.

YES

Read the notes for the supplementary pages that you need to fill in and the parts of this Guide for filling in sections F and G of form **IHT200**.

If you do not have all the values and information that you need to fill in form **IHT200** and the supplementary pages, see about getting it now.

Fill in the supplementary pages and sections F and G of form **IHT200**.

You will need to use form **D17*** if there is not enough room on form **IHT200** or the supplementary pages.

Do you wish to work out the tax that is payable with form **IHT200** yourself?

YES — Read the guide *"How to fill in form IHT(WS)"* and fill in the form using the values on form **IHT200** and the supplementary pages.

Follow the instructions on form **IHT(WS)** and copy the figures to sections H and J of form **IHT200**.

NO

Fill in section K of form **IHT200**.

Read the declaration at section L on form **IHT200**. If you are satisfied that all the information in form **IHT200** and the supplementary pages is correct sign and date the form.

Page 29 of this Guide tells you what to do when you have signed form **IHT200**.

* If you are applying for a grant of Confirmation in Scotland, you will also need to fill in an Inventory, form **C1**. As this form lists each asset individually, you do not need to repeat this information on **D17**.

What values to include

The law says that for inheritance tax, you have to value all assets as if each item had been **sold** on the date the deceased died. We call this the 'open market value'. As you work through this Guide, it tells you how to obtain the right value to include in form **IHT200**. Round the value of assets and liabilities down to the nearest £.

Estimated values

You should make full enquiries to find out the exact value for each item in the estate. However, if you are having difficulty with one or two items, such as an income tax repayment or household bill, or perhaps details of foreign tax or income due from a trust, the law says that you may include a provisional estimate. You should make the best estimate that you can. You will need to list the boxes that contain provisional estimates in section L of form **IHT200**.

It is your responsibility to tell us what the correct figure is as soon as you know it.

Supporting documents

You do not need to send us copies of documents, for example, a letter from a bank with the balance in an account, evidence of household bills etc, unless we specifically ask you to provide a copy in this Guide. However, you must keep safe all documents that you have used to fill in form **IHT200** and the supplementary pages as we may ask you for some or all of them after you have obtained the grant.

Original documents

If you have had to return an original document, such as a life insurance policy, please make sure you have kept a copy of the document and any other papers that are linked with it, such as a deed of trust or a loan agreement.

Things to keep in mind

There are some types of asset that may be included in more than one section of form **IHT200** and the supplementary pages. This applies especially to stocks and shares and to assets owned jointly. Please make sure you have read all the appropriate notes before you include details of such assets so that you can put them in the right section of the form. Also, do not include the same asset in more than one section.

Where can I get help

If you need any help in filling in the forms, working out the tax, or have any questions about inheritance tax you should contact our

- Nottingham office, if you live in England or Wales,
- Edinburgh office, if you live in Scotland, and
- Belfast office, if you live in Northern Ireland.

Our addresses and telephone numbers are on page 2 of this Guide.

How to fill in section A

A1 Write in the name of the probate registry, Sheriff Court District or Commissary Office where you will apply for your grant. If you are applying for a grant in England and Wales or Northern Ireland without the help of a solicitor, enter the name of the registry (or the name of the registry that controls the local office) where you want your interview to take place.

You can find out the name of the registry that you need from the booklet **'How to obtain Probate'** (form PA2), which you can get from your local probate registry.

How to fill in section B

B1 Write in the deceased's title ('Mr', 'Mrs', 'Dr' etc). If there is not enough room, for example, for a peer of the realm, include the title in box B2.

B2 Write in the deceased's surname.

B3 Write in the deceased's first name(s).

B4 Write in the deceased's date of birth in the format dd/mm/yyyy

B5 Write in the deceased's date of death in the format dd/mm/yyyy

B6 Say whether the deceased was 'Married', 'Divorced', 'Widowed' or 'Single' at the time of their death.

B7 Write in the address of the property where the deceased was normally living before they died. Include the postcode, if you know what it was.

B8 Tick this box if their husband or wife survived the deceased.

B9 Tick this box if any of their brother(s) or sister(s) survived the deceased.

B10 Tick this box if any of their parent(s) survived the deceased.

B11 Write in **the number** of children who survived the deceased.

B12 Write in **the number** of grandchildren who survived the deceased.

B13 Tick this box if the address that you have shown in B7 was a nursing home or other residential care home.

B14 A person's domicile is usually the country where their main home is. The United Kingdom is not a "country" when establishing a person's domicile. So a person will have a domicile in England and Wales, **or** Scotland **or** Northern Ireland. But to keep things simple, we refer to all three countries as the United Kingdom (UK) in these notes.

Say in this box wheth er the deceased was domiciled in 'England and Wales', 'Scotland', 'Northern Ireland', or write in the name of the foreign country.

The Channel Islands and the Isle of Man are foreign countries when considering domicile.

Even though the deceased may have been domiciled abroad, there are some special rules that mean we can treat the deceased *as if* they were domiciled in the UK. We tell you more about this in form **D2(Notes)** and in our leaflet **IHT18**. You should still write the name of the foreign country in this box, but fill in the rest of the form as if the deceased was domiciled in the UK.

B15 Write in the deceased's occupation, if you know what it was, and say whether or not they were retired.

B16 Write in the deceased's National Insurance number. If the deceased had retired, you can find this on their State pension book. If the State pension was paid directly to a bank or building society, you can find the number on the letter from the Benefits Agency (form BR2199), which told the deceased how much money would be paid into their account. The Benefits Agency reference *is* the National Insurance number.

If the deceased was still working, you can find the National Insurance number on their payslip, form P60 or on letters from the Revenue such as a notice of coding.

B17 Write in the name of the tax district that dealt with the deceased's affairs.

B18 Write in the income tax reference or unique 10-digit Self Assessment number. You should find these details on any correspondence the deceased had with the Inland Revenue. Leave boxes B17 and B18 blank if you cannot find this information.

How to fill in section C

C1 Write in the name and address of the firm or person that we should contact. If possible, please include the postcode.

C2 The DX code only applies to solicitors or other firms and organisations that are members of the Document Exchange system. Write in the DX number and town.

C3 If you have given the name of a firm in box C1, write in the name and reference of the person we should contact.

C4 Write in a **daytime** telephone number for the person we should contact.

C5 If appropriate, write in a fax number for the person we should contact.

Confidentiality

You have a right to the same high degree of confidentiality that all taxpayers have. We have a legal duty to keep your affairs completely confidential and cannot give information to others about an estate, trust or transfer even if they have an interest in it, unless the law permits us to do so. This means we may only discuss a taxpayer's affairs with that person, or with someone else that the taxpayer has appointed to act for them. In the case of someone who has died, this means that we can only discuss an estate with the people (or person) who have signed and delivered form **IHT200**, that is the executors or administrators, or another person appointed to act for them; usually a solicitor or an accountant.

So if, for example, you are applying for a grant without the help of a solicitor or accountant to act for you and it is difficult for us to contact you by telephone during the day, we cannot discuss the estate with another person without your written authority. You may want us to write to you, but for someone else - perhaps a husband, wife or other relative - to be able to deal with telephone calls. If so, you should either include their name in box C1 as well, or enclose a separate written authority when you send the form **IHT200** to us.

How to fill in section D

- **Tick the appropriate box to answer each of the questions in section D. If you have said that the deceased was domiciled abroad, you should answer the questions for UK assets only. The following notes will help you to answer the questions.**

The Will

- Fill in form **D1** if the deceased left a Will and attach a copy of the deceased's Will to the form if required.

Domicile outside the United Kingdom

- If you have said that the deceased was domiciled in a foreign country or if the deceased is only treated as domiciled in the UK, fill in form **D2**. Where this applies, you **must** send form **IHT200** to us before you apply for a grant (see page 29 of this Guide).

Gifts and other transfers of value

- You can answer "No" to this question and do not need to provide any details if the **only** gifts made by the deceased were
  - to their husband or wife and spouse exemption applies (see page 36 of this Guide)
  - **outright** gifts to any individual which do not exceed £250 in any one year (the small gifts exemption)
  - **outright** gifts to any individual of money or quoted stocks and shares which are **wholly** covered by the annual and/or gifts out of income exemptions described in form **D3(Notes)**.

  If the deceased had made any other gifts or "transfers of value" since 18 March 1986, including transfers into settlement and payment of insurance premiums for the benefit of another person (other than the deceased's spouse), or advances out of a trust fund or any assets that were taken out of a trust before death, you must fill in form **D3**. In general, a "transfer of value" is any transaction where the deceased did not receive full value in exchange.

Joint assets

- Bank and building society accounts, stocks and shares, household goods, freehold and leasehold property are the assets most usually owned in joint names. We call all the assets that are owned jointly "joint property". Fill in form **D4** as appropriate if the deceased owned any **UK** assets in joint names with one or more people.

Nominated assets

- Some bank accounts and assets such as National Savings certificates can be 'nominated'. This means that the owner has given instructions for the asset to go to a particular person when the owner dies. (But this does not include legacies in the Will). Nominated assets remain part of the owner's estate for inheritance tax when they die. Fill in section 3 of form **D4** if the deceased had nominated any assets during their lifetime.

Assets held in trust

- We call assets that are held in trust "settled property". Where the deceased had the right to
  - the income from assets (for example dividends from shares, interest from a bank account, or rent from let property) **or**
  - payments of a fixed amount each year, often in regular instalments **or**

- live in a house or use the contents without paying any rent

they had a right to benefit from settled property and you should fill in form **D5**.

Pensions

▸ Fill in form **D6** if

- the deceased was being paid a pension from an employer or a personal pension scheme or a retirement annuity contract
- a lump sum became payable from such a source as a result of the deceased's death or
- the deceased had made any changes to their pension provision in the 2 years before they died.

Stocks and shares

▸ Fill in form **D7** to give details of all the stocks and shares owned by the deceased.

Debts due to the estate

▸ If the deceased lent any money to someone which had not been repaid at the time of death, fill in form **D8**. You should also use this form to give details of any debts owned to the deceased by a business or company, including their own business or company.

Life insurance and annuities

▸ Fill in form **D9** if the deceased paid either regular, monthly, or lump sum premiums for

- insurance policies which are payable to the estate
- a mortgage protection policy (form **D4(Notes)** tells you more about a joint mortgage protection policy)
- unit-linked investment bonds with insurance companies or other financial service providers which pay out 101% of the value of the units to the estate
- investment or re-investment plans, bonds or contracts with financial service providers which pay out to the estate on death
- insurance policies and unit-linked investment bonds etc which are payable to beneficiaries under a trust and do not form part of the estate
- joint life insurance policies under which the deceased was one of the lives assured *but which remain in force after the death*
- insurance policies on the life of another person but under which the deceased was to benefit
  or
- if the deceased received any payments under an annuity which continued after death, or under which a lump sum was payable as a result of the their death.

Household and personal goods

▸ Fill in form **D10** to give details of the household and personal goods owned by the deceased in their own name.

11

Interest in another estate

▸ The deceased may have had the right to a legacy or a share of an estate of someone who had died before them. If they died before receiving the full legacy or share of the estate, fill in form **D11**.

Land, buildings and interests in land

▸ Fill in form **D12** to give details of the land and buildings owned by the deceased.

Agricultural relief

▸ If the deceased owned a farm or farmland you may be able to deduct agricultural relief against the value of the agricultural property. Fill in form **D13** if the estate includes agricultural property and you wish to deduct agricultural relief. Form **D13(Notes)** and our leaflet **IHT17** tell you more about agricultural relief.

Business interests

▸ Fill in form **D14** to give details of the deceased's business interest(s), holdings of unquoted shares or assets used in a business.

Business relief

▸ You may be able to deduct business relief against certain holdings of shares, business interests or assets used in a business. Fill in form **D14** if you wish to deduct business relief. Form **D14(Notes)** and our leaflet **IHT17** tell you more about business relief.

Foreign assets

▸ Fill in form **D15** to give details of any overseas assets owned by the deceased, including any jointly owned overseas assets. Do **not** include here details of foreign shares which are quoted on the London Stock Exchange, see the note for box F1. We call all the assets that the deceased owned overseas "foreign property". Remember the Channel Islands and the Isle of Man are foreign countries so assets held there are foreign property.

Debts owed by the estate

▸ Fill in form **D16** to give details of any

- money which the deceased had borrowed from close friends or relatives
- money which close friends or relatives had spent on behalf of the deceased and is to be repaid from the estate
- other loans and overdrafts or
- guarantee debts

which you are deducting from the estate.

How to fill in section E

▸ Section E of form **IHT200 only** applies if the deceased died domiciled in **Scotland**. Tick the box if the deceased's husband or wife or any of their children or grandchildren have indicated that they wish to claim or discharge their legal rights. If you have answered "Yes", please fill in the number of the deceased's children who are under 18 and the number who are 18 and over.

Please use form **D17** if you need to provide any other information about a claim for legal rights.

12

How to fill in section F

- You must include in section F all the assets described in boxes F1 to F23 that were owned in the UK by the deceased in their own name when they died. You should also include the funeral expenses and other debts that the deceased owed when they died.

Stocks and shares

- There are many different types of stocks and shares. If you have a professional valuation, please attach a copy. If not, you will need to fill in form **D7** (or Inventory form **C1** in Scotland) giving details of the stocks, shares and other such investments belonging to the deceased.

  You can help us by dividing the stocks and shares into the categories listed on the next page for boxes F1 to F4. It will also help us if you list the stocks and shares in the order they appear in the Stock Exchange Daily Official List, in the Financial Times or other newspaper. Your local library may have back issues of newspapers.

Underwriters at Lloyds

- If the deceased was an Underwriter with Lloyds of London, they may have had both personal and business portfolios of stocks and shares. You should keep the personal portfolio and business portfolio separate. You should include the stocks and shares in the personal portfolio in section F of form **IHT200**. You should include a value for the deceased's business as an Underwriter in box G8.1, see page 24 of this Guide.

Where to include stocks and shares

- You may pay inheritance tax on certain shareholdings by instalments. If you want to do so, the shares owned by the deceased must meet a number of conditions. If the shares meet the conditions, you may include those shares in section G on page 5 of form **IHT200**. The basic conditions are that

  - the number of shares owned by the deceased gave them control of the company. A person controls a company for inheritance tax if they could **control** the majority (more than 50%) of the voting powers on *all* questions affecting the company as a whole or

  - the shares are **not quoted** on the Stock Exchange and their value exceeds £20,000. The notes for boxes F3 and F4 list the different types of shares that are treated as not quoted for this rule.

  There are other, more detailed rules that apply to shares **not quoted** on the Stock Exchange. You should telephone our Helpline for more information if the shares owned by the deceased meet this second rule and you want to pay the tax on the shares in instalments. In certain circumstances, you may be able to pay tax by instalments even if the value of the shares is less than £20,000. Telephone our Helpline for more information.

  If the shares do not meet either of these rules, you **must** include the shares in section F on page 3 of form **IHT200**.

13

F1 Quoted stocks, shares and investments

Include in this box the total value for

- all stocks, shares, debentures and other securities listed in the Stock Exchange Daily Official List
- unit trusts
- investment trusts
- Open-Ended Investment Companies
- Personal Equity Plans
- shares which are part of an Individual Savings Account (ISA)
- foreign shares which are listed on the London Stock Exchange.

F2 UK Government securities ('gilts') and municipal securities

Include in this box the total value for

- Treasury Bills, Treasury Annuities, Treasury Stock, Exchequer Stock, Convertible Stock, Consolidated Stock and Loan, Funding Stock, Savings Bonds, Victory Bonds, War Loan
- Government Stock held on the Bank of England Register (previously held on the National Savings Register)
- cities or towns, dock, harbour and water boards, Port of London Authority, Agricultural Mortgage Corporation, Northern Ireland municipal stock.

F3 Unquoted stocks, shares and investments

Include in this box the total value for

- unlisted stocks and shares in private limited companies
- shares held in a Business Expansion Scheme (BES) or in a Business Start-up Scheme (BSS).

F4 Traded unquoted stocks and shares

Include in this box the total value for

- shares listed on the Alternative Investment Market (AIM)
- shares traded on OFEX
- shares traded on the Unlisted Securities Market (USM).

F5 Dividends or Interest

Include in this box dividends and interest on the assets in boxes F1 to F4 or G10 to G12 that were due at the date of death but have not yet been paid.

How to value stocks and shares

Form **D7(Notes)** tells you how to value the different types of stocks and shares. The notes also provide more information about stocks and shares generally. You can find out the value of stock held on the Bank of England register by writing to

Registrar's Department, Southgate House,
Southgate Street, Gloucester, GL1 1UW.

F6 Premium Bonds

Include in this box the total value for any Premium Bonds owned by the deceased. Include any unclaimed or uncashed prizes as well.

F7 National Savings investments

List each investment separately on form **D17** (or Inventory form **C1** in Scotland) and include in this box the total for items such as

- National Savings Certificates
- National Savings Capital or Deposit Bonds
- National Savings Income Bonds
- Pensioners Guaranteed Income Bonds
- Children's Bonus Bonds
- First Option Bonds
- Save As You Earn Contracts
- Year Plans.

You should include a National Savings Bank account in box F8.

How to value National Savings Investments

You can find out the value of all National Savings investments by sending off form DNS 904. You can get this form from the Post Office. If the reply gives separate figures for capital and for interest owed, but not paid, up to the date of death, please show them separately on form **D17**. Put the total in box F7.

F8 Bank and building society accounts

List each account or investment separately on form **D17** (or Inventory form **C1** in Scotland) and include in this box the total for

- current, deposit, high interest, fixed interest, term, bond and money market accounts with a bank, building society, mutual, friendly or co-operative society
- accounts with supermarkets or insurance companies
- National Savings Bank account
- TESSA account
- cash in an Individual Savings Account.

How to value bank and building society accounts, etc

▸ The bank or building society will be able to tell you how much was in each account when the deceased died and how much interest was due, but not paid, up to the date of death. If you have separate figures for capital and interest, please show them separately on form **D17**. Put the total in box F8.

F9 Cash (not at bank)

Include in this box

- any cash held by the deceased or kept at home or elsewhere such as safe deposit boxes
- cash held for deceased by someone else, for example, a stockbroker
- travellers cheques
- any uncashed cheques made out to the deceased.

How to value travellers cheques

▸ Sterling travellers' cheques should be included as capital at face value. If the travellers' cheques are in one of the major foreign currencies, you should convert them to sterling using the closing mid-price at the date of death from the "Pound Spot Forward against the Pound" table in the Financial Times. Otherwise convert them at the rate shown in the 'FT Guide to World Currencies' which is published every week in the Financial Times on Monday.

F10 Debts due to the deceased and secured by mortgage

Include in this box any money the deceased had lent to someone which was secured by a mortgage and had not been repaid at the date of death. You will need to fill in form **D8** to give details of each mortgage.

F11 Other debts due to the deceased

Include in this box

- money which the deceased had lent personally to someone and which had not been repaid at the date of death
- money which the deceased had lent to trustees linked to a life insurance policy held in trust
- money for which the deceased held a promissory note
- money for which the deceased held an "IOU"
- money owing to the deceased from a director's loan account or current account with a company.

You will need to fill in form **D8** to give details of each sum owed to the deceased.

16

F12 Rents due to the deceased

Include in this box the gross amount of any rent from let property that was due to the deceased, but had not been paid at the date of death. Include the property itself separately on form **D12**.

F13 Accrued income

Include in this box income from settled property where the trustees had received the income but had not paid it over to the deceased before the deceased died.

F14 Apportioned income

Include in this box any income that has arisen on settled property but had not been received by the trustees between the date when income was last paid to the deceased and the date of death.

Note

The trustees of the settlement should be able to tell you the figures to include in boxes F13 and F14.

F15 Other income due to the deceased

Include in this box

- any money owed in salary, wages, director's fees or *arrears* of pension
- benefits or arrears of pension due but unclaimed from the Benefits Agency
- guaranteed payments due to the estate from a pension scheme or policy (you should also fill in form **D6** to give details of payments due)
- guaranteed payments due to the estate under a purchased life annuity (you should also fill in form **D9** to give details of payments due)

F16 Life insurance policies

Include in this box the total payable

- from life insurance policies, including bonuses
- under mortgage protection policies (form **D4(Notes)** tells you more about joint mortgage protection policies)
- under unit-linked investment schemes which pay 101% of the unit value on death
- under investment or re-investment plans, bonds or contracts with a financial services provider which pay out on death

17

- for the value of the deceased's interest in joint life insurance policies under which the deceased was one of the lives insured, *but which remain in force after the death*
- for the value of insurance policies on the life of another person but under which the deceased was to benefit and
- from insurance policies which are part of an Individual Savings Account.

You will need to fill in form **D9** to give details of each insurance policy.

F17	Private health schemes	Include in this box any payments due to the deceased under private medical insurance to cover hospital or other health charges incurred before death.
F18	Income tax or capital gains tax repayment	Include in this box any income tax or capital gains tax actually repaid to the estate or a reasonable estimate of any sum that might be repayable to the deceased. An income tax repayment may be due if the deceased died early in the tax year and received a pension and other income where tax was deducted at source.
F19	Household and personal goods (sold)	Include in this box the **gross** sale price for the items that have been sold.
F20	Household and personal goods (unsold)	Include in this box the total value of all household and personal goods remaining unsold. Include pictures, china, clothes, books, jewellery, stamp, coin and other collections, motor cars, boats etc. You will need to fill in form **D10** to give details of the household and personal goods.
F21	Interest in another estate	The deceased may have had the right to a legacy or share of an estate of someone who died before them. If the deceased died before receiving the full legacy or share from that estate, you should include a value in this box for the assets that they still have to receive. You will need to fill in form **D11** to give details of this interest.

18

F22 Interest in expectancy (reversionary interest)

The deceased may have been entitled to some assets in a trust or settlement but someone else is receiving the benefit from them during that person's life. For example, the dividends from stocks and shares, or the right to live in a house without paying any rent. The deceased's estate will not receive the assets until after the other person has also died.

Include in this box an estimated value for the assets. Use form **D17** to give

- the name and date of death (or date of settlement) of the person who set up the trust and
- the name and age of the person who is receiving the benefit.

(It is unlikely that you will have to pay any tax on this item, as most reversionary interests are "excluded property" (see page 40 of this Guide) but we still need to know that the deceased was entitled to it.)

F23 Other personal assets

Include in this box

- any refunds from gas, electricity or water suppliers
- any insurance premium or licence refunds
- lump sums payable to the estate from an annuity, pension scheme or policy
- money due to the deceased from the sale of real and leasehold property where the contract for sale had been exchanged before the death but the sale had not been completed by the time the deceased died
- any other assets not included elsewhere.

Use form **D17** (or Inventory form **C1** in Scotland) to list the items included in this box.

F24 Add together boxes F1to F23 and write the total in this box.

Debts and liabilities

▸ You should only include debts that the deceased actually owed at the date they died. You must **not** include fees for professional services carried out **after** death. This means that probate fees, any solicitor's or estate agent's fees and any valuation fees incurred in dealing with the deceased's estate cannot be deducted.

Liabilities

F25 List all the debts owed by the deceased at the date they died. You should fill in the name of the person or organisation that is owed the money and say briefly why the money is owed. If you include a deduction for solicitors' or accountants' fees, give the dates for the period during which the work was done. Add up all the liabilities and write the total in this box.

Particular types of debt

▸

Loans and overdrafts	Fill in form **D16** to give details of any overdrafts or loans made to the deceased.
Uncleared cheques	If you include cheques written by the deceased, but which had not cleared before they died, please say who the cheques were written out to and for what goods or services.
Money being repaid to relatives	Fill in form **D16** to give details about money being repaid to relatives.
Guarantee debts	Fill in form **D16** to give details about any guarantee debts.
Deficit	If there is a deficit in either section G on form **IHT200** or in box FP5 on form **D15**, you may include that deficit here – we tell you what to do with a deficit on page 41 of this Guide.

Funeral expenses

F26 You may include a deduction for funeral expenses and a reasonable deduction for the mourning expenses of the close family. You may also deduct the cost of a tombstone or headstone marking the site of the deceased's grave. Describe the items you wish to deduct, add up all the funeral expenses and write the total in this box.

Total liabilities and funeral expenses

F27 Add box F25 to box F26 and write the total in this box.

Net assets

F28 Take boxes F27 away from box F24 and write the answer in this box.

What you should do if box F28 results in a minus figure

- If the figure in box F27 is more than the assets in box F24, you should make a note of the deficit. You should write '0', rather than the minus figure in boxes F28 and F30.

  We tell you what you should do with a deficit at page 41 of this Guide.

Exemptions and reliefs

- There are a number of exemptions and reliefs that are available to reduce the value of the estate on which you need to pay tax. We tell you more about exemptions and reliefs starting on page 36 of this Guide. To deduct any exemptions or reliefs against the assets listed in boxes F1 to F23 you should write the title of the exemption or relief and the amount that you want to deduct in the space provided.

Exclusions

- Inheritance tax is not charged on any assets that are "excluded property". Details of the exclusions start at page 40 of this Guide. If any of the deceased's assets listed in boxes F1 to F23 is "excluded property" you should say which exclusion applies and write the amount in the "Exemptions and reliefs" box.

F29 Add up all the exemptions, reliefs and exclusions and write the total in this box.

Chargeable value

F30 Take box F29 away from box F28 and write the answer in this box. This box must not contain a minus figure. Taking away exemptions and reliefs may only reduce the figure in box F28 to '0'.

Copy the figure from this box to box WS1 on form **IHT(WS)**.

How to fill in section G

- You must include in section G all the assets described in boxes G1 to G12 that were owned in the UK by the deceased in their own name when they died. You may pay the tax on the assets included in section G by instalments. We tell you more about this option on page 13 of the guide "*How to fill in form IHT(WS)*". If you want to pay the tax on the assets in section G by instalments, you should tick the box at the top of page 5 of form **IHT200**.

Land and buildings

- You must include here all real, leasehold, heritable and other immovable property owned by the deceased in the UK. If you have a professional valuation, please attach a copy. You will need to fill in form **D12** giving details of each item of land anyway.

Do not include here any land that the deceased owned jointly with someone else and which land passes by survivorship. Form **D4(Notes)** tells you what to do with such land.

You can help us by dividing the land into the categories listed for boxes G1 – G6.

G1	Deceased's residence	Include in this box the value for the deceased's home. If the deceased had moved to a nursing or other residential home shortly before they died and their home was vacant, you should include the property in this box and not box G2 below.
G2	Other residential property	Include in this box the value of any other residential property owned by the deceased which was either let, or could be let but was vacant when they died. You **should** include the deceased's home here if it was let at death.
G3	Farms	Include in this box the value of all the farmland, farmhouses and farm buildings owned by the deceased. If the deceased lived on a farm, you should include the value of the farmhouse here and not in box G1. Include farms, farm buildings and farmland in this box whether you are deducting agricultural relief or not.
G4	Business property	Include in this box the value of any property owned by the deceased from which they ran a business, either alone or in partnership, (for example a hotel, a shop, or a factory). If it was a farming business, include the property in box G3.

G5 Timber and woodland

Include in this box the value of any timber and woodland owned by the deceased that is not part of a farm. Most farms will include coppices, small woods and belts of trees that shelter the land. Include these in the one value for the farm in box G3.

G6 Other land and buildings

Include in this box the value of any other land not included in boxes G1 to G5 (for example, lock-up garages, redundant land, derelict property, quarries, airfields etc) and any other rights, for example fishing rights, that are attached to land.

How to value land and buildings

- If you do not have a professional valuation, you need to take all reasonable steps to put a value on the land and buildings. Advertisements in local estate agents and local papers for properties that are very similar to the deceased's may help you to make a realistic estimate of the value of the deceased's property.

You should take account of the state of repair of the property. (This may decrease its value.) But you must also take account of any features that might make it attractive to a builder or developer, for example large gardens or access to land that is suitable for development. (This is likely to increase its value.)

Business interests

- You will need to fill in form **D14** to give details of any business interests owned by the deceased.

G7 Farming business

Include in this box the net value of the deceased's interest in a farming business. If the deceased was in partnership, write the value in box G7.2. If they ran the business personally, write the value in box G7.1. If the deceased took part in more than one farming business, you may need to fill in a separate form **D14** for each business. Write the total value of all the farming businesses in the appropriate box and the overall total in box G7.

G8 Other business interests

Include in this box the net value of the deceased's interest in a business other than a farming business. If the deceased was in partnership, write the value in box G8.2. If they ran the business personally, write the value in box G8.1. If the deceased took part in more than one business, you may need to fill in a separate form **D14** for each business interest. Write the total value of all the business interests in the appropriate box and the overall total in box G8.

23

G9 Business assets

Include in this box any assets that the deceased owned, which were not included as part of a business in boxes G7 and G8, but were still used by the deceased for business activities. If the assets were used in a farming business, write the value in box G9.1, if they were used for another business write the value in box G9.2. Write the total in box G9.

How to value a business interest

- Ideally, accounts for the business should be prepared at the date of death. If this is not practical, (for example, where the deceased was a member of a partnership and the business continues) you should use the last set of accounts prepared before the death. The value of the deceased's capital and current accounts with the business will be the starting point. Form **D14(Notes)** gives you more help in valuing an interest in a business.

Stocks and shares

- Page 13 of this Guide told you which stocks and shares could be included in this section. If the deceased was an Insurance Underwriter with Lloyds, include the net value of the deceased's assets with Lloyds as a business interest in box G8.1. Do not include the separate holdings of shares anywhere else in sections F or G.

G10 Quoted shares and securities

You may **only** include stocks and shares listed on the Stock Exchange here if the holding gave the deceased control of the company. A person controls a company for inheritance tax if they could control the majority (more than 50%) of the voting powers on *all* questions affecting the company as a whole. Write the value of the holding in box G10.

Fill in details of the shares on form **D7**, section 1, but keep them separate from other shares being included in section F. **Do not add the value of these shares to the total in box SS1.**

G11 Unquoted shares

Include in this box the value of any stocks and shares that are not listed on the Stock Exchange. The types of shares are listed in the notes for box F3. If the shares gave the deceased control of the company, write the value in box G11.1. If not, include the value in box G11.2.

Fill in details of the shares on form **D7**, section 3.

24

G12 Traded unquoted shares

You should **only** include unlisted stocks and shares that are traded on exchanges in this box. The exchanges are listed in the notes for box F4. If the shares gave the deceased control of the company, write the value in box G12.1. If not include the value in box G12.2.

Fill in details of the shares on form **D7**, section 4.

G13 Add together boxes G1 to G12 and write the total in this box.

How to value stocks and shares

- Form **D7(Notes)** tells you how to value shares that are listed on the Stock Exchange. The same rules apply for traded unquoted shares that are dealt on various exchanges.

For unquoted shares, you should estimate the value on the best evidence available to you. You should not include a nominal or par value for the holding of shares, unless that value is appropriate. You have to try to establish what the shares might have been sold for if they had been sold on the open market at the date of death. The company may be able to give you some idea of the value of the shares.

We will usually ask our Shares Valuation Division to consider the value of unquoted shares. Their Helpline number is 0115 974 2222.

Debts and liabilities

- The notes at page 20 of this Guide gave some information about debts. You should only include here debts that are specifically linked to the assets shown on this page.

G14 Mortgages

Include in this box any money that was secured by a mortgage on the land shown on this page. If the deceased had a mortgage protection policy, you should include the mortgage on this page and include the money due to the estate from the policy in box F16.

You will need to fill in form **D16** to give details of the mortgage.

G15 Other liabilities

Include in this box other sums that were owed by the deceased at the death. You may also need to fill in **D16** to give details about the debt.

25

Deficit — If there is a deficit in either section F on form **IHT200** or in box FP10 on form **D15**, you should include that deficit here – we tell you what to do with a deficit on page 41 of this Guide.

Net assets

G16 Take boxes G14 and G15 away from G13 and write the answer in this box.

What you should do if box G16 results in a minus figure

- If the total of all the liabilities in boxes G14 and G15 is more than the assets in box G13, you should make a note of the deficit. You should write '0', rather than the minus figure in boxes G16 and G18.

  We tell you what you should do with a deficit on page 41 of this Guide.

Exemptions and reliefs

- There are a number of exemptions and reliefs that are available to reduce the value of the estate on which you must pay tax. We tell you more about exemptions and reliefs starting on page 36 of this Guide. To deduct any exemptions or reliefs against the assets listed in boxes G1 to G12 you should write the title of the exemption and the amount that you want to deduct in the space provided.

Exclusions

- Inheritance tax is not charged on any assets that are "excluded property". Details of the exclusions start at page 40 of this Guide. If any of the deceased's assets listed in boxes G1 to G12 are "excluded property" you should say which exclusion applies and show the amount in the "Exemptions and reliefs" box.

G17 Add up the total of exemptions, reliefs and exclusions and write the total in this box.

Chargeable value

G18 Take box G17 away from box G16 and write the answer in this box. This box must not contain a minus figure. Taking away exemptions and reliefs can only reduce the figure in box G16 to '0'.

Copy the figure from this box to box WS6 on form **IHT(WS)**.

Working out the tax that is due

When you have filled in form **IHT200** up to section G and any supplementary pages that are necessary, you are ready to start to work out the total tax that is due. You can then go on to work out the tax (and any interest) that you will need to pay before you can apply for a grant.

Go to the guide *"How to fill in form IHT(WS)"* and form **IHT(WS)** provided with form **IHT200**. Follow the guide to work out the different figures.

If you are applying for a grant without the help of a solicitor or other agent, you do not have to work out the tax if you do not want to. You can send the forms to us and we will make a provisional calculation of the tax that is due based on the information on the form.

You do not need to fill in form IHT(WS) and you should leave sections H and J of form IHT200 blank. Continue to fill in form IHT200 at section K.

How to fill sections H and J

When you have filled in form **IHT(WS)** and worked out the tax, if any, to pay you will need to copy some of the figures to sections H and J of form **IHT200**. Follow the instructions on form **IHT(WS)** and copy the figures to form **IHT200**.

How to fill in section K

If a repayment of inheritance tax becomes necessary, the cheque will be made out in the names of all the people who have signed the form. If you do not have a bank account in those names, it may be difficult for you to cash the cheque.

To avoid this difficulty, you can say here how you would like the cheque made out. If there are three or four executors and you want the cheque made out to just one or maybe two of them, write the name(s) of the people here. If a solicitor or other agent is acting on your behalf and the cheque is to be made out to their firm, write the name of the firm here.

How to fill in section L

L1 Write the type of grant that you are applying for in this box. The most common types of grant are

- Grant of Probate - where the deceased has left a Will.
- Grant of Confirmation - where the deceaseddied in Scotland.
- Grant of Letters of Administration - where the deceased died without leaving a Will
- Grant of Letters of Administration with Will annexed - where the deceased left a Will but either failed to appoint an executor, or all the executors appointed in the Will have died.

There are other types of grant, but they are only used in special circumstances. We tell you more about these on page 42 of this Guide.

Supplementary pages

L2 List the supplementary pages that make up the account in this box. If you have filled in more than one copy of the same supplementary pages show it, for example, as "D17x2".

Provisional estimates

L3 Show the boxes that contain a provisional estimate, either on form **IHT200** or on the supplementary pages by writing their box number here.

Signing form IHT200

▸ **All the people who will be named on the grant as executors or administrators must now carefully read the declarations and warnings on page 8. Each person should give their full name and address, sign and date the form in the space provided.**

In signing the form, each person confirms that they have read the declaration and warnings and that they agree that the information given in form IHT200, the supplementary pages and any other supporting papers is correct.

Form D18 (England, Wales and Northern Ireland)

▸ If you are applying for a grant in England, Wales or Northern Ireland, you **must** fill in form **D18** for every estate. It tells the probate registry what values you have included on form **IHT200**. The probate registry needs this information before it can issue a grant. You should fill in form **D18** after you have filled in and signed form **IHT200**. Read form **D18(Notes)** before you fill in the form.

Inventory form C1 (Scotland)

▸ If you are applying for a grant of Confirmation in Scotland, you **must** fill in form **C1** for every estate. The Sheriff Court needs the form before it can issue a grant.

When you have filled in and signed all the forms

When you have filled in and signed form **IHT200** and filled in any supplementary pages, including form **D18** or an Inventory form **C1**, use the checklist, form **CHK1**, to make sure that you have got all the papers that you need to send to us. You should then follow the notes below that apply to you.

When you must send form IHT200 to us before doing anything else

There are three situations when form **IHT200**, all the supplementary pages and any other supporting documents must be sent to IR Capital Taxes **before you go any further**. In particular, if you are applying for a grant without the help of a solicitor you should **not** apply to the Probate Registry for an interview before we have written to you and returned form **D18**. These are if

- you have filled in box B14 on page 1 of the form to say that the deceased died domiciled outside the UK, or that the deceased was only treated as domiciled in the UK (if there is any tax to pay, please include your payment as well)
- you want to pay the tax from a National Savings Bank account, or the proceeds from other National Savings investments (see page 13 of the guide *"How to fill in form IHT(WS)"*)
- the grant is needed for land which was settled property before the deceased's death and which remains settled property after the death (we tell you more about this on page 42 of this Guide).

Our addresses are given on page 2 of this Guide. We tell you which office to contact below. When we have looked at the papers, we will tell you what to do next.

Which office should I use

When you are ready to apply for a grant, or you need to send the forms to us before you can apply for the grant, you should send the papers to our

- Edinburgh office, if you are applying for Confirmation in Scotland or a grant at the Newcastle probate registry
- Nottingham office, if you applying for a grant anywhere else in England and Wales or
- Belfast office, if you are applying for a grant in Northern Ireland.

Which procedure should I follow

There are different procedures to follow depending on whether you are applying for a grant in England, Wales and Northern Ireland, or in Scotland. Please follow the steps that apply to you.

If you are applying for a grant in **England, Wales or Northern Ireland**, the follow the notes starting on page 30. The notes for **Scotland** start on page 32.

England, Wales and Northern Ireland

If you are applying for a grant without the help of a solicitor and you want us to work out the tax for you

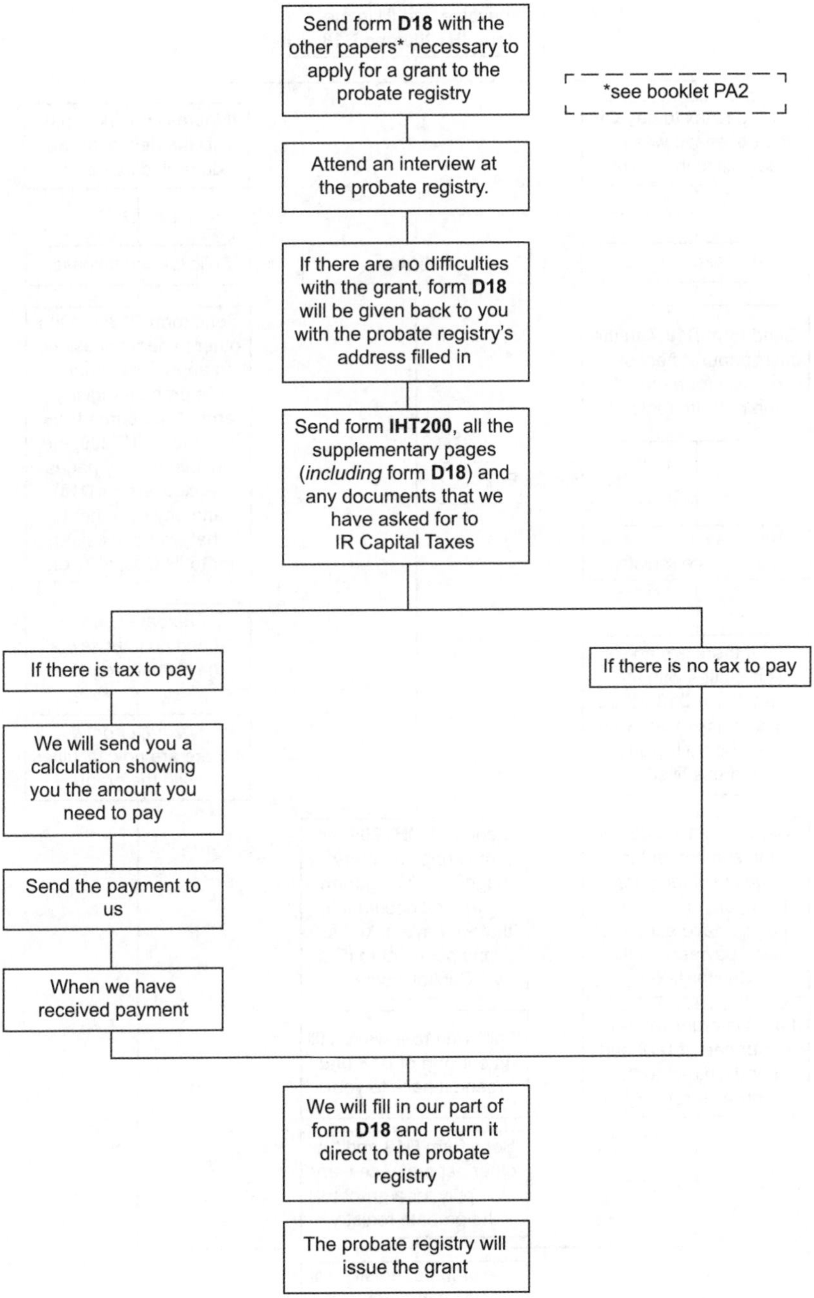
Send form D18 with the other papers* necessary to apply for a grant to the probate registry
*see booklet PA2
Attend an interview at the probate registry.
If there are no difficulties with the grant, form D18 will be given back to you with the probate registry's address filled in
Send form IHT200, all the supplementary pages (including form D18) and any documents that we have asked for to IR Capital Taxes
If there is tax to pay
If there is no tax to pay
We will send you a calculation showing you the amount you need to pay
Send the payment to us
When we have received payment
We will fill in our part of form D18 and return it direct to the probate registry
The probate registry will issue the grant

30

If you are a taxpayer or solicitor working out the tax

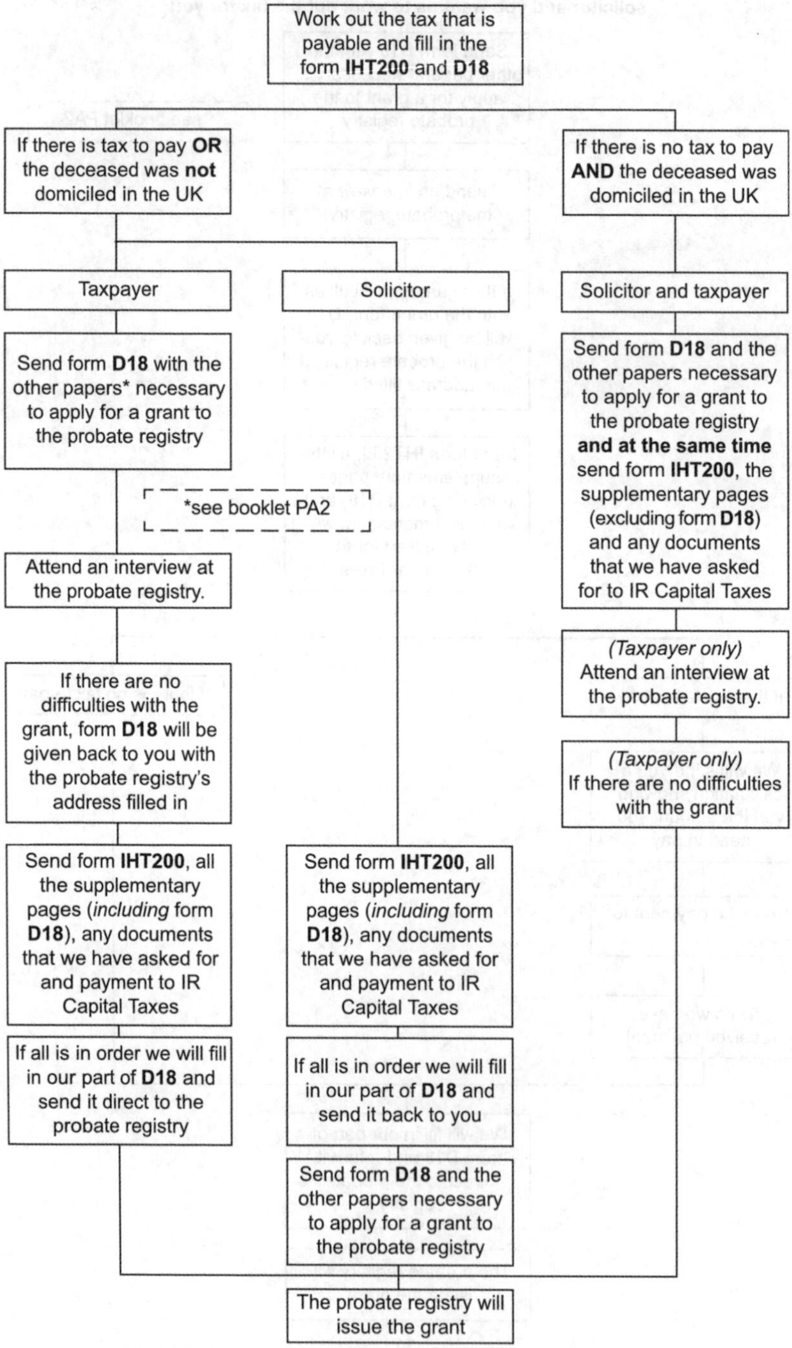
Work out the tax that is payable and fill in the form IHT200 and D18
If there is tax to pay OR the deceased was not domiciled in the UK
If there is no tax to pay AND the deceased was domiciled in the UK
Taxpayer
Solicitor
Solicitor and taxpayer
Send form D18 with the other papers* necessary to apply for a grant to the probate registry
*see booklet PA2
Attend an interview at the probate registry.
If there are no difficulties with the grant, form D18 will be given back to you with the probate registry's address filled in
Send form IHT200, all the supplementary pages (including form D18), any documents that we have asked for and payment to IR Capital Taxes
If all is in order we will fill in our part of D18 and send it direct to the probate registry
Send form IHT200, all the supplementary pages (including form D18), any documents that we have asked for and payment to IR Capital Taxes
If all is in order we will fill in our part of D18 and send it back to you
Send form D18 and the other papers necessary to apply for a grant to the probate registry
Send form D18 and the other papers necessary to apply for a grant to the probate registry and at the same time send form IHT200, the supplementary pages (excluding form D18) and any documents that we have asked for to IR Capital Taxes
(Taxpayer only) Attend an interview at the probate registry.
(Taxpayer only) If there are no difficulties with the grant
The probate registry will issue the grant

31

Scotland

If you are applying for a grant without the help of a solicitor and you want us to work out the tax for you

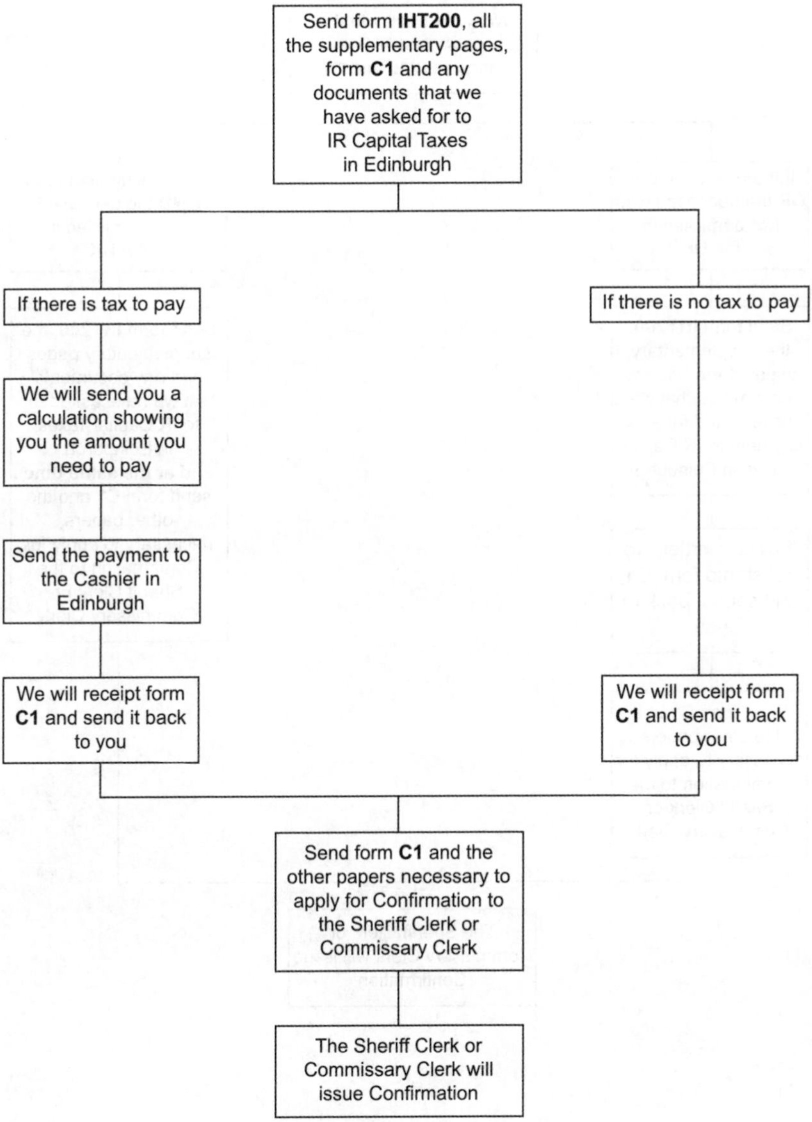
Send form **IHT200**, all the supplementary pages, form **C1** and any documents that we have asked for to IR Capital Taxes in Edinburgh
If there is tax to pay
If there is no tax to pay
We will send you a calculation showing you the amount you need to pay
Send the payment to the Cashier in Edinburgh
We will receipt form **C1** and send it back to you
We will receipt form **C1** and send it back to you
Send form **C1** and the other papers necessary to apply for Confirmation to the Sheriff Clerk or Commissary Clerk
The Sheriff Clerk or Commissary Clerk will issue Confirmation

If you are a taxpayer or solicitor working out the tax

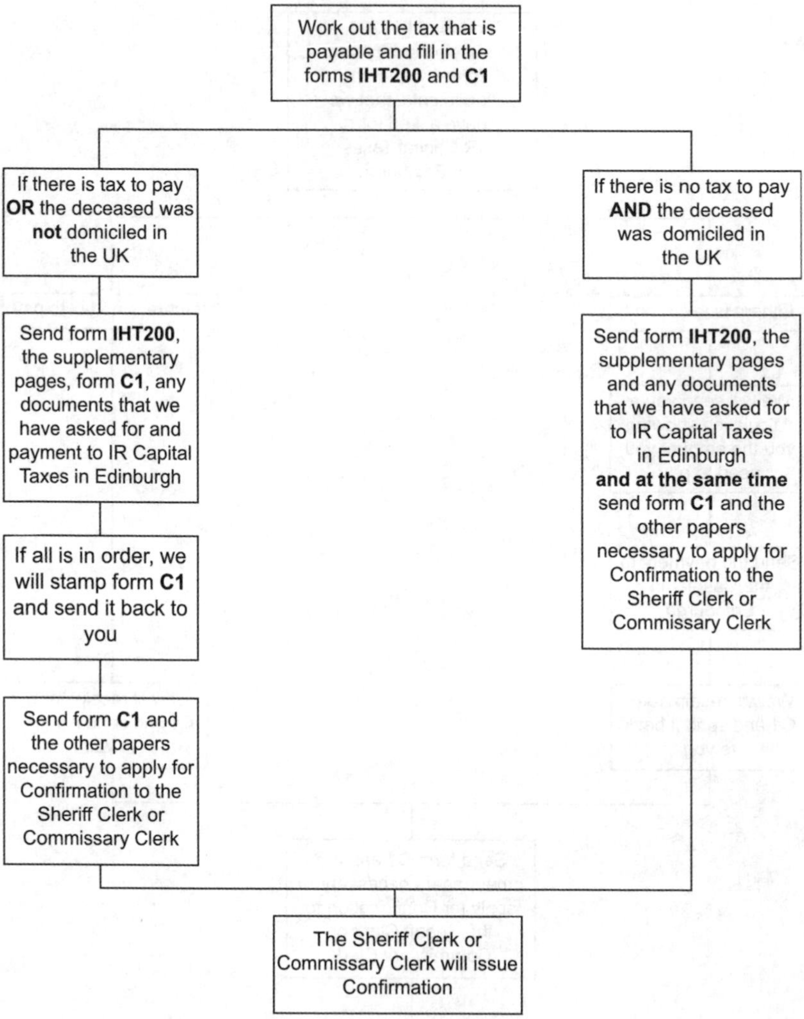
Work out the tax that is payable and fill in the forms IHT200 and C1
If there is tax to pay OR the deceased was not domiciled in the UK
If there is no tax to pay AND the deceased was domiciled in the UK
Send form IHT200, the supplementary pages, form C1, any documents that we have asked for and payment to IR Capital Taxes in Edinburgh
If all is in order, we will stamp form C1 and send it back to you
Send form C1 and the other papers necessary to apply for Confirmation to the Sheriff Clerk or Commissary Clerk
Send form IHT200, the supplementary pages and any documents that we have asked for to IR Capital Taxes in Edinburgh and at the same time send form C1 and the other papers necessary to apply for Confirmation to the Sheriff Clerk or Commissary Clerk
The Sheriff Clerk or Commissary Clerk will issue Confirmation

33

What happens after I get the grant

- You can begin to deal with the estate by collecting the assets and paying debts.

The inheritance tax on the estate may change

- When you have got the grant, it does not mean that you have paid all the inheritance tax and interest on the estate. If you sent us the form before the grant, we look at the details you have given and if there are no obvious errors, we will accept the tax that you have shown us is due.

  Once we have returned form **D18** or the Inventory form **C1** we will look at form **IHT200** in more detail. We may ask you questions to help us understand what you have said on the form and any supplementary pages. We may discuss the value of any assets in the estate and question whether any debts are properly deducted. We will look carefully at any deduction for exemptions, reliefs and exclusions you have made.

  We may also send you statements that show you the tax and interest you must pay, particularly if you have said that you wish to pay some of the tax by instalments.

Provisional estimates

- If you have included provisional estimates in form **IHT200** or on any of the supplementary pages, it is your responsibility to tell us what the final figures are as soon as you know them.

You must tell us about other changes to the estate

- If the value of any asset or debt changes, you must tell us. You can help us by giving us our reference if you can, otherwise tell us the full name and date of death of the deceased.

Payment in advance

- If you think more tax will be payable, you can make a payment on account. If you do we will not charge you interest on the amount you have paid from the date we receive it. You can help us by giving us our reference if you can, otherwise tell us the full name and date of death of the deceased. If you pay too much on account, we will pay you interest when we return the money to you.

  We tell you how to make a payment on account on page 11 of the guide *"How to fill in form IHT(WS)"*.

What happens if quoted shares or land are sold for less than their value on form IHT200

- If

  - shares listed on the Stock Exchange are sold within **one** year of the date of death or
  - land and buildings are sold within **four** years of the date of death

  for less than the value included on form **IHT200**, we may be able to reduce the inheritance tax. Telephone our Helpline if this applies to you and we will tell you what you have to do.

How can I be sure there is no more tax to pay

- If you have worked out that there is no tax to pay and would like to know that we agree, you should fill in form **D19** and send it to us with form **IHT200**. Make sure you fill in all the white boxes on the form.

If there is some tax to pay on the estate, then when you think that the value of all the assets and debts in the estate is settled and you have paid all the tax and interest, you may ask us for a clearance certificate. We will send you an application form (form **IHT30**). The certificate stops us from charging any more tax and interest on the assets you have told us about.

35

Exemptions and reliefs

- The two most important reliefs are agricultural relief and business relief. Forms **D13(Notes)** and **D14(Notes)** tell you about these reliefs. We now tell you about the other exemptions and reliefs that may be available to the estate.

Some exemptions and reliefs reduce the value of an asset or part of an estate to zero, for example, agricultural relief and business relief if the relief is due at 100% or the exemption for transfers between husband and wife. Even though no tax will be payable because of the exemption or relief, **you must still include the assets in the estate at the proper value and then deduct the exemption or relief in full.**

Where to deduct exemptions and reliefs

- Most exemptions and reliefs apply to particular assets. So the amount of the exemption etc. is limited to the value of the asset after any liabilities have been taken away. You should deduct the exemption or relief from the section of the account where the asset is included. Some exemptions, for example, charity relief, may apply to the estate as a whole. You should deduct the exemption from whichever part of the estate the legacy is being paid.

Gifts between husband and wife

- There is no limit to this exemption unless at the date of death the deceased is domiciled in the United Kingdom and the deceased's spouse is not. If this applies, the exemption is limited to £55,000. Gifts made by the deceased to their spouse before the death will be taken into account to find out whether the limit to the exemption applies.

Note

If you are deducting spouse relief, you should give the full name, the date of birth and the domicile of the deceased's spouse on form **D17**.

If the deceased had the right to benefit from a trust set up by the Will or intestacy of a spouse or former spouse who died before 13 November 1974, the capital value is not taken into account if

- Estate Duty was paid or was treated as paid on the earlier death in respect of those assets and
- the deceased was "not competent to dispose" of the assets. For example, if the deceased was given the power to say how the settled property should be dealt with either during their lifetime or on their death, they would be competent to dispose of the assets and the exemption would not apply.

Note

If you are deducting this exemption from the assets in a trust, any apportioned income included in box F14 is also exempt. However, the exemption does **not** apply to any accrued income that had not been paid to the deceased and included in box F13.

Gifts to charities established in the UK

- Gifts to charities in the UK are exempt, as long as the money passes directly to the organisation and the Will does not restrict how the money should be used. If there are lots of gifts to different charities and some of them are not well known, you can help us by listing the charities and giving their Registered Charity Number on form **D1** or form **D17**. For Scottish charities you should give the recognition number on the Scottish Charities Index.

Relief for successive charges

- This relief applies where one person has inherited assets on the death of another and the two deaths occur within five years of each other. If inheritance tax was paid by the estate of the first person to die, the tax payable on the second death will be reduced. The reduction is a percentage of the tax paid on the assets inherited by the second person as shown in the table below.

Period between deaths	%
Within I year	100
Between 1 & 2 years	80
Between 2 & 3 years	60
Between 3 & 4 years	40
Between 4 & 5 years	20

This relief may be relevant to the deceased's estate if you have had to fill in form **D11**. There are some examples of how to work out this relief starting on page 14 of the guide *"How to fill in form IHT(WS)"*. This relief can only reduce the tax payable on the deceased's estate to 'NIL', it cannot give rise to a repayment of tax.

Note

If you have deducted successive charges relief, copy the calculation of the relief on form **IHT(WS)** to form **D17**. If you are not filling in form **D11**, use form **D17** to tell us the name and date of death of the person who died before the deceased. Give our reference for their estate if you know what it is.

Double taxation relief

- This relief applies where the deceased's estate includes some foreign property **and** a foreign tax, similar to UK inheritance tax, has been paid on those assets. You may deduct relief up to the maximum amount of UK inheritance tax payable on the same assets. The amount of the relief is the amount in sterling needed to pay the foreign tax, up to that maximum.

The exchange rate used is the London Selling Rate as shown in the Financial Times **at the date the foreign tax was paid**. If the foreign currency was only available at a premium, you should include the premium. There is an example of how to work out this relief on page 16 of the guide *"How to fill in form IHT(WS)"*.

There are arrangements between some countries for a formal exchange of information about the assets that have been declared for tax and the amount of tax that has been paid. If this applies to this estate, we will help you to go through the right procedures once you have got a grant.

Note

If you have deducted double taxation relief, copy the calculation of the relief on form **IHT(WS)** to form **D17**.

Gifts to political parties

- A political party qualifies for this exemption if two of its members were elected to the House of Commons at the last general election before the gift, or if one of its members was elected and at least 150,000 votes were cast for its candidates. If the gifts were made before 15 March 1988 either on death or within one year of death, there is a limit of £100,000 on the amount of the exemption.

Gifts to registered housing associations

- If the deceased made a gift of land and buildings in the UK to a registered housing association after 14 March 1989, the gift is exempt.

Gifts to national museums etc

- Gifts to national museums and local authority museums, universities and other public bodies are exempt. The qualifying bodies are listed in Schedule 3 of the Inheritance Tax Act 1984. You should telephone our Heritage section Helpline (0115 974 2488) for help if you think a gift under the deceased's Will may qualify for this exemption.

  If the body concerned is not listed in Schedule 3, it may be that we will not be able to give you an immediate answer. If that is the case, we will let you know how long it may take before we can give you an answer.

Limitation on gifts to charities, political parties and public bodies

- The exemptions for gifts to charities, political parties and public bodies may be limited if the gift was not made to the organisation outright. If you are not sure whether one of these exemptions should apply because the money does not pass direct to the organisation or if the Will restricts how the money should be used, you should telephone our Helpline and explain the circumstances.

National Heritage exemptions

- There are a number of exemptions available for gifts of heritage and other historic property. The rules and conditions that the different exemptions impose are complicated. There is a corresponding relief from capital gains tax. The exemption, which must be claimed within two years after the deceased died, may be available for

  - property transferred into a settlement for the maintenance of qualifying heritage property or
  - specific property, for example works of art, historic houses or other land of a sufficient standard that may qualify for conditional exemption on the death of the deceased.

38

If you would like more information about this please write to our Heritage section at the Nottingham office or telephone our Heritage section Helpline (0115 9742488).

If you are claiming exemption under one of the National Heritage exemptions and the item has already been granted exemption on an earlier death or lifetime transfer, please fill in form **D17** and tell us

- the name of the person who died earlier or who made the gift
- the date of death or the date of birth of the person
- any IR Capital Taxes reference concerning this previous occasion.

If you are in doubt about whether a National Heritage exemption previously applied, please write to our Heritage section in Nottingham who might be able to help you from their records.

Woodlands relief

This relief may apply if any part of the deceased's estate includes land on which trees are growing, but which does not qualify for agricultural relief. The trees may qualify for woodlands relief if all the following conditions are met

- the land must be in the UK
- it must not qualify for agricultural relief
- the deceased must have owned the land throughout the five years up to death or
- have acquired the land other than by buying it **and**
- you must formally claim the relief within two years after the death.

If all the conditions are met, you may deduct the value of the trees as the amount of the relief. When the trees are either sold or given away later, there may be some inheritance tax to pay. We tell you more about woodlands relief in leaflet **IHT17**.

Ex-gratia payments to Britons held prisoner by the Japanese during World War II

If the deceased's received such a payment during their lifetime, you should reduce the amount of tax charged on the estate by the smaller of

- 40% of the payment(s) received, or
- the amount of tax payable before allowing the deduction.

To apply the reduction, you should include the figure above in box WS21 on form IHT(WS) so that it is carried to box J6 on form IHT200. Applying the reduction can only reduce the tax liability to nil; it cannot result in a repayment of tax.

If the deceased died having made a claim but before they received the payment, you should include £10,000 for the right to make a claim in box F23 and then reduce the tax as above.

You should enclose a copy of the letter from the War Pensions Agency confirming the deceased's claim was successful.

39

Exclusions

The most common exclusions are described below.

Reversionary interests

The note for box F22 tells you what a reversionary interest is. You should include an estimated value in that box. A reversionary interest is excluded property if it

- has not at any time been sold or exchanged
- does not arise under a settlement made after 16 April 1976 where the settlement was made by the deceased or the deceased's spouse
- does not involve a lease of a property for life that is treated as a settlement for inheritance tax.

As long as none of the above apply, you may deduct the value of the reversionary interest in box F29.

Settled property

If the deceased had the right to benefit under a trust and

- the assets in the trust are outside the UK and
- the person who set up the trust was domiciled outside the UK when the assets were put into trust

the assets are excluded property. Form **D5(Notes)** tells you what information is needed.

Domicile outside the UK

If you have said that the deceased was domiciled outside the UK when they died, any assets (apart from settled property) that are outside the UK are "excluded property". There is no need to give details of the foreign assets on form **IHT200**, but you can help us by including an estimated value for all the foreign property at question 6 on form **D2**.

If the deceased was domiciled outside the UK and was not resident or ordinarily resident in the UK when they died, foreign currency bank accounts held with certain banks in the UK are "excluded property". A foreign currency account with any of "High Street" banks, such as Lloyds, Barclays, Abbey National Plc, Halifax etc will qualify. Foreign currency accounts with other banks such as

- ANZ Grindlays Bank Plc
- Banque Nationale de Paris Plc
- Italian International Bank Plc
- Wesleyan Savings Bank Plc

will also qualify. Telephone our Helpline if you need to check whether or not a foreign currency account qualifies as "excluded property". You should include the bank accounts in box F8 of form **IHT200**, but deduct the value in box F29.

40

If the deceased was not ordinarily resident in the UK when they died, UK government securities that are authorised as exempt from tax, for example, 9% Conversion Loan 2001 or 7% Treasury Stock 2006, are excluded property. You should include the securities in box F2 of form **IHT200**, but deduct the value in box F29.

If the deceased died before 6 April 1998, such securities are only exempt if the deceased was also domiciled outside the UK.

Domicile in the Channel Islands or Isle of Man

▸ If the deceased was domiciled in the Channel Islands or Isle of Man when they died, the following are also excluded property

- War Savings Certificates
- National Savings Certificates or Ulster Savings Certificates
- Premium Bonds
- certain certified contractual savings schemes (usually described as Save As You Earn or SAYE schemes, the prospectus will tell you if the scheme qualifies)
- deposits with the National Savings Bank.

You should include the assets in the appropriate boxes in section F of form **IHT200**, but deduct the value in box F29.

How to deal with a deficit

▸ You may find that there are not enough assets in one part of the estate to cover the debts you need to deduct. If so, you may carry the deficit forward and deduct it from other parts of the estate as follows.

Deficit in section F

▸ If the figure in box F28 would be a minus figure, you should write '0' in that box and in box F30. You can carry the deficit forward and deduct it in box G15.

If there are not enough assets in section G to cover the deficit, you may carry any balance forward and deduct it from any foreign property the deceased owned (unless the foreign property itself is also in deficit). Include the deficit in box FP4 on form **D15**.

Deficit in section G

▸ If the figure in box G16 would be a minus figure, you should write '0' in that box and in box G18. You can carry the deficit back and deduct it in box F25.

If there are not enough assets in section F to cover the deficit, you may carry any balance forward and deduct it from any foreign property the deceased owned (unless the foreign property itself is also in deficit). Include the deficit in box FP9 on form **D15**.

41

Special types of grant

There are a number of special types of grant that may apply in certain circumstances. For example

- a grant for limited period of time, perhaps while there is a legal dispute about the validity of a will,
- a grant that is limited to certain assets, perhaps where the estate consists of perishable goods that need to be preserved, or where the deceased has appointed an executor in respect of certain assets; for example an author might appoint a literary executor.

Your local Probate Registry can tell you more about these special types of grant and whether they might be of use in dealing with the deceased's estate. They will also tell you the name of the grant concerned. You should make sure you write this name in box L1 on page 8 of form **IHT200**.

You will still need to fill in form **IHT200** in full where the grant is for a limited period time. Where the grant is limited to certain assets, we tell you how to fill in form **IHT200** below.

When form IHT200 need not be filled in completely

There are certain types of grant where you do not have to fill in form **IHT200** completely. These are

- when the proposed grant is to be limited to certain assets. In this case you should include the assets to be covered by the grant in pages 3 – 5 of form **IHT200**. All the other assets that are part of the deceased's estate, but are to be excluded from the grant, should be included in box WS11 on form **IHT(WS)**. You should fill in pages 1,6,7 & 8 and answer the questions on page 2 of form **IHT200**. You should only fill in (at this stage) any supplementary pages that apply to the assets for which the grant is required
- when the grant is required only for settled land. In this case, you should include the land in the appropriate box on page 5 of form **IHT200**. You should fill in form **D12** and any other supplementary pages that are needed. All the other property that is part of the deceased's estate should be included in box WS11 on form **IHT(WS)** and carried to box H11 on page 6 of form **IHT200**. You should fill in pages 1,6,7 & 8 and answer the questions on page 2 of form **IHT200**, as they relate to the settled land.
- when the deceased left no estate and the grant is required only for assets (not settled land) of which the deceased was only a trustee. You only need to fill in pages 1 & 8 and answer the questions on page 2 of form **IHT200**. You do not need to include the assets in the account, or fill in pages 6 & 7 of form **IHT200**.

Changes to the administration of an estate

Where there are to be changes in the administration of an estate, you can apply for a grant to allow the administration to continue, provided the assets concerned were included in an earlier grant. You **must** use form **A5-C** if you are applying for a:

England, Wales and Northern Ireland

- Grant of Double Probate - Where an executor (perhaps due to ill health) was not party to the initial grant, but on regaining health the executor wishes to take up office.
- Grant de bonis non administratis - When the only or last surviving executor dies without fully dealing with estate.

When you have filled in the form, you should send the form to the probate registry. There is no need to send the form to us first.

Scotland

If you need an "Eik to Confirmation" for additional assets or to amend an estate, you should fill in a Corrective Inventory on form **C4** (which you can get from our Edinburgh office) and send it to us. After we have looked at it, we will stamp and return the form to you so you can send it to the Sheriff or Commissary Clerk. If you need an "Eik to Confirmation *ad non executa*" (where the estate has not been fully administered and none of the original executors, or substitutes remain in office) you should get form **X-1** from the Sheriff or Commissary Clerk. Once you have filled it in, you should return it direct to the Sheriff or Commissary Clerk.

Excepted estates

If the deceased's estate is below a certain limit (currently £210,000) and also satisfies some other conditions, you may be able to get a grant without filling in form **IHT200**. Such estates are called "excepted estates". If you are applying for a grant without the help of a solicitor or other agent you can find out if you can use this procedure by following the notes below, depending on which part of the UK you live in. This will tell you whether you can apply for a grant as an "excepted estate" or whether you will need to fill in form **IHT200** to apply for a grant.

England & Wales

Read the booklet **IHT206** and, if necessary, fill in form **IHT205**. Both are available from your local probate registry.

Scotland

Read form **C3** and, if necessary, fill in Inventory form **C1**. Both forms are available from our Edinburgh office.

Northern Ireland

Contact the Probate and Matrimonial Office in either Belfast (028 9072 4679) or Londonderry (028 7136 3448 ext 250) who will send you a copy of their booklet.

Data Protection Act

▸ The Inland Revenue is a Data Controller under the Data Protection Act. We hold information for the purposes specified in our notification made to the Data Protection Commissioner, and may use this information for any of them.

We may get information about you from others, or we may give informaton to them. If we do, it will only be as the law permits, to

- check accuracy of information
- prevent or detect crime
- protect public funds

We may check information we receive about you with what is already in our records. This can include goverment departments and agencies and overseas tax authorities. We will not give information about you to anyone outside the Inland Revenue unless the law permits us to do so.

Index of items that often make up an estate

45

Useful IHT leaflets

IHT2	Lifetime gifts
IHT3	Introduction to IHT
IHT8	Alterations to an inheritance following death
IHT11	Payment of IHT from National Savings
IHT11(S)	Payment of IHT from National Savings (Scotland)
IHT13	Penalties
IHT14	The personal representatives' responsibilities
IHT15	How to calculate the liability
IHT16	Settled property
IHT17	Businesses, farms and woodlands
IHT18	Foreign aspects
IR45	What to do about tax when someone dies
IR120	You and CTO
IR156	Our Heritage – your right to see tax exempt works of art
SVD1	Shares Valuation Division (an introduction)

The Will

Form D1

▸ Please read the Will and answer **ALL** the questions on form **D1**.

How to fill in form D1

1 If deceased's residence shown on page 1 of the **IHT200** is different from their address given in the Will, please say what has happened to the property given as the deceased's residence in the Will. If the Will was signed before 18 March 1986 and the deceased's address shown in the Will has been replaced a number of times, there is no need to list the chain of events. Just say that the property has been replaced by the property that is included in the estate as the deceased's address at death.

If the deceased owned the property shown as their address in the Will at some time but no property is included as part of the estate, please say what has happened to the property and if it was sold, say where the money is included as part of the estate.

2 Quite often, a Will includes a number of specific legacies, for example, leaving a particular item to a beneficiary, or writing off a loan that is still outstanding at death. The deceased may also refer to gifts they have made during their lifetime.

If there are no such specific bequests etc, you should tick the N/A box. Otherwise, tick the appropriate box and give a brief explanation of what happened to any item listed in the Will that *does not* appear in the estate.

If the item was given away, please say when the gift was made, to whom and the value of item at the time of the gift.

If the item was sold, please give details of the sale and say where the money is included in the estate. There is no need to give details of all the various bank accounts and investments that the money has passed through, just say which assets included in form **IHT200** represent the sale proceeds.

3 Pages 36 to 41 of the guide *"How to fill in form IHT200"* give details of the exemptions, exclusions and reliefs that apply to inheritance tax. Please remember to deduct exemptions that are due on form **IHT200** and/or the supplementary pages.

If the legacy or bequest is to the deceased's spouse, please tell us either here or on form **D17** the full name of the spouse, their date of birth and say what their domicile is.

If the legacy or bequest is to one of the less well-known charities,

D1(Notes)

you can help us by giving the Charity Registration Number or, for Scottish charities, the recognition number on the Scottish Charities Index, in this box.

Is a copy of the Will needed?

You must always send the original Will to the Probate Registry, Commissary Court or Sheriff Court. But you do not always need to enclose a copy for us.

If you have answered "Yes" to questions 1 & 2 (including N/A to question 2) and the gross value of the estate is below the tax threshold, you do not need to provide a copy of the Will for us. We tell you what the tax thresholds are on page 6 of the guide *"How to fill in form IHT(WS)".* **In all other circumstances, please attach a copy of the Will you are submitting for probate/Confirmation and any codicils to form D1.**

The gross value of the estate is the value of all the assets in the estate and the value of any gifts the deceased made *before* deducting debts, liabilities, exemptions, reliefs and exclusions.

If an Instrument of Variation or Disclaimer, which varies either the terms of the Will or the distribution of an estate under intestacy, has been signed, please attach a copy of the deceased's Will (if appropriate) and a copy of the Instrument of Variation or Disclaimer to form D1, irrespective of the value of the estate.

Instruments of Variation

There are more details about Instruments of Variation in our leaflet IHT8 *"Alterations to an inheritance following a death".* If you do not need to send us a copy of the Will with form **IHT200**, but an Instrument of Variation is completed later, please send us a copy of the Will and the Instrument when you tell us about it.

Domicile outside the United Kingdom

Form D2

You **must** fill in form **D2** if you have said that the deceased was domiciled **outside** the UK when they died.

Usually, the country where you have your main home is where your domicile is. It is the country whose laws decide, for example, whether a Will is valid, or how the estate of a person who has not made a Will is dealt with when they die.

Everybody has a domicile. At birth, you have a "domicile of origin". This is normally the same country as your father's domicile, so it is not always the country you were born in. You keep this domicile until you acquire a different domicile – a domicile of choice or of dependence.

The United Kingdom is not a "country" when establishing a person's domicile. So a person will have a domicile in England and Wales, **or** Scotland **or** Northern Ireland. But to keep things simple, we refer to all three countries as the United Kingdom (UK) in these notes.

Domicile is not the same as "residence" or "nationality". You may be "resident" in more than one country, but UK law says that you can only have one domicile at any one time.

However, there are some special rules that apply for inheritance tax

- if a person has lived in the UK for a long time, so that they were resident for income tax purposes for at least 17 of the 20 years ending with the tax year in which they died, **or**
- if a person was domiciled in the UK under English law at any time in the three years before they died,

the law says that we can treat the deceased as if they were domiciled in the UK when they died. This means that we can charge inheritance tax on the deceased's worldwide estate, even though they were not domiciled in the UK when they died.

Also, if the terms of a Double Taxation Convention or Agreement apply (we tell you more about these at note 7), a person may be treated as having more than one domicile. The terms of the convention or agreement will say which domicile is to be used.

There is more help about domicile in our leaflet **IHT18**. And the Inland Revenue leaflet **IR20** has more help about residence.

*Remember that the Channel Islands and the Isle of Man are **not in the UK**.*

D2(Notes)

How to fill in form D2

1 If the deceased's domicile has already been agreed for other Revenue purposes, please state the name and reference number of the office concerned.

If not, the history should give details of

- the nationality of the deceased and where they were born
- an outline of their educational and employment history
- the date(s) they left the UK and set up their main home abroad
- the date(s) they returned to the UK
- how long they stayed in the UK
- the purpose of their stay.

You should also say why the deceased did not intend to remain in, or return to, the UK at the date of death and give details of the evidence you have used to arrive at this conclusion.

If the deceased was a widow, please give the full name of her husband, his date of death and where he was domiciled when he died. You should include a similar history for the deceased's husband if necessary.

2 Tick the box to answer this question. If you answer "Yes" to this question, the deceased will be treated as domiciled in the UK when they died. If the deceased is treated as domiciled in the UK, you should fill in form **IHT200** with details of their world-wide estate.

3 Tick the box to answer this question. Long term residence in the UK for income tax purposes is another of the circumstances when a person may be treated as domiciled in the UK for inheritance tax. If you have answered "Yes" to this question, we will have to establish how long the deceased was resident in the UK over the last 20 years. Include in this box the periods that the deceased was resident. You can help us by making sure that you have completed boxes B16 to B18 on page 1 of form **IHT200**.

4 When someone dies abroad, it is usually the law of the country of domicile that says how the deceased's estate should be dealt with. In some countries, the law may say that the deceased's estate must be divided in a particular way, even though they have left a Will.

If the deceased's estate is to be distributed according to the terms of the Will, please say so. You do not need to give any more details, but please provide a copy of the Will.

If all or part of the deceased's estate is to be distributed in some other way, please say how the estate is to be dealt with and who is to benefit.

5 Tick the box to answer this question. If you have answered "Yes", we may need to take the foreign law into account in deciding how inheritance tax should be charged.

In the UK, assets can be owned jointly between two or more people. It does not matter whether the people are married; the law is the same for both married and unmarried joint owners. In some other countries, the law may say that a husband and wife share their property through what is called the "community of property". When one of them dies, the foreign law may say that this "shared" property has to be dealt with in a special way.

5a You should list the assets that will be passing to the deceased's widow or widower.

5b Tick the box to answer this question. A community of property may be set up as a result of the deceased signing a marriage contract or just because the deceased got married. If you have answered "Yes", you should give details of the rights that each person had under the community. For example, was there

- full or universal community of property
- community of gains
- community of chattels and gains, or
- some other means of dividing the property.

You should also say which country's law applies to the community of property.

If there is a written contract or agreement, you should provide a copy when you first send form **IHT200** and the supplementary pages to us. If obtaining a copy might delay sending the papers to us, you can send them without the agreement. But we will need to see the agreement after you have obtained the grant before we can accept that the assets should be dealt with under a community of property.

5c Tick the box to answer this question. The law of the foreign country that has set up the community of property may say that it overrides UK law and applies to assets in the UK. If you have answered "Yes", you should list the assets in the UK that are affected by the community of property.

5d Tick the box to answer this question. You should fill in form **IHT200** to show the community of property.

6 Tick the box to answer this question. If the deceased was domiciled outside the UK when they died, any assets they owned abroad will not be liable to inheritance tax. Even so, you can help us to deal with this estate more quickly if you can give us a rough idea of the value of all of the deceased's estate outside the UK.

7 If a person owns assets in two different countries it is possible that both countries will want to charge tax when the deceased died. There are formal agreements, called Double Taxation Conventions or Agreements, between some countries to stop this from happening. There are presently agreements with: Republic of Ireland, South Africa, United States of America, Netherlands, Sweden, Switzerland, France, Italy, India and Pakistan. Tick the box to answer this question.

As both countries may have the right to tax the assets, these agreements usually have rules that say which country may tax the different assets. We will not give up our right to tax any assets until we have evidence from the foreign authority that the assets have been included for tax in the foreign country and tax has been paid. If you feel that certain assets should not be taxed in the UK because an agreement says so, you should let us have evidence that foreign tax has been paid on the assets as soon as you can.

8 You may find that you have to pay foreign tax on assets in the UK as a result of the deceased's death. Tick the box to answer the question. If you have answered "Yes", you will need to send us evidence of the payment, such as a copy of the receipt from the foreign authorities, and tell us when the payment was made. You do not have to provide this information when you apply for a grant, but we will need these details afterwards.

Note

If you have paid, or expect to pay foreign tax as a result of the deceased's death and you are also paying inheritance tax on the same assets, you may be able to deduct double taxation relief. We tell you more about this relief on page 37 of the guide *"How to fill in form IHT200"*. There is an example of how to work out how much relief you can deduct on page 16 of the guide *"How to fill in form IHT(WS)"*.

Gifts and other transfers of value

Form D3

You **must** fill in form **D3** if the deceased gave away or transferred any assets since 18 March 1986. We may have to add the value of those assets to the estate at death so we can work out the total value on which tax must be charged. To keep things simple, we refer to all types of transfer made by the deceased as gifts.

Exempt gifts

You **do not** need to fill in form **D3** (and should answer "No" to the question about gifts on page 2 of form **IHT200**) if the **only** gifts made by the deceased were

- to their husband or wife and spouse exemption applies (see page 36 of the guide *"How to fill in form IHT200"*)
- **outright** gifts to any individual which do not exceed £250 in any one year (the small gifts exemption)
- **outright** gifts of money or quoted stocks and shares to any individual which are **wholly** covered by the annual and/or gifts out of income exemptions described on pages 2 and 3 of these notes.

Time limits

There are certain time limits that apply. The most important is the period of seven years before the deceased died. But it is possible that other gifts made before that period may also affect the amount of tax that is payable as a result of the deceased's death. These notes contain an outline of the circumstances in which a gift may need to be added to the estate at death. There is more help in our leaflets **IHT2** and **IHT15**.

What kind of gifts need to be included

It is not just outright gifts, such as giving a cheque for £10,000 to someone on a special occasion, that are relevant for inheritance tax. The law says that there will be a gift whenever there is "a loss to the donor" (the "donor" is the person making the gift). This can happen in different ways. For example, a parent may sell a house to a son or daughter for less than they could sell the property on the open market. This will be a loss to the donor. A person may hold some shares that gives them control of a company. They may sell only a few shares to a relative but losing control of the company reduces the value of their other shares. This too will be a loss to the donor. If you are not sure whether you should include details of a particular gift, please telephone our Helpline.

Gifts with reservation of benefit

Sometimes the person making the gift may retain an interest in the assets being given away, or the person receiving the gift may not take full ownership or possession of the assets. Such a gift is called a "gift with reservation of benefit". There is more about this sort of gift on page 6 of these notes. You should include details of any such gifts in section 2 of form **D3**.

Who must tell us about any gifts

We need to know the value of any gifts made by the deceased in case the value needs to be added to the estate at death to work out how much tax is payable. You must include full details on form **D3** of all the gifts that the deceased made which are not exempt gifts.

However, if we need to know any more information, or if we need an account of the gifts to be sent in, or if there is any tax to pay on the gifts themselves we will contact the person who received the gift. This is because it is the recipient of the gift who should send in an account and who must pay any tax that is due on the gift.

Exemptions and reliefs for gifts

The exemptions, reliefs (apart from woodlands relief) and exclusions beginning on page 36 in the guide *"How to fill in form IHT200"* also apply to gifts, although there may be some additional conditions to be satisfied. There are also other exemptions that apply to gifts only. These are described below.

Gifts in consideration of marriage

If the gift was made

- on or shortly before the marriage
- to one or both parties to the marriage, and
- to become fully effective on the marriage taking place

it will be exempt up to the following limits

- £5,000 if the deceased was a parent to one of the people getting married
- £2,500 if the deceased was a grandparent or more remote ancestor of one of the people getting married, or
- £1,000 in any other case.

If you are deducting the marriage exemption, say on form D17 how the person who received the gift was related to the deceased and give the date of marriage.

Gifts out of income

If the gifts are unconditional **and you can show if we ask you** that they

- formed part of the deceased's usual expenditure
- were made out of income, and
- left the deceased with sufficient income to maintain their normal standard of living

they will be exempt.

"Usual expenditure" means that the payments were a regular part of the deceased's expenditure. Examples are where the deceased was paying a regular premium on an insurance policy for the benefit of another person, (see the notes for question 1c) or perhaps where they were making a monthly or other regular payment to someone else.

2

A one-off payment, even if it was out of income will not be exempt.

If the gifts meet these conditions, are outright gifts to another individual and do not exceed £3,000 in total each year, you do not need to give any details on form D3. If you are deducting more than £3,000 per year, please give the date and amount of each gift and the amount of exemption you wish to deduct. We may ask for more information after you have obtained the grant.

Small gifts exemption

Gifts to any one person which do not exceed £250 in any one tax year to 5 April are exempt. This exemption covers gifts at birthdays and Christmas.

You cannot use this exemption in conjunction with the annual exemption below. This exemption is **only** available if **all** the gifts made to the same person in one tax year do not exceed £250.

Annual exemption

Gifts not exceeding £3,000 in any one tax year to 5 April are exempt. This can apply to one gift or the total of a number of gifts and is addition to the other exemptions described above. If the gifts made in one year fall short of £3,000, any surplus can be carried forward to the next year (but no further) and can be used once the exemption for that year has been used up in full. The exemption cannot be carried back to earlier years.

If the gifts are outright gifts to another individual and wholly covered by the small gifts or the annual exemption you do not need to give any details on form D3.

When the exemptions may not apply

If you have answered "Yes" to question 1d on form **D3**

- you cannot deduct the exemption for gifts in consideration of marriage or the annual exemption from such a gift unless the deceased gave notice to the trustees that the exemption was available within 6 months of the date of gift, and
- you cannot deduct the exemption for gifts out of income or for small gifts at all.

Gifts which exceed exemptions

Where the gifts made by the deceased are not **wholly** covered by any of the exemptions or reliefs, fill in form **D3** to give details of the gifts made. Use more than one form, if there is not enough space to list all the gifts.

3

How to fill in form D3

1 This section of form **D3** is for details of gifts made within 7 years of the deceased's death. Tick the boxes to answer each of these four questions. If you answer "Yes" to any of them, you must fill in the table in this section of form **D3**.

1a You should answer "Yes" to this question where the deceased has made any gift or transfer of value that is not wholly covered by exemptions. This will include straightforward gifts of cash or other assets and any other arrangements that have given rise to a "loss to the donor". As well as the examples on page 1, this can include things like

- granting a lease at less than a full market rent
- re-arranging the shares in a private company, or altering the rights attaching to the shares
- agreeing to act as a guarantor for someone else's debts.

If you are not sure whether to include details of a particular transaction, please discuss the circumstances with our Helpline.

1b You should answer "Yes" to this question where the deceased has either set up a new trust or settlement or has transferred more assets to an existing trust or settlement. Again, this will include straightforward gifts of cash or other assets as well as any other arrangements with the trustees that may have given rise to a "loss to the donor" and transferred value to the trust or settlement.

1c You should answer "Yes" to this question where the deceased has made a gift by paying the premium(s) on a life insurance policy for the benefit of someone else, but you can ignore policies where the only person to benefit will be the deceased's spouse.

You should provide a copy of

- the life insurance policy, and
- any related documents such as trust deeds and loan agreements

with form **IHT200**. If there is more than one insurance policy and they are all identical, you only need to send a copy of one policy.

You must include details of all premiums paid and provide copies of the policy etc even if you are deducting exemption as gifts made out of income.

In some circumstances, the deceased may have purchased an annuity as well as paying the premiums on a life insurance policy for the benefit of someone else. There are complicated rules that might apply in such circumstances and the exemption as gifts made out of income may not be available against the premiums. If the deceased had

- purchased an annuity (at any time), and
- paid the premiums on a life insurance policy for the benefit of some one else, and
- the life insurance policy was taken out after 27 March 1974

you should provide a copy of the annuity documents as well as the life insurance policy.

1d The deceased may have been entitled to benefit from the assets held in a trust or settlement (see page 10 of the guide *"How to fill in form IHT200"*), but during their lifetime, that entitlement came to an end, either in whole or in part. It may have been the terms of the trust that brought their entitlement to an end, or the deceased may have asked the trustees to alter or terminate their entitlement. You should answer "Yes" to this question where the deceased ceased to have the right to benefit from any assets held in trust for whatever reason.

Date of gift

▶ Write in the date of gift showing the day, month and year if possible.

Name and relationship of recipient, description of assets

▶ Write in the name of the person receiving the gift and their relationship to the deceased. Describe the asset(s) that have been given away. For example, cash, the address of a house, the number of shares in a particular company, the premium paid on an insurance policy.

Value at date of gift

▶ Write in the value of the asset(s) that have been given away **at the date of gift**. The rules for valuing gifts are the same as the rules for valuing assets owned by the deceased (see pages 15 and 23–25 of the guide *"How to fill in from IHT200"*, form **D7(Notes)** and form **D10(Notes)**).

Amount and type of exemption

▶ Write in the amount and type of exemption that you wish to deduct from the value of the asset. If you are deducting the annual exemption, please say which tax years' exemption you are deducting.

If you are claiming heritage exemption or any of the assets given away have at any previous time benefited either from heritage exemption or from an approved maintenance fund, you can help us to deal with this aspect of the estate by filling in form **D17** to give us

- the name of the person who died earlier or who made the gift
- the date of death or the date of birth of the person
- any CTO reference concerning this previous occasion.

Net value after exemptions

▶ Deduct the exemptions from the value of the asset and write the answer in this column.

5

LT1 Add up all the figures here and write the answer in this box. Copy the figure from this box to box WS14 on form **IHT(WS)**. Below is an example of what section 1 of form **D3** might look like.

Date of gift	Name and relationship of recipient and description of assets	Value at date of gift	Amount and type of exemption claimed	Net value after exemptions
12/6/97	Robert Smith (son) Cash	10,000	6,000 (annual 97/98 & 96/97)	4,000
16/3/98	Stephen Smith (son) Cash	10,000	5,000 (marriage)	5,000
14/10/98	Robert Smith (son) Cash	4,000		
14/10/98	Stephen Smith (son) Cash	4,000		
14/10/98	James Smith (gndson) Cash	1,000 9,000	3,000 (annual 98/99)	6,000
			Total LT1	£ 15,000

Other exemptions and reliefs

There are two other exemptions that apply to gifts. These only apply if the total of gifts made during the deceased's lifetime is more than the tax threshold when the deceased dies so that there is some tax to pay on the gifts themselves.

Taper relief

If there is any tax to pay on a gift, the tax is reduced by a sliding scale for gifts made more than three but less than seven years before the death. There is more about taper relief on page 17 of the guide *"How to fill in form IHT(WS)"*.

Fall in value relief

If the value of the assets given away has fallen between the date of gift and the date of death, tax may be charged on the lower value at death. The relief only applies if the value of the gifts exceed the tax threshold. There are some other complicated rules and you should telephone our Helpline if you think this relief may apply. If you wish to claim this relief, you should include the date of death value in the "description of assets" column, but do not alter the value at the date of gift. We will look at the claim after the grant.

Gifts with reservation

A gift with reservation is one where the person receiving the gift does not fully own it **or** where the person making the gift either reserves or takes some benefit from it. Where this happens, the law says that we can include the assets as part of the deceased's estate at death. The rule only applies to gifts made on or after 18 March 1986, but there is no seven year limit as there is for outright gifts.

One of the most common examples is where the deceased gives their house to their child but continues to live there. Another is where a bank or building society account is put in the name of a child, but the interest the money produces continues to be paid to the deceased.

However, if arrangements are made, such as payment of a market rent, then the donor will not reserve a benefit and you should include the gift in section 1 of form **D3**.

What happens if the reservation ceases

▸ A gift may start off as a gift with reservation, but some time later, the reservation ceases. For example, if the deceased gave their house to their daughter, but continued to live there without paying any rent, that would be a gift with reservation. If, after two years, the deceased started to pay a market rent, the reservation would cease when the rent was first paid. Once the reservation ceases, the gift becomes an outright gift at that point and the seven year period starts to run from the date the reservation ceased.

If the deceased died within the seven year period, the gift should be included in section 1 of form **D3**. You should include the value of the property at the time the reservation ceased. However, the law says that where a gift with reservation becomes an outright gift, you **cannot** deduct any of the exemptions from the value of the gift.

There are other more complicated rules that can apply to a gift with reservation. You should telephone our Helpline if you not sure how to include a gift on form **D3**.

2 This section of form **D3** is for details of gifts with reservation of benefit where the reservation remained in place at the deceased's death. Tick the boxes to answer each question. If you answer "Yes" to either question, you must give details in the table in this section of form **D3**.

2a You should answer "Yes" to this question if the deceased made a gift but the person receiving the gift did not take full ownership or possession of the assets given.

2b You should answer "Yes" to this question if the deceased made a gift of land and continued to benefit from the property without any contractual or other arrangement, for example, by simply continuing to live there.

You should also answer "Yes" to this question if the deceased made a gift of land on or after 9 March 1999, and the deceased or their spouse continued to benefit from, or enjoy, the property through a lease or trust or similar right, or through any arrangement.

2c You should answer "Yes" to this question if the deceased made a gift of any other asset apart from land, but continued to receive some benefit from all or part of the asset given.

Follow the guidance on the previous pages to fill in this section of the form, but with the following changes.

Value at date of death

▶ Because the law says we include a gift with reservation as part of the deceased's estate, we need to value it **at the date of death**. Write in the value at the date of death.

Amount and type of exemption

▶ The law says that the exemption for gifts out of income and the annual exemption do not apply to a gift with reservation.

LT2 Add up the figures here and write the answer in this box. Copy the figure from this box to box WS12 on form **IHT(WS)**.

Earlier gifts

▶ This section of form **D3** is about any gift that the deceased made before the gifts you have included in sections 1 and 2. To work out whether tax is payable on any gift, the law says that we must add it to any *chargeable* gifts made in the seven years before the gift concerned. This means that if the deceased made a gift 6 years before they died, we need to add that gift to any *chargeable* gifts made in the seven years before the gift was made.

What is a *chargeable* gift

▶ A chargeable gift is, broadly, any gift which is not wholly covered by exemptions and

- was made before 18 March 1986, **or**
- was made on or after 18 March 1986 and was given to a company or the trustees of a discretionary trust .

This means that gifts from one person to another are **not** *chargeable* gifts and you should not include such gifts in this section of form **D3**.

3 You should answer "Yes" to this question if the deceased had made any chargeable gifts in the seven years *before the earliest date of the other gifts you have entered on the form.* You should give details of such gifts in the table in this section of form **D3**. Fill in the table following the guidance on the previous pages.

The form does not allow you to include these earlier gifts with the estate on death because they are only relevant in working out any tax payable on the gifts in section 1 and 2 of form **D3**. We will take any earlier gifts into account when looking at the gifts in section 1 and 2 after you have taken out the grant.

8

Joint and nominated assets

Form D4

You **must** fill in form **D4** to give details of all of the UK assets the deceased owned jointly with other people. Where assets are owned by two or more people, the way in which they own the assets will affect how the assets must be dealt with on the death of one of the joint owners.

This difference in the way assets can be jointly owned is very important for inheritance tax and affects the way in which you should fill in the forms.

Property may be owned by two or more people in such a way that

- the share of the first to die passes automatically to the other joint owners. Where this applies we say that the shares passes *'by survivorship'*. Or
- each joint owner may decide to give their share to someone else under their Will (or if they did not make a Will, under the rules of intestacy).

These two principles apply throughout the UK, but are described differently in English and Scots law. It is a complex area of law under both legal systems and these notes only give broad guidance.

English law

Joint tenants

If all the joint owners intended that when one of them died, their share would pass automatically to the other joint owners, the asset is owned as *'joint tenants'*. Assets owned by joint tenants are always owned equally and the deceased's share passes to the other joint owners by survivorship.

Tenants in common

If all the owners intended that when one of them died, their share would pass to someone else under their Will (or if they did not make a Will, under the rules of intestacy), the asset is owned as *'tenants in common'*. Tenants in common can, but do not always, have unequal shares in the asset. The share of a tenant in common is usually in proportion to the money they put in to buy the joint property.

Scots law

Assets passing by survivorship

If assets are owned in the names of the joint owners *'and the survivor'* (this is called special or survivorship destination), or if their is any mention of survivorship in the deeds to heritable property, the share of the first to die will normally pass by survivorship to other joint owners.

Assets passing by Will or under intestacy

If there is no mention of special destination or survivorship so that the assets are in just the names of the joint owners, the share of each owner will pass by their Will or under intestacy.

D4(Notes)

1

Can the way assets are jointly owned change ?

Under English law, if joint owners buy an asset such as a house between them equally, the property will be held as joint tenants unless the owners say otherwise. Joint bank and building society accounts are also usually held as joint tenants. It is possible for joint tenants to "sever" the joint tenancy. If this happens, the owners will then hold the joint asset as tenants in common.

Under Scots law, if joint assets are held with no special destination each owner can dispose of their share of a joint asset as they think fit. Where, however, there is a special destination it may be possible for each joint owner to "evacuate" the destination so that it no longer applies. But the matter is complex, especially where the joint ownes have paid equally for assets and each situation will need to be considered on it's facts, where it will have bearing on the amount of tax to be paid.

Establishing the deceased's share

Where land and buildings are owned in joint names, the deeds to the property will usually set out the share of each joint owner. With other assets, each joint owners share will usually correspond to their contribution to the asset. Where the deceased's share does not correspond to their contribution to the asset you will need to explain why the deceased's share is different.

Where all the money was provided by the deceased

Sometimes assets may be owned jointly with another person, but only one person provided all the money either in the account or to buy the asset. For example, an elderly person who has difficulty getting out may add the name of a relative to an account for convenience so that the relative may draw out money on the deceased's behalf.

If the deceased provided all the money **and you include the value of the whole of the asset**, you only have to give the name of the joint owner, a description of the asset and its value. No further information about the history of the joint ownership is necessary. Remember, however, that if the other joint owner has withdrawn money from a joint bank account for their own use, such withdrawals may be gifts and you may need to include them on form **D3**.

It follows from this that if someone dies with their name on a joint account but they did not provide any of the funds in the account, then unless the other joint owner has made a gift to the deceased, no part of the account should be included in the deceased's estate.

Scots law

Under Scots law, if the deceased provided all the money in a joint account or provided all the money to buy an asset then you **must** include the whole value at the date of death as if it had belonged only to the deceased, unless there is clear evidence that the deceased intended to make a gift to the other joint owner(s). Any gift should be reported on form **D3** if appropriate.

2

Assets owned jointly between husband and wife

▸ If the other joint owner was the deceased's spouse **and** the asset now passes to the spouse by survivorship, you only need to give the name of the spouse, a brief description of the asset and its approximate value. No further information about the history of the joint ownership is necessary. Remember to deduct spouse exemption from such asset(s).

Where the deceased owned more than one joint asset

If the deceased owned a number of assets jointly with the same person and the circumstances of the ownership of each item are the same, you may include them all on one form. But, if a person owns some assets jointly with the same person and one asset is owned as joint tenants (or subject to special destination) and another as tenants in common (with no special destination) you should fill in separate forms.

How to fill in form D4
Where the assets pass by survivorship

1 You should answer each of the questions giving details of the history of the joint item. Then go on to fill in the boxes to show details of the assets, any liabilities and any exemptions or reliefs that you feel are due.

JP1 List the assets owned jointly where the tax may not be paid by instalments (the same type of assets included in section F of form **IHT200**). Show the value of the whole of the asset and the value of the deceased's share. Add up all the figures and write the total in this box.

JP2 List any liabilities that are to be deducted from the assets. Add up all the figures and write the total in this box.

JP3 Take box JP2 away from box JP1 and write the answer in this box. If this figure is a minus figure, do not fill in box JP4 and write '0' in box JP5 .

JP4 List any exemptions or reliefs (see pages 36-40 of the guide *"How to fill in form IHT200")* that you wish to deduct from the joint property. Add up all the figures and write the total in this box.

JP5 Take box JP4 away from box JP3 and write the answer in this box. Copy this figure to box WS2 on form **IHT(WS)**.

2 You should answer each of the questions giving details of the history of the joint item. Then go on to fill in the boxes to show details of the assets, any liabilities and any exemptions or reliefs that you feel are due.

Tick the box at the top of the page if you wish to pay the tax on these assets by instalments.

JP6 List the assets owned jointly where the tax may be paid by instalments (the same type of assets included in section G of form **IHT200**). Show the value of the whole of the assets and the value of the deceased's share. Add up all the figures and write the total in this box.

3

JP7 List any liabilities that are to be deducted from the assets. Add up all the figures and write the total in this box.

JP8 Take box JP7 away from box JP6 and write the answer in this box. If this figure is a minus figure, do not fill in box JP9 and write '0' in box JP10 .

JP9 List any exemptions or reliefs (see pages 36-40 of the guide *"How to fill in form IHT200")* that you wish to deduct from the joint property. Add up all the figures and write the total in this box.

JP10 Take box JP9 away from box JP8 and write the answer in this box. Copy this figure to box WS7 on form **IHT(WS)**.

How to fill in form D4
Where the assets pass under Will or intestacy

1 You should answer each of the questions giving details of the history of the joint item. Then go on to fill in the boxes to show details of the assets and liabilities.

JP1 List the assets owned jointly where the tax may not be paid by instalments (the same type of assets included in section F of form **IHT200**). Show the value of the whole of the asset and the value of the deceased's share. Add up all the figures and write the total in this box.

JP2 List any liabilities that are to be deducted from the assets. Add up all the figures and write the total in this box.

Do not fill in boxes JP3, JP4 or JP5. Include the figures from boxes JP1 and JP2 in the appropriate boxes in section F on form ***IHT200.*** *Deduct any exemptions or reliefs on form* ***IHT200*** *only.*

2 You should answer each of the questions giving details of the history of the joint item. Then go on to fill in the boxes to show details of the assets and liabilities.

Tick the box at the top of the page if you wish to pay the tax on these assets by instalments.

JP6 List the assets owned jointly where the tax may be paid by instalments (the same type of assets included in section G of form **IHT200**). Show the value of the whole of the assets and the value of the deceased's share. Add up all the figures and write the total in this box.

JP7 List any liabilities that are to be deducted from the assets. Add up all the figures and write the total in this box.

Do not fill in boxes JP8, JP9 or JP10. Include the figures from boxes JP6 and JP7 in the appropriate boxes in section G on form ***IHT200.*** *Deduct any exemptions or reliefs on form* ***IHT200*** *only.*

4

Household goods

- If the deceased was a joint owner of household goods and effects they should be included here as joint property. Group the items together following the groups on form **D10**. The value of the jointly owned household goods and effects should be included on form **D4** and not on form **D10**.

  If the household goods and effects were owned jointly with the deceased's spouse you may include an approximate value. Remember to deduct spouse exemption from the assets.

Houses and land

- If the deceased owned any houses or land jointly, you should also fill in form **D12** giving details of the properties. You may include jointly owned properties on the same form **D12** that gives details of properties that the deceased owned on their own.

Insurance policies and bonds

- If you have deducted any money owed under a joint mortgage in box JP7 and a joint mortgage protection policy was assigned to repay the mortgage, you should include the value of the deceased's share of the policy proceeds as an asset in box JP1.

  If the deceased was entitled to benefit from a joint life insurance policy (other than a mortgage protection policy) of the type described at question 2 on form **D9**, you should include details of the deceased's interest in the policy on that form.

Businesses

- You should **not** include any business assets owned jointly by a partnership on this form. Such assets should be included on form **D14** and in boxes F7 or F8 on page 5 of form **IHT200** as appropriate.

Foreign property

- The way in which assets may be owned jointly in the UK does not usually apply in other countries. You should **not** include any jointly owned foreign property on this form. You should fill in form **D15** giving details of the foreign property and fill in form **D17** giving answers to the questions on this form for the foreign assets.

How to value joint property

- The rules for valuing joint property are the same as the rules for valuing assets owned by the deceased alone (see pages 14 - 25 of the guide *"How to fill in form IHT200"*, form **D7(Notes)** and form **D10(Notes)**). In the case of bank and building society accounts, stocks and shares etc, you should find out the whole value and then include the value of the deceased's share. For example, the deceased owned a joint account with two other people that was worth £9,000 at the date of death. They had all contributed equally to the money in the account. The value of the deceased's share would be an arithmetical one-third share of the whole or £3,000.

However, in the case of a house or land not owned as an investment, the open market value of a share is likely to be less than a share calculated in this way, as a discount may be appropriate.

The amount of the discount will vary depending on the circumstances of each property. To give us a starting point, you may reduce the arithmetical share of the value of the whole of the property by 10%. This will give us an indication of the value of the share of the property. **This figure of 10% is only to give us a starting point. The amount of the discount, as well as the value estimated for the whole of the property may need to be changed after the grant has been issued.**
For example, the deceased owned a house worth £120,000 jointly with one other person. The arithmetical value of the deceased's share is £60,000 and this may be reduced by 10% or £6,000. The value to include is £54,000.

You may **not** deduct a discount if the other joint owner is the deceased's spouse. Special rules prevent this discount from applying, so you should include the deceased's arithmetical share of the whole value of the house or land.

How is the value of land and buildings agreed?

▸ We will usually ask the Valuation Office to give us their opinion of the value of the deceased's property. They will take into account the circumstances of any jointly owned property and amount of discount to be allowed. If the Valuation Office cannot agree with the figures you have used, they will try to agree a value with you. If the agreed value is more than the figure that you have suggested, you may have to pay some more tax (and interest).

Nominated assets

3 You should also use this form to give details of any nominated assets that pass on the deceased's death. You must give the name of the person who is to receive the asset(s), a description of the assets and include the whole value on the form.

*You should include the value of the nominated assets, in the appropriate box in section F of form **IHT200**. However, you should deduct the value of the nominated assets from the value in box F24 that you carry forward to box PS1 on form **D18**.*

Assets held in trust (settled property)

Form D5

The law says that if someone has the right to benefit from assets held in a trust, they are treated for inheritance tax as if they owned those assets personally. A person may benefit from assets held in a trust by receiving the income from the assets or being allowed to use the asset, for example living in a house. These assets must be included as part of the deceased's estate. We call assets held in a trust "settled property".

You **must** fill in form **D5** to give details of, and a value for, all the settled property in which the deceased had a right to benefit. If it is easier, you can fill in a separate form for each trust. You must give details of all settled property including

- settled property which is overseas and is held in a trust made by a person who was domiciled in the United Kingdom at the time the trust was set up
- settled property in the United Kingdom which is held in a trust made by a person who was domiciled outside the United Kingdom at the time the trust was set up, and
- settled property over which the deceased had a general power of appointment **and** the deceased exercised that power in the **Will**.

Foreign trusts

If the deceased had a right to benefit from settled property where the assets are overseas **and** the person who set up the trust was domiciled **outside the United Kingdom** when the trust was created, please answer question 1 only.

Discretionary trusts

Sometimes, a trust will give the trustees a choice about who can benefit under the trust. These trusts are called "discretionary trusts". As no one has a *right* to benefit from a discretionary trust, you should not fill in form **D5** for such a trust, even if the deceased has been receiving some benefit.

Settled land grant

If you need to apply for a Settled Land Grant, you should fill in form **IHT200**, see page 42 of the guide *"How to fill in form IHT200"*.

Who should tell us about a trust

It is the trustees of the settlement who must give full details of assets and liabilities that make up the trust and who must pay any inheritance tax that is due. However, we need to know at least the total net value of any settled property so that we can work out the total tax that is due. If you have details of the assets and liabilities of the trust, you should include the details on form **D5**. **If the trustees will only give you a total value for the trust fund, you only need to include that value in box SP5 or SP10.**

If the trust assets are exempt from inheritance tax, again you only need to include a total figure in box SP3 or box SP8. Deduct the exemption in box SP4 or box SP9.

D5(Notes)

Sometimes, the trustees want to pay the tax at the same time as you apply for a grant. This often happens where the trustees of the trust and the personal representatives are the same people. If this applies here, you can help us by giving full details of all the assets and liabilities on the form and sending a copy of the deed of trust.

How to fill in form D5

1 You should fill in this box with the details that we ask for on the form.

2 If you have details of the assets and liabilities of the trust fill in the boxes below.

SP1 List the assets held in the trust where the tax may not be paid by instalments (this is the same type of assets included in section F of form **IHT200**) and their value. Add up all the figures and write the total in this box. If you use form **D7** to schedule stocks and shares remember not to carry these figures to section F of form **IHT200**.

SP2 List any liabilities that are to be deducted from the assets. Add up all the figures and write the total in this box.

If you include a deduction for income that was due to the deceased but had not been paid in their lifetime, remember to include the same figure in either box F13 or F14 in form **IHT200**. If there is a minus figure in box SP8, you may include the deficit here.

SP3 Take box SP2 away from box SP1 and write the answer in this box. If this figure is a minus figure, do not fill in box SP4 and write '0' in box SP5.

SP4 List any exemptions or reliefs (see pages 36-40 of the guide *"How to fill in form IHT200")* that you wish to deduct from the settled property. Add up all the figures and write the total in this box.

SP5 Take box SP4 away from box SP3 and write the answer in this box.

If the trustees wish to pay the tax on these assets when you apply for a grant, copy this figure to box WS4 on form **IHT(WS)**. If the trustees do not want to pay the tax on these assets when you apply for a grant, copy this figure to box WS11 on form **IHT(WS)**.

3 If you have details of the assets and liabilities of the trust fill in the boxes below.

Tick the box at the top of the page if the trustees wish to pay the tax on these assets by instalments.

SP6 List the assets held in the trust where the tax may not be paid by instalments (this is the same type of assets included in section G of form **IHT200**) and their value. Add up all the figures and write the total in this box.

SP7 List any liabilities that are to be deducted from the assets. Add up all the figures and write the total in this box. If there is a minus figure in box SP3, you may include the deficit here.

SP8 Take box SP7 away from box SP6 and write the answer in this box. If this figure is a minus figure, do not fill in box SP9 and write '0' in box SP10.

SP9 List any exemptions or reliefs (see pages 36-40 of the guide *"How to fill in form IHT200")* that you wish to deduct from the settled property. Add up all the figures and write the total in this box.

SP10 Take box SP9 away from box SP8 and write the answer in this box.

If the trustees wish to pay the tax on these assets when you apply for a grant, copy this figure to box WS9 on form **IHT(WS)**. If the trustees do not want to pay the tax on these assets when you apply for a grant, copy this figure to box WS11 on form **IHT(WS)**.

How to value settled property

- The rules for valuing settled property are the same as the rules for valuing assets owned by the deceased (see pages 14 - 25 of the guide *"How to fill in form IHT200"*, form **D7(Notes)** and form **D10(Notes)**).

Insurance policies held in trust

- If the deceased had the right to benefit under an insurance policy held in trust, you should fill in the names and addresses of the trustees, the value of the deceased's interest in the policy and attach a copy of the policy to form **D5**.

Accounts from trustees

- If the trustees and the personal representatives are the same people and you do give us full details of the settled property on form **D5**, we may still ask for a formal account to be filled in and signed by the trustees at a later date. But we will only do this in exceptional circumstances.

  If the trustees are different people or if you have only been able to give brief details on form **D5**, we will ask the trustees to deliver a separate account.

Heritage exemption

- If you are aware that the trustees intend to claim heritage exemption or any asset of the trust has at any previous time benefited either from heritage exemption or from an approved maintenance fund, you can help us to deal with this aspect of the estate by filling in form **D17** to give

  - the name of the person who died earlier or who made the gift
  - the date of death or the date of birth of the person
  - any CTO reference concerning this previous occasion.

Pensions

Form D6

▸ You **must** fill in form **D6** if the deceased either received or had made provision for a pension, other than the State pension, from either an employer or under a personal pension scheme or policy.

Personal pension policies replaced retirement annuity contracts with effect from 1 July 1988. What we say here about personal pension policies also applies to retirement annuity contracts. If the deceased owned a retirement annuity contract, you should fill in form **D6** as if it was a personal pension policy.

For income tax purposes, pension schemes and personal pension policies are either **approved** or **unapproved** (the scheme papers or policy documents will say whether or not it is an approved scheme). If the benefits are payable under an **unapproved** scheme, please give details on form **D17** of the benefits payable under the scheme and those taken by the deceased as well as answering the questions on form **D6**.

Pensions Helpline

▸ Deciding whether inheritance tax is payable on pension benefits can be difficult. If you need to discuss a particular situation with us please telephone 0131 777 4204.

How to fill in form D6

1 In most cases, the payment of a pension or other benefit will cease when the person dies. In some cases, the pension may be guaranteed for a fixed period and the person dies before the end of that period. The payments may then continue to be paid to the estate. The value of the right to receive the remainder of the payments should be included on this form and on form **IHT200**.

You can answer "No" to this question if

- the deceased was due only a small arrears of pension for the period from their last monthly payment to the date of death (include this money in box F15, form **IHT200**), or
- payments continue to be made, usually in the form of a reduced widower's or widow's pension to the deceased's husband or wife (such payments do not form part of the deceased's estate).

If you have answered "Yes" to this question, fill in

- the name of the pension scheme or title of the personal pension policy
- whether the scheme/policy is approved for income tax purposes
- the annual gross amount that was payable
- how often the payments were made
- the date of the final guaranteed payment, and

D6(Notes)

- details of any increase in the payments during the remaining guaranteed period.

2 Some pension schemes or personal pension policies pay out a lump sum benefit when the person dies. This is often referred to as the death benefit. If the lump sum is

- payable to the deceased's personal representatives either by right or because there is no-one else who qualifies for the payment, **or**
- the deceased could, right up until their death, have signed a "nomination" (either for the first time or after having revoked an existing "nomination"), which *bound* the trustees of the pension scheme to make the payment to the person named by the deceased

you must include the lump sum as an asset of the deceased's estate. You should fill in

- the name of the pension scheme or title of the personal pension policy
- whether the scheme/policy is approved for income tax purposes
- the amount of the lump sum payment
- the name of the person who received the lump sum payment

and include the lump sum in box PA2.

A binding nomination is different from a "letter of wishes". A letter of wishes records what the deceased would *like* to happen with the death benefit and does not bind the trustees of the pension scheme to follow the deceased's wishes.

It is important to find out whether or not the deceased could bind the trustees with a nomination. Many pension schemes and policies provide a form that is called a nomination, but which usually goes on to say that the trustees are not bound to follow the deceased's wishes. If the deceased signed such a form, they have a signed a letter of wishes and not a binding nomination.

If you have answered "Yes" to this question and the trustees could choose who received the lump sum, you should fill in

- the name of the pension scheme or title of the personal pension policy
- whether the scheme/policy is approved for income tax purposes
- the name of the person who received the lump sum payment.

Say that the payment was made at the trustees discretion and **do not** include the lump sum in box PA2.

3 Most pension schemes and personal pension policies allow the member to dispose of the death benefits and to make changes to the benefits that they are entitled to under the scheme or policy. Usually, the member can

- nominate or appoint the death benefits to someone else
- assign the death benefits into a trust, or
- make changes to the pension benefits they intend to take and when they intend to take them (there are some examples of the sort of changes that might be made later).

If the deceased made a nomination, appointment or assignment or made any changes to the pension benefits **in the 2 years before they died** a liability to inheritance tax may have arisen. If this applies to the deceased, please fill in

- the name of the pension scheme or title of the personal pension policy
- whether the scheme/policy is approved for income tax purposes
- when the benefit was nominated, appointed or assigned, and
- who the benefit was given to, or
- when any changes were made and what those changes were.

Examples of changes in benefits

Some examples of changes in benefit that might be made are

- where the deceased reaches pension age and decides not to take the payment of their pension at that time or chooses to take "income drawdown", or

- where the deceased having got to pension age and chosen to take "income drawdown" decides at a later date and whilst in ill health to reduce the level of income taken or

- where the deceased having got to pension age and chosen to take "phased retirement" decides at a later date, and whilst in ill health to reduce the number of segments taken.

"Income drawdown" is a particular situation where the deceased has reached pension age but has chosen not to buy an annuity that will provide their pension. Instead, they decide to "draw" a certain level of income from the retirement fund with a view to buying an annuity at a later date.

"Phased retirement" is where the deceased has divided their pension entitlement into a series of segments and has agreed a plan on retirement with their pension provider to take so many segments each year.

Where the deceased has given away any benefits, or has made some changes to the benefits they were entitled to, it is possible that they may have made a transfer of value. You should give the details we ask for above on form **D6** and we will look at what you have said after the grant has been issued. If we think there has been a transfer of value, we will discuss the value with you.

If you wish to include your own value for the benefits given away, you should include a figure on form **D3**. Use form **D17** to show how you have arrived at your value.

Valuing the benefits given away

The value of the benefits given away or the impact of the changes made will depend to a large extent on the deceased's health at the date of the nomination, appointment or change. So that we can establish the value, please provide some evidence of the deceased's state of health and life expectancy at that time. A letter from the deceased's doctor is the best sort of evidence.

If obtaining a letter from the deceased's doctor will delay your application for a grant; you do not have to have it before you send form **IHT200** to us. However, we will need to see the letter as soon as you receive it after the grant has been issued.

Stocks and shares

Form D7

You **must** fill in form **D7** to give details of all the stocks and shares owned by the deceased. You should give the details we ask for in each column for each holding of shares. We explain how to value the shares and what else to look out for on the next page. If

- you have a stockbroker's valuation, or
- you have filled in Inventory form **C1** (Scotland only),

you only need to copy the totals for each category of share to form **D7**. Please attach a copy of the valuation and write "see attached valuation" across form **D7**. (The Inventory will be sent to us after Confirmation.)

How to fill in form D7

1 You should include the following shares in these columns

- all stocks, shares, debentures and other securities quoted in the Stock Exchange Daily Official List
- unit trusts
- investment trusts
- Open-Ended Investment Companies
- Personal Equity Plans
- shares which are held in an Individual Savings Account
- foreign shares which are listed on the London Stock Exchange.

2 You should include the following securities in these columns

- Treasury Bills, Treasury Annuities, Treasury Stock, Exchequer Stock, Convertible Stock, Consolidated Stock and Loan, Funding Stock, Savings Bonds, Victory Bonds, War Loan,
- Government Stock held on the Bank of England Register (previously held on the National Savings Register)
- all UK municipal securities, mortgages, debentures and stock in counties, cities or towns, dock, harbour and water boards, Port of London Authority, Agricultural Mortgage Corporation, N.Ireland municipal stock.

3 You should include the following shares in these columns

- unquoted shares and securities in private limited companies
- shares held in a Business Expansion Scheme (BES) or in a Business Start-up Scheme (BSS).

4 You should include the following shares in these columns

- shares listed on the Alternative Investment Market (AIM)
- shares traded on the Unlisted Securities Market (USM)
- shares traded on OFEX (an unregulated trading facility for dealing in unquoted shares).

D7(Notes)

1

How to value stocks and shares listed on the Stock Exchange

▸ The value for inheritance tax of quoted stocks and shares is either

- one quarter up from the lower to the higher limit of the prices quoted, or
- halfway between the highest and lowest bargains recorded for the day, but excluding bargains at special prices.

The Financial Times (FT)

▸ The FT contains prices for many UK and foreign shares, for unit trusts and investment trusts and for insurance linked investment products. The extract from the FT below explains which figures you should take to work out the value of the deceased's shares. There is example of working out the value on the next page.

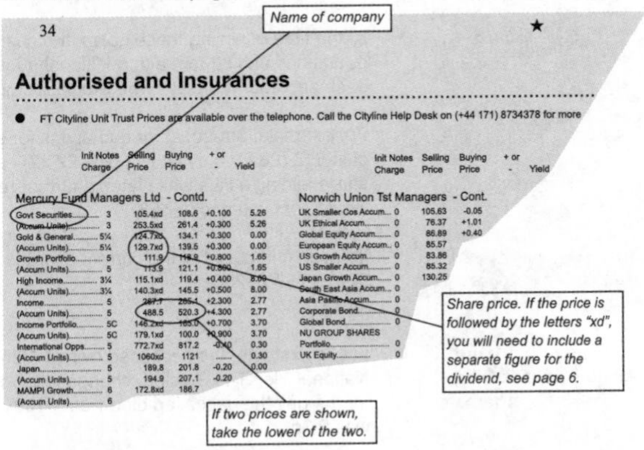

34 ★

Authorised and Insurances

● FT Cityline Unit Trust Prices are available over the telephone. Call the Cityline Help Desk on (+44 171) 8734378 for more

Mercury Fund Managers Ltd - Contd.

	Init Notes Charge	Selling Price	Buying Price	+ or -	Yield
Govt Securities	3	105.4xd	108.6	+0.100	5.26
(Accum Units)	3	253.5xd	261.4	+0.300	5.26
Gold & General	5¼	124.7xd	134.1	+0.300	0.00
(Accum Units)	5¼	129.7xd	139.5	+0.300	0.00
Growth Portfolio	5	111.9	118.9	+0.800	1.65
(Accum Units)	5	113.9	121.1	+0.800	1.65
High Income	3¼	115.1xd	119.4	+0.400	8.00
(Accum Units)	3¼	140.3xd	145.5	+0.500	8.00
Income	5	267.7	285.1	+2.300	2.77
(Accum Units)	5	488.5	520.3	+4.300	2.77
Income Portfolio	5C	146.2xd	165.0	+0.700	3.70
(Accum Units)	5C	179.1xd	100.0	+0.900	3.70
International Opps	5	772.7xd	817.2	-0.40	0.30
(Accum Units)	5	1060xd	1121	......	0.30
Japan	5	189.8	201.8	-0.20	0.00
(Accum Units)	5	194.9	207.1	-0.20	
MAMPI Growth	6	172.8xd	186.7		
(Accum Units)	6				

Norwich Union Tst Managers - Cont.

	Init Notes Charge	Selling Price	Buying Price	+ or -	Yield
UK Smaller Cos Accum	0	105.63	-0.05		
UK Ethical Accum	0	76.37	+1.01		
Global Equity Accum	0	86.89	+0.40		
European Equity Accum	0	85.57			
US Growth Accum	0	83.86			
US Smaller Accum	0	85.32			
Japan Growth Accum	0	130.25			
South East Asia Accum	0				
Asia Pacific Accum	0				
Corporate Bond	0				
Global Bond	0				
NU GROUP SHARES					
Portfolio	0				
UK Equity	0				

Extract from the Financial Times dated 4 August 1999.
Reproduced by kind permission of the Financial Times.

If you are using a newspaper to value the shares, remember to use the prices given in the paper published on the day *after* the deceased died.

The Stock Exchange Historic Price service

▸ Another way to find out about share prices is to use the London Stock Exchange Historic Price service. The Stock Exchange can tell you what the end of day quotation (price) was for all the stocks and shares on the Stock Exchange Daily Official List. If the shares are marked "xd" (see page 6) the Stock Exchange can also tell you the dividend per share that was to be paid to the deceased. There is a charge for this service.

How to use the historic price service

▸ If you choose to use this service, write to the Stock Exchange and give a full description of the stocks and shares you need a quotation for. For example, do not say "Abbey National shares" but give the full name and nominal value - "Abbey National Plc 10p ordinary shares". You will also need to give the date of death and enclose a cheque to cover the fee.

2

Your cheque should be made payable to "London Stock Exchange". All requests **must** be made in writing. The Stock Exchange will not accept any requests to provide quotations over the telephone.

The Stock Exchange will reply by letter (or by fax if you ask them to) and will give the end of day quotation. If the shares are marked "xd", they will also give you dividend per share. The address to write to is

Historic Price Service
4th Floor Tower
London Stock Exchange
Old Broad Street
LONDON EC2N 1HP

Charges ▶ At the time of writing these notes, the charges are £8 for the first five quotations and £2 for each additional quotation. The charges apply to each separate request to the Stock Exchange.

For example, a request for quotations for seven holdings of shares would cost £12 (£8 for the first five plus £2 x2). If you discovered a further shareholding a little while later, a further request to the Stock Exchange would cost you another £8.

You can find out what the current charges are by telephoning 0207 - 797 - 1206.

How to work out the value of the shares ▶ In this example, the deceased owned 1,250 10p ordinary shares in Abbey National Plc. The Stock Exchange tells you that the end of day quotation for the day the deceased died was "p1091 - 1101xd" and the dividend was 2.3p.

The value of the shares ▶ To work out the value of the shares, you should multiply the number of shares by the "quarter-up" price. The "quarter-up" price is the lower price (1091) plus ¼ of the difference between the two prices (¼ of 10p or 2½p). The "quarter-up" price is 1091+2½ = 1093½p. So the value of the shares will be 1,250 x £10.93½ = £13,668.75.

The value of the dividend ▶ To work out the value of the dividend, multiply the number of shares by the dividend per share. The value of the dividend will be 1,250 x 2.3p = £28.75.

Sometimes the dividend may be given as a percentage, say 2.6%. Where this is the case, you can work out the dividend by finding out the percentage of the nominal value of the stock. So if the deceased had owned £400 of loan stock, the dividend would be 2.6% of £400 or £10.40.

Filling in form D7

The example below shows how the Abbey National example should appear on form **D7**.

1 Quoted stocks, shares and investments *(see box 2 for government securities)*

Name of company and type of shares or stock, or **full** name of unit trust and type of units	Number of shares or units or amount of stock held	Market price at date of death	Total value at date of death	Dividend or interest due to date of death	For CTO use only
Abbey National 10p ords	**1,250**	**1093½**	**13,668.75**	**28.75**	

If the deceased died at a weekend or on a Bank Holiday

If the deceased died on a day when the Stock Exchange was closed, you may take the price for either the next day or the last day when the Stock Exchange was open. For example, if the deceased died on a Sunday, you may take the price for either the Monday after or the Friday before. You may use whichever day gives the lowest valuation.

Dividends and interest

You must include any dividends and interest on the assets in boxes 1-4 that were due at the date of death, but have not yet been paid. There is more help about dividends at page 6.

Unit Trusts

For unit trusts, investment trusts and open-ended investment companies the newspapers may show two prices. Take the lower of the two prices. If there was no price published on the day the person died, take the last price published before they died. Newspapers do not show dividends due on unit trusts. You will need to ask the fund managers what you should include as the declared dividend.

Personal Equity Plans (PEPs)

If the deceased owned a PEP you should obtain a valuation from the PEP managers. You can attach it to the form and write "see attached valuation" across the form. Copy the value of the shares in the PEP to the appropriate part of the form, but do not include any deductions for manager's fees. If you cannot obtain a valuation, list the shares held in the PEP on the form and value them in the same way as other shares. You must include a figure for any uninvested cash held in the PEP with the value for the shares.

Individual Savings Accounts (ISAs)

Only shares listed on a recognised stock exchange may be held in an ISA. If the deceased held any shares in an ISA, you should include those shares in either box 1 or 2 on the form. List the shares on the form and value them in the same way as other shares. You must include a figure for any uninvested cash held in the ISA, but **do not** include any other cash or insurance policies held in an ISA with the value for the shares.

The guide *"How to fill in form IHT200"* tells you where to include cash (page 15, box F8) or insurance policies (page 18, box F16) held in an ISA.

Shares listed on a foreign stock exchange may also be held in an ISA. You should include foreign shares (other than those listed on the London Stock Exchange) on form **D15**.

Things to look out for

▶ You should take particular care with the 'unit of quotation' shown in the stock exchange list. Because of company reorganisations the units on the share certificates, for example £1 ordinary shares, may be different from the unit quoted at the date of death. If this is the case, the company's registrar should be able to tell you how many shares of the new unit the deceased owned.

With unit trusts etc, listed in the Financial Times under the 'FT Managed Funds Service' take care to find the right management group. Many companies will be listed more than once because they offer a large variety of investments. If you are filling in form **D7**, please write out the full name of the unit trust, for example "AXA Equity & Law Unit Trust Mangers, Pacific Basin Trust Accumulation Units".

Unusual shares

▶ You will also find prices for shares traded on the markets below listed in the Financial Times

- AIM, the Alternative Investment Market, include any shares in table 4
- NASDAQ, the National Association of Securities Dealers Automated Quotations, include any shares on form **D15**
- EASDAQ, the European Association of Securities Dealers Automated Quotations, include on form **D15**
- OFEX, an unregulated trading facility for dealing in unquoted shares, include any shares in table 4
- USM, the Unlisted Securities Market. This is only relevant if the deceased died before December 1996, include any shares in table 4
- Transactions under Stock Exchange Rule 535 or 4.2. This is only relevant if the deceased died before September 1995, include the shares in the appropriate table.

Foreign shares

▶ Foreign shares listed on the London Stock Exchange may have their nominal value given in the currency of their country, for example $10. However, the price shown will be in sterling. You can value these shares as described above.

Stock Exchange markings

▶ The Stock Exchange Daily Official List includes a number of markings that may affect the value of the stocks and shares. Some of the markings increase the value of the shares. You will need to include this adjustment in box F5 on form **IHT200**. Some markings decrease the value and you will need to deduct the adjustment from the value you include for the shares. Others show that the deceased was entitled to some new shares at the date of death.

Markings which increase the value of the shares

- 'xd' (ex-dividend) – the dividend that is due remains payable to the deceased. Include the net value of the dividend on form **D7**.
- 'IK' ('gilts' plus interest) - the interest that has accrued is part of the value at the date of death. Include the gross interest that has accrued from the date interest was last paid up to date of death on form **D7**.
- 'IM' (fixed interest securities, loan and debenture stock plus interest) – this is the same as 'IK', but applies to a different type of security. Include the gross interest that has accrued from the date interest was last paid up to date of death on form **D7**.

Carry the total for all dividends to box F5 on form **IHT200**.

Markings which decrease the value of the shares

- 'IK...X' ('gilts' minus interest) – interest due from the date of death to the date of payment of interest is deducted from the value at the date of death. Take the gross interest that has accrued from the date of death to the date interest was paid *away* from the value of the stock. If a separate interest payment has been received, include the net amount of the interest payment on form **D7**.
- 'IM...X' (fixed interest securities, loan and debenture stock minus interest) - this is the same as 'IK...X', but applies to a different type of security. Take the gross interest that has accrued from the date of death to the date interest was paid *away* from the value of the stock. If a separate interest payment has been received, include the net amount of the interest payment on form **D7**.

Markings which mean the deceased was entitled to new shares

- 'XC' (ex-capitalisation) – include the new shares
- 'XR' (ex-rights) – account for the value of the new shares or rights
- 'XE' (ex-entitlement) – include the new shares or warrants, if any.

If you do not know how many new shares, rights or warrants to include, the company's registrar should be able to tell you. Include the new shares, rights or warrants with the original holding in boxes F1 to F4 on form **IHT200**.

Debts due to the estate

Form D8

▶ You **must** fill in form **D8** if the deceased had any debts owing to them at the date of death. If the deceased was owed money from more than one source, please fill in a separate form for each debt. If the money owed to the deceased was a director's loan account or current account with a company or other business, you only need to answer questions 3 and 4.

How to fill in form D8

1 Write the date the deceased made the loan in this box.

2 Write the amount of money that was loaned in this box

3 Write the amount of the loan that remained outstanding when the deceased died. If interest was being paid, make sure you include a figure for the capital to be repaid and any interest still to be paid when the deceased died.

4 The law says that if the deceased was owed some money when they died, you must assume that the debt will be repaid in full. On this basis, you must include the full value of the capital and interest outstanding. If, however, it is impossible or not reasonably possible for the money to be repaid, you may include a reduced figure.

You must explain why you have included the reduced figure and show how the figure has been worked out. Use form **D17** if necessary. You must have evidence to show why you are including a reduced figure.

5 Please state the name(s) of the borrowers and if they were related to the deceased, please describe the relationship between the deceased and the borrower(s).

6 If you have answered "Yes" to this question please say what evidence there is. For example, a mortgage deed will show that the loan was secured on a property. But other evidence may be a letter between the deceased and the person borrowing the money. Please provide a copy of any evidence that exists. If there is no evidence, give brief details of the terms of the loan, for example, the period of the loan and whether it was repayable on demand.

A number of insurance-linked products include a loan from the deceased to the trustees of a settlement or policy. If the loan is to be repaid to the estate by the trustees of such a scheme, please provide a copy of the loan agreement and any settlement or policy connected to it.

D8(Notes)

7 If you have answered "Yes" to this question, please say what rate interest was charged at and over what period. How often was the interest paid to the deceased?

8 If you have answered "Yes" to this question, please say how much capital was repaid and when. You should say whether money was actually repaid to the deceased or whether the "repayment" was by the deceased writing off some of the debt. If the deceased wrote off some or all of the debt, please provide a copy of the Deed(s) of Release.

If some, or all, of the debt has been written off, this will change that part of the loan to a gift. You should fill in form **D3** to give details. Normally, a loan **must** be written off by a Deed.

Life insurance and annuities

Form D9

▸ You **must** fill in form **D9** if the deceased was paying premiums on any life insurance policies. This includes premiums paid at regular intervals, for example monthly or quarterly as well as lump sum premiums. It does not matter whether the policies were on the deceased's life or someone else's life or whether the policies were for the deceased's benefit.

There are many different types of life insurance policy. The guide *"How to fill in form IHT200"*, pages 17 and 18 describes the sort of policies that you should include on this form.

Mortgage protection policies

▸ If the policy is a mortgage protection policy, you should include the property, the mortgage and the policy as separate items.

If the deceased owned the property in their own name, you should include the policy in box 1 below.

If the deceased owned the property jointly, you should include the policy along with the property and the mortgage on form **D4**. Form **D4(Notes)** tells you how to fill form **D4**.

How to fill in form D9

1 If the estate received payments from any life insurance policies, you must include the value received including any bonuses that were payable. You should fill in the

- name of the insurance company
- policy number, and
- amount paid under the policy.

In Scotland, the policies will be listed on the Inventory form **C1**. You do not need to list the policies again here, but please include their total in box IP1.

2 The deceased may have been entitled to benefit from a life insurance policy that does not pay out following their death. If so, the deceased's interest in the policy is part of their estate and should be included here. The most common examples are

2a Where the policy is held in the names of two or more people and only pays out on the death of the last of the lives assured. These are often described as "joint life and survivor" policies.

2b Where the deceased will benefit from the policy when another person dies. Quite often policies of this sort will have been purchased "second hand".

D9(Notes)

In both instances, you should include the value of the deceased's interest in the policy as provided by the insurance company. Please also provide a copy of the insurance policy.

If the deceased has paid all the premium(s) on a joint life policy, you may need to fill in form **D3** – see question 5 as well.

3 Most payments under a purchased life annuity will cease when the person dies. In some cases, the payments may be guaranteed for a fixed period even if the person dies before the end of that period. The payments may then continue to be paid to the estate. The value of the right to receive the remainder of the payments should be included on this form and on form **IHT200**.

If you have answered "Yes" to this question, fill in

- the name of the company that sold the policy
- the annual gross amount payable
- what part of the gross annual amount is treated as income (and so liable to income tax) and what part is treated as a repayment of capital (and so tax free)
- how often the payments were made
- the date of the final guaranteed payment
- details of any increase in the payments during the remaining guaranteed period, and
- the value of the right to receive the remainder of the payments.

4 In certain circumstances, often where the deceased has died shortly after purchasing a life annuity, there may be a lump sum payable to the estate. If such a payment has been received, you should fill in

- the name of the company that sold the policy
- how the lump sum has been worked out (if known)
- the amount of the lump sum payable.

If the lump sum is **not** payable to the estate, please say when and how the deceased disposed of the right to receive the lump sum.

5 If the deceased was paying premiums on life insurance policies for the benefit of someone, other than themselves or their spouse, each premium paid within 7 years of the deceased's death will be a transfer of value. Quite often, such transfers will be exempt, but if you answer "Yes" to this question, you should read form **D3(Notes)** and provide the information that we ask for.

6 Life insurance policies taken out on one person's life may be held in a trust for the benefit of others. Parents and grandparents may often take out a life insurance policy but put it in trust for their children or grandchildren. Business partners or the directors of a company may also take out insurance on their lives but for the benefit for their partners or co-directors.

So, if the deceased died whilst they were still working, or they died before their parent(s), there is a possibility that they may have a right to benefit under a policy held in trust.

If the deceased had the right to benefit under a life insurance policy held in trust, that right may be settled property. You will need to fill in form **D5** giving details of the names and addresses of the trustees and, if possible, details of the life insurance policies concerned.

Household and personal goods

Form D10

You **must** fill in form **D10** if the deceased owned any household or personal goods. If the deceased owned any household or personal goods jointly, you should include the value of any such items on form **D4** and not on this form.

By household and personal goods we mean

- antiques and works of art including paintings, drawings, sculpture, porcelain, glass, silver etc
- jewellery
- collections of any kind including books, stamps, coins, medals, wines and spirits etc
- cars (including classic cars), caravans, boats etc
- TV, audio and video equipment, cameras and other specialist equipment
- all other furniture, household and domestic items including electrical items, clothes, garden equipment,tools etc.

Husband and wife

If any items are passing to the deceased's spouse under the Will there is no need to provide details of the items concerned. You need only provide an approximate value for such items. Remember to deduct spouse exemption on page 4 of form **IHT200.**

How to fill in form D10

1 Fill in the **gross** proceeds of any items that have already been sold before you applied for the grant in box HG1. If any items have been sold at below the market value, you must increase the figure in box HG1 to reflect the open market value of the items concerned.

2 If you have a professional or specialist valuation, please attach a copy. If you have not had the items valued, you should group the items together according to the list above and include a value for each group. Add up all the figures and write the total in box HG2.

If the deceased owned a motor car, including classic or vintage cars, you should include details of the make, exact model, year of registration and the registration number. If the registration number has a value, please include it separately. You should include similar details as necessary if the deceased owned a caravan, boat or aeroplane etc.

3 Tick the box to answer this question. You must tell us about any sales of household and personal goods by you or the beneficiaries that take place within a reasonable time after the death and where the gross sale price is different from the value you included in box HG2. You should tell us what value was included in box HG2 for

D10(Notes)

the item(s) sold and the gross sale price that the item(s) were sold for.

4 If the unsold items have not been professionally valued, you should tell us how you have arrived at the values you have included. If the value of any unsold item has been reduced or discounted, or if a nil value has been included, you should tell us why in this box.

How to value household and personal goods

Remember that the value of any asset that you or your valuers give should be the price that you would expect the item to sell for in the open market. For household and personal goods, such a sale often takes place at auction. Or items might be advertised in the local paper or sold at a car boot or other such sale. If you have a professional valuation, it is only acceptable if the instructions to the valuer were for an open market value.

A valuation for a "forced sale" is not acceptable. A valuation "for insurance", although a good place to start, may be the cost to replace the items and not necessarily a realistic price for which the items might be sold.

As a rough guide, it might be worth having any individual items specifically mentioned in the Will and any other items that individually are thought to be worth more than £500 valued.

Heritage exemption

If you are claiming heritage exemption or any asset has at any previous time benefited either from heritage exemption or from an approved maintenance fund, please fill in form **D17** and tell us

- the name of the person who died earlier or who made the gift
- the date of death or the date of birth of the person
- any CTO reference concerning this previous occasion.

Interest in another estate

Form D11

▸ You **must** fill in form **D11** if the deceased had the right to a legacy or a share in the estate of someone who had died before them, but they did not receive that legacy or share before they died. You should fill in a separate form for each of the other estate(s).

How to fill in form D11

1 Write in the full name of the person who died earlier.

2 Write in the date of death of the person who died earlier.

3 You can help us by giving our reference number for the earlier estate. If you do not know the reference, give the date of the grant for the earlier death.

4 Describe what the deceased's right to benefit from the other estate was. For example, was it a legacy of money, was it a specific item, perhaps, of furniture or a holding of shares, or was the deceased entitled to the remainder of the estate for their own use.

5 The deceased may have received part of their legacy or share of the estate before they died. Tick the box to answer the question. If the answer is "Yes", give details of what they had received here.

6 Write in this box the details of the legacy or share of the estate that was still to be paid to the deceased when they died.

If the deceased was entitled to a legacy of money or a specific item, please describe the asset and give its value at the date the deceased died.

However, if the deceased was entitled to the remainder of the estate, there are special rules that apply to value the deceased's interest. You will need to find out details of the assets and liabilities that the personal representatives of the person who died earlier held at the date the deceased died, including any legacies or other payments still to be made. You will then need to value those assets at the deceased's date of death (in the same way as you value the deceased's own assets). You should take away any liabilities or legacies that have still to be paid out under the Will of the person who died earlier.

It may be that you are unable to obtain such details before you are ready to apply for a grant. If so, please fill in the form with as much

D11(Notes)

information as you can and include an estimate for the value.

Add up all the figures and write the net total in box UE1. Copy this figure to box F21 in form **IHT200**

Successive charges relief

Remember that if the estate of the person who died earlier is paying inheritance tax **and** there are fewer than five years between the two deaths, you may be able to deduct successive charges relief, see page 37 of the guide *"How to fill in form IHT200"*.

Land, buildings and interests in land

Form D12

You **must** fill in form **D12** to give details of all the land and buildings or interests in land and buildings owned by the deceased. If you have a professional valuation, please attach a copy.

How to fill form D12

1 We will usually ask the District Valuer to help us with the value of land and buildings. Fill in the details of the person to contact from section C of form **IHT200.** The District Valuer will make any necessary arrangements to inspect the property or discuss values through this contact.

2 Fill in the table, giving details of each item of property. If necessary, you can continue over the page. If the deceased owned a large number of properties, use more than one form. You may include property in the deceased's own name as well as property owned jointly with someone else on the same form.

Column A — Please number each item of property.

Column B — Give a full description of the property with the postcode, so we can identify it easily. If the property is not numbered, or it is farmland or other land without an address, you should **attach a plan** that shows the boundaries of the property clearly.

If the property is jointly owned, write the deceased's share under the description of the property.

Column C — Say whether the deceased owned the property outright or had a lease and any rent being paid.

Column D — If the property was let, you should provide a copy of the lease, or sub-lease, business or agricultural tenancy agreement. If the lease etc does not say so, or there is no written agreement, please fill in this column to say

- the date the tenancy/lease began
- how long the property was let for
- what rent is payable, and whether the rent can be reviewed
- who is responsible for the outgoings on the property, and
- the name of the tenant.

If the property was unoccupied at the date of death, please write "vacant" in this column.

D12(Notes)

Column E — If you are deducting agricultural relief, woodlands relief or claiming heritage exemption, write in the value of the property which you say qualifies for relief.

If you are claiming heritage exemption and the property has at anyprevious time benefited either from heritage exemption or from an approved maintenance fund, please fill in form **D17** and tell us

- the name of the person who died earlier or who made the gift
- the date of death or the date of birth of the person
- any CTO reference concerning this previous occasion.

Column F — Write in the open market value of the property at the date of death. Remember that the basis of valuation that you or your valuers use is the price at which the asset might be sold on the open market. A valuation "for Probate" will only be acceptable if it is based on the open market value. If the property was jointly owned, give the value of the deceased's share. Show how you have worked out the value of the share.

Show the total value of all the properties in the boxes at the foot of columns E and F. Page 5 of form **IHT200** breaks property down into 6 categories. Include the properties in the relevant boxes and make sure that the figures in boxes G1-G6 in form **IHT200** total the same as the figure at the foot of column F, excluding any jointly owned property passing by survivorship that you have included on form **D4**.

3 If any of the properties is suffering from any major damage, its value may be affected. Things like a poor state of internal and external decoration are not so important. But if the property is damaged in a way that is covered by buildings insurance, we have to value the property in a special way.

Tick the box to answer this question. If you have answered "Yes", show the item number from column A in the first column and give details of the damage in the box. If you have a survey or structural engineer's report, please provide a copy.

You should say whether the deceased's insurance policy covered all or part of the repairs and whether you will make a claim under the policy. If you are intending to make a claim under the policy, please provide a copy of any correspondence you may have had with the insurers or loss adjusters.

4 If you are going to be selling any of the deceased's properties within a reasonable time after the death, the sale price will usually be a good indication of the value at the date of death.

Tick the box to answer this question. If you have answered "Yes", fill in the table giving the information that we ask for.

Column G — Use the same item number as column A above.

Column H — Say whether the property

- has already been sold
- is on the market for sale or
- is to be sold later on.

If the property has been sold, please include the date on which contracts were exchanged (or, in Scotland, when missives have been concluded).

You only need to fill in columns I to L if the property has actually been sold before you apply for a grant.

Column I — Write in the asking price, or the price agreed for the sale. The costs of selling the property should not be taken off the price.

Column J — Say whether the sale was at "arm's length" to a stranger or whether it was to a relative, friend or perhaps business colleague.

Column K — If the sale price you have shown in column I includes fixtures and fittings, carpets, curtains etc, say how much of the sale price was for these items.

Column L — Say whether you want to use the sale price as the value at the date of death.

Agricultural relief

Form D13

You **must** fill in form **D13** if you are deducting agricultural relief from some or all of the land included in the deceased's estate. You can help us by **sending a plan of the property** with form **IHT200**. Fill in a separate form if you deducting agricultural relief from a lifetime transfer.

When is agricultural relief available

Agricultural relief is available for transfers of agricultural property and certain shareholdings in farming companies. There are three basic rules

- the property must be agricultural property
- the deceased must have owned the property for a minimum number of years, and
- the property must have been used for agricultural purposes.

Our leaflet **IHT17** tells you more about agricultural relief.

What is the rate of relief

Provided the asset qualifies for relief, the rate at which relief is allowed is shown in the table below. The relief is given by deducting the relevant percentage of the capital value of the asset. So, if the property qualifies for 100% relief, you should include the value of the asset in box G3 on form **IHT200**. You should deduct the relief using the same figure in box G17.

	Date of death on or after 10 March 1992	Date of death up to 9 March 1992
Land with vacant possession	100	50
Land that is let	50	30
Land that was let after 31/8/1995	100	Not applicable

There are some circumstances where the higher rate of relief can apply to land that was let. The notes for question 6 explain this a little more. However, the rules are complicated and our leaflet **IHT17** gives more details.

How to fill in form D13

1 Fill in the address of the property as shown on form **D12**.

2a Tick the box to answer this question. If you have answered "Yes", go to question 3. You do not need to answer questions 5a – 5c. If you have answered "No", go to question 2b.

2b Tick the box to answer this question. If you have answered "Yes", go to question 3. You do not need to answer question 4. If you have answered "No", go to question 2c.

D13(Notes)

2c If you have answered "No" to questions 2a and 2b, the deceased has not owned the property for long enough to qualify for agricultural relief. However, there are detailed rules under which agricultural relief may still be available. Broadly these apply where

- the deceased inherited the property on the death of another person, or
- the property had replaced other agricultural property.

Our leaflet **IHT17** tells you more about the conditions that must be met.

If you feel that relief is due, please say why in this box and then carry on filling in the form.

3 Give details of when and how the deceased acquired the property. For example, did the deceased inherit the property or buy it themselves?

4 Describe the agricultural activities that the deceased carried out. Do not use vague phrases like "general farming". Say whether it was

- an arable, pastoral or mixed farm
- the type of crops usually grown, and
- the type of livestock that grazed the land.

If a variety of livestock grazed the land, give some idea about the number of animals and acreage used by each type.

You should also tell us here if the deceased left the property or stoppedthe agricultural activity. Say when this happened and why. Agricultural relief may still be due if the property was managed under an agro-environmental or habitat scheme arrangement.

Our Helpline can tell you what the conditions are for the agro-environmental or habitat scheme arrangement.

5a Say here who has been occupying the property throughout the 7 years up to the death. Please list all the different people who have occupied the land (this can include the deceased) and the date(s) of their occupation.

5b Describe the agricultural activities carried out by each occupier. Do not use vague phrases like "general farming". Say whether it was

- an arable, pastoral or mixed farm
- the type of crops usually grown, and
- the type of livestock that grazed the land.

If a variety of livestock grazed the land, give some idea about the number of animals and acreage used by each type.

You should also tell us if the agricultural activity stopped at any time. Say when this happened and why. Agricultural relief may still be due if the property was managed under an agro-environmental or habitat scheme arrangement.

5c If the letting began after 31 August 1995, please say when the tenancy started and provide a copy of the tenancy agreement. You can ignore question 6 and go to question 7.

If the letting began before 1 September 1995, give details of the letting, particularly when the letting started, how long the property was let for, what rent was charged. If there is a written lease or agreement for the letting, please provide a copy.

6 It is possible that the higher rate of relief may be available for let land. The first situation this may apply to is where the deceased would have been able to obtain vacant possession within 24 months of the date of death. If you have answered "Yes" to this question, please say how the deceased would have been able to obtain vacant possession. For example, were they a freeholder or was a tenancy coming to an end.

If you have answered "No" to this question, relief may still be available if the tenancy began before 10 March 1981. There are three other conditions that apply. They are that

- the deceased has owned the land since before 10 March 1981, **and**
- the land would have qualified for full agricultural relief under the law at that date, **and**
- the deceased did not have and could not have had the right to vacant possession between 10 March 1981 and the date of death.

If you think that the higher rate of relief may apply to land that was let before 10 March 1981 you should telephone our Orderline and ask for form **220**. This tells you more about the law as at 10 March 1981. You should fill in form **220** and send it with form **IHT200**.

7 Agricultural relief is only available for agricultural property that is occupied for the purposes of agriculture. Whether each house or cottage will qualify for relief depends on who lived in each property. You should identify each house or cottage on the farm separately and say

- who lived there at the date of death, and how long they had lived there

- if the house or cottage was let, describe the type of tenancy, for example, agricultural tenancy, assured shorthold
- how much rent was paid
- why the occupier lived there, and
- why you consider the house or cottage to be "of a character appropriate" to agricultural property.

8 If, before the deceased died, all or part of the property was subject to a binding contract for sale where contracts have been exchanged(or, in Scotland, when missives have been concluded), but the sale had not been completed, agricultural relief will not be due. You should give details of the sale, and clearly identify the part of the property that was sold on the plan.

9 If you are deducting agricultural relief in connection with a lifetime transfer, you should fill in a separate form **D13** to give the details we ask for as at the date of gift. There are also additional conditions that must be met before the relief is due. Please answer each of the questions so we can decide whether or not the relief is due.

For this purpose, "relevant period" means the period between the date of the lifetime transfer and the date of death of the deceased (or death of the person who received the gift if they died first).

Note If the conditions for both agricultural relief and business relief are met, agricultural relief is allowed in preference to business relief. Business relief is not allowed instead of or in addition to agricultural relief.

Business relief, business interests or partnerships

Form D14 You **must** fill in form **D14** if the deceased owned

- shares in a company and you are deducting business relief, or
- a business or part of a business, or
- an asset used in a business and you are deducting business relief.

If necessary, fill in a separate form for each holdings of shares, business or assets used in a business.

When is business relief available The relief is available for transfers of certain types of business and business assets and certain types of shares. The deceased must have owned the assets for a minimum period, generally two years, and the assets must also qualify for the relief under a number of other quite complicated rules. Our leaflet **IHT17** tells you more about business relief.

What is the rate of relief If the asset qualifies for relief, the rate at which relief is allowed is shown in the table below. The relief is given by deducting the relevant percentage of the capital value of the asset. So, if the asset qualifies for 100% relief, you should include the value of the asset in one of boxes at G7 to G12 on form **IHT200**. You should deduct the relief using the same figure in box G17.

	Date of death after 6 April 1996	Date of death between 10 March 1992 and 5 April 1996	Date of death between 17 March 1987 and 9 March 1992
A business or interest in a business	100%	100%	50%
Control holding of shares in an 'unquoted' company	100%	100%	50%
Substantial holding of shares in an 'unquoted' company	100%	100%	50%
Other shares in an 'unquoted' company	100%	50%	30%
Control holding of shares in a 'quoted' company	50%	50%	50%
Land, buildings or plant and machinery used in a business	50%	50%	30%
Land, buildings or plant and machinery held in a trust	50%	50%	30%

D14(Notes)

1

Definitions -

Quoted company ▸ This means a company that is listed on a recognised stock exchange. This includes shares traded on the American NASDAQ and European EASDAQ for deaths after 9 March 1992.

Unquoted company ▸ This means a company that is not listed on a recognised stock exchange. Some companies although they are listed in the Stock Exchange Daily Official List are still "unquoted" for business relief. This includes shares

- shares listed on the Alternative Investment Market (AIM)
- shares listed on the Unlisted Securities Market (USM), although thereare some complicated rules that apply to deaths before 10 March 1992. You should telephone our Helpline if the deceased owned shares listed on the USM and the date of death, or date of gift, is before 10 March 1992.

Control holding ▸ This means a holding of stocks and shares that gives a person control of a company. For inheritance tax a person controls a company if they can control the majority (more than 50%) of the voting powers on *all* questions affecting the company as a whole.

Substantial holding ▸ This means a holding of stocks and shares that gives the owner more than 25% of the voting powers on *all* questions affecting the company as a whole.

Used in a business ▸ Land, buildings or plant and machinery will only qualify for business relief if it is used in a business in which the deceased was a partner at the date of death or if it was used by a company which was controlled by the deceased.

Held in trust ▸ Land, buildings or plant and machinery held in trust will only qualify for business relief if the deceased had the right to benefit from the trust *and* the asset was used in a business carried on by the deceased.

How to fill in form D14

1 Tick one of the boxes to show the type of asset the deceased owned.

2 Tick the box to answer this question. If you have answered "No", the deceased has not owned the property for long enough to qualify for business relief. However, there are detailed rules where business relief may still be available. Broadly these apply where

- the deceased inherited the property on death, or
- the property has replaced other property that qualified for business relief.

Our leaflet **IHT17** tells you more about the conditions that must be met.

3 If, before the deceased died, all or part of the shares, business interest or business assets was subject to a binding contract for sale, but the sale had not been completed, business relief will not be due. You should give details of the sale, and clearly identify the assets that had been sold.

4a Write in the name of the company, the number and type of shares, for example, 100 £1 ordinary shares, A Company Ltd, and give their value. Say what the activity of the company is. You can help us by writing down the company's registration number if you know it. You do not need to provide a copy of the company accounts now, although we may ask you for these and other information later. We will write to you if we need any other information.

If the company owed the deceased any money, often through a loan account, it does not qualify for business relief. You should give details on form **D8** and include the value of the loan account in box F11, page 3, form **IHT200**.

If the deceased owed any money to the company, please say why and include the debt as a liability on page 4, form **IHT200**.

If the deceased's spouse owned any shares in the company, give the number and type of shares they owned on form **D17**.

4b Tick this box to answer the question. If you have answered "Yes", please give the date of the winding up or brief details of the stage the liquidation had reached at the date of death (or gift) in the box above. If a company is being wound up or is in the process of liquidation, it is possible that business relief will not be due. We will discuss the matter with you further after the grant has been issued.

5a The last set of accounts prepared before the deceased died is the best starting point for valuing a business. The value of the business or the deceased's interest in the business will be the sum of the deceased's capital and current accounts. Please attach a copy of the last two years' accounts.

Business accounts sometimes include land as an asset of the business when in fact the properties in question were actually owned by the deceased. If this is the case, you should include the land separately in boxes G1 to G6 in form **IHT200** and adjust the value of business. We help you to do this in the section called "*How to value the business*".

If the business owed any money to the deceased, often through a loan account, you must **not** add that value to the value of the capital and current accounts. A loan account does not qualify for business relief. You should give details on form **D8** and include the value of the loan account in box F11, page 3, form **IHT200**.

3

If the deceased owed any money to the business, you must **not** deduct that value from the capital and current accounts. Include the debt as a liability on page 4, form **IHT200**.

5b Business relief is not available for businesses, partnerships and companies that deal in properties or investments. Please give

- the name of the business, and
- say what the main activity of the business was at the date of death.

If the activity has changed in the two years before the date of death, please give details of the earlier activity.

How to value the business

If you are deducting business relief at 100% from the value of the deceased's business or interest in a business, there is no need to adjust the value taken from the accounts. Write this value in box BR1. Copy the figures to the appropriate box on page 5 of form **IHT200**. Remember to deduct the relief using the same figure at the foot of page 5.

If you are not deducting business relief at 100% from the value of the deceased's business or interest in a business, you will need to adjust the value taken from the accounts. You will need to adjust the value where the assets are included in the accounts at "book value" or where the assets are included separately in form **IHT200**.

Other than land, the assets most commonly included in business accounts at book value are business stock and goodwill. You may be including the land separately in form **IHT 200** in one of boxes G1 to G6. If so, you will need to take that value, or the deceased's share of the value, *away* from the value of the deceased's interest in the business.

If not, you will need to obtain open market values for land and any other assets included at "book value" such as stock and goodwill. If the open market value is more than the "book value", *add* the increase in value, or the deceased's share of that increase, to the value of the deceased's interest in the business. If the open market value is less than the "book value", *deduct* the decrease in value, or the deceased's share of that decrease, from the value of the deceased's interest in the business.

You should show how you have arrived at your value for the business or interest in a business on form **D14** (use form **D17** if you need more space) and write the value in box BR1.

5c Tick the box to answer this question. If you have answered "Yes", please attach a copy of the partnership agreement that shows the terms of the partnership at the date of death. If there is no agreement, please give details of the terms on which the partnership was carried on such as

- when it began
- who provided the capital and in what shares, and
- how the profits from the partnership were shared.

4

5d Tick the box to answer this question.

6a Please describe the assets that were owned by the deceased but that were used by a business or company and give their value.

6b Please say what the main activity of the business was and to what extent the deceased was involved with the business concerned. Business relief will **only** be available if the deceased was a partner in the partnership that used the asset or if they controlled the company that used the asset.

7 If you are deducting business relief in connection with a lifetime transfer you should fill in form **D14** to give the details that we ask for as at the date of gift. There are also additional rules that have to be met before the relief can be allowed. You must answer each of the questions so we can decide if the relief is due.

To answer question 7b, you must consider whether, *if* the person who received the gift had made a transfer of the property at the date of death, the transfer would have qualified for business relief.

If shares were given away, you may answer "Yes" to question 7b without having regard to a notional transfer by the person who received the gift where the

- shares were quoted at the time of the gift and were a control holding or came out of a control holding, or
- the death occurred on or after 6 April 1996 and shares were unquoted at the time of the gift and they remained unquoted throughout the period between the gift and the death of the deceased (or death of the person who received the gift if they died first).

If the death occurred before 6 April 1996, the second bullet only applies to gifts out of control holdings of shares, so you will need to consider a notional transfer by the person who received the gift if the gift was from a minority holding of shares.

If the gift was made between 18 March 1986 and 16 March 1987 inclusive, you will need to consider a notional transfer for all gifts, irrespective of the assets transferred.

For this purpose, "relevant period" means the period between the date of the lifetime transfer and the date of death of the deceased (or death of the person who received the gift if they died first).

Note

If the conditions for both agricultural relief and business relief are met, agricultural relief is allowed in preference to business relief. Business relief is not allowed instead of or in addition to agricultural relief.

5

Foreign assets

Form D15

- You **must** fill in form **D15** if the deceased was domiciled in the UK when they died and they owned assets abroad. You should give details of all the foreign assets and liabilities.

  In some circumstances, you may find it easier to fill in more than one form. For example, if the deceased left a separate Will to deal with all or part of their foreign estate they may have appointed different personal representatives. These assets will still form part of the deceased's estate.

Domicile

- Usually, the country where you have your main home is where your domicile is. It is the country whose laws decide, for example, whether a Will is valid, or how the estate of a person who has not made a Will is dealt with when they die.

  Everybody has a domicile. At birth, you have a "domicile of origin". This is normally the same country as your father's domicile, so it is not always the country you were born in. You keep this domicile until you acquire a different domicile – a domicile of choice or of dependence.

  The United Kingdom is not a "country" when establishing a person's domicile. So a person will have a domicile in England and Wales, **or** Scotland **or** Northern Ireland. But for the sake of simplicity, we refer to all three countries as the United Kingdom (UK) in these notes.

  Remember that the Channel Islands and the Isle of Man are ***not in the UK.***

Domicile outside the UK

- You may have said that the deceased was not domiciled in the UK. If so, you should not include details of any assets that the deceased owned abroad on this form. Instead you should include an approximate value for all the assets that the deceased owned abroad in answer to question 6 on form **D2**. However, you should include details of assets that are outside the UK under general law if they are treated as situated in the UK by reason of a Double Taxation Agreement or Convention.

  If you have said that the deceased was not domiciled in the UK, but they owned assets in the UK, you may have to treat some of those assets as "foreign assets" and give details on this form.

D15(Notes)

So, if you have said that the deceased was not domiciled in the UK, you should

- if applying for a grant in England and Wales, give details on form **D15** of any assets the deceased owned in Scotland or Northern Ireland,
- if applying for confirmation in Scotland, give details on form **D15** of any assets the deceased owned in England and Wales or Northern Ireland, and
- if applying for a grant in Northern Ireland, give details on form **D15** of any assets the deceased owned in England and Wales or Scotland.

Deemed domicile

There are also some special rules that apply for tax

- if a person has lived in the UK for a long time, so that they were resident for income tax purposes for at least 17 of the 20 years ending with the tax year in which they died, **or**
- if a person was domiciled in the UK under English law at any time in the three years before they died,

the law says that we can treat the deceased as if they were domiciled in the UK when they died. This means that we can charge inheritance tax on the deceased's worldwide estate. You will need to fill in form **D15** to give details of all the assets owned by the deceased outside the UK.

How to fill in form D15

1 The rules about the type of assets where tax may be paid by instalments are the same for foreign assets as they are for assets in the UK. If the asset would have been included in section F of form **IHT200**, include it in section 1 of this form.

FP1 Give details of any foreign stocks and shares on which tax may not be paid by instalments. You will find a number of foreign stocks and shares are listed in the Financial Times. Shares listed on the World Stock Markets or on NASDAQ or EASDAQ should be included in box FP1. **Do not include here foreign stocks and shares that are listed on the London Stock Exchange and reported under the London Share Service** (see pages 13 and 14 of the guide *"How to fill in form IHT200"*).

Add up the stocks and shares and write the total in this box.

FP2 List any other foreign assets such as bank accounts on which the tax may not be paid by instalments.

Add up the assets and write the total in this box.

FP3 Add up boxes FP1 and FP2 and write the total in this box.

FP4 The rules about debts and liabilities in general (see page 20 of the guide *"How to fill in form IHT200"*) also apply to debts and liabilities deducted from foreign assets. List any debts and liabilities that are to be deducted from these assets. Add up all the figures and write the total in this box.

Special rules for foreign deductions

▸ There are two special rules for deductions from foreign assets.

- Normally, debts due to anyone who lives abroad should be deducted here. If, however, the debt arose in the UK or it is charged on property in the UK, you should deduct it at box F25 or G15.

- You may also include a deduction in box FP4 for any additional expenses that you incur in dealing with assets that are held abroad. The amount must be worked out using the actual cost of dealing with the assets abroad less the likely costs of dealing with similar assets in this country. The amount must be worked out in this way because it is only the *additional* cost of dealing with the assets abroad that you can deduct. The deduction must not exceed 5% of the gross value of all foreign assets in the estate.

If there is a deficit in either section F on form **IHT200** or box FP10 of this form, you may include that deficit here.

FP5 Take box FP4 away from box FP3 and write the answer in this box. If this figure is a minus figure, you should make a note of the deficit and write '0' in this box and in box FP7.

FP6 List any exemptions, reliefs or exclusions (see pages 36 - 40 of the guide *"How to fill in form IHT200"*) that you wish to deduct from the foreign assets. Add up all the figures and write the total in this box.

FP7 Take box FP6 away from box FP5 and write the answer in this box. Copy the total from box FP7 to box WS3 on form **IHT(WS)**. This box must not contain a minus figure. Taking away exemptions and reliefs can only reduce the figure in box FP5 to '0'.

2 If the asset would have been included in section G of form **IHT200**, include it in section 2 of this form.

Tick the box at the top of the page if you wish to pay the tax on these assets by instalments.

FP8 Give details of the foreign assets where tax may be paid by instalments. Add up all the figures and write the total in this box.

FP9 List any liabilities that are to be deducted from the assets including either of the special deductions described at box FP4. Add up all the figures and write the total in this box.

If there is a deficit in either section G on form **IHT200** or box FP5 on this form, you may include that deficit here.

FP10 Take box FP9 away from box FP8 and write the answer in this box. If this figure is a minus figure, you should make a note of the deficit and write '0' in this box and in box FP12.

FP11 List any exemptions, reliefs or exclusions (see pages 36 - 40 of the guide *"How to fill in form IHT200"*) that you wish to deduct from the foreign assets. Add up all the figures and write the total in this box.

FP12 Take box FP11 away from box FP10 and write the answer in this box. Copy the total from box FP12 to box WS8 on form **IHT(WS)**. This box must not contain a minus figure. Taking away exemptions and reliefs can only reduce the figure in box FP10 to '0'.

How to value foreign assets and debts

▶ You should show the value of the asset in its foreign currency. Then, show how you have converted that value to £ sterling. Major currencies should generally be converted at the closing mid-point figure given in the "Pound Spot Forward against the Pound" table shown in the Financial Times. Less common currencies may be converted at the rates shown in the 'FT Guide to World Currencies', published weekly in the Financial Times on Mondays.

Jointly owned foreign assets

▶ If the deceased owned any foreign assets jointly, you should include those assets on this form and not on form **D4**. Use form **D17** to answer the questions on form **D4** about the jointly owned foreign assets.

Debts owed by the estate

Form D16

▶ You **must** fill form **D16** if you are including a deduction on form **IHT200** for

- a loan from a close friend or a relative
- any money that had been spent on behalf of the deceased and which is to be repaid out of the estate
- any other loans or overdrafts, or
- any guarantee debts.

How to fill in form D16

1 If the deceased had borrowed money from a close friend or relative you should say for each loan

- the name of the individual who has lent money to the deceased
- the date of the loan, and
- why the loan was made.

If there are any papers that provide written evidence of the loan and its terms, you should attach a copy to form **D16**. If the money was used for a specific purpose you should say why the deceased's own money was not used. If the deceased had made a gift to the person who had lent the money to the deceased, you should read the notes for box 4 below

If someone else had spent some money on behalf of the deceased it is unlikely that there will be any evidence to show the amount of money that is owed. For each such sum deducted from the estate you should

- give the name of the person who has spent the money
- say what the money was spent on
- say why the deceased's own money was not used, and
- say why the money was not repaid during the deceased's lifetime.

2 If the deceased had a loan or overdraft with a bank, other financial service provider, or the trustees of a life insurance policy, you should give

- the date the loan or overdraft was agreed
- whether or not the lender held any security, for example, a mortgage over the deceased's property, and
- where the money that was borrowed is reflected in the assets of the estate.

D16(Notes)

3 A guarantee debt is where one person promises to pay the debts of another person (who we call the debtor) should that person not be able to repay those debts. The first person will only have to pay the debts if the debtor cannot pay and the individual or organisation that is owed the money calls the guarantee in.

If the deceased had guaranteed to pay the debts of someone you should

- give the name of that person
- explain the circumstances behind the deceased giving the guarantee
- say whether or not the deceased had been called upon to pay to debts, and if not
- say why you feel the guarantee should be included as a deduction from the estate.

4 There are complicated rules that apply if

- the deceased had borrowed money from someone after 18 March 1986 (even if the debt had been repaid in full before death), **and**
- at any time, they had made a gift to that same person, **or**
- a liability is in anyway related to a policy of life insurance and the sum assured is not fully reflected in the deceased's estate.

If the other person was a close friend or a member of the deceased's family or the money was borrowed from trustees in connection with a life insurance policy, you should have already given details in either box 1 or box 2. If you have not included the loan in either box, you should give details of the loan in this box.

You may have filled in details of the gift on form **D3**. If so, identify the gift concerned in this box. If you have not included the gift on form **D3** you should give details of the gift in this box.

Note

The rules that apply when the deceased has both borrowed money from someone and made a gift to that same person are very complicated. You should follow the notes here and include both the debt and the gift, or just the debt alone. However, we will look at the papers in more detail after you have obtained the grant and we may need to alter either or both of the values. If this happens, we will explain what we are doing and why.

Additional information

Form D17

▸ Form **D17** is available for you to give us

- any additional information that we have asked for, or
- anything else you would like us to take into account when we look at form **IHT200.**

Where, in Scotland, you may have already included the details on Inventory form **C1**, there is no need to repeat the information here.

Below are cross references to the other guides and notes where we ask you to provide more detail on this form.

IHT 210 "*How to fill in form IHT 200*"

Pg12 Give details about any claim for or discharge of legal rights (Scotland only).

Pg15 List each National Savings Investment separately and show the total carried to box F7.

Pg15 List each bank and building society account separately and show the total carried to box F8.

Pg19 Interest in expectancy - give the name and date of death (or date of settlement) of the person who set up the trust and the name and age of the person who is receiving the benefit from the trust.

Pg19 Other personal assets - list the items separately and show the total carried to box F23.

Pg36 Spouse exemption - give the full name, date of birth and domicile of the deceased's husband or wife, if not already given on form **D1**.

Pg37 If there is not enough room on form **D1**, list any less well known charities that are receiving legacies under the Will and give their registration number, if known.

Pg37 Copy the calculations for successive charges relief shown on form **IHT(WS)** to this form. If you are not filling in form **D11**, tell us the name and date of death of the person who died before the deceased. Please also give us our reference number for their estate, if you know what it is.

D17(Notes)

Pg37 Copy the calculations for double taxation relief shown on form **IHT(WS)** to this form.

Pg38 If one of the National Heritage exemptions applies to the estate, tell us the name and date of death of the person who died before the deceased or who made the gift and their date of death or birth. Please also give us our reference number for their estate, if you know what it is.

IHT 213 "*How to fill in form IHT WS*"

- If you are paying the tax on a lifetime transfer at the same time as you apply for a grant, please show the calculations you have made and say how the payment you are sending should be used.

D1(Notes)

- If there is not enough room on form **D1**, list any less well known charities that are receiving legacies under the Will and give their registration number, if known.

D3(Notes)

- If you are deducting marriage exemption, say how the person receiving the gift was related to the deceased and give the date of marriage.

  If one of the National Heritage exemptions applies to a lifetime transfer, tell us the name of the person who died before the deceased or who made the gift and their date of death or birth. Please also give us our reference number for their estate, if you know what it is.

D5(Notes)

- If one of the National Heritage exemptions applies to settled property, tell us the name and date of death of the person who died before the deceased or who made the gift and their date of death or birth. Please also give us our reference number for their estate, if you know what it is.

D6(Notes)

- If the pension scheme was an unapproved scheme give details of the benefits payable under the scheme and the benefits taken by the deceased.

  If you have answered "Yes" to question 3 and you wish to include your own figure for the value of the benefits given way, show how you have worked out that figure here.

D8(Notes)

- If you are including a reduced figure for the value of money owed to the deceased, show here how you have worked out that figure.

D10(Notes)

- If one of the National Heritage exemptions applies to household and personal goods, tell us the name and date of death of the person who died before the deceased or who made the gift and their date of death or birth. Please also give us our reference number for their estate, if you know what it is.

D12(Notes)

- If one of the National Heritage exemptions applies to the land or buildings, tell us the name and date of death of the person who died before the deceased or who made the gift and their date of death or birth. Please also give us our reference number for their estate, if you know what it is.

D14(Notes)

- If business relief at 100% does not apply and you need more space to show how you have worked out the value of the business, show here how you have worked out the figure.

  If both the deceased and their spouse owned shares in an unquoted company give the number and type of shares owned by the spouse.

D15(Notes)

- If any of the foreign assets were jointly owned give answers to the questions on form **D4** about the joint foreign assets here.

Probate summary

Form D18

You **must** fill in form **D18** if you are applying for a grant in England and Wales or Northern Ireland.

If you are applying for a grant without the help of a solicitor or other agent, **do not fill in section A.** Fill in sections B and C only, following the notes below.

How to fill in section A

Copy the name and address (or DX code and town) from section C and the name of the probate registry from box A1 on page 1 of form **IHT200**.

How to fill in section B

Copy the deceased's title, surname, first name(s), date of death, domicile and last usual address from section B on page 1 of form **IHT200**.

How to fill in section C

Copy the figures from the boxes in form **IHT200** as described below. If you have filled in form **D5** and the deceased had **and had exercised** a general power of appointment over the settled property, you should add the value of such assets and liabilities to the figures in the relevant boxes below.

PS1 Copy the value from box F24, page 3, form **IHT200**, having deducted the value of any nominated property included in section F, form **IHT200**.

PS2 Copy the value from box G13, page 5, form **IHT200**.

PS3 Add together boxes PS1 and PS2 and write the answer in this box.

PS4 Copy the value from F27, page 4, form **IHT200**. If this figure includes the balance of liabilities from box G15, you should deduct that balance before including a value in this box.

PS5 Copy the value from boxes G14 and G15, page 5, form **IHT200**. If this figure includes the balance of liabilities from box F27, you should deduct that balance before including a value in this box.

PS6 Take boxes PS4 and PS5 away from box PS3 and write the answer in this box.

PS7 If you have worked out the tax that is payable and will be sending payment of tax with the other papers to us, copy the figure from box J19, page 7, form **IHT200** here. If you want us to work out the tax for you leave this box blank for us to put in the figure.

If there is no tax to pay, write "0" in this box.

If you have worked out the tax in box PS7, sign and date the form. Please include the contact name or reference from section C on page 1 of form **IHT200.**

Follow the instructions starting at page 29 in the guide *"How to fill in form IHT200"* to apply for your grant.

D18(Notes)

How to fill in form IHT(WS)

- This Guide has step by step instructions to help you work out the tax that is due. It will help you to fill in form **IHT(WS)**.

If you are applying for a grant without the help solicitor or other agent, you do not have to work out the tax. You can send form **IHT200** and the other papers that go with it to us and we will do the calculation for you. In certain circumstances, we recommend that you let us work out the tax for you. We tell you more about this at page 19 of this Guide.

If you are a solicitor or other agent acting on behalf of the personal representatives, you must work out the tax before sending the form to us. If, *exceptionally*, you need help in working out the tax, send form **IHT200** and the other papers that go with it to us and say what the problem is.

We tell you which office you should contact on page 29 of the guide *"How to fill in form IHT200"*.

You will find instructions for paying the tax starting on page 11 of this Guide.

IHT 213

Contents

Key steps in working out the tax that is due

1 **Work out the value of the "chargeable estate".**

A person's estate may be made up of lots of different parts. You may have filled in sections F and G of form **IHT200** as well as some of the supplementary pages, for example, for joint property and assets in a trust. It does not matter how many different parts make up the estate, inheritance tax is charged on the sum of all those parts, which we call the "chargeable estate". The tax bill is then divided up between the different parts of the "chargeable estate".

2 **Work out the value of the "aggregate chargeable transfer".**

If the deceased had made any transfers during their lifetime, the chargeable value of those transfers will be added to the chargeable estate. We call this the "aggregate chargeable transfer".

3 **Take away the tax threshold to give the value on which tax is charged.**

The tax threshold is usually changed each year in the budget. For deaths after 15 March 1988, tax is charged at 40% on the amount by which the aggregate chargeable transfer is above the tax threshold. We tell you what the different thresholds are on page 6 of this Guide.

4 **Work out the tax that is due.**

5 **Work out whether any tax is due on the lifetime transfers.**

This is **only** relevant if the chargeable value of any lifetime transfers is more than the tax threshold at death. If so, take any tax due on the lifetime transfers away from the tax at 4.

6 **Take away any relief for successive charges.**

We tell you how to work out this relief on page 14 of this Guide.

7 **Divide the result between the different parts of the chargeable estate – which does not include the value of lifetime transfers.**

How to fill in form IHT(WS)

You will need to copy some of the figures from form **IHT200** and the supplementary pages to form **IHT(WS)**. When you have worked out the tax and any interest that is due, you will need to copy certain figures back to form **IHT200**.

The value for the assets being taxed should be rounded down to the nearest £. **But the figures for tax and interest must include pence.**

If you have filled in more than one supplementary page for the same type of assets, there is space on form **IHT(WS)** to add up the different figures.

Working out the tax that is due

WS1 Copy the figures from box F30 on form **IHT200** to this box.

WS2 If you have filled in form **D4** and the joint assets pass by survivorship, copy any figures from box JP5 to this box.

WS3 If you have filled in form **D15**, copy the figures from box FP7 to this box.

WS4 If you have filled in form **D5** *and the trustees want to pay the tax that is due on the settled property now,* copy the figures from box SP5 to this box.

If only *some* of the tax that is due on the settled property is to be paid now, write the figures from box SP5 on the relevant forms **D5** in the space provided. You will include figures from the other forms **D5** where tax is *not* to be paid now in box WS11.

WS5 Add together boxes WS1 to WS4 and write the total in this box.

WS6 Write the figures from box G18 on form **IHT200** in this box.

WS7 If you have filled in form **D4** and the joint assets pass by survivorship, copy any figures from box JP10 to this box.

WS8 If you have filled in form **D15**, copy the figures from box FP12 to this box.

WS9 If you have filled in form **D5** *and the trustees want to pay the tax that is due on the settled property now,* copy the figures from box SP10 to this box.

If only *some* of the tax that is due on the settled property is to be paid now, write the figures from box SP10 on the relevant forms **D5** in the space provided. You will include figures from the other forms **D5** where tax is *not* to be paid now in box WS11.

WS10 Add together boxes WS6 to WS9 and write the total in box WS10.

WS11 If you have filled in form **D5**, and the trustees are **not** paying the tax now, copy the figures from boxes SP5 and SP10 to this box.

WS12 If you have filled in form **D3**, copy any figure from box LT2 to this box.

WS13 Add together boxes WS5, WS10, WS11 and WS12 and write the total in this box.

Working out the aggregate chargeable transfer

WS14 If you have filled in form **D3**, copy any figure from box LT1 to this box.

WS15 Add together boxes WS13 and WS14 and write the total in this box.

Working out the tax that is payable on the chargeable estate

WS16 Copy the figure from box WS15 to this box.

WS17 Write the tax threshold that applies at the date the deceased died in this box.

Date of event on or between	Tax threshold
15 March 1988 and 5 April 1989	£110,000
6 April 1989 and 5 April 1990	£118,000
6 April 1990 and 5 April 1991	£128,000
6 April 1991 and 9 March 1992	£140,000
10 March 1992 and 5 April 1995	£150,000
6 April 1995 and 5 April 1996	£154,000
6 April 1996 and 5 April 1997	£200,000
6 April 1997 and 5 April 1998	£215,000
6 April 1998 and 5 April 1999	£223,000
6 April 1999 and 5 April 2000	£231,000
6 April 2000 and 5 April 2001	£234,000
6 April 2001 and 5 april 2002	£242,000
6 April 2002 and after	£250,000

Telephone our Helpline if the date of death or transfer is not shown in the table.

WS18 Take box WS17 away from box WS16. Write the answer in this box.

If this answer is a minus figure, write "0" in this box. You do not need to fill in any more of this form as there will be no tax to pay. Follow the instructions on form IHT(WS) and copy the figures to section H and J on form IHT200. Write "0" in box J19.

Working out the tax that is due

WS19 Multiply the figure in box WS18 by 40%. Write the answer in this box.

Working out the tax on any lifetime transfers

WS20 If the figure in box WS14 is more than the figure in box WS17, you will need to work out the amount of tax that is due on the lifetime transfers. Follow the notes for boxes LT3 to LT6 below. Otherwise write "0" in this box and go on to box WS21.

LT3 Copy the figure from box WS14 to this box.

LT4 Copy the figure from box WS17 to this box.

LT5 Take box LT4 away from box LT3. Write the answer in this box. If this answer is a minus figure, write "0" in this box and in boxes LT6 and WS20.

LT6 Multiply the figure in box LT5 by 40%. Write the answer in this box. Copy the figure from box LT6 to box WS20.

WS21 Write the figure for any successive charges relief due in this box. There are examples of how to calculate this relief at pages 14 and 15 of this Guide. If you have used form **IHT(WS)** to work out this relief, copy the figure from box SC6 to this box.

You should copy details of your calculations to form **D17**, see page 37 of the Guide *"How to fill in form IHT200"*.

WS22 Take boxes WS20 and WS21 away from box WS19 and write the answer in this box.

If this answer is a minus figure, write "0" in this box. You do not need to fill in any more of this form as there will be no tax to pay. Follow the instructions on form IHT(WS) and copy the figures to section H and J on form IHT200. Write "0" in box J19.

Dividing the tax between the different parts of the estate

The tax on the chargeable estate is divided up between the different parts of the estate. For example, if

- the value of part of the estate was A
- the value of the chargeable estate was B, and
- the tax on the chargeable estate was C

the tax that is due on A can be worked out with the formula

$$A \times \frac{C}{B}$$

Using this formula, you can work out the minimum tax that has to be paid to apply for a grant. The following pages help you to work out the tax and interest to pay.

Working out the tax and interest to be paid when you apply for a grant

TX1 Copy the figure from box WS5 to this box.

TX2 Copy the figure from box WS22 to this box.

TX3 Copy the figure from box WS13 to this box.

TX4 Work out the tax due with the sum $TX1 \times \frac{TX2}{TX3}$ and write the figure in this box.

TX5 Write the figure for any double taxation relief due in this box. There is an example of how to calculate this relief at page 16 of this Guide. If you have used form **IHT(WS)** to work out this relief, copy the lower of boxes DT2 and DT3 to this box.

You should copy details of your calculations to form **D17**, see pages 37 and 38 of the Guide *"How to fill in form IHT200"*.

TX6 Take box TX5 away from box TX4. Write the answer in this box.

TX7 To work out whether or not any interest is payable look at table 1 on page 20 of this Guide. Work out the date that tax is due. Write the date in box IT1. *If that date is in the future there will be no interest pay.* Write "0" in this box and go on to box TX8.

If that date has passed, you will need to work out the interest that is due. Follow the notes starting at page 20 of this Guide and write any interest that is payable in this box.

TX8 Add together box TX6 and box TX7. Write the answer in this box.

The figure in box TX8 is the minimum tax you must pay before you can get a grant.

Working out the tax and interest that may be paid by instalments

If there is tax that may be paid by instalments, you may choose whether to pay the tax

- in one lump sum at the same time as you apply for the grant
- in one lump sum before the due date for tax or
- by one equal instalment each year for ten years.

You should have ticked the box on page 5 of form **IHT200** and on any relevant supplementary page to show whether you wish to pay any of the tax by instalments. We tell you more about paying tax by instalments on page 13 of this Guide.

If you want to pay the tax by instalments **and** you are applying for a grant **more than 1 month before** the date the tax is due (see box IT1), write "0" in each of boxes TX12 – TX19. Go on to box TX20.

If you want to pay tax by instalments and the **tax is due within 1 month**, you should fill in boxes TX9 – TX19 to pay the first instalment when you apply for a grant.

If you want to pay all the tax that is payable at the same time as you apply for a grant **or** the date the tax is due has passed, continue to fill in boxes TX9 – TX19.

TX9 Copy the figure from box WS10 to this box.

TX10 Copy the figure from box WS22 to this box.

TX11 Copy the figure from box WS13 to this box.

TX12 Work out the tax due with the sum $TX9 \times \frac{TX10}{TX11}$ and write the figure in this box.

TX13 Write the figure for any double taxation relief due in this box. There is an example of how to calculate this relief at page 16 of this Guide. If you have used the working sheet to calculate this relief, copy the lower of boxes DT2 and DT3 to this box.

9

You should copy details of your calculations to from **D17**, see pages 37 and 38 of the Guide *"How to fill in form IHT200"*.

TX14 Take box TX13 away from box TX12. Write the answer in this box.

TX15 If you want to pay tax by instalments, write the number of instalments that are due in this box. If you want to pay all the tax that is payable by instalments when you apply for a grant, write "10" in this box

TX16 Work out the tax now payable by multiplying the figure in box TX14 by the fraction in box TX15. Write the answer in this box. For example

• Net tax payable *(TX12 - TX13)*		TX14 45,000
• Number of instalments being paid now	TX15 2 / 10 (Copy to box J14 on IHT200)	
• Tax payable now *(TX14 x TX15)*		TX16 9,000 (Copy to box J15 on IHT200)

• Net tax payable *(TX12 - TX13)*		TX14 45,000
• Number of instalments being paid now	TX15 10 / 10 (Copy to box J14 on IHT200)	
• Tax payable now *(TX14 x TX15)*		TX16 45,000 (Copy to box J15 on IHT200)

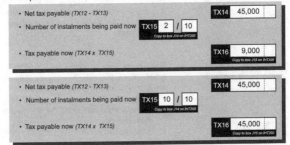

TX17 If you decided that there was no interest to pay on the tax in box TX6, *there will be no interest to pay here either.* Write "0" in boxes TX17 and TX18 and go on to box TX19.

If you have included some interest in box TX7 (or the tax in box TX6 was "Nil" and the date in box IT1 has passed), you will need to work out the interest to include in this box. There is more help to work out interest starting at page 20 of this Guide.

TX18 We tell you how to work out any interest to include in this box at page 25 of this Guide.

TX19 Add together boxes TX16, TX17 and TX18 and write the answer in this box.

TX20 Add together boxes TX8 and TX19 and write the answer in this box.

This is the tax and interest that you must pay when you apply of the grant.

10

Figures to copy to form IHT200

When you have filled in form **IHT(WS)**, follow the instructions on the form to copy the figures to section H and J of form **IHT200**.

Payment of inheritance tax

Inheritance tax is due six months after the end of the month in which the person died. If the tax is not paid by that date, **the law says that we must charge interest on any unpaid tax.** But, you do not have to pay all the tax that is due to be able to apply for a grant. There is more information about interest on page 20 of this Guide.

The minimum amount of tax to be paid

You **must** pay the tax that is due on the assets included in section F of form **IHT200** before you can apply for a grant. You may also have to pay some or all of the tax that is due on any joint property or foreign property. In addition, if you are applying for a grant more than six months after the end of the month in which the deceased died, you will have to pay some of the tax on the assets included in section G of form **IHT200**.

Options for payment

If you wish, you can pay all the tax that is due when you apply for a grant. If not, you may pay the tax that is due on the assets included in section G of form **IHT200**

- in one lump sum before the six months is up (to avoid any interest charges), or
- in ten instalments.

There is more information about instalments on page 13 of this Guide.

You can also pay the tax on other assets

When you apply for a grant, you may also pay tax on other assets if the people who are liable for the tax provide the funds for you to do so.

Payment in advance

If you do not expect to able to apply for a grant within six months of the death, you can make a payment on account at any time. If you do, we will not charge you interest on the amount paid from the date we receive it. Please make sure you tell us the full name of the deceased and the date of death. If you pay too much on account, we will pay you interest when we return the money.

How to make payment

You can pay the tax that is due either by cheque, by electronic transfer, by Bank Giro Credit, or by using National Savings investments owned by the deceased.

11

By cheque

▸ Write out your cheque to "Inland Revenue only" and

- put a line through any space left on the "Pay" line
- cross your cheque "A/c payee"
- write the full name of the deceased and the date of death on the back of the cheque.

You should send your cheque with any papers to one of the three branches of Capital Taxes Office. We tell you which branch to use at page 29 of the guide *"How to fill in form IHT200".* You will find our addresses on page 2 of that guide. You should address the envelope specifically to the cashiers in the office as follows

- Nottingham – address the envelope to "Section K". If you use the DX system, there is a special number DX 701205 Nottingham 4
- Edinburgh – address the envelope to "The Cashier"
- Belfast – address the envelope to "The Cashier".

By electronic transfer (CHAPS/ BACS)

▸ You should contact your bank to find out how to make payment in this way. You will need to give your bank details of the bank account for the office which is handling your case. These are

Office	Bank	Sort Code	Account number
Nottingham	Bank of England	10-53-92	23430303
Edinburgh	Royal Bank of Scotland	83-06-08	00132961
Belfast	Bank of Ireland	90-21-27	999 42208

You should give the full name of the deceased, transferor or settlement, where appropriate, the date of death or settlement and Capital Taxes reference number if you know what it is.

By Bank Giro Credit

▸ Fill in the Giro slip with

- Bank of England sort code 10-53-92
- our account number 23430303
- the name of the account "Commissioners of Inland Revenue – Capital Taxes", and
- the full name of the deceased and the date of death.

Note

There may be a delay before the Bank of England notifies us of payment by either an electronic transfer or Giro. So, if you use either of these methods of payment, it may be a few days before we can let you have you confirmation that the tax has been paid.

Payment at the Stamps Office

▸ You may also pay tax by taking form **IHT200** and supporting papers, form **D18** and your cheque to the Stamps Office, South West Wing, Bush House, Strand, London.

You can use National Savings to pay inheritance tax

You can pay some or all of the tax and interest that needs to be paid before you can apply for a grant by using National Savings investments owned by the deceased. However, it can take up to four weeks to process a payment made in this way. Our leaflet **IHT11** gives more details of this scheme.

You can pay inheritance tax by transferring assets to the Crown

You can offer to pay some or all of the tax and interest for which you are liable by transferring national heritage property to the Crown. The rules are complicated. In particular, we cannot accept property from you before you have taken out a grant of representation. But if we do accept a transfer of property as payment of tax, we will repay the money to you up to the value of the property we accept.

For a full explanation of the rules, please refer to the separate booklet **IR67.** Alternatively, you can write to or telephone our Heritage Section Helpline. Page 39 of the guide *"How to fill in form IHT200"* tells you the number of our Heritage Section Helpline and tells you how you can get a copy of **IR67**.

Paying tax by instalments

You may pay tax on land and buildings, some business interests and some unquoted shares in ten instalments. The instalments are one a year, for ten years. The first instalment will be payable when the tax is due (see table 1 on page 20 of this Guide), the second twelve months after that and so on.

For example, if the deceased died on 7 February 1998, tax is due is 31 August 1998. The first instalment will be due on that date; the second will be due on 31 August 1999 and so on.

Normally, you will still have to pay interest on the tax that remains unpaid at the time each instalment falls due. As more of the tax is paid, the interest will reduce over the years as each instalment reduces the amount unpaid, providing that the rate of interest remains unchanged.

If you are paying the tax by instalments on

- some businesses
- certain unquoted shares, or
- land that qualifies for agricultural relief

you may qualify for some interest relief. If so, interest is only charged on each instalment as it becomes due. This means that provided each instalment is paid on time, no interest will be paid on the tax on that asset. The rules to qualify for this relief are quite complicated and you should telephone our Helpline if you want more information.

Sale of assets where tax is being paid by instalments

- You **must** tell us if you sell any of the assets on which tax is being paid by instalments. The option to pay by instalments comes to an end when an asset is sold and the tax remaining unpaid is due immediately. You should tell us when the sale of the asset was completed. We will work out and tell you how much tax and interest is due to clear the liability.

Changing your mind

- Even though you may choose to start paying some of the tax by instalments, you may decide later to pay off all the tax. You should tell us if you want to do this. We will work out and tell you how much tax and interest is due to clear the liability.

  You should be aware, however, that once you have paid all the tax that may be paid by instalments, you cannot ask for the money back and start paying by instalments again.

Examples of how to work out relief for successive charges

- The deceased had inherited a legacy of £100,000 from a relative who died on 4 March 1997. The relative's estate was worth £425,000 legacies of £150,000 and inheritance tax of £90,000 were paid.

  The deceased died on 23 November 1998, within five years of the relative dying. The executors may claim relief to stop the money the deceased inherited being taxed twice in a short period of time. The figures to use in form **IHT(WS)** as follows.

SC1 Write in this box the value of the estate of the first person to die; in this example it is £425,000.

SC2 Write in this box the total amount paid out in legacies from the estate of the first person to die. This is the total amount, not just any legacies that the deceased received. In this example it is £150,000.

SC3 Write in this box the amount of inheritance tax paid by the estate of the first person to die. In this example it is £90,000

SC4 Write in this box, the value of the deceased's entitlement. In this example it is £100,000.

SC5 Write in this box, the percentage of relief that will be allowed, see page 37 of the guide *"How to fill in form IHT200"*. In this example, as the deceased died more than one but less than two years after the first person to die, it is 80%.

SC6 Copy the figures from boxes SC1 to SC5 into the formula and work out the sum. Write the answer in this box. Copy this figure to box WS21 on form **IHT(WS)**.

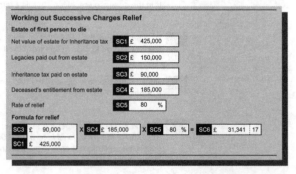

Working out Successive Charges Relief

Estate of first person to die

Net value of estate for Inheritance tax	SC1	£ 425,000
Legacies paid out from estate	SC2	£ 150,000
Inheritance tax paid on estate	SC3	£ 90,000
Deceased's entitlement from estate	SC4	£ 100,000
Rate of relief	SC5	80 %

Formula for relief

SC3 £ 90,000 / SC1 £ 425,000 X SC4 £ 100,000 X SC5 80 % = SC6 £ 16,941 17

In the example above, the deceased received a legacy of £100,000. If the deceased had received the remainder of the estate after legacies of £150,000 had been paid to other people, the figure box SC4 would have been different. The example below shows this difference.

The deceased's entitlement should be worked out as follows

Value of estate	425,000
Less: legacies paid	-150,000
tax paid	-90,000
Deceased's inheritance	£185,000

The figures will the same for boxes SC1 to SC5 apart from box SC4 that will contain £185,000. The entries on the working sheet are as below.

Working out Successive Charges Relief

Estate of first person to die

Net value of estate for Inheritance tax	SC1	£ 425,000
Legacies paid out from estate	SC2	£ 150,000
Inheritance tax paid on estate	SC3	£ 90,000
Deceased's entitlement from estate	SC4	£ 185,000
Rate of relief	SC5	80 %

Formula for relief

SC3 £ 90,000 / SC1 £ 425,000 X SC4 £ 185,000 X SC5 80 % = SC6 £ 31,341 17

15

An example of how to work out double taxation Relief

- The deceased died on 17 April 1998, leaving an estate of £500,000. Of that value, £50,000 was in the USA and tax of $16,000 was paid on those assets. The amount of sterling needed to pay the foreign tax was £10,000.

DT1 Write in this box the value of the foreign property on which you have paid foreign tax.

DT2 Write in this box the amount of sterling needed to pay the foreign tax.

DT3 Copy the figures from boxes WS22 and WS13 on form **IHT(WS)** and from box DT1 into the formula and work out the sum. Write the answer in this box.

If the foreign property is included in box WS3 on form **IHT(WS)**, copy the lower of boxes DT2 and DT3 to box TX5.

If the foreign property is included in box WS8 on form **IHT(WS)**, copy the lower of boxes DT2 and DT3 to box TX13.

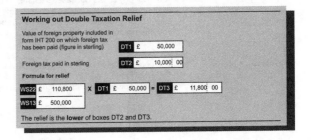

Working out Double Taxation Relief

Value of foreign property included in form IHT 200 on which foreign tax has been paid (figure in sterling) — DT1 £ 50,000

Foreign tax paid in sterling — DT2 £ 10,000 00

Formula for relief

WS22 £ 110,800 / WS13 £ 500,000 x DT1 £ 50,000 = DT3 £ 11,800 00

The relief is the **lower** of boxes DT2 and DT3.

Note

This is a simple example of how double taxation relief works. Depending on the reason why the relief is allowed, it may be worked out differently. Our leaflet **IHT18** tells you more about double taxation relief.

If you need more help with this relief, you should telephone our Helpline.

Taper relief

Taper relief is available where there is tax to pay on any lifetime gifts made by the deceased and the gifts were made between 3 and 7 years before the death. *If the total of all the gifts made by the deceased does not exceed the tax threshold that applies at the date of death, there can be no taper relief.* The relief is given by reducing the *tax* payable on the gift by the percentage in the table below

Date of gift	%
More than 3, but 4 or less years before the death	20
More than 4, but 5 or less years before the death	40
More than 5, but 6 or less years before the death	60
More than 6, but 7 or less years before the death	80

The tax must be paid by the person who received the gift so the relief would not normally be relevant in working out the tax that must be paid before you can apply for a grant.

However, if the person who received the gift would like to pay their tax when you apply for a grant, you can send the payments together. You must still follow all the steps on form **IHT(WS)** to work out the tax that you must pay on the deceased's estate. The example here helps you to work out the tax that is payable on a lifetime transfer. Please show the calculations you have made on form **D17** and say how the payment you are sending should be used.

An example of how taper relief works

The deceased died on 17 April 1998, leaving an estate of £500,000. They had made 3 gifts in the seven years before they died, each to a different person, which after deducting exemptions, were

12 May 1991	52,000
14 July 1993	105,000
16 March 1995	104,000
	£261,000

None of the tax on the deceased's estate could be paid by instalments so the figures in form **IHT(WS)** will be

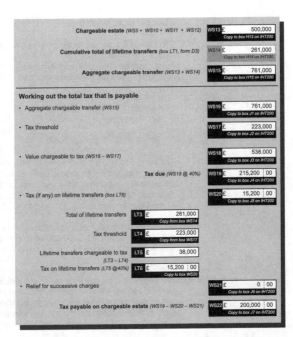

Chargeable estate *(WS5 + WS10 + WS11 + WS12)*	WS13	£ 500,000	*Copy to box H13 on IHT200*
Cumulative total of lifetime transfers *(box LT1, form D3)*	WS14	£ 261,000	*Copy to box H14 on IHT200*
Aggregate chargeable transfer *(WS13 + WS14)*	WS15	£ 761,000	*Copy to box H15 on IHT200*

Working out the total tax that is payable

• Aggregate chargeable transfer *(WS15)*	WS16	£ 761,000	*Copy to box J1 on IHT200*
• Tax threshold	WS17	£ 223,000	*Copy to box J2 on IHT200*
• Value chargeable to tax *(WS16 – WS17)*	WS18	£ 538.000	*Copy to box J3 on IHT200*
Tax due *(WS18 @ 40%)*	WS19	£ 215,200 : 00	*Copy to box J4 on IHT200*
• Tax (if any) on lifetime transfers *(box LT6)*	WS20	£ 15,200 : 00	*Copy to box J5 on IHT200*
Total of lifetime transfers	LT3	£ 261,000	*Copy from box WS14*
Tax threshold	LT4	£ 223,000	*Copy from box WS17*
Lifetime transfers chargeable to tax *(LT3 – LT4)*	LT5	£ 38,000	
Tax on lifetime transfers *(LT5 @40%)*	LT6	£ 15,200 : 00	*Copy to box WS20*
• Relief for successive charges	WS21	£ 0 : 00	*Copy to box J6 on IHT200*
Tax payable on chargeable estate *(WS19 – WS20 – WS21)*	WS22	£ 200,000 : 00	*Copy to box J7 on IHT200*

As none of the tax on the deceased's estate could be paid by instalments, the whole of the £200,000 must be paid before applying for the grant.

If the people who received the lifetime gifts want to pay the tax at the same time, the total tax of £15,200 would need to be reduced by taper relief. The tax on each gift is worked out separately and then taper relief deducted.

First gift on 12 May 1991.

The chargeable amount of the gift was £52,000. The tax threshold to apply is the threshold at death (£223,000). As the gift is below the threshold, there is no tax to pay on this gift and so there can be no taper relief.

Second gift on 14 July 1993

The chargeable amount of the gift was £105,000. The first gift must be added to it to establish the total value (£157,000) on which tax is charged. The tax threshold to apply is the threshold at death (£223,000). As the value is below the threshold, there is no tax to pay on this gift and so there can be no taper relief.

Third gift on 16 March 1995.

The chargeable amount of the gift was £104,000. The first two gifts must be added to it to establish the total value (£261,000) on which tax is charged. The tax threshold to apply is the threshold at death (£223,000). The tax payable on the third gift is

Taxable value	261,000
Less threshold	-223,000
Chargeable value	£38,000
Tax at 40 %	£15,200

The tax of £15,200 is payable only by the person who received the third gift, it should not be divided between all three people. The third gift was made more than three, but less than four years before the deceased died so taper relief is due at 20%. 20% of £15,200 is £3,040, so the tax to be paid is £15,200 – 3,040 = £12,160.

So, to pay all the tax that is due when applying for a grant, a payment of £212,160 is required, £200,000 of which will be for the tax on the deceased's estate and £12,160 will be for the tax on the gift.

More complicated calculations

Working out the tax that is payable, and including the correct figures in form **IHT200** can become quite complicated when the deceased leaves part of their estate (other than outright legacies) to an exempt beneficiary, such as their spouse or a charity. The situation is even more complicated if a relief, such as agricultural or business relief is due as well.

For example, the deceased's Will may contain a number of cash legacies to relatives and charities and leaves the remainder of the estate to family. The tax can be worked out quite easily after deducting the exemption for the legacies to charities.

If, after giving a number of legacies, it is part of the remainder of the estate that is exempt, for example, ½ of the remainder to charity and ½ to the family, the calculations can become much more difficult. And the complications increase if a relief is due as well.

If these circumstances apply to you and you are applying for a grant without the help of a solicitor, we recommend that you send the papers to us and let us work out the tax for you.

Otherwise, there is a separate booklet IHT214, which contains examples of these more complicated calculations.

Interest

Inheritance tax is due to be paid six months after the end of the month in which the deceased died. It does not matter that you have not got a grant by then. Nor does it matter that we have not contacted you or anybody else, for example, the trustees of a settlement or someone who received a gift from the deceased. The law says that interest will be added to any unpaid tax after this date. Interest is charged at a daily rate. The tables below tell you

- the date interest will start to run for each month of the year
- the rates of interest that are in force and for what period, and
- the daily rate of interest, which will allow you to work out any interest that is due when you make your payment.

Starting date for interest

1

Month of death	Tax is due to be paid by	Interest starts from
January	31st July	1st August
February	31st August	1st September
March	30th September	1st October
April	31st October	1st November
May	30th November	1st December
June	31st December	1st January
July	31st January	1st February
August	28/29th February	1st March
September	31st March	1st April
October	30th April	1st May
November	31st May	1st June
December	30th June	1st July

Rates of interest

2

Interest period			Days in period	Interest rate
6th June 1987	to	5th August 1988	427	6%
6th August 1988	to	5th October 1988	61	8%
6th October 1988	to	5th July 1989	273	9%
6th July 1989	to	5th March 1991	608	11%
6th March 1991	to	5th May 1991	61	10%
6th May 1991	to	5th July 1991	61	9%
6th July 1991	to	5th November 1992	489	8%
6th November 1992	to	5th December 1992	30	6%
6th December 1992	to	5th January 1994	396	5%
6th January 1994	to	5th October 1994	273	4%
6th October 1994	to	5th March 1999	1611	5%
6th March 1999	to	5th February 2000	337	4%
6th February 2000	to	5th May 2001	455	5%
6th May 2001	to	5th November 2001	184	4%
6th November 2001	to	date		3%

Interest charge per £1 per day

3

Interest rate	Interest charge per £1 per day
3%	0.000081967
4%	0.000109290
5%	0.000136612
6%	0.000163934
7%	0.000191257
8%	0.000218579
9%	0.000245902
10%	0.000273224
11%	0.000300546

Working out the interest on tax not being paid by instalments

TX7 Work out the interest that is due as follows

- write the date that interest starts from in box IT1
- write the date that you expect to be sending the papers and tax to us in box IT2.

Interest will be charged for the period between these two dates, including the two days themselves. You can now work out the interest that is due by filling in table IT3.

Look at table 2 on the previous page to see how the period for charging interest in the deceased's estate compares to the different interest periods. Then, in table IT3

1 Write the start and finish dates in column 1.

2 Work out the number of days between the dates. Write this number in column 2, remembering to include both start and finish days.

3 Look at table 3 above. Write the daily interest rate that matches the rate of interest to be charged in column 3.

4 To work out the interest that is due, multiply the number of days by the daily rate and then multiply that answer by the tax due (box TX6). Write the interest payable in column 4.

5 Copy the total interest payable to box TX7.

Example 1

▶ The deceased died on 7 February 1997. The papers and tax were sent to us on 14 November 1997. The tax due was £5,000. So, following the steps above

Step 1 Write the start and finish dates in column 1.

The date interest starts from for a death in February is 1 September in the same year. The start date is 1 September 1997 and the finish date 14 November 1997

IT3 Col 1	Col 2	Col 3	Col 4
Start and end dates for interest periods	No. of days	Daily rate	Interest payable
1/9/97 – 14/11/97			
		Total	£

Step 2 Work out the number of days between the dates. Write this number in column 2, remembering to include both start and finish days.

Days in September	=	30
Days in October	=	31
Days to 14 November	=	14
Total		75

IT3 Col 1	Col 2	Col 3	Col 4
Start and end dates for interest periods	No. of days	Daily rate	Interest payable
1/9/97 – 14/11/97	75		
		Total	£

Step 3 Look at the table 3 on page 21 of this Guide. Write the daily interest rate that matches the rate of interest to be charged in column 3.

The rate of interest to be charged for the period 1/9/97 – 14/11/97 is 5%. So, the daily rate of charge is 0.000136612

IT3 Col 1	Col 2	Col 3	Col 4
Start and end dates for interest periods	No. of days	Daily rate	Interest payable
1/9/97 – 14/11/97	75	0.000136612	
		Total	£

Step 4 Multiply the number of days by the daily rate and then multiply that answer by the tax due (box TX6). Write the interest payable in column 4.

75 x 0.000136612 x 5,000 = 51.23.

IT3 Col 1	Col 2	Col 3	Col 4	
Start and end dates for interest periods	No. of days	Daily rate	Interest payable	
1/9/97 – 14/11/97	75	0.000136612	51	23
		Total	£ 51	23

Step 5 Copy £51.23 to box TX7.

Example 2 ▶ The deceased died on 14 July 1993. The papers and tax were sent to us on 21 January 1995. The tax due was £10,000. Following the same steps.

Step 1 Write the start and finish dates in column 1.

The date interest starts from for a death in July 1993 is 1 February in the next year. The start date is 1 February 1994 and the finish date 21 January 1995. Comparing this period to table 2, it covers the last two interest periods. So, there will be two interest periods.

- from 1 February 1994 to the end of the 4% interest period (5 October 1994), and
- the start of the next interest period (6 October 1994) to the finish date 21 January 1995.

IT3 Col 1	Col 2	Col 3	Col 4	
Start and end dates for interest periods	No. of days	Daily rate	Interest payable	
01/02/94 - 05/10/94				
06/10/94 - 21/01/95				
		Total	£	

Step 2 Work out the number of days between the dates. Write this number in column 2, remembering to include both start and finish days.

23

Days between 1/2/94 and 5/10/94

Days in February	=	28
March	=	31
April	=	30
May	=	31
June	=	30
July	=	31
August	=	31
September	=	30
Days to 5 October	=	5
		247

Days between 6/10/94 and 21/10/95

Days from 6/10/95 to 31/10/95	=	26
Days in November	=	30
Days in December	=	31
Days to 21 January	=	21
		108

IT3 Col 1	Col 2	Col 3	Col 4
Start and end dates for interest periods	No. of days	Daily rate	Interest payable
01/02/94 - 05/10/94	247		
06/10/94 - 21/01/95	108		
		Total	£

Step 3 Look at the table 3 on page 21 of this Guide. Write the daily interest rate that matches the rate of interest to be charged in column 3.

The rate of interest to be charged for the period 1/2/94 – 5/10/94 is 4%. So, the daily rate of charge is 0.000109290. The rate for the period 6/10/94 – 21/1/95 is 5%, so the daily rate of charge is 0.000136612.

IT3 Col 1	Col 2	Col 3	Col 4
Start and end dates for interest periods	No. of days	Daily rate	Interest payable
01/02/94 - 05/10/94	247	0.000109290	
06/10/94 - 21/01/95	108	0,000136612	
		Total	£

Step 4 Multiply the number of days by the daily rate and then multiply that answer by the tax due (box TX6). Write the interest payable in column 4.

247 x 0.000109290 x 10,000 = 269.95
108 x 0.000136612 x 10,000 = 147.54

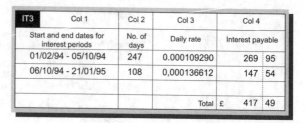

IT3 Col 1	Col 2	Col 3	Col 4	
Start and end dates for interest periods	No. of days	Daily rate	Interest payable	
01/02/94 - 05/10/94	247	0.000109290	269	95
06/10/94 - 21/01/95	108	0,000136612	147	54
		Total	£ 417	49

Step 5 Copy £417.49 to box TX7.

Working out the interest on tax being paid by instalments

TX17 If there is tax to pay in box TX16 and you have included some interest in box TX7, you will need to work out the interest to include in this box.

The interest that is due on the tax on box TX16 will be charged in exactly the same way as the interest that is due on the tax in box TX7. You can copy the details from the table IT3 into table IT4 and then work out the interest that is payable here. Copy the total interest that is payable to box TX17.

However, if more than one instalment is due, the interest charges in this box and in box TX18 will be different. Examples 3 and 4 explain this difference.

What happens if more than one instalment is due

TX18 If more than one instalment of tax is due, (in other words, if you will be applying for a grant more than 18 months after the deceased died) you will need to include some additional interest charges. You can follow the same process as for table IT3, although you will need to work out different start and end dates. The type of additional charge will depend on the type of asset on which the tax is being paid (see page 13 of this Guide).

If the asset is land or buildings that does not qualify for agricultural relief, the additional interest charge arises on the whole of the tax that is to be paid by instalments (box TX14) and is included in box TX18. The charge starts from the date tax first became due and ends on the date the most recent instalment now being paid was due. Fill in the interest table and work out the interest that is payable. To avoid a double charge to interest, the interest charge in box TX17 starts from the date the interest charge in box TX18 stops.

Example 3

▶ The deceased died on 6 July 1994. The date tax is due is 28 February 1995. The tax being paid by instalments is £10,000. The first instalment of £1,000 is due on that date, the second on 29 February 1996 and so on.

The application for a grant was made on 18 June 1996 so that two instalments had to paid at that time.

The interest charge in box TX17 will be on the tax for two instalments (£2,000). The interest charge starts from 1 March 1996 rather than 1 March 1995.

IT4 Col 1	Col 2	Col 3	Col 4	
Start and end dates for interest periods	No. of days	Daily rate	Interest payable	
01/03/96 - 18/06/96	110	0.000136612	30	05
		Total	£ 30	05

The additional interest charge in box TX18 will be on the whole of the tax being paid by instalments (£10,000) from 1 March 1995 to 29 February 1996.

IT5 Col 1	Col 2	Col 3	Col 4	
Start and end dates for interest periods	No. of days	Daily rate	Interest payable	
01/03/95 - 29/02/96	366	0.000136612	500	00
		Total	£ 500	00

Example 4 ▸ If the assets qualify for a reduced interest charge, see page 13 of this Guide, interest is only charged on each instalment as it falls due. You should include a separate interest charge in box TX18 for each instalment that is being paid. In column 1, the start date will be the date that each separate instalment is due. The end date for all the instalments will be the date that you expect to be sending the papers and tax to us. Work out the interest that is payable and copy the total interest that is payable to box TX18.

Using the figures from the example above, there would be no interest charge in box TX17 and a charge for each of first two instalments of £1,000 in box TX18 as follows.

IT5 Col 1	Col 2	Col 3	Col 4	
Start and end dates for interest periods	No. of days	Daily rate	Interest payable	
01/03/95 - 18/06/96	476	0.000136612	65	03
01/03/96 - 18/06/96	110	0.000136612	15	02
		Total	£ 80	05

Examples of inheritance tax calculations

- This Guide contains some examples that show you how to work out inheritance tax when some of the exemptions and reliefs apply either alone or together.

It also shows you how to carry the results over to form **IHT200**.

Our leaflet **IHT15** contains more information about calculating the liability

IHT 214

Contents

Example 1

This is an example of the calculations necessary when the deceased leaves specific legacies that do not bear their own tax and the residue is partly exempt.

The deceased died on 28 February 1999, leaving an estate as follows

Personal estate	500,000
Joint property (with wife)	50,000
Real estate	250,000
Settled estate	300,000
	£1,100,000

By Will, he left

- pecuniary legacies of £100,000 to his son free of tax
- charitable legacies of £10,000
- ½ of the realty to his wife absolutely and
- the residue to be shared equally between his wife and son.

The joint property passes to his wife by survivorship.

During his lifetime, he made gifts that gave rise to a cumulative total of £150,000.

Stage 1

Gross up the value of the chargeable legacies paid free of tax at their own rate.

Cumulative total of lifetime gifts	150,000	(A – see note 1)
Legacies free of tax	100,000	
	250,000	(B – see note 2)
Less threshold at death	-223,000	
Excess over threshold	27,000	
Multiply 27,000 x 5/3	45,000	
Value of legacies	100,000	
Plus (45,000 – 27,000)	18,000	
Grossed up value of legacies	£118,000	

Notes

1. **If the value at A exceeds the threshold, you simply need to multiply the value of the chargeable legacies that are free of tax by 5/3 to arrive at the grossed value of the legacies and then move to stage 2.**

2. **If the total value at B does not exceed the threshold, move directly to stage 2 and use the actual value of the legacies.**

4

Stage 2 ▶ Determine the initial value of the chargeable estate

Personal estate	500,000
Real estate	250,000
	750,000
Less	
Grossed up chargeable legacies	-118,000
Charitable legacy	-10,000
½ real estate to wife	-125,000
	497,000
½ residue exempt	-248,500
Chargeable residue	248,500
Chargeable estate	
½ residue	248,500
Pecuniary legacy	118,000
	£366,500

Note

Property not passing under same title, that is the joint property passing by survivorship and the settled property, is excluded from the calculation.

Stage 3 ▶ Gross up the value of the chargeable legacies paid free of tax at the initial rate

Tax on initial estate	
Cumulative total of gifts	150,000
Initial estate	366,500
	516,500
Less threshold	-223,000
	293,500
Tax 293,500 @ 40%	117,400

Re-gross the chargeable legacies paid free of tax

$$100{,}000 \quad \times \quad \frac{366{,}500}{(366{,}500 - 117{,}400)} \quad = \quad \underline{£147{,}129}$$

5

Stage 4 ▸ Determine the final value of the chargeable estate

Personal estate	500,000
Real estate	250,000
	750,000
Less	
Grossed up legacy to son	-147,129
Charitable legacy	-10,000
½ real estate to wife	-125,000
	467,871
½ residue exempt	-233,936
Chargeable residue	233,935
Chargeable estate	
½ residue	233,935
Pecuniary legacy	147,129
	£381,064

How would these calculations be carried forward to form **IHT200** and the supplementary pages?

1. The joint property should be included on form **D4**. Only brief details need be given and the exemption should be claimed.

2. The settled property should be included on form **D5**, reporting as much information as the trustees have made available.

3. The extent of the spouse exemption in the personal estate is worked out as

Value of Personal estate	500,000	
Grossed up legacies	-157,129	(147,129+10,000)
	342,871	
½ residue	£171,436	

Extract of form IHT200, Section F

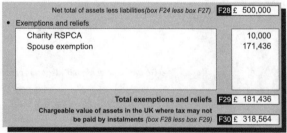

Net total of assets less liabilities*(box F24 less box F27)*	F28	£ 500,000
• Exemptions and reliefs		
Charity RSPCA		10,000
Spouse exemption		171,436
Total exemptions and reliefs	F29	£ 181,436
Chargeable value of assets in the UK where tax may not be paid by instalments *(box F28 less box F29)*	F30	£ 318,564

6

Extract of form IHT200, Section G

Net total of assets less liabilities *(box G13 less boxes G14 and 15)*	G16	£ 250,000
• Exemptions and reliefs		
Spouse exemption (1/2 realty)		125,000
Spouse exemption (1/2 residue)		62,500
Total exemptions and reliefs	G17	£ 187,500
Chargeable value of assets in the UK where tax may be paid by instalments *(box G16 less box G17)*	G18	£ 62,500

Extract of form IHT200, Section H

Assets where tax may not be paid by instalments		
• Estate in the UK *(box WS1)*	H1	£ 318,564
• Joint property *(box WS2)*	H2	£
• Foreign property *(box WS3)*	H3	£
• Settled property on which the trustees would like to pay tax now *(box WS4)*	H4	£
Total of assets where tax may not be paid by instalments *(box WS5)*	H5	£ 318,564
Assets where tax may be paid by instalments		
• Estate in the UK *(box WS6)*	H6	£ 62,500
• Joint property *(box WS7)*	H7	£
• Foreign property *(box WS8)*	H8	£
• Settled property on which the trustees would like to pay tax now *(box WS9)*	H9	£
Total of assets where tax may be paid by instalments *(box WS10)*	H10	£ 62,500
Other property taken into account to calculate the total tax		
• Settled property *(box WS11)*	H11	£ 300,000
• Gift with reservation *(box WS12)*	H12	£
Chargeable estate *(box WS13)*	H13	£ 681,064
Cumulative total of lifetime transfers *(box WS14)*	H14	£ 150,000
Aggregate chargeable transfer *(box WS15)*	H15	£ 831,064

7

Example 2 ▶ This is an example of the calculations necessary when the deceased leaves an estate that

- is partly exempt
- contains property that is entitled to agricultural or business relief
- contains at least one specific legacy of non-relievable property and
- not all the relievable property is specifically given.

The deceased died on 28 February 1999, leaving an estate as follows

Personal estate	500,000	(chattels £20,000)
Farmland	300,000	(agricultural relief due at 50%)
Unquoted shares	500,000	(business relief due at 100%)
Residence	200,000	
Settled property	250,000	
	£1,750,000	

By Will, he left

- pecuniary legacies to his daughters of £200,000 free of tax
- the unquoted shares to his son
- charitable legacies of £50,000
- the chattels and residence to his widow and
- the residue of his estate equally between his widow and three children.

The "interaction" of the spouse exemption with business and agricultural relief means that the provisions of section 39A IHTA 1984 are relevant.

During his lifetime, he made gifts that gave rise to a cumulative total of £150,000.

Stage 1 ▶

Establish the value of the property passing under the Will and deduct	1,500,000
Agricultural relief	-150,000
Business relief	-500,000
	850,000

Stage 2 ▶

Establish the value of any specific legacies of relievable property after relief	Nil (unquoted shares qualify for relief at 100%)

8

Stage 3 ▸ As there is other relievable property (the farmland) that is not specifically given, establish the fraction to proportionately reduce all other specific gifts.

Fraction =

Value of estate after AR/BR (less specific legacies of relievable property at reduced value)	850,000 – Nil
Value of estate before AR/BR (less specific legacies of relievable property at unreduced value)	1,500,000 – 500,000

Reduce other legacies

$$200{,}000 \times \frac{850{,}000}{1{,}000{,}000} = 170{,}000$$ (reduced value of pecuniary legacies)

$$50{,}000 \times \frac{850{,}000}{1{,}000{,}000} = 42{,}500$$ (reduced value of charitable legacy)

$$220{,}000 \times \frac{850{,}000}{1{,}000{,}000} = 187{,}000$$ (reduced value of legacies to spouse - chattels 17,000, residence 170,000)

Stage 4 ▸ Gross up the *reduced* value of the chargeable legacies paid free of tax at their own rate.

Stage 1

Cumulative total of gifts	150,000	(see note 1, example 1)
Reduced value of gifts free of tax	170,000	
	320,000	(see note 2, example 1)
Less threshold at death	-223,000	
	97,000	
Multiply 97,000 x 5/3	161,667	
Value of legacies	170,000	
Plus (161,667 – 97,000)	64,667	
Grossed up value of legacies	£234,667	

9

Stage 2

Determine the initial value of chargeable estate

Personal estate	500,000
Farmland (after relief at 50%)	150,000
Unquoted shares (after relief at100%)	0
Residence	200,000
	850,000
Less	
Unquoted shares to son	0
Grossed up legacies	-234,667
Reduced charitable legacy	-42,500
Reduced legacy to spouse	-187,000
	385,833
¼ residue exempt	-96,458
Chargeable residue	289,375
Chargeable estate	
¾ residue	289,375
Grossed up legacies	234,667
	£524,042

Stage 3

Gross up the *reduced* value of chargeable legacies paid free of tax at the initial rate

Tax on initial estate	
Cumulative total of gifts	150,000
Initial estate	524,042
	674,042
Less threshold	-223,000
	451,042
Tax 451,042 @ 40%	180,417

Re-gross the chargeable legacies paid free of tax

$$170{,}000 \times \frac{524{,}042}{(524{,}042 - 180{,}417)} = \underline{\pounds 259{,}257}$$

10

Stage 5 ▸ Calculate the residue using the reduced values

Value of estate after relief	850,000
Less	
Unquoted shares to son	0
Grossed up legacies	-259,257
Reduced charitable legacy	-42,500
Reduced legacy to spouse	-187,000
	361,243
¼ residue exempt	-90,311
Chargeable residue	£270,932

Stage 6 ▸ Calculate chargeable estate

Chargeable estate	
¾ residue	270,932
Grossed up legacies	259,257
	£530,189

How would these calculations be carried to the **IHT200**?

1. Exemption for the reduced value of the legacies to the spouse and the charity can be deducted against the appropriate section.

2. Agricultural and business relief can be deducted against the property in section G.

3. The residue at £361,243 contains both personal estate and real estate and ¼ of it is exempt. The legacies to be paid from the personal estate are

   - Chattels (at reduced value) £17,000
   - Grossed up value of pecuniary legacies £259,257
   - Legacy to charity (at reduced value) £42,500

   These total £318,757, leaving a residue of £181,243 (500,000 – 318,757), ¼ of which is £45,311.

   The legacies to be paid from the real estate are

   - Residence to spouse (at reduced value) £170,000
   - Legacy of farmland to son (after relief) £150,000

   These total £320,000, leaving a residue of £180,000 (500,000 – 320,000), ¼ of which is £45,000.

Extract of form IHT200, Section F

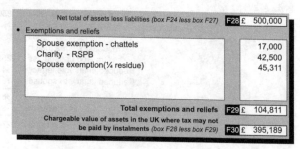

Net total of assets less liabilities *(box F24 less box F27)*	F28	£ 500,000
• Exemptions and reliefs		
Spouse exemption - chattels		17,000
Charity - RSPB		42,500
Spouse exemption(¼ residue)		45,311
Total exemptions and reliefs	F29	£ 104,811
Chargeable value of assets in the UK where tax may not be paid by instalments *(box F28 less box F29)*	F30	£ 395,189

Extract of form IHT200, Section G

Net total of assets less liabilities *(box G13 less boxes G14 and G15)*	G16	£ 1,000,000
• Exemptions and reliefs		
Spouse exemption (realty)		170,000
Business relief (unquoted shares 100%)		500,000
Agricultural relief (farmland 50%)		150,000
Spouse exemption (¼ residue)		45,000
Total exemptions and reliefs	G17	£ 865,000
Chargeable value of assets in the UK where tax may be paid by instalments *(box G16 less box G17)*	G18	£ 135,000

12

Extract of form IHT200, Section H

Assets where tax may not be paid by instalments

Estate in the UK *(box WS1)*	H1	£ 395,189
Joint property *(box WS2)*	H2	£
Foreign property *(box WS3)*	H3	£
Settled property on which the trustees would like to pay tax now *(box WS4)*	H4	£
Total of assets where tax may not be paid by instalments *(box WS5)*	H5	£ 395,189

Assets where tax may be paid by instalments

Estate in the UK *(box WS6)*	H6	£ 135,000
Joint property *(box WS7)*	H7	£
Foreign property *(box WS8)*	H8	£
Settled property on which the trustees would like to pay tax now *(box WS9)*	H9	£
Total of assets where tax may be paid by instalments *(box WS10)*	H10	£ 135,000

Other property taken into account to calculate the total tax

Settled property *(box WS11)*	H11	£ 250,000
Gift with reservation *(box WS12)*	H12	£
Chargeable estate *(box WS13)*	H13	£ 780,189
Cumulative total of lifetime transfers *(box WS14)*	H14	£ 150,000
Aggregate chargeable transfer *(box WS15)*	H15	£ 930,189

13

Example 3

This is an example of calculations necessary to work out the tax payable on lifetime transfers where both taper relief and "fall in value relief" (section 131 IHTA 1984) apply. There is no provision to deduct either relief on form **IHT200** or its supplementary pages since in the vast majority of estates we will issue calculations for such tax once the grant has been issued. If, however, the donee wishes to pay this tax at the same time as you apply for the grant, you will need to go through the calculations in this example.

Remember that taper relief can only apply if the lifetime transfers are taxable in their own right and fall in value relief only applies to reduce the tax on the transfer that qualifies for relief – it does not serve to reduce the value that cumulates with other transfers or the estate on death.

Extract from form D3

If the answer to any part of question 1 is "Yes", fill in the details we ask for below

Date of gift	Name and relationship of recipient and description of assets	Value at date of gift	Amount and type of exemption claimed	Net value after exemptions
14/10/93	David Smith (son) 74 Acacia Gardens Nottingham	100,000	6,000 (annual 93/94 and 92/93)	94,000
16/01/95	Robert Smith (son) Cash	200,000	3,000 (annual 94/95)	197,000
17/04/96	David Smith 74 Acacia Gardens Nottingham (s131 relief claimed, value at date of death £130,000)	150,000	6,000 (annual 96/97 and 95/96)	144,000
			Total LT1	£ 435,000

14

The deceased died on 14 July 1999. You would need to go through the following calculations.

First gift 14 October 1993

The chargeable amount of the gift was £94,000. The tax threshold to apply is the threshold at death (£231,000). As the gift is below the threshold, there is no tax to pay on this gift so there can be no taper relief.

If the market value of the property had fallen between the date of gift and the date of death to, say £80,000, there would be no benefit in claiming fall in value relief because the gift is below the threshold. The value that cumulates with all other transfers remains at £94,000.

Second gift 16 January 1995

The chargeable amount of the gift was £197,000. The first gift must be added to it to establish the total value (£291,000) on which tax is charged. The tax threshold to apply is the threshold at death (£231,000). The tax payable on the second gift is

Taxable value	291,000
Less threshold	-231,000
Chargeable value	£ 60,000
Tax at 40%	£ 24,000

The second gift was made more than four, but less than five years before the deceased died so taper relief is due at 40%. 40% of £24,000 is £9,600, so the tax to be paid is £24,000 – 9,600 = £14,400.

Third gift 17 April 1996

The chargeable amount of the gift was £144,000. The first two gifts must be added to it to establish the total value (£435,000) on which tax is charged. The tax threshold to apply is the threshold at death (£231,000). The tax payable on the third gift is

Taxable value	435,000
Less fall in value relief	-20,000
Less threshold	-231,000
Chargeable value	£ 184,000
Tax at 40%	£ 73,600
Less tax on second gift	-24,000
Tax to pay	49,600

The third gift was made more than three, but less than four years before the deceased died so taper relief is due at 20%. 20% of £49,600 is £9,920, so the tax to be paid is £49,600 – 9,920 = £39,680.

Fall in value has been deducted in working out the tax that is payable on the third gift, but it does not reduce the value of the gifts that are added to the estate at death. This remains at £435,000.

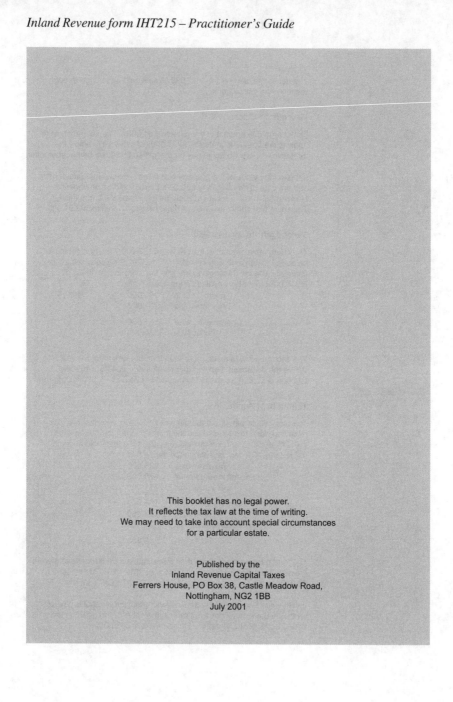

This booklet has no legal power.
It reflects the tax law at the time of writing.
We may need to take into account special circumstances
for a particular estate.

Published by the
Inland Revenue Capital Taxes
Ferrers House, PO Box 38, Castle Meadow Road,
Nottingham, NG2 1BB
July 2001

Appendix 4

District probate registries and sub-registries – contact details

Registries	*Sub-registries*	*Addresses, telephone numbers, fax numbers and document exchange (DX) numbers*
Birmingham		The Priory Courts, 33 Bull Street, Birmingham B4 6DU Tel: 0121 681 3400 Fax: 0121 236 2465 DX 701990 Birmingham 7
	Stoke on Trent	Combined Court Centre, Bethesda Street, Hanley, Stoke on Trent ST1 3BP Tel: 01782 854065 Fax: 01782 274916 DX 20736 Hanley
Brighton		William Street, Brighton BN2 2LG Tel: 01273 684071 Fax: 01273 625845 DX 98073 Brighton 3
	Maidstone	The Law Courts, Barker Road, Maidstone ME18 8EW Tel: 01622 202048/7 Fax: 01622 754384 DX 130066 Maidstone 7
Bristol		Ground Floor, The Crescent Centre, Temple Back, Bristol BS1 6EP Tel 1: 0117 927 3915 Tel 2: 0117 926 4619 Fax: 0117 925 3549 DX 94400 Bristol 5
	Bodmin	Market Street, Bodmin, Cornwall PL31 2JW Tel: 01208 72279 Fax: 01208 269004 DX 81858 Bodmin
	Exeter	Finance House, Barnfield Road, Exeter EX1 1QR Tel: 01392 274515 Fax: 01392 493468 DX 8380 Exeter

Cardiff – **Probate Registry of Wales**		PO Box 474, 2 Park Street, Cardiff CF1 1ET Tel: 029 2037 6479 Fax: 029 2037 6466 DX 122782 Cardiff 13
	Bangor	Council Offices, Ffordd Gwynedd, Bangor LL57 1DT Tel: 01248 362410 Fax: 01248 364423 DX 23186 Bangor 2
	Carmarthen	14 King Street, Carmarthen SA31 1BL Tel: 01267 236238 Fax: 01267 229067 DX 51420 Carmarthen
Ipswich		8 Arcade Street, Ipswich IP1 1EJ Tel: 01473 284260 Fax: 01473 231951 DX 3729 Ipswich
	Norwich	Combined Court Building, The Law Courts, Bishopsgate, Norwich NR3 1UR Tel: 01603 728267 Fax: 01603 627469 DX 5202 Norwich
	Peterborough	1st Floor, Crown Buildings, Rivergate, Peterborough PE1 1EJ Tel: 01733 562802 DX 112327 Peterborough 1
Leeds		3rd Floor, Coronet House, Queen Street, Leeds LS1 2BA Tel: 0113 243 1505 Fax: 0113 247 1893 DX 26451 Leeds (Park Square)
	Lincoln	360 High Street, Lincoln LN5 7PS Tel: 01522 523648 Fax: 01522 539903 DX 703233 Lincoln 6
	Sheffield	PO Box 832, The Law Courts, 50 West Bar, Sheffield S3 8YR Tel: 0114 281 2596 Fax: 0114 281 2598 DX 26054 Sheffield 2
Liverpool		Queen Elizabeth II Law Courts, Derby Square, Liverpool L2 1XA Tel: 0151 236 8264 Fax: 0151 227 4634 DX 14246 Liverpool 1
	Chester	5th Floor, Hamilton House, Hamilton Place, Chester CH1 2DA Tel: 01244 345082

		Fax: 01244 346243 DX 22162 Northgate
	Lancaster	Mitre House, Church Street, Lancaster LA1 1HE Tel: 01524 36625 Fax: 01524 35561 DX 63509 Lancaster
Manchester		9th Floor, Astley House, 23 Quay Street, Manchester M3 4AT Tel: 0161 834 4319 Fax: 0161 832 2690 DX 14387 Manchester 1
	Nottingham	Butt Dyke House, Park Row, Nottingham NG1 6GR Tel: 0115 941 4288 Fax: 0115 950 3383 DX 10055 Nottingham
Newcastle upon Tyne		2nd Floor, Plummer House, Croft Street, Newcastle upon Tyne NE1 6NP Tel: 0191 261 8383 Fax: 0191 230 4868 DX 61081 Newcastle upon Tyne 14
	Carlisle	Courts of Justice, Earl Street, Carlisle CA1 1DJ Tel: 01228 521751 DX 63034 Carlisle
	Middlesbrough	Teesside Combined Court Centre, Russell Street, Middlesbrough TS1 2AE Tel: 01642 340001 DX 60536 Middlesbrough
	York	1st Floor, Castle Chambers, Clifford Street, York YO1 9RG Tel: 01904 666777 Fax: 01904 666776 DX 720629 York 21
Oxford		Combined Court Building, St Aldates, Oxford OX1 1LY Tel 1: 01865 793050 Tel 2: 01865 793055 Fax: 01865 793090 DX 96454 Oxford
	Gloucester	2nd Floor, Combined Court Building, Kimbrose Way, Gloucester GL1 2DG Tel: 01452 834966 Fax: 01452 834970 DX 98663 Gloucester
	Leicester	90 Wellington Street, Leicester LE1 6HG Tel: 0116 285 3380 Fax: 0116 285 3382 DX 17403 Leicester 3

Winchester		4th Floor, Cromwell House, Andover Road, Winchester SO23 7EW Tel 1: 01962 897024 Tel 2: 01962 897029 Fax: 01962 840796 DX 96900 Winchester 2

District probate registries and sub-registries are open every weekday, from 9.30 am until 4.00 pm.

The probate department of the Principal Registry of the Family Division is at:

First Avenue House
42–49 High Holborn
London WC1V 6NP
Tel: 020 7947 7431
Fax: 020 7947 6946/7454
DX 941 London/Chancery Lane

The department is open every weekday from 10.00 am until 4.30 pm.

Index

U.W.E.L. LEARNING RESOURCES

U.W.E.L. LEARNING RESOURCES